WHAT SHOULD CONSTITUTIONS DO?

Edited by

**Ellen Frankel Paul, Fred D. Miller, Jr.,
and Jeffrey Paul**

D1354975

CAMBRIDGE
UNIVERSITY PRESS

CAMBRIDGE UNIVERSITY PRESS
Cambridge, New York, Melbourne, Madrid, Cape Town,
Singapore, São Paulo, Delhi, Tokyo, Mexico City

Cambridge University Press
32 Avenue of the Americas, New York, NY 10013-2473, USA

www.cambridge.org
Information on this title: www.cambridge.org/9780521175531

First published 2011
Reprinted 2011

A catalog record for this publication is available from the British Library.

Library of Congress Cataloging in Publication Data

What Should Constitutions Do?
edited by Ellen Frankel Paul, Fred D. Miller, Jr., and Jeffrey Paul.
    p. cm. "The essays . . . have also been published, without introduction and index,
in the semiannual journal Social Philosophy & Policy,
volume 28, number 1"–T.p. verso.
Includes bibliographical references and index.
ISBN 978-0-521-17553-1 (pbk.)
1. Constitutional law–Philosophy. 2. Political science. I. Paul, Ellen Frankel. II. Miller,
Fred Dycus, 1944– III. Paul, Jeffrey. IV. Title.
K3165.W435 2010
342.0201–dc22   2010043704

ISBN 978-0-521-17553-1 Paperback

The essays in this book have also been published, without introduction and index, in
the semiannual journal Social Philosophy & Policy, Volume 28, Number 1,
which is available by subscription.

CONTENTS

INTRODUCTION

"In framing a government which is to be administered by men over men," James Madison wrote, "the great difficulty lies in this: you must first enable the government to control the governed; and in the next place oblige it to control itself."[1] The task of a constitution is to solve this difficulty by setting out the structure of the government and establishing its powers and limits. But how extensive should those powers be, and where should their limits lie? What are the legitimate functions of government, and what is their proper justification? Should a nation's constitution aim at securing the general welfare of its citizens, and, if so, how is the general welfare to be defined? What protections should a constitution afford to individual rights, and how should these rights be specified?

The essays in this volume—written by prominent philosophers, political scientists, and legal scholars—address these questions and explore related issues. Some essays examine the basic purposes of constitutions and their status as fundamental law. Some deal with specific constitutional provisions: they ask, for example, which branches of government should have the authority to conduct foreign policy, or how the judiciary should be organized, or what role a preamble should play in a nation's founding document. Other essays explore questions of constitutional design: they consider the advantages of a federal system of government, or the challenges of designing a constitution for a pluralistic society—or they ask what form of constitution best promotes personal liberty and economic prosperity.

The collection opens with several essays on the functions of a constitution and the relationship between constitutional law and ordinary law. In "What Are Constitutions, and What Should (and Can) They Do?" Larry Alexander begins with the observation that the principal function of law is to settle questions about what people are obligated to do: that is, to determine which of our moral obligations are enforceable through coercion. By establishing a system of determinate legal rules, we are able to peacefully resolve disagreements and coordinate our actions with the actions of others. Likewise, Alexander argues, the function of constitutional law is to settle the most basic questions about how to organize our society and our government. Constitutional law is more fundamental than ordinary law in two senses: first, ordinary law must conform to constitutional law; and second, constitutional law is more firmly entrenched and more difficult to change than ordinary law. In addition to establishing

---

[1] James Madison, *Federalist No. 51*, in Alexander Hamilton, James Madison, and John Jay, *The Federalist Papers*, ed. Clinton Rossiter (New York: New American Library, 1961), 322.

the powers and responsibilities of the various branches of government, constitutions usually contain provisions that safeguard the rights of citizens, and Alexander goes on to discuss how these rights should be understood. He argues that the incorporation of moral rights within a constitution poses a danger: given that people disagree about the exact nature of moral rights, their incorporation in a constitution will likely undermine the law's aim of settling questions about what enforceable obligations we have. In light of this, Alexander contends, moral rights should be subordinated to constitutional structures, which can provide procedures for determining the content of those rights. He concludes with a discussion of the role of courts in providing authoritative interpretations of the meaning of constitutional provisions.

John David Lewis draws on the experience of ancient Athens to illuminate the nature of constitutional law in his essay, "Constitution and Fundamental Law: The Lesson of Classical Athens." During the fifth century B.C., Lewis notes, the Athenians instituted radical changes to their political system, undermining the influence of the established nobility and the traditional laws, and placing political power directly into the hands of an Assembly made up of the entire body of male citizens. Under this new system, there were virtually no limits to the Assembly's power, and this led to a number of problematic practices. For example, the Assembly could vote to exile anyone suspected of gathering too much personal power, and persuasive orators used this mechanism to eliminate their political rivals. The Assembly could also audit government officials at the end of their terms, demanding that they account for their actions. And the Assembly had the authority to elect military commanders, which meant that Athenian generals were subject to the Assembly's decisions and were less likely to follow their own best judgment in military matters. Lewis argues that these factors weakened the city-state of Athens and led to its defeat by the Spartans in the Peloponnesian War. This defeat, however, ushered in a movement in Athens to rediscover the traditional laws established by Solon and other lawgivers, as a means of establishing proper limits on the actions of the Assembly. The Greek term *nomos* came to signify a fundamental law inscribed in public view—as distinguished from *psephisma*, a decree of the Assembly. On this understanding, a *nomos* was viewed as a fixed standard, which could not be overridden by the arguments of orators in the Assembly. Lewis concludes by drawing parallels between the Athenian case and the American understanding of the importance of a written constitution to serve as a fundamental law and to limit the power of the legislature and other branches of government.

The grounding of constitutional government in the consent of the governed is the subject of Loren E. Lomasky's contribution to this volume, "Contract, Covenant, Constitution." Lomasky begins with a discussion of social contract theory, which occupies a central place in the Western liberal understanding of the origins of government. According to the social contract view, individuals living in a pre-political "state of nature" find themselves beset by scarcity and rampant violence. In order to secure a peaceful coexistence, they agree to establish a government with the power to defend them from aggression and resolve disputes that arise among them. The social contract model, Lomasky argues, has several defects. Since no actual historical agreement has occurred, the social contract must be understood to be hypothetical, and its terms are thus subject to disagreement. Even if specific historical individuals were thought to have consented to the formation of a government, important questions would remain. For example, can the consent of one generation bind members of future generations? And what methods exist for interpreting the obligations of citizens? Given these shortcomings of social contract theory, Lomasky proposes an alternative way of understanding the establishment of government in terms of "covenant"—on the model of the biblical covenant enacted between the Israelites and their god at Sinai. Lomasky goes on to argue that the U.S. Constitution can be understood as a kind of covenant. Like a covenant, and unlike a hypothetical social contract, the U.S. Constitution represents an agreement entered into by specific people (the American colonists, represented by their delegates) at a specific time and place. Unlike a hypothetical contract, the Constitution's terms are spelled out in detail. Moreover, the Constitution has within itself the resources to resolve some of the other problems faced by social contract theory. The fact that the Constitution contains provisions for its own amendment strengthens the case for believing that future generations should be bound by its terms (since they have the opportunity to alter those terms as they see fit). Likewise, the Constitution provides for an independent judiciary with the power to interpret the nature and extent of individual citizens' obligations. Lomasky concludes that constitutional government might be better understood in terms of covenant than in terms of social contract.

In "Constitutionalism in the Age of Terror," Michael Zuckert and Felix Valenzuela argue that constitutions have two primary aims that may sometimes come into conflict with each other. On the one hand, a constitution must limit and control the power of government so that it does not harm the citizens who live under its rule. On the other hand, a constitution must ensure that the government has sufficient power to achieve the common good and to safeguard its citizens against aggression. The tension between these two aims becomes especially apparent in emergency situations (e.g., when government must confront the threat of terrorism). In such situations, it is tempting to say that limits on governmental power (especially limits on the power of the executive branch) must be set aside so that the government may quickly and effectively respond to the threat at hand. Zuckert and Valenzuela examine four models for understanding how a constitution should channel and control governmental power in situations of emergency. The Whig model (which takes its name from the seventeenth-century English political party) maintains that there must be strict limits on governmental power, and especially on executive power, even in emergencies. The Jeffersonian model rejects the inclusion of emergency powers within the constitution, but acknowledges that it may sometimes be necessary for the executive to act outside the bounds of the constitution in extraordinary situations. The Hamiltonian model maintains that the powers required to confront extraordinary circumstances should be contained within the constitution itself, and looks to the executive to exercise these powers. The Madisonian model agrees that extraordinary powers should be provided for within the constitution, but holds that these powers should be vested in the legislature rather than in the executive. Zuckert and Valenzuela discuss each of these models in detail, relating them to contemporary debates over the limits of governmental power in the context of the war on terror. They conclude that the Madisonian model does the best job of limiting government while at the same time giving it the power it needs to confront the dangers of the modern world.

The collection continues with three essays that focus on specific parts or provisions of a constitution. In "The Liberal Constitution and Foreign Affairs," Fernando R. Tesón attempts to outline the foreign-relations clauses that should ideally be included in the constitution of a liberal society. On his view, an ideal constitution should enable the government to implement a morally defensible foreign policy, which implies a commitment to the defense of human liberty and prosperity. A government defends liberty by protecting its citizens and its territory from aggression, but also by protecting its liberal institutions against outside forces that would attempt to undermine them. A commitment to liberty also implies that a liberal government should promote the advancement of freedom around the globe—when this is possible and when the cost is not prohibitive. At the very least, a liberal government should seek to ally itself with other like-minded governments and should refrain from cooperating with tyrannical regimes. Moreover, a liberal government should promote prosperity by fostering free trade at home and abroad. Tesón goes on to apply these general principles to the design of a liberal constitution. He argues that a constitution's war-power provisions should be designed to secure combat-readiness and to allow for a flexible executive who will be able to respond to threats readily and effectively. At the same time, Tesón recommends that the legislative branch should have a role in authorizing all large-scale uses of military force. In terms of promoting free trade, he argues that the government should be prohibited from adopting protectionist economic policies. He concludes with a discussion of international treaties and an analysis of when it is appropriate to incorporate international law into domestic law. He suggests that principles of international law should be adopted and applied by domestic courts only when those principles reflect genuine, long-standing international customs, and when they do not conflict with liberal constitutional principles.

The practice of including preambles in written constitutions is the subject of Sanford Levinson's essay, "Do Constitutions Have a Point? Reflections on 'Parchment Barriers' and Preambles." Levinson begins by pointing out that constitutional provisions generally serve one of two purposes. Some provisions offer definitive answers to specific questions, such as when elections should be held or whether the legislature should have one chamber or two. But other provisions address issues that do not lend themselves to definitive solutions. The latter provisions may seek to protect certain rights (e.g., freedom of speech, or equal protection of the laws), but the exact nature and extent of these rights may remain open to dispute. Rather than providing a clear-cut settlement of a given controversy, these provisions serve as the basis for an ongoing legal conversation, in which lawyers and constitutional scholars debate the meaning of the rights and protections in question. As Levinson notes, however, constitutional preambles do not fall easily into either of these two categories. On his view, preambles can serve a variety of expressive purposes. For example, a preamble may set out the ends to be attained by the constitution (as the preamble of the U.S. Constitution sets out the ends of establishing justice, ensuring domestic tranquility, providing for the common defense, and so on). Or the authors of the preamble may wish to express the essence of a people or a nation, in terms of their shared history, religion, language, ethnicity, or values. In the course of his essay, Levinson analyzes the preambles of a number of contemporary constitutions. He argues that the desire of constitutional authors to use a preamble to describe (or create) national unity is sometimes at odds with the reality of contemporary societies, which are often made up of diverse peoples with differing values. At their worst, he suggests, preambles may be used to attempt to impose uniformity where none exists, or to marginalize ethnic or religious minorities.

One of the central features of the U.S. Constitution is its establishment of an independent judiciary, in which the federal courts constitute a separate branch of the national government, federal judges enjoy tenure during good behavior, and their salaries cannot be diminished while they hold office. In "The Origins of an Independent Judiciary in New York, 1621–1777," Scott D. Gerber explores the development of the concept of judicial independence in New York State and traces its influence on the drafters of the federal constitution. Gerber recounts New York's judicial history through four periods. From 1621 to 1664, the territory was administered by the Dutch West India Company under a charter from the Dutch government. During this period, the Company established "schout" courts in various parts of the territory, courts made up primarily of mayors and aldermen, whose members exercised both legislative and judicial power. In 1664, the Dutch ceded control of the territory to England, and from

1664 to 1685 New York was under the authority of James, the Duke of York, brother of Charles II, the King of England. In contrast with the earlier period, legislative and judicial powers were divided. The duke established a judicial system consisting of: town courts (with jurisdiction over minor civil disputes); a court of sessions (with jurisdiction over more significant civil disputes, as well as noncapital criminal cases); and a court of assizes, which handled capital cases and appeals from the lower courts. After the death of Charles II in 1685, the Duke of York became King James II, and New York became a royal colony. This period (from 1685 to 1776) saw the establishment of county courts of common pleas, as well as a supreme court whose justices were appointed by the colony's governor and served at his pleasure. Finally, during the early state period, after the adoption of the New York Constitution of 1777, significant steps were taken toward increasing the independence of the judiciary. Judges of the supreme court and the county courts were selected by a council of appointment—rather than by the governor—and they held office during good behavior (though they faced an age limit of sixty years). The history of the judiciary in New York, Gerber concludes, represents a slow and imperfect progress toward the ideal of judicial independence, an ideal that would become more fully realized with the institution of an independent federal judiciary in the United States Constitution of 1787.

The collection concludes with five essays that address various issues relating to constitutional design. In "Foot Voting, Political Ignorance, and Constitutional Design," Ilya Somin argues that a federal constitutional system that limits the power of the central government has the potential to enhance citizen welfare and democratic accountability. Under a federal system in which people are free to move from one jurisdiction to another, regional and local governments have incentives to enact policies that citizens find attractive. When citizens relocate, they are, in effect, "voting with their feet," and this foot voting, Somin contends, has significant advantages over conventional ballot box voting. Ballot box voters have strong incentives to be "rationally ignorant" about the candidates and policies they vote on, because the chance that any one vote will have a decisive impact on an electoral outcome is vanishingly small. For the same reason, they also have little or no incentive to make good use of the information they do possess. In contrast, "foot voters" choosing a jurisdiction in which to live have much stronger incentives to acquire information and use it rationally: the choices they make will have a decisive impact on their lives and the lives of their families. Indeed, Somin suggests that under a decentralized system, even members of disadvantaged minority groups with little education are able to acquire the information they need to practice effective foot voting. For example, African Americans in the Jim Crow era South were able to learn from relatives about employment opportunities and better living conditions in the North, and the resulting migration benefited both the migrants and those African

Americans who were left behind. Since African Americans were an important source of labor for white-owned farms and businesses in the South, the governments of southern states were forced to take steps toward providing better educational opportunities and enhanced protection of civil liberties. Failure to do so only encouraged more outbound migration. Somin concludes that an appreciation of the advantages of foot voting should lead us to design political institutions that limit the power of the central government and encourage competition among regional and local governments.

In "Pluralist Constitutionalism," William A. Galston explores the ways in which a broadly pluralist outlook can help illuminate long-standing issues relating to constitutional design. He bases his discussion on the account of value pluralism offered by Isaiah Berlin, an account that recognizes cultural diversity and a diversity of reasonable conceptions of the good life. On Berlin's view, there is no single highest good, but rather a variety of goods that might be ranked differently by various people in various circumstances. Galston goes on to show how this pluralist framework is consistent with the maintenance of social order within a viable political community. He contends that those who embrace divergent conceptions of the good life can nevertheless agree on certain minimum conditions of public order, including the rule of law, a stable system of property rights, an economic system that provides genuine opportunities for the poor to improve their condition, and a sense of political community that is strong enough to override ethnic and religious differences. These minimum conditions, Galston suggests, contribute to the existence of a civil order within which individuals will remain largely free to live according to their own beliefs about what makes life worth living. Applying this analysis to constitutional design, Galston argues that there is no single constitutional system that is preferable to all others, but that constitutions can nonetheless be judged according to three criteria: realism, coherence, and congruence. A constitution is realistic if it does not put undue burdens on its citizens; it is coherent if the values it embraces are not too diverse to coexist within the same community; and it is congruent if its general outlines correspond to the moral sentiments of the citizens who live under it. Galston concludes with a discussion of how constitutional authority should be exercised in a pluralistic society, arguing that public officials charged with resolving disputes should avoid winner-take-all solutions whenever possible and should strive to accommodate a range of worthwhile ways of life.

In "Deliberative Democracy and Constitutions," James S. Fishkin examines the role deliberation might play in processes of higher law making, either for the founding of a constitution or for amending an existing constitution. Fishkin begins by setting out four principles that are central to the design of democratic institutions. Ideally, all citizens should have the opportunity to participate in political decision-making (i.e., there should be *mass participation*), and every citizen's voice should have the same weight in determining the outcome (*political equality*). Moreover, decisions should be made after citizens hear arguments for various positions and have an opportunity to weigh and discuss the merits of different alternatives (*deliberation*), and the majority should not choose policies that impose severe burdens on the minority (*non-tyranny*). As Fishkin notes, however, it is difficult to satisfy all of these principles simultaneously. The two processes most commonly used to establish or amend a constitution are elite deliberation (often in the form of a constitutional convention where representatives of the people gather and debate various proposals) and plebiscitary mass democracy (where citizens vote directly on a proposal through a referendum). The former process employs deliberation without mass participation, while the latter emphasizes mass participation without genuine opportunities for public deliberation. A better alternative, Fishkin argues, might be one in which a proposal formulated by a constitutional convention could be debated by citizens in small groups over the course of a day, after which the proposal would be put to a vote. Fishkin describes in detail how such a process might work in practice. He acknowledges that it would be difficult to implement, since it would involve a national holiday and perhaps the compensation of citizens for their participation in deliberations. Nonetheless, he concludes that it would be an effective way to realize the goals of political equality, deliberation, and mass participation.

Guido Pincione argues that a constitution that fosters economic liberty is the best way to protect individuals from being dominated by others. In "The Constitution of Nondomination," Pincione defines domination in terms of arbitrary interference with individuals' freedom of action. The most extreme example of domination would be the institution of slavery, yet domination may also occur when some entity (whether a government, a corporation, or an individual citizen) holds a legal monopoly over some essential resource (e.g., potable water) and is able to set the terms on which the resource may be obtained. Some political theorists argue that state interference with private markets is necessary to prevent this sort of domination, but Pincione contends that the dispersal of market power that comes with economic liberty is a better mechanism for combating domination. Free markets with low barriers to entry into the marketplace encourage competition and result in a plurality of suppliers of goods and services, so that no single supplier has the power to dominate consumers. In the course of his essay, Pincione addresses the idea that governmental regulation is the best way to limit concentrations of power, and he maintains that the constitutional provisions needed to implement this idea would necessarily be subject to interpretation and would open the door to increased domination by governmental regulatory agencies themselves. He goes on to suggest that market freedoms are best protected by procedural rules for political decision-making, rather than by constitutional guarantees of property rights. Constitutional guarantees of rights are typically vague and subject to debate regarding their proper extent and limits; they are therefore prone to manipulation by politicians and bureaucrats seeking to expand their own power. In contrast, procedural rules may be less subject to manipulation. Pincione concludes by sketching procedural rules that he believes would be likely to lead to the maintenance of a free market. These would include (1) a supermajority voting rule in the national legislature, which would increase the costs for interest groups seeking subsidies and special favors, and (2) a federal constitutional system in which state governments set most tax and spending policies and are forced to compete with one another by tailoring their policies to attract investment and citizens.

Richard A. Epstein defends a Lockean, limited-government model of constitutional design in the collection's final essay, "Can We Design an Optimal Constitution? Of Structural Ambiguity and Rights Clarity." Epstein begins with the assumption that individuals and groups are self-interested, and that in a world of scarce resources they will seek to use the power of the state to pursue their own advantage. In order to counter this tendency, a constitution should provide for a separation of powers among the various branches of government, along with a system of checks and balances, so that special interest groups will find it more difficult to use governmental power to impose their will on others. Epstein allows that the optimal structure of the government will vary from case to case, depending on the size of the nation, its level of economic development, and the existence of ethnic divisions within it. Nonetheless, he argues that any constitution should provide strong protections for individual rights, including both personal liberties (e.g., freedom of speech and religion, and freedom from invidious discrimination) and economic liberties (e.g., property rights and freedom of contract). Epstein maintains that the protection of these negative rights will tend to reduce the level of conflict within a society, whereas attempts to provide for positive rights (e.g., entitlements to housing, jobs, health care, or welfare payments) will tend to increase conflict. Efforts to create systems of positive entitlements are bound to fail, on his view, because of their detrimental effects on wealth creation and because of the difficulty involved in defining and limiting the scope of such entitlements. Epstein concludes that the best strategy for constitutional designers is to limit the number of decisions that government must make by emphasizing the state's role in preventing coercion, fraud, and the development of monopolies, while at the same time shying away from the redistribution of wealth and the creation of positive rights.

The proper organization of a nation's government is a central issue in political philosophy—and one with profound implications in practice. The essays in this volume address essential questions concerning constitutional theory and constitutional design.

ACKNOWLEDGMENTS

The editors wish to acknowledge several individuals at the Social Philosophy and Policy Center, Bowling Green State University, who provided invaluable assistance in the preparation of this volume. They include Program Managers John Milliken and Ben Dyer, Graduate Research Assistant Christoph Hanisch, Pamela Phillips, Mary Dilsaver, and Terrie Weaver.

The editors also extend special thanks to Administrative Editor Tamara Sharp, for her patient attention to detail, and to Managing Editor Harry Dolan, for providing editorial assistance above and beyond the call of duty.

CONTRIBUTORS

Larry Alexander is Warren Distinguished Professor at the University of San Diego School of Law. He is the author, coauthor, or editor of eleven books and more than 170 published essays on various topics in jurisprudence, constitutional law, criminal law, and moral/social philosophy. His most recent books are *Crime and Culpability: A Theory of Criminal Law* (with K. K. Ferzan, 2009), *Demystifying Legal Reasoning* (with E. Sherwin, 2008), and *Is There a Right of Freedom of Expression?* (2005).

John David Lewis is Visiting Associate Professor in the Philosophy, Politics, and Economics Program at Duke University. He received his Ph.D. in Classics from the University of Cambridge and is the author of *Solon the Thinker: Political Thought in Archaic Athens* (2006), *Early Greek Lawgivers* (2007), and *Nothing Less Than Victory: Decisive Wars and the Lessons of History* (2010). He is Senior Research Scholar in History and Classics at the Social Philosophy and Policy Center, Bowling Green State University, and has published in journals that include *Polis*, *Dikē*, and *Bryn Mawr Classical Review*.

Loren E. Lomasky is Cory Professor of Political Philosophy, Policy, and Law at the University of Virginia, where he directs the Political Philosophy, Policy, and Law Program. He previously taught at Bowling Green State University and the University of Minnesota, Duluth, and has held visiting positions at Virginia Polytechnic Institute, Australian National University, the Australian Defence Force Academy, and the National University of Singapore. He is the author of *Persons, Rights, and the Moral Community* (1987), for which he was awarded the 1990 Matchette Prize. His other books include *Democracy and Decision: The Pure Theory of Electoral Preference* (coauthored with Geoffrey Brennan, 1993), and *Politics and Process: New Essays in Democratic Theory* (coedited with Geoffrey Brennan, 1989).

Michael Zuckert is Nancy R. Dreux Professor of Political Science at the University of Notre Dame. He has written extensively on the liberal tradition in political philosophy and American constitutionalism. He is currently completing a book entitled *Natural Rights and American Constitutionalism*.

Felix Valenzuela is a doctoral candidate in Political Science at the University of Notre Dame. He holds a J.D. degree from Yale Law School and is currently at work on a critical study of the recent literature on constitutional failure.

Fernando R. Tesón is Tobias Simon Eminent Scholar at Florida State University College of Law. A native of Buenos Aires, Argentina, he is known for his scholarship relating political philosophy to international law and for his work on political rhetoric. He is the author of *A Philosophy of International Law* (1998), *Humanitarian Intervention: An Inquiry into Law and Morality* (3d ed., 2005), and *Rational Choice and Democratic Deliberation* (with Guido Pincione, 2006). Before joining Florida State University in 2003, he taught for seventeen years at Arizona State University. He has served as a visiting professor at Cornell Law School, Indiana University School of Law, and the University of California Hastings College of Law, and is Permanent Visiting Professor at Torcuato Di Tella University, Buenos Aires.

Sanford Levinson is W. St. John Garwood and W. St. John Garwood Jr. Centennial Chair in Law at the University of Texas Law School. He is also Professor of Government at the University of Texas at Austin. He holds a Ph.D. from Harvard University and a J.D. from Stanford University Law School. He has taught at Princeton University and has held visiting appointments at the Harvard, Yale, New York University, Georgetown, and Boston University law schools, as well as law schools in France, Hungary, Israel, New Zealand, and Australia. Among his books are *Constitutional Faith* (1988) and *Our Undemocratic Constitution: Where the Constitution Goes Wrong (and How We the People Can Correct It)* (2006). He is the author of more than 250 articles in professional and popular journals and was elected to membership in the American Academy of Arts and Sciences in 2001.

Scott D. Gerber is Ella and Ernest Fisher Chair in Law and Professor of Law at Ohio Northern University, and Senior Research Scholar in Law and Politics at the Social Philosophy and Policy Center. He received his Ph.D. and J.D. from the University of Virginia, and his B.A. from the College of William and Mary. His published works include six books and nearly one hundred articles, book reviews, and op-eds. He clerked for U.S. District Judge Ernest C. Torres of the District of Rhode Island and practiced with a major Boston-based law firm. He is a member of the Massachusetts, Colorado, and Virginia bars, as well as the U.S. Supreme Court bar. In both 2002 and 2009, he received the Fowler V. Harper Award for excellence in legal scholarship, and in 2008, he was appointed to a two-year term on the Ohio Advisory Committee of the U.S. Commission on Civil Rights. He teaches constitutional law and American legal history.

Ilya Somin is Associate Professor of Law at George Mason University School of Law. His research focuses on constitutional law, property law, and the study of popular political participation and its implications for constitutional democracy. His work has appeared in numerous scholarly journals, including the *Yale Law Journal, Stanford Law Review, Northwestern University Law Review, Georgetown Law Journal,* and *Critical Review.* He has served as a visiting professor at the University of Pennsylvania Law School; the University of Hamburg, Germany; and Torcuato Di Tella University in Buenos Aires, Argentina; and as an Olin Fellow at Northwestern University School of Law.

William A. Galston is Ezra Zilkha Chair of the Governance Studies Program at the Brookings Institution, where he serves as a Senior Fellow. He is also College Park Professor at the University of Maryland. Prior to January 2006, he was Saul Stern Professor at the School of Public Policy, University of Maryland, director of the Institute for Philosophy and Public Policy, and founding director of the Center for Information and Research on Civic Learning and Engagement (CIRCLE). From 1993 until 1995, he served as Deputy Assistant to President Clinton for Domestic Policy. He is the author of eight books, the most recent of which are *Liberal Pluralism* (2002), *The Practice of Liberal Pluralism* (2004), and *Public Matters* (2005). A winner of the American Political Science Association's Hubert H. Humphrey Award, he was elected a Fellow of the American Academy of Arts and Sciences in 2004.

James S. Fishkin is Janet M. Peck Chair in International Communication at Stanford University, where he is also Chair and Professor of Communication and Professor of Political Science (by courtesy). He is the director of Stanford's Center for Deliberative Democracy and is the author of a number of books, including *When the People Speak: Deliberative Democracy and Public Consultation* (2009), *The Voice of the People: Public Opinion and Democracy* (1995), *The Dialogue of Justice* (1992), and *Democracy and Deliberation* (1991). He is the coauthor, with Bruce Ackerman, of *Deliberation Day* (2004).

Guido Pincione is Professor of Philosophy and Law at Torcuato Di Tella University, Buenos Aires, and was Visiting Professor of Philosophy at Bowling Green State University in 2009–2010. He has taught previously at Buenos Aires University Law School and was a visiting scholar at Arizona State University College of Law, Australian National University, the Center for Ethics and Public Affairs at Tulane University, Corpus Christi College at Oxford University, Florida State University College of Law, Mannheim University, Université de Montreal Faculté de Droit, and University of Toronto Faculty of Law. He is the coauthor, with Fernando R. Tesón, of *Rational Choice and Democratic Deliberation* (2006), and has published articles on moral, political, and legal philosophy in journals such as *Utilitas, The Journal of Philosophy,* and *Philosophy and Phenomenological Research.*

Richard A. Epstein is James Parker Hall Distinguished Service Professor of Law and a director of the John M. Olin Program in Law and Economics at the University of Chicago. He has been the Peter and Kirsten Bedford Senior Fellow at the Hoover Institution since 2000 and a visiting law professor at New York University Law School since 2007. He is a member of the American Academy of Arts and Sciences and a Senior Fellow of the Center for Clinical Medical Ethics at the University of Chicago Medical School. He has served as editor of the *Journal of Legal Studies* and the *Journal of Law and Economics*, and is the author of numerous books, including *Cases and Materials on Torts* (9th ed., 2008), *Supreme Neglect: How to Revive Constitutional Protection for Private Property* (2008), *Overdose: How Excessive Government Regulation Stifles Pharmaceutical Innovation* (2006), and *Skepticism and Freedom: A Modern Case for Classical Liberalism* (2003).

ACKNOWLEDGMENT

The editors gratefully acknowledge Liberty Fund, Inc., for holding the conference at which the original versions of many of these papers were presented and discussed.

WHAT ARE CONSTITUTIONS, AND WHAT SHOULD (AND CAN) THEY DO?

By Larry Alexander

I. Introduction

A constitution is, as Article VI of the United States Constitution declares,[1] the fundamental law of the land, supreme as a legal matter over any other nonconstitutional law. But that almost banal statement raises a number of theoretically vexed issues. What is law? How is constitutional law to be distinguished from nonconstitutional law? How do morality and moral rights fit into the picture? And what are the implications of the answers to these questions for questions regarding how and by whom constitutions should be interpreted? These are the issues that I shall address.

I proceed as follows: In Section II, I take up law's principal function of settling controversies over what we are morally obligated to do. In Section III, I relate law's settlement function to the role of constitutional law. In particular, I discuss how constitutional law is distinguished from ordinary law. I also discuss the role of constitutions in establishing basic governmental structures and enforcing certain moral rights. In Section IV, I address the topic of constitutional interpretation, and in Section V the topic of judicial review. Finally, in Section VI, I discuss constitutional change, both change that occurs through a constitution's own rules for amendments and change that is the product of constitutional misinterpretations and revolutions.

II. Law and the Settlement of Moral Controversy

What is the principal function of law—all law? I would argue, and have argued,[2] that law's principal function is to settle what we are obligated to do. More precisely, law's principal function is to settle what our moral obligations are that are properly subject to coercive enforcement. Even if we were all motivated to fulfill our enforceable moral obligations, our disagreements about what those obligations are and what they entail in particular situations would produce huge moral costs. Because of our

---

[1] See U.S. Constitution, art. VI: "This Constitution . . . shall be the supreme Law of the Land. . . ."

[2] See, e.g., Larry Alexander and Emily Sherwin, *The Rule of Rules: Morality, Rules, and the Dilemmas of Law* (Durham, NC: Duke University Press, 2001), 11–25; and Larry Alexander, "'With Me, It's All or Nuthin'': Formalism in Law and Morality," *University of Chicago Law Review* 66 (1999): 530 (hereinafter "Formalism").

moral disagreements, we could not predict with any certainty what others were going to do. And because what is the morally correct conduct for me often depends upon what others are doing, my inability to predict and coordinate with others will lead me to do what is morally wrong even if I am trying to do what is morally right. Legal settlement of what I and others are obligated to do allows me to coordinate my acts with others' acts and avert the moral costs of colliding good intentions.

Legal settlement also can improve moral decision-making through giving decision-makers the benefits of others' expertise. I may know that polluting is wrong, but I may not know whether the substance I am about to dump in the river is a pollutant. I may know that I should not operate equipment that endangers others, but I may be ignorant of the fact that this particular piece of equipment is dangerous. Good intentions without factual expertise can be as problematic, in terms of morally significant consequences, as bad intentions are. Legal settlement can improve our moral decision-making if the law makes use of expertise.

Legal settlement also makes moral decision-making more efficient in terms of time and other resources. Even if I could eventually acquire expertise and the ability to predict how others will act, my decisions regarding what I am morally obligated to do, if unaided by law, may require a great deal of time and energy that could be put to better use if there were a legal settlement of the issue that was clear and easily accessible.

Thinking of law in terms of settlement of what we are enforceably morally obligated to do explains how law and morality coexist on the same terrain. Both purport to tell us what we are obligated, forbidden, or permitted to do. So the question might be asked, "Why do we need law, given that we already have morality?" Why do we have many volumes chock-full of laws rather than only the one, Spike Lee law, "Do the right thing"?[3] The answer is that although the Spike Lee law is in one sense perfect, and would be appropriate for a society of omniscient gods, in another sense, in our world of less than omniscient humans, "Do the right thing" is not "the right thing." Although we are neither gods nor angels, law is a response to the fact that we are not gods—not to the fact that we are not angels.[4] If we were omniscient gods, but some of us were not angels, "Do the right thing" would suffice. If one of us did the wrong thing, others, being omniscient, would know the right thing to do in response.[5] But if we were angels but not gods—always motivated to do the right thing, but uncertain of and disagreeing about the right thing to do—specific laws settling what we should do would effect a moral improvement over the Spike Lee law. It is paradoxical perhaps, but true

---

[3] Spike Lee is an American movie director, one of whose movies was entitled "Do the Right Thing." I am playing off this title, although the movie itself was not about law.

[4] See Alexander, "Formalism," 530.

[5] After all, we have moral theories about the appropriate responses to moral wrongdoing. See ibid.

nonetheless, that the perfect Spike Lee law is morally inferior to a regime of quite specific and likely imperfect laws.

Of course, to fulfill its settlement function and improve upon Spike Lee, law will have to consist of determinate rules. It is determinacy that produces settlement and its moral benefits of coordination, expertise, and efficiency.[6] Standards—those legal norms that are not determinate rules but rather instruct us to do what is "reasonable," "fair," or "just"—leave matters unsettled. In effect, they tell us to "do the right thing" within the region of decision-making subject to them. They fail to fulfill the settlement function. Rather, they defer settlement.

III. The Nature and Functions of Constitutional Law

If law's function is to settle what ought to be done through determinate rules, constitutional law's function is to settle the most basic matters regarding how we ought to organize society and government.[7] One can think of a constitution's being basic law through at least two different prisms. Looked at in terms of legal validity, constitutional law is the law that is highest in the validity chain. It validates lower-level law. Just as an administrative law may be valid only if it is authorized by a statute, a statute may be valid only if it is authorized by the constitution. The constitution is the highest law there is, and is neither valid nor invalid but just accepted.[8]

The second way to think of a constitution's being basic law is to think of it in terms of relative entrenchment against change. Typically,

---

[6] Determinacy, required for settlement, entails that rules, no matter how ideally crafted, will inevitably diverge from what morality requires in a range of cases (the over- and under-inclusiveness problem). In such cases, those subject to the rules will be faced with a choice between complying with the requirements of the rules and complying with the requirements of morality as they perceive those requirements. Settlement requires that they believe complying with the rules trumps complying with morality as they perceive it; and, as previously stated, morality itself suggests that there be settlement. Yet, if moral reasons are those reasons for acting that are always overriding, then it looks as if following rules when they appear to conflict with morality is acting against reason. If that is true, then rules cannot settle what we are morally obligated to do, which in turn means that settlement, however morally desirable, is not rationally achievable. This problem—we morally must seek but cannot morally achieve settlement—is nothing other than the perennial problem of law's normativity, or whether there can ever be an obligation to obey the law because it is the law.

I view the problem of law's normativity as part and parcel of law's settlement function. But in this essay I assume the settlement function is possible and put aside the paradox that it engenders. That paradox is given exhaustive (but inconclusive) treatment in Alexander and Sherwin, *The Rule of Rules*, 53–95.

[7] This view is relatively orthodox, but there are dissenters. For example, Michael Seidman believes a constitution's function is to *unsettle* matters. See Louis Michael Seidman, *Silence and Freedom* (Stanford, CA: Stanford University Press, 2007).

[8] Even if a constitution has not been ratified according to its terms, if it is accepted by the people as the highest law (minus its ratification provisions), then it *is* the highest law.

a constitution is more entrenched against change than a statute, an administrative rule, or a common law court decision.[9]

Usually the law that is highest in the validity chain is also the most entrenched. The reason for this is obvious. If lower-level laws like statutes were more entrenched than the higher-level constitutional laws that authorized such statutory entrenchments, one could repeal the entrenched statutes by the easier route of repealing the less entrenched constitution's authorization of the statutory entrenchment. So it makes sense to have higher-level law be more entrenched than lower-level law. Nevertheless, it is theoretically possible to have a lower-level law be more entrenched than the higher-level law that validates it.

Constitutions, as I said, lay down the ground rules for governance. They "constitute" the government. They set up structures, offices, and lawmaking procedures. Constitutions such as the U.S. Constitution and the Canadian Charter also entrench "rights."

When a constitution promulgates the structures, offices, and procedures for governance—the rules about how laws are to be made, how offices are to be filled, and which level of government and which officials within government are to have jurisdiction over which matters—the constitutional provisions in question are similar to assembly instructions that accompany gadgets or toys that we buy. They are instructions for "how to assemble a government." But if this is how we should conceptualize the structural provisions of the constitution, how should we conceptualize those provisions that constitutionalize certain rights?

As I see it, there are three, and only three, possibilities here. First, the constitutional authors might be creating rights or making certain rights more determinate by means of rules granting various specific liberties and immunities. Second, the constitutional authors might not be creating or specifying rights through rules but might instead be incorporating real moral rights as they exist in the moral realm[10]—that is, making certain real moral rights legally as well as morally binding on the government and enforceable by the judiciary. Third, the constitutional authors might be inventing

---

[9] The question of how much constitutions should be entrenched against change—and for that matter, the question of how much subconstitutional laws should be entrenched against change—is an important, complex, and controversial matter. I call it the problem of legal transitions, and it finds constitutional expression in doctrines relating to takings of property, impairments of contracts, and deprivations of vested interests. It finds meta-constitutional expression in discussions over how easily amendable constitutions should be. For a general discussion, see the symposium "Legal Transitions: Is There an Ideal Way to Deal with the Non-Ideal World of Legal Change?" *The Journal of Contemporary Legal Issues* 13 (2003). See also Alexander and Sherwin, *The Rule of Rules*, 151–56.

[10] In speaking of "real moral rights" or of "the moral realm," I am referring throughout to a conception of morality that views it as independent of norms created by individuals or societies, as a matter of discovery rather than invention, as a set of norms that human norms seek to mirror and by which they can be criticized. I believe that such a conception of morality, sometimes referred to as "critical morality," is metaethically modest and neutral among several metaethical positions.

or creating rights but without translating them into determinate rules. I shall take up the implications of these three possibilities in turn.

The first possibility—creating a right, or making an existing right determinate, through a determinate rule—is unproblematic and unremarkable. In the U.S. Constitution, the so-called right against self-incrimination was most likely meant by the authors of the Fifth Amendment to be no more than a rule granting defendants an immunity from being compelled, on pain of contempt, to testify in court.[11] It was an invented right, as there probably is no corresponding moral right against self-incrimination. And the scope of this invented right was coterminous with the rule that embodied it.

Likewise, some scholars believe that the "freedom of speech" referred to in the First Amendment was meant to be a determinate rule forbidding Congress from requiring licensing of speakers and publishers—that is, a determinate rule against prior restraints.[12] If there is a general right of free expression, on this view, the First Amendment was making determinate and constitutionalizing only a portion of the more general right. Something similar might be said of the rights against takings of property without just compensation[13] and against impairing the obligations of contracts:[14] the constitutional provisions protecting these rights might be said to be rules that make determinate (and constitutionalize) portions of a more general moral right against upsets of legitimate expectations engendered by law.

Other rights, such as the right in the First Amendment to petition the government, might be seen as rules that are corollaries of the type of governmental structure created by the Constitution—a representative democracy—and not as moral rights that exist prior to that structure.[15]

Let me now turn to the second possibility for constitutionalizing rights, namely, incorporating by reference real moral rights. Ronald Dworkin, for example, believes that this is what the authors of the U.S. Constitution were doing when they wrote into the Constitution a right against cruel and unusual punishments, a right to equal protection, a right to the free exercise of religion, and other rights.[16] There are three aspects of such an enterprise worth careful consideration.

---

[11] See U.S. Constitution, amend. V: "No person shall . . . be compelled in any criminal case to be a witness against himself."

[12] See U.S. Constitution, amend. I: "Congress shall make no law . . . abridging the freedom of speech." See also Leonard Levy, *Legacy of Suppression: Freedom of Speech and Press in Early American History* (Cambridge, MA: Belknap Press of Harvard University Press, 1960).

[13] See U.S. Constitution, amend. V: "[N]or shall private property be taken for public use, without just compensation."

[14] See U.S. Constitution, art. I, sec. 10: "No State shall . . . pass any . . . Law impairing the Obligation of Contracts."

[15] See U.S. Constitution, amend. I: "Congress shall make no law . . . prohibiting . . . the right of the people peaceably to assemble, and to petition the Government for a redress of grievances."

[16] See Ronald Dworkin, *Freedom's Law: The Moral Reading of the American Constitution* (Cambridge, MA: Harvard University Press, 1996), 7–12.

First, if one is going to incorporate real moral rights into a constitution, then one is going to have to subordinate those rights to the various rules setting up the structure of the government and also subordinate them to decisions regarding their content that are supposed to be legally authoritative—that is, decisions that are supposed to settle the question of what the content of those moral rights is for purposes of the legal system.[17]

Let me elaborate briefly on this point about subordinating moral rights. Within morality, moral rights are not subordinate to human institutions and human decisions. Rather, the contrary is the case. Human institutions and decisions are subordinate to moral rights. If moral rights were incorporated into a constitution without making them subordinate to other aspects of the constitutional regime, then they might completely overturn that regime.[18] For there is never any guarantee that a constitutional structure is consistent with moral rights as they really are. After all, the constitutional structure is an artifact produced by human beings possessing fallible moral beliefs.

Moreover, because the content of real moral rights is controversial, incorporating real moral rights into a constitution would make the content of constitutional law—and thus all law—incapable of being authoritatively determined. For the content of real moral rights cannot be settled by any institution's decision regarding that content, whether it is the decision of the legislature or the decision of the Supreme Court. Therefore, incorporation of real moral rights into a constitution will undermine the settlement function of law unless it is understood that those rights are legally (if not morally) subordinate to some institution's determination of their content. If that were not true, decisions of the legislature and the Supreme Court regarding moral rights would fail to be *law* in the eyes of those who disagreed with the decisions, because they would see those decisions as inconsistent with real moral rights.[19]

Thus, the first point about incorporating real moral rights is that they must be subordinated to constitutional structures and to authoritative determinations of their content. The second point about incorporation of real moral rights is related: A decision must be made regarding which institution's *view* of real moral rights should be treated as authoritative for purposes of the legal system. To narrow the focus to the usual suspects, should the legislature's view of real moral rights be authoritative, or should the authoritative view be that of the courts?

Keep in mind that everyone—the legislature, the courts, and the people themselves—is subject to the requirements imposed by real moral rights. So the question is never whether the legislature is *morally* free to disregard

---

[17] See generally Larry Alexander and Frederick Schauer, "Law's Limited Domain Confronts Morality's Universal Empire," *William and Mary Law Review* 48 (2007): 1579.

[18] Ibid., 1595.

[19] Ibid., 1595–96.

real moral rights, or whether the courts are *morally* free to do so. The question is whose view of what those rights require should be the authoritative view within the legal system.

Some democrats believe that the legislature's view should be authoritative.[20] However, because the legislature is always subject to the constraints of real moral rights, and can always tailor its legislation to the requirements of real moral rights as it perceives them whether or not those rights are incorporated into the constitution, it is pointless to incorporate them unless one plans to make them judicially enforceable against the legislature (whether or not the legislature is able thereafter to override that determination). I repeat: Constitutionalizing real moral rights only makes sense alongside judicial authority to determine their content and enforce them against the legislature. That is not because courts are superior to legislatures when it comes to determining the content of moral rights; rather, it is because legislatures are already supposed to make their legislation consistent with real moral rights, whether or not those rights are constitutionalized. Incorporating those moral rights as legal rights, but then making the legislature's view of their content legally supreme over the view of the courts, thus accomplishes nothing. (I take no view here on whether courts *are* superior to legislatures in determining the content of real moral rights.[21] I tend to be skeptical of either institution's ability in this regard, though no more skeptical than I am of law faculties' or philosophy departments' ability.) Nonetheless, as I said, if courts are *not* superior to legislatures in determining the content of real moral rights, either epistemically or motivationally, it makes no sense to constitutionalize those rights. They apply to the legislature whether or not they are constitutionalized.

So if real moral rights are to be incorporated into a constitution, they must be subordinated to the constitutional structures and to some institution's determination of their content. Therefore, an institution must be chosen that will have the authoritative say regarding that content, though incorporation of real moral rights strongly implies that the chosen authoritative institution will be the courts.

The third thing to note about incorporating real moral rights is that there is no guarantee that the moral realm as it actually is will contain the specific moral rights referred to in the constitutional text. There may not be any moral right of equality,[22] or of freedom of expression,[23] or of

---

[20] See Jeremy Waldron, *Law and Disagreement* (Oxford: Clarendon Press; New York: Oxford University Press, 1999).

[21] For an analysis of the competence of courts to decide moral matters, see Jeremy Waldron, "Judges as Moral Reasoners," *I-Con* 7 (2009): 2; and Wojciech Sadurski, "Rights and Moral Reasoning: An Unstated Assumption—A Comment on Jeremy Waldron's 'Judges as Moral Reasoners,' " *I-Con* 7 (2009): 25.

[22] See Peter Westen, "The Empty Idea of Equality," *Harvard Law Review* 95 (1982): 537.

[23] See Larry Alexander, *Is There a Right of Freedom of Expression?* (Cambridge and New York: Cambridge University Press, 2005).

freedom of religion.[24] Or those rights may just be aspects of some moral right that is not named in the constitution. Or the correct moral theory might be a consequentialist one, like utilitarianism or egalitarianism, in which the only moral "right" is that all actions conform to the consequentialist norm. If constitutional authors wish to constitutionalize real moral rights, they had better be certain that the rights they name *are* real moral rights. But, of course, they cannot be certain.[25] They might be better off just telling the courts to enforce against the legislature whatever moral rights there actually are, without attempting to name them. For in naming moral rights that do not exist, they might lead the courts to be more confused about what rights there are than would be the case if they had left moral rights unnamed.

I have now discussed two of the three possibilities constitutional authors might have in mind in constitutionalizing rights. They might be creating specific rights in the form of determinate rules that define the rights, such as a rule forbidding judicially compelled incriminating testimony or a rule forbidding requiring a license to speak. Or they might be attempting to incorporate by reference real moral rights rather than defining those rights through determinate rules or creating them. The third and final possibility is that in constitutionalizing a right, the constitutional authors are inventing or creating the right, but without giving it any determinate form—that is, without embodying it in a rule or set of rules. Rather, the right is supposed to function as a principle or value, with weight,[26] not as a specific rule such as the rule against requiring a license to speak.

There is only one problem with this third possibility, but it is a doozy. This possibility is in truth an impossibility. One cannot, however hard one tries, create a right that is not coterminous with a determinate rule. If there is nothing in the world preexisting the constitution to which this right refers—if this right comes into being only by virtue

---

[24] Ibid., chap. 8.

[25] I have said that referring to actual moral principles is a risky business. One reason, already mentioned, is that moral principles, unless cabined, can overrun all positive law, including those decisions meant to settle the controversial content of moral principles themselves. However, another reason is that there is no relation between the number of moral principles our vocabularies reveal and the number of moral principles there actually are. We have all sorts of moral principles as a matter of vocabulary. Thus, we can refer to freedom of speech, protection against cruel and unusual punishment, equal protection, and so on. But suppose utilitarianism is the correct moral theory. There are no such "joints" in utilitarianism. Seeking to enact only a limb, we may have enacted an entire beast. In short, if there are objective referents for our moralized enactments, there is no reason to assume that morality has the joints our terms reflect, or, if it does, that morality deems it morally permissible that it be carved at such joints.

[26] What does it mean to say a principle or value has "weight"? It means that the principle or value is supposed to incline one to reach a certain result but, unlike a rule, it does not mandate that result. Rules either apply or do not apply; and if they apply, then they determine what should be done. Principles or values, in contrast, are supposed to be always applicable but can be outweighed by other principles or values that incline one in the opposite direction.

of its being mentioned in the constitution—then its contours and weight cannot be assessed nonarbitrarily, as there is nothing in the world that would make any such assessment true. The courts would be making it up if they were to declare that such a constitutional right applied or did not apply, outweighed the government's interest in its legislation or did not outweigh it.

I shall give one illustration of the problem that will stand in for every possible illustration. Suppose that we wish to create a right that does not exist in the moral realm—say, a right to fine art. We do not, however, specify through determinate rules just what the right entails: Does it entail government funding of art, and if so, how much, and how is this funding to be balanced against other governmental resource needs? Does it entail a legally enforceable obligation of talented artists to produce such art, and if so, how is this obligation to be balanced against artists' right to liberty? And may government suppress fine art that threatens public order, and if so, of what magnitude must the threat be? Suppose that instead of resolving these questions through detailed determinate rules, we simply say that we will let the courts resolve these questions. Well, how will the courts resolve them other than according to judicial preference? There is no right to fine art in the moral realm which they can consult. When they resolve these questions, then, there will be no criteria available to determine if their resolutions are correct or incorrect. We made up the right, and they will have to make up its contours in deciding cases rather than looking to independently existing contours that could render their decisions right or wrong. They will be in the position of one who is told that a nonexistent creature—say, a unicorn—has a horselike body and a horn on its head, but is then asked to give its height, weight, color, and speed. One would protest, "This is an invented creature, and its inventor hasn't given me this information—so how would I know?" The same applies to invented rights not embodied in determinate rules.

My point is this: Rights that do not exist in the moral realm can only be created through and fully embodied in determinate rules. The enactment of nondeterminate "principles" that are supposed to function as weighty considerations cannot create rights and their weights, if those rights and weights have no pre-enactment existence. Put differently, there are no *legal* principles, legal norms that are neither determinate rules nor references to preexisting *moral* principles. If incorporation of actual moral principles is not what the enactment of legal principles represents, can legal principles be created merely through enactment? The answer is "no." For there is no way to "create" by an act of human will a real principle, namely, a norm that is not a determinate rule with a canonical formulation but is instead a norm that possesses weight.[27]

---

[27] Again, real moral principles are themselves not human creations. See note 10 above. I take no position here on whether real moral principles actually have weight, or whether

To see that this is impossible, assume that there is, in the moral realm, no free speech principle. Then put yourself in the position of the lawmaker who wishes to create a free speech principle. How can he accomplish this (again, keeping in mind that there is no such moral principle for him to refer to and incorporate by reference). He could, of course, write out a set of instructions for how to apply the "principle," but in that case he will merely have reduced it to a rule with canonical form that is either applicable or inapplicable but lacks weight. And I see no way that lawmakers can create weight, except by issuing instructions for how the principle applies in every conceivable case—which is not only impossible, but if possible would just be the enactment of a weightless rule, albeit an infinitely lengthy and complex one.

If I am correct, then direct enactment of legal principles is not an option. If lawmakers believe that they are enacting legal principles, they are mistaken. If, for example, there is no free speech principle in the moral domain available for incorporation in the legal domain, then enacting a free speech principle is an impossibility, and lawmakers who believe *that* is what they are doing must be doing something else.[28]

---

instead they are complex algorithms whose complexity is taken for weight. (I lean heavily toward the latter position.)

[28] In a recent essay, Tara Smith argues that when lawmakers refer to "concepts" in their enactments, the meaning those concepts possess is not the list of things the lawmakers had in mind, nor is it the criteria the lawmakers were employing in constructing that list. Rather, the meaning of such concepts is the things in the world that the concepts themselves pick out. So when the lawmakers use terms like "cruel," "speech," or "equal protection" in the laws they enact, correct interpretation requires looking not at what the lawmakers meant by those terms but at what sorts of things in the world are really cruel, speech, or equal protection. See Tara Smith, "Why Originalism Won't Die: Common Mistakes in Competing Theories of Judicial Interpretation," *Duke Journal of Constitutional Law and Public Policy* 2 (2007): 159, 189–92. I do not want to get into the deep waters of what concepts are and what the relationship is between words and concepts, between criteria and concepts, or among natural, artifactual, and fictional kinds as they relate to concepts. (Is there an "objective" concept of, say, a unicorn or a table that possibly differs from users' criteria?) I want to restrict my comments here to the kinds of concepts that Smith uses as her examples. For one might be tempted to believe that *these* are what legal principles are: that is, legal principles are the normative concepts referred to in legal enactments.

I have conceded that real moral principles can be referred to in legal enactments and thereby be incorporated into the law, though I have also alluded to the risks of doing so. I shall return to this possibility momentarily.

What I want to consider first is whether there are moral concepts that can exist apart from being part of morality as it actually is. For example, suppose, as I have argued elsewhere (see note 23 above), that there really is no defensible principle of freedom of expression. Is there nonetheless an objective "concept" of freedom of expression to which a user of this term could be referring? Or suppose the normative idea of equality is "empty" (see, e.g., Westen, "The Empty Idea of Equality"). Is there nonetheless an objective "concept" of "equal protection"?

Of course, even if there are no objective moral concepts other than those picked out by correct moral theory, we can refer to incorrect moral *theories*. I may not believe utilitarianism is correct as a moral theory, but I can refer to it and apply it. What is important, however, is that I can do these things based on the criteria that I and others use to define utilitarianism. Apart from the criteria that define it, utilitarianism *as a false moral theory* has no other

If legal principles cannot be created directly by enactment, perhaps they can be created indirectly. Indeed, indirect creation is precisely the account given by Ronald Dworkin, whose description of legal principles I am employing. For Dworkin, legal principles are not enacted as such. Rather, they arise out of those legal rules and judicial decisions that *are* directly enacted.[29]

Legal principles—again, legal norms that lack canonical form and have the dimension of weight—are those principles and their weights that "fit" (would justify) a sufficient number of legal rules and decisions and that have a sufficient degree of moral acceptability. Put differently, legal principles are those principles that are the most morally acceptable of the principles that are at or above the requisite threshold of fit.

On Dworkin's account, legal principles may turn out to be less than morally ideal. That is, legal principles will not be moral principles. For legal principles, unlike moral principles, are constrained by the requirement that they fit the legal rules and decisions, at least to a certain degree. That is why Dworkinian legal principles are not just moral principles consulted by judges. (Dworkin's argument for legal principles, which relies on the notion of fit, both synchronic and diachronic,[30] actually implies that legislatures and constitutional authors, no less than judges, should be bound by legal principles.)

Over a decade ago, Ken Kress and I wrote an article attacking Dworkin's account of legal principles.[31] The article was long and complex, and I shall give only a very abbreviated version of it here. The nub of the argument, however, was that (1) the moral acceptability axis would dictate whatever threshold of "fit" correct *moral* principles will satisfy and thus make legal principles identical to moral ones, and (2) Dworkinian legal principles, if not identical to moral principles, would be quite unattractive norms by which to be governed.

With respect to the first point, suppose a jurisdiction has a number of legal rules and judicial decisions on the books that are morally infelicitous or even iniquitous. Moral principles would tell us to follow only those

---

ontological status. There is no independently existing "concept" of utilitarianism sitting in some ontological warehouse waiting for someone to come along and refer to it.

My view, then, is that the one possibility that is open is that when lawmakers use a moralized term like "freedom of speech" or "equal protection," they are either enacting a determinate rule that is fixed by the specific criteria they have in mind, or they are referring to and incorporating actual moral principles. Legal principles, in other words, could just be actual moral principles referred to by laws.

[29] See Ronald Dworkin, *Taking Rights Seriously* (Cambridge, MA: Harvard University Press, 1977), 81–130; and Ronald Dworkin, *Law's Empire* (Cambridge, MA: Belknap Press of Harvard University Press, 1986), 176–275.

[30] Synchronic fit is fit with currently existing posited legal materials, such as the constitution, statutes, and administrative rules. Diachronic fit is fit with past legal decisions. Dworkin's legal principles must fit legal materials along both dimensions.

[31] Larry Alexander and Ken Kress, "Against Legal Principles," in Andrei Marmor, ed., *Law and Interpretation: Essays in Legal Philosophy* (Oxford: Clarendon Press; New York: Oxford University Press, 1995), 279–328.

legal rules and decisions that were morally sound or to follow unsound
legal rules and decisions only when doing so is warranted according to
correct moral principles—in other words, follow moral principles.

It might be objected that if we ignored legal rules and decisions that
were morally infelicitous, various bad things would happen. People who
relied on infelicitous rules and decisions would have their expectations,
on which they may have relied in costly ways, dashed. Coordination with
others would become more difficult and costly. And so on.

But notice that if those costs are morally cognizable, which is plausible,
then *application of correct moral principles will have taken those costs into
account.* Put differently, if a morally incorrect legal rule or decision is
enacted, its enactment changes the facts in the world to which *correct*
moral principles apply. So it may be morally correct to follow a legal rule
that it would have been morally better not to have enacted *ab initio.*

Therefore, the moral acceptability axis will always dictate a threshold
of fit that is precisely what following correct moral principles would
produce. That means that *unless the threshold of fit is determined independently of moral acceptability, legal principles will turn out to be identical to
moral principles.*

The alternative of the threshold's being independent of moral acceptability is quite unattractive, however. Any threshold of fit less than one
hundred percent looks arbitrary. More importantly, however, if the threshold is independent of moral acceptability, legal principles will be normatively unattractive. For on this accounting, legal principles will lack the
determinacy virtue of legal rules and decisions—they will have all of the
indeterminacy of moral principles (because they can be ascertained only
by recourse to morality and will therefore be as controversial as morality)—
and they will lack, as well, the moral correctness virtue of moral principles (because they must fit morally incorrect legal rules and decisions).
Legal principles will be neither determinate and predictable nor morally
correct. They will have nothing to recommend them as norms, and thus
there will never be any reason to consult them.

If a norm is not a norm of morality, and if it is not determinate and
cannot coordinate behavior, then it has no normative virtues. And if a
norm lacks normative virtues, then I would argue it does not exist as a
norm. Indirectly enacted Dworkinian legal principles do not satisfy this
existence condition.

Robert Alexy's conception of legal principles is very similar to that of
Dworkin.[32] On Alexy's conception, principles have no specific canonical
form, and they have the dimension of weight.[33] When they conflict, one
principle can outweigh the other in the circumstances of the case at hand,

---

[32] See Robert Alexy, *A Theory of Constitutional Rights* (Oxford and New York: Oxford
University Press, 2002).
[33] Ibid., 50–54.

but the outweighed principle continues to exist and may outweigh the other principle in different circumstances.[34] (When rules conflict, however, one rule is either invalid altogether or at a minimum invalid in the circumstances of conflict and thus modified.)[35] Alexy conceives of legal principles as values to be optimized—realized to the greatest extent possible consistent with their weight vis-à-vis the weight of competing values, including the value of following democratically enacted rules.[36] Alexy departs from Dworkin—who distinguishes principles from collective goals (policies)—by treating both as principles, the realization of which is to be optimized.[37]

How do principles become part of the law on Alexy's account? Alexy nowhere suggests that, as Dworkin contends, legal principles emerge from the mating of legal rules and legal decisions with moral principles— that is, that legal principles are the most morally acceptable principles that "fit" (to an unspecified degree) with the extant legal rules and decisions.

That leaves on the table the possibility that legal principles are posited by lawmaking acts intended to bring those principles into the law. Again, there are two ways principles might be deliberately made part of the law. First, lawmakers might wish to incorporate real moral principles into the law, either in legal standards, or as necessary or sufficient conditions for legal validity. Second, lawmakers might wish to create principles and enact their own creations. To repeat what I said earlier, real moral principles incorporated into standards are hemmed in by rules and subordinated to those rules and to judicial decisions regarding the content of the moral principles. They are thoroughly domesticated and incapable of undermining the settlement function of law—although they do nothing to further it. However, law's settlement function *is* undermined when real moral principles are incorporated as necessary or sufficient conditions of legal validity but are not subordinated to posited rules and judicial decisions.

In any event, Alexy provides ample evidence that incorporation of real moral principles is not what he is envisioning in the positing of legal principles. For example, he mentions the possibility of positing morally obnoxious principles, such as the "principle" of racial segregation.[38] Obviously, that is not a real moral principle, a principle that true morality contains. Nor is the principle, cited by Alexy, of the "maintenance and support of the manual arts"[39] likely to be a real moral principle rather than, at most, a relevant consideration under some general moral theory.

---

[34] Ibid.
[35] Ibid., 49.
[36] Ibid., 47–48, 80–81 n. 143, 86, 92.
[37] Ibid., 66.
[38] Ibid., 61.
[39] Ibid., 81.

In still other passages, Alexy speaks of *enactment* of a principle.[40] I conclude, therefore, that Alexy views legal principles and their weights as
capable of being *created* by deliberate enactment (as opposed to being
incorporated from an independent moral realm).

If I have read Alexy correctly, then his position is subject to my earlier
critique of the direct enactment of legal principles. Weight cannot be enacted.
There may be *moral* principles that have that dimension; that would depend
on whether the best moral theory is one in which there is a plurality of principles that are not lexically ordered. And a complex *rule* with a number of
qualifications and conditions on its application may mimic the dimension
of weight. But real weight—and hence legal principles—cannot be enacted.
Both direct and indirect enactment of principles with weights are impos-
sibilities. Therefore, there are no legal principles. If that is true, then when
courts purport to decide cases by alluding to legal principles and their relative weights, they are making it up. There is no independent realm of legal
principles and their weights to which they can be referring.

Well, one might ask, what about legal *standards*—legal norms that are
not determinate rules? Do standards not require judges to fill in their
requirements? I would answer that standards do require judges to fill in
their requirements, but to fill them in by consulting reasons that preexist
the legal system, most notably, moral reasons. A standard essentially
instructs the judge to do what is morally best within the space left open
by legal rules.[41] Standards do *not* create the reasons on which judges are
to rely in fleshing them out.

---

[40] See, e.g., ibid., 83.

[41] Standards are delegations to future decision-makers to engage in first-order practical
reasoning and (unlike rules) do not themselves authoritatively settle controversies over the
deliverances of such reasoning. But is this true of standards that require the future decision-
maker to consider certain factors or criteria?

To answer this, one should distinguish two types of multifactor standards. One type
requires the decision-maker to consider certain factors (criteria) but does not preclude the
decision-maker from also considering other factors that the decision-maker may think relevant to the correct all-things-considered judgment. Such a multifactor standard is *not* a
counterexample to the claim that standards invite first-order practical reasoning. The factors
are merely things the standard promulgator thinks will probably bear on that reasoning. But
the future decision-maker is not precluded from taking into account *any* factor that bears on
that reasoning. A standard issued by the owner of a major league baseball team to the team's
general manager instructing him, when trading ball players, to consider batting average,
fielding percentage, and salary, *among other factors*, leaves the general manager unconstrained in making the best all-things-considered baseball decision. He can give the named
factors whatever weight he believes they possess.

The second type of multifactor standard requires the future decision-maker to consider
nothing but the mentioned factors. This type of standard is really a combination of a standard
and a rule. It essentially directs the decision-maker to make an all-things-considered judgment (a standard) but, in doing so, to screen out all considerations but the named factors (a
rule). The decision-maker would, in essence, be bound by the rule portion to assume that all
the relevant factors he is *not* supposed to consider are in equipoise, even if they really are
not. It would be like a directive from the owner to the general manager to determine trades
based *only* on batting, fielding, and salary, and to assume therefore that all the players are
equal in leadership qualities, tendencies to injury, fan appeal, and so on.

IV. Constitutional Interpretation

I have argued that constitutional provisions creating governmental structures are like assembly instructions for toys and gadgets. They are assembly instructions for creating a government. Constitutional rights provisions, I have argued, can be of two types: determinate rules creating the rights; or incorporation by reference of real moral rights. Finally, I have argued that creating rights other than through determinate rules is an impossibility.

So what do these points suggest is the proper way to interpret constitutions? Let us consider first the interpretation of structural provisions. Consider what the constitutional enterprise *is* in this regard. We have asked the constitutional authors to tell us how we should construct our government. How should the legislative branch be structured and chosen? How should the other branches be structured and chosen? What should be the respective powers of the federal and provincial governments? And so on. The constitutional authors have communicated their resolutions of these issues to us through symbols—marks on pages, in the case of written constitutions. It would make sense, would it not, to interpret those symbols as meaning what the constitutional authors intended them to mean—that is, by reference to the constitutional authors' intended meaning. After all, we charged them with the task of producing governmental assembly instructions, and these symbols were meant by them to convey what they had produced. It would be decidedly odd to have one group write assembly instructions but then to take the symbols the group used and "interpret" those symbols as if they had been produced by some other group with different intended meanings. Why should we read the Canadian Charter or the United States Constitution as if they were written in English if we do not care about the intended meanings of their actual authors? Why not imagine that the marks on the pages are not English but are in some special code that means what we would like it to mean? No mark or sound has any inherent meaning. Marks, sounds, and other symbols used by someone or some group to communicate their ideas to others have only the meanings that those who produce them intend them to convey. And although for any set of symbols produced by one author with a given intended meaning, we can always treat those symbols as if they were produced by a different author with a different intended meaning, doing so with constitutional provisions makes the whole process of authoring them and adopting them bizarre. When I read assembly instructions for a toy or gadget, I try to discern what those who wrote them intended, not what someone else might have intended by those symbols, much less what I would have intended. Looking for the authors' originally intended meaning is the only thing that makes sense when it comes to constitutions' structural provisions.

Someone might object that I have overstated my case. They might argue that interpretation of structural constitutional rules can properly depart from the authors' intended meaning so long as the symbols in the constitution can bear an alternative meaning. But this is a confusion on several levels.

First, to repeat, giving some people the job of coming up with structural rules but then disregarding the meanings *they* intended their chosen symbols to convey seems quite bizarre and verges on unintelligibility.

Second, it is a mistake to imagine that a given set of symbols can bear only a limited number of meanings. Any symbol can convey an indefinite number of meanings. Even if we artificially decree that a certain set of symbols must be treated as if it were English (and no set of symbols itself declares what standard language, if any, it is in), words and phrases in English can bear an indefinite number of meanings, again depending on the intentions of their users and the understandings of those intentions by the audience. At some point in time, the word "bad" came to convey the meaning "good," as in, "That's a really bad car you're driving." At some point in time, "He's a really cool cat" came to refer not only to the tabby by the air conditioner but to a jazz musician in sweltering New Orleans. Symbols, languages, codes, idiolects—they can convey any meaning so long as the intended meaning is understood by its audience.

Moreover, it is only the intended meaning of its authors that gives a constitutional text its unity, so that the Canadian or American constitution reprinted in one book is the same constitution as that in another book, and the same as that in the national archives. What I mean is this: If a constitution contains an ambiguous word or phrase, and we can resolve the ambiguity either by reference to the authors' intended meaning or by reference to other possible meanings (meanings someone other than the authors could have intended to convey), then the different possible interpretations represent different constitutions. For suppose the ambiguous word or phrase in English has no counterpart in, say, Italian. Rather, there is a separate Italian word for each of the possible meanings. In that case, when translators translate the constitution into Italian, if they resolve the ambiguity differently from one another, they will produce Italian versions that are *symbolically* different one from another. The only thing that makes a given set of symbols the same text as a different set of symbols is that they have the same authorially intended meaning.

Someone might object to my assertion that seeking the authorially intended meaning of structural rules is the only thing that makes sense of the enterprise of asking some group to author such rules. She might claim that I have conflated the Constitution as a set of structural rules drafted and ratified by identifiable people at a specific time in history with "The Constitution" that is our fundamental law. The latter refers not to the specific instructions communicated to us by their drafters/ratifiers but to our *practice* of constitutional argument. Within that practice, we might invoke the intended meanings of the actual authors. But we might also invoke the plain meaning of the text, historical developments, morality, prudence, and so forth. Each argumentative modality is part of our constitutional practice.[42] Originally intended meanings occupy no preferred position among such modalities.

There is a sense in which this claim is true, and there is a sense in which it seems deeply confused. It is true that one can find constitutional arguments framed in all of these ways, and one can find Supreme Court opinions that exhibit this modal diversity as well.

Nonetheless, each modality corresponds to a different constitution. The originally intended constitution is different from the textualist one, which is in turn different from the historical and moral ones, and so on. If rendered in Italian, each would be symbolically distinct. So different modalities entail different constitutions.

But then, when a litigant invokes one modality in an argument and her opponent invokes another, what exactly are they arguing about? To answer "the Constitution" is wrong on the modalities account, as there are different constitutions, not *the* Constitution. The litigants appear to be arguing past each other and thus not in fact disagreeing. They are each engaged in "the practice" of constitutional argument and cannot be said to be disagreeing about *that*.[43]

What, then, is the argument about, on the modalities account? Perhaps it is not an argument over what *the* Constitution means but rather an argument about *which* constitution the Supreme Court should endorse as *the* Constitution. Perhaps this is true—although those endorsing the modalities approach tend not to see it as one in which litigants offer up alternative constitutions from which the Supreme Court is to choose. For one thing, if the Court does, as it must, choose one modality to resolve the

---

[42] See Philip Bobbitt, *Constitutional Fate: Theory of the Constitution* (New York and Oxford: Oxford University Press, 1982); and Mitchell N. Berman, "Constitutional Theory and the Rule of Recognition: Toward a Fourth Theory of Law," in Matthew D. Adler and Kenneth Einar Himma, eds., *The Rule of Recognition and the U.S. Constitution* (New York and Oxford: Oxford University Press, 2009), 269–94.

[43] Mitch Berman has recently argued that "the Constitution" is really our practice of constitutional argument. See Berman, "Constitutional Theory and the Rule of Recognition." But this "argumentative practice" conception of the Constitution seems to me to entail a category mistake. The fact that we argue about the Constitution's meaning does not mean that the Constitution is itself the practice of constitutional argument. To assert the latter would be to confuse the external perspective on what constitutional lawyers are doing— "they're *arguing* about constitutional meaning"—with the internal perspective of the participants themselves—"we're arguing *about* constitutional meaning." If Berman's view were correct, then when scientists argue about string theory or elementary particles, we would be justified in saying that string theory and elementary particles *are* argumentative practices. That would, however, be obviously absurd.

Berman has also recently argued that constitutional meaning is a matter of achieving reflective equilibrium among our various "constitutional intuitions," intuitions that are independent of our views about authorially intended meaning. See Mitchell N. Berman, *Reflective Equilibrium and Constitutional Method: The Case of John McCain and the Natural Born Citizenship Clause* (forthcoming). I deny that we have independent constitutional intuitions of the type required by the methodology of reflective equilibrium. For the full argument against this position, see Larry Alexander, "Simple-Minded Originalism" (forthcoming).

case, that choice is not supposed to establish the supremacy of that modality in any other case. All of the losing constitutions are supposed to remain available for use in future cases.

More importantly, on what basis is the Court to choose among the modalities? There is no meta-modality to govern choice among the modalities. Any choice among them will thus be an exercise of judicial will and nothing more.

There is only one "modality" that makes sense of the enterprise of drafting and ratifying a constitution. Seeking any "meaning" other than the meaning that the actual drafters/ratifiers intended to convey through whatever symbolic medium they employed renders the project of constitution-making quite bizarre. We might as well make anagrams out of the letters in a constitution (though in what language?)!

When it comes to a constitution's structural rules, therefore, those rules have a fixed meaning, the meaning their authors intended at the time the rules were promulgated. Any other interpretive approach is tantamount to reauthoring the structural rules. The "dead hand" of the authors' original intended meaning must control, lest the enterprise of designing a constitutional structure be upended.

How do these remarks about interpreting structural rules bear on the interpretation of constitutional rights? If the rights are embodied in determinate rules, then what I have said about interpreting structural rules applies equally to interpreting rules that create rights. If those rules are given meanings as if they had been authored by someone other than their actual authors, someone who did not mean by them what their actual authors meant by them, then the constitutional rights will have been amended by the courts. If the rules meant on day one what their authors meant by them—and, to repeat, it would be an odd enterprise to have some group come up with rights-creating rules but then assign meanings to those rules that are different from the authors' intended meanings— then the rules continue to mean the same thing on day two and day three and today. Any "living tree" or other approach is as inapplicable to rules specifying rights as it is to rules structuring the government.

What about constitutional rights that represent incorporation by reference of real moral rights? Well, with such provisions, interpretation begins and ends with discovering that the authors intended to refer to real moral rights. Once the courts get into the business of spelling out the content of those rights, they are no longer interpreting the constitution but doing moral philosophy. It would be inapt to describe this enterprise as "living tree" interpretation, or any other kind, because it is not interpretation at all. And based on what I said earlier about incorporating real moral rights and making them judicially enforceable, there is room to doubt that the rights mentioned in the U.S. Constitution or the Canadian Charter were invitations to the courts to consult moral reality and apply their findings as fundamental law.

As I have already noted, the final possibility, the creation of rights other than through determinate rules—that is, through the promulgation of legal principles—is an impossibility.

Therefore, if a court is interpreting a constitution, it is interpreting *rules* laid down by those authorized to do so and is seeking their authorially intended meaning. Originalism, in the sense of seeking the authorially intended meaning, is the only option in a constitutional system that does not allow judicial amendment.

This is not to say that the courts should never engage in first-order moral reasoning. Even if we put aside the incorporation of real moral rights, even the most determinate set of constitutional rules will undoubtedly leave some matters open; that is, there will inevitably be a realm consisting of standards rather than determinate rules. Moreover, the courts will have to implement even the determinate constitutional rules through development of their own doctrines, and in doing so they will have no choice but to consult first-order moral and prudential reasons. Nevertheless, their doing so will be hemmed in by the rules laid down by the constitutional authors.

Moreover, I am not denying that discerning the originally intended meaning of a constitutional rule will often be difficult. It will often be difficult for the authors themselves, when faced with a rule's application that was not in mind at the time of the rule's promulgation, to distinguish whether they intended the rule to apply but now regret that they did, or did not intend the rule to apply, or possibly had no intention at all with respect to the matter. In other words, it will be difficult, even aided by ordinary norms of conversational implicature, for the authors themselves, as well as their interpreters, to determine what meaning they intended in some range of cases. It will likewise frequently be difficult for the authors themselves, as well as their interpreters, to distinguish what is implied *in* their rules from what is implied *by* their rules but not in them.

Despite these difficulties in determining authors' intended meanings, determining those meanings is what *interpreting* legal directives issued by legal authorities *is*. Anything else is not interpretation and substitutes some fictitious author for the authors who have the authority to make law, whether constitutional or subconstitutional.[44]

V. JUDICIAL REVIEW

What do these observations about law, constitutions, structures, rights, and interpretation suggest regarding the practice of judicial review, par-

---

[44] I should mention as well the famous "Kripkenstein" puzzle regarding how a quite limited momentary mental state—the mental state to which authorially intended meaning refers—can cover a limitless number of applications not present to the author's mind at the moment of communication. See Alexander and Sherwin, *The Rule of Rules*, 112–14. However that puzzle is to be resolved, it nonetheless seems to be true that we can justifiably assert that an author did or did not intend his promulgated norm to cover cases not present to his mind at the moment of the norm's utterance.

ticularly the strong and much mooted form of that practice that makes constitutional decisions by the highest court authoritative for all other officials?[45] Can judicial review be justified, and if so, on what assumptions?

First, to the extent that the constitution consists of *rules*, there is surely a case for making courts' interpretations of those rules supremely authoritative within the legal system. A democratic legislature is, in almost all conceivable circumstances, inferior to a court when it comes to interpreting legal rules, including constitutional rules. The question is not whether the will of a current democratic majority should be subordinated to the will of a nondemocratic body. *That* question has already been answered in the affirmative by the adoption of a consti- tution. No matter how democratic the composition of its authors and ratifiers, their rules are not those of current democratic majorities. (And even states like Great Britain without formal constitutions have unwrit- ten "constitutional" rules defining Parliament, its operation, and its powers that even Parliament cannot override.) The only question is which institution is better able to interpret the constitutional rules cor- rectly; and in the case of a written, consciously created constitution, courts seem to be better constructed to get the meaning of rules right. This is true whether the rules are rules about structure or rules creating and elaborating rights. For the meaning of the rules is a matter of historical fact: what their authors' intended meaning was. And ascer- taining historical facts is right in the wheelhouse of courts.

Even if the desideratum for rules is that their meaning not be controversial—after all, their function is to settle controversy and avert its costs—authorially intended meanings will often not be clear to every- one and thus will often leave matters unsettled unless authoritatively interpreted. The hope then is that even if the constitutional authors' intended meaning is not clear enough to avert controversy, the courts rendering of that meaning will be.

If a constitution contains standards, matters are different. Standards tell a decision-maker to do "the right thing" within a decisional area cabined by rules. There is no reason to assume that courts are necessarily better reasoners about morality and policy than legislatures or the executive. However, I see no reason of democratic principle against leaving the authoritative fleshing out of standards to courts. Although Jeremy Waldron disagrees,[46] the question for me is what mix of democratic and nondem- ocratic institutions is most likely to "do the right thing." If courts are epistemically and motivationally superior to legislatures in fleshing out standards, then good constitutional design will give that task to them.

In any event, even if a constitution were all rules and no standards, courts would have to consult moral and other practical considerations in

---

[45] See *Cooper v. Aaron*, 358 U.S. 1 (1958).
[46] See Waldron, *Law and Disagreement*.

designing doctrines to implement those rules. For, as Mitch Berman and others have pointed out,[47] judicial enforcement of a constitution's rules will require the creation of doctrines—rules—regarding burdens of proof and other similar matters. These doctrines could themselves be contained in constitutional rules, but often they are not.[48]

Thus, courts are likely to need to resort to moral and prudential practical reasoning in fleshing out (rulifying) constitutional standards and in constructing doctrines for implementing both constitutional rules and constitutional standards. If courts are not superior to democratic legislatures in such first-order practical reasoning, then perhaps the judicially created doctrines for fleshing out constitutional standards and for implementing constitutional rules and standards should not be finally authoritative within the legal system, but should be subject to legislative overrides. Again, the principal reason would be one of relative competence, not Waldron's reason that there is a moral right to have controversial moral issues resolved by a democratic vote.

Finally, what if a constitution refers to preexisting moral rights, notwithstanding the perils of incorporating morality to which I have alluded? As I have said, if that is what a constitution does, then this would imply that such moral rights are to be enforced by the judiciary. After all, the legislature and the executive are always supposed to make their actions consistent with moral requirements, whether or not those requirements are also found in the constitution. So explicitly referring to preexisting moral requirements in a constitution signals not merely that such requirements bind the government but also that they are to be enforced by the courts. Whether or not it is wise as a matter of constitutional design to make courts the moral censors of government action is a question about which reasonable minds can disagree. (A body with the responsibility of hearing individual moral complaints about proposed and enacted legislation and advising the legislature on the legislation's moral propriety might be a better design than judicial enforcement of the judicial view of that propriety.) Moreover, judicial moral oversight can vary from *de novo* consideration to highly deferential review. Once more, the issue for me is not one of democratic right but rather one of wise political design.

---

[47] See Mitchell N. Berman, "Constitutional Decision Rules," *Virginia Law Review* 90 (2004): 1; and Kermit Roosevelt, "Constitutional Calcification: How the Law Becomes What the Court Does," *Virginia Law Review* 91 (2005): 1649.

[48] An issue of great importance, not to my knowledge discussed anywhere in the literature, is how to constrain courts from crafting implementing doctrines that undermine constitutional rules with which they disagree. For if courts must resort to moral reasoning in crafting implementing doctrines, and if courts believe the constitutional rules they are implementing offend morality, then they will be prone to craft doctrines that make application of such rules extremely difficult. For example, they may impose a very high burden of proof on litigants claiming that those constitutional rules have been violated. The lesson here is that constitutional authors would do well to protect their constitutional rules by also authoring implementing doctrines, thereby giving unfriendly courts less room to maneuver.

VI. Constitutional Change, Organic or Otherwise

Constitutions usually provide for their own amendment. When they are amended, we can describe that as an organic change in the constitution, a change authorized by the constitution itself.

Constitutions change in ways other than organic ones. One of the most obvious of these is through decisions by the highest legal authority—in the United States, the U.S. Supreme Court—that misinterpret some constitutional provisions. Because law's function is to settle what we are obligated to do—or so I have claimed—when there is disagreement over the *law's* meaning, it is important that the law provide a means of settling *that* dispute. So any constitution whose provisions' intended meanings are at all disputable should designate some institution as having the authority to settle disputes over those meanings.[49]

When the highest legal authority misinterprets the intended meaning of a constitutional provision, we now have a conflict between the constitution itself and the authoritative interpretation of it. Which is the "supreme law"? Although some disagree,[50] the better view is that the authoritative interpreter's interpretation settles what we are obligated to do. What is more vexing, however, is what the authoritative interpreter should do when it comes to believe its interpretation of the constitution was mistaken. This is the issue in U.S. constitutional law of whether the Supreme Court should always, never, or sometimes follow its own constitutional precedents that it now regards as mistaken. My own opinion is that "sometimes" is the correct answer, and that the Court should overrule its own constitutional precedents only if (1) it believes them to be erroneous and (2) it believes that overruling them will not create a great deal more mischief than leaving the incorrect precedent intact. (Overruling a mistaken decision upholding the constitutionality of paper money would produce disastrous consequences;[51] overruling *Roe v. Wade*[52] would not, the plurality in *Casey* notwithstanding.)[53]

It is also possible that the highest legal authority's mistakes regarding the constitution's intended meaning—or the authority's deliberate refusal to seek the intended meaning and its substitution of a "meaning" it prefers for the intended meaning—will meet with public approval and

---

[49] See Larry Alexander and Frederick Schauer, "On Extrajudicial Constitutional Interpretation," *Harvard Law Review* 110 (1997): 1359. On most interpretations, the United States Constitution does not do this.

[50] See Michael Stokes Paulsen, "The Intrinsically Corrupting Influence of Precedent," *Constitutional Commentary* 22 (2005): 289; and Gary Lawson, "Mostly Unconstitutional: The Case Against Precedent Revisited," *Ave Maria Law Review* 5 (2007): 1.

[51] See *Legal Tender Cases*, 79 U.S. 457 (1870).

[52] *Roe v. Wade*, 410 U.S. 113 (1973).

[53] See *Planned Parenthood of Southeastern Pennsylvania v. Casey*, 505 U.S. 833, 843–901 (1992). One should compare the *Casey* plurality's treatment of *Roe* as precedent with the same justices' treatment of the precedent of *Bowers v. Hardwick*, 478 U.S. 186 (1986) in *Lawrence v. Texas*, 539 U.S. 538 (2003).

will be accepted by the public as fundamental law, much in the way the public accepts the constitution qua the originally intended meaning. The public's acceptance as fundamental law of those deviations from the originally intended meaning will result in the constitution's having been changed nonorganically.

In other words, it is always possible for there to be some sort of bloodless constitutional revolution. Constitutions are fundamental law only if they are accepted by the people as fundamental law, and the people may wake up tomorrow and begin accepting as fundamental law some new instrument. The U.S. Constitution was not an organic continuation of the Articles of Confederation. (The constitutional convention that produced it was itself created under the authority of the Articles of Confederation, but the convention was not authorized to produce a new constitution, only to amend the Articles.) The Constitution was just run up a flagpole, and the people saluted. If they had not saluted, the Constitution would have no more authority today than do the original Articles of Confederation or the Constitution of the Confederate States of America.

Therefore, if justices depart from the intended meanings of the constitutional authors, and the people accept these new judicial "amendments" as fundamental law, then we will have had several constitutional revolutions.[54] Several new constitutions, superficially resembling but actually different from one another, will have come into being through successive judicial "amendments" and popular acceptance of those "amendments." But the real question then is whether the people are actually aware of what is going on. Is their acceptance itself dependent on their belief that the courts are not amending the constitution from the bench but are interpreting it?[55] If so, then a constitutional crisis perhaps awaits.

VII. Conclusion

I have argued that thinking about what constitutions should and can do is best facilitated by attending to the following factors. The first is the settlement function of law and its requirement of determinate rules as opposed to standards. The second is the danger of incorporating by reference real moral rights and the need to "domesticate" those rights within the legal system by subordinating them to the rules regarding constitutional structures and processes and to the determinations of their content by those who possess the final legal authority within the system. (Otherwise, morality would run roughshod over the rules con-

---

[54] See Frederick Schauer, "Amending the Presuppositions of a Constitution," in Sanford Levinson, ed., *Responding to Imperfection: The Theory and Practice of Constitutional Amendment* (Princeton, NJ: Princeton University Press, 1995), 145–61.

[55] See Larry Alexander and Frederick Schauer, "Rules of Recognition, Constitutional Controversies, and the Dizzying Dependence of Law on Acceptance," in Adler and Himma, eds., *The Rule of Recognition and the U.S. Constitution*, 175–92.

stituting the government, and the controversial nature of morality's content would undermine law's settlement function.) The third factor is the impossibility of legal principles—legal norms directly or indirectly created by lawmakers that are not canonical rules but are values with some degree of "weight." The fourth is that interpretation of rules is recovering the meaning intended by the rules' authors. The fifth is that courts are probably better equipped than other governmental actors for interpreting rules. The sixth is that constitutionalizing real moral rights through incorporation implies judicial review. Finally, the moral reasoning required for courts to flesh out constitutional standards, to formulate doctrines for judicial enforcement of constitutional rules, and to resolve the meaning of any real moral rights that have been constitutionalized does not offend any putative right to make such decisions legislatively. However, if the legislature is better equipped epistemically and motivationally to do such moral reasoning than are the courts, that is a reason not to incorporate real moral rights into the constitution (since incorporation implies judicial review); it is also a reason to minimize the use of standards and to make judicial doctrines fleshing out standards and implementing constitutional rules (as opposed to interpreting them) subject to legislative override. When strong judicial review extends beyond ascertaining authorially intended meanings, its epistemological and motivational justification is at best controversial.

Law, University of San Diego

CONSTITUTION AND FUNDAMENTAL LAW: THE LESSON OF CLASSICAL ATHENS

By John David Lewis

I. Introduction: The Constitution as Fundamental Law

One of the major innovations that the American Founders brought to constitutional thought was their conception of a constitution as a written, *fundamental law*—the supreme "law of the land" that defines the organization of government and serves as the ruling principle for the proper exercise of power by legislators, officials, and judges.[1] This conception of what a constitution should do stood against centuries of European history, in which constitutions were shaped by traditions, circumstances, and bloody warfare,[2] legislative acts and the decrees of kings had constitutional force,[3] and constitution-making usually involved upheaval by violence and revolution. With the American constitutional revolution, a written constitution was no longer a description of a political system, but a prescriptive plan of government and a law to govern its operation, enacted by rational deliberation and used as a legal standard.

This American legal conception also ran counter to the premises of Greek political thought, which defined basic constitutional forms and grappled with constitutional change, but never theorized about a written constitution as a fundamental law. Although the figure of the lawgiver

[1] U.S. Constitution, Article VI: "This Constitution ... shall be the Supreme Law of the Land ..." The phrase "law of the land" is in the Magna Carta: see G. R. C. Davis, *Magna Carta*, rev. ed. (London: British Library, 1985), sections 39, 42, 55. See also Paul Vinogradoff, *Villainage in England: Essays in English Mediaeval History* (Oxford: Clarendon Press, 1892; reprint, Clark, NJ: The Lawbook Exchange, 2005), 100 (for aspects of "the general law of the land, maintaining actionable rights of free persons"); and Richard A. Posner, "Modesty and Power" (review of Philip Hamburger, *Law and Judicial Duty*), in *The New Republic Online*, January 15, 2009, http://www.tnr.com.

[2] In *Federalist No. 1*, Alexander Hamilton asked "whether societies of men are really capable or not, of establishing good government from reflection and choice," or whether they will be forever dependent "on accident and force." Alexander Hamilton, James Madison, and John Jay, *The Federalist* (1788), ed. Jack Richon Pole (Indianapolis, IN: Hackett, 2005), 1.

[3] Ernst Freund, "Constitutional Law," in *The Encyclopedia of the Social Sciences*, ed. Edwin R. A. Seligman (New York: MacMillan, 1951), 4:247: any Act of Parliament is "legally superior to the constitution." Reflecting centuries of prior history, the German Weimar Constitution was amendable by the legislature, which produced "a formal confusion between constitutional and ordinary law" (ibid., 4:248). See also Ulrich K. Preuss, "The Political Meaning of Constitutionalism: British, French, and American Perspectives," in John Arthur and William H. Shaw, eds., *Readings in the Philosophy of Law* (Upper Saddle River, NJ: Prentice-Hall, 2001), 503 (in France, "the concept of an eternal, paramount, or supreme law never arose").

looms large in ancient Greek political history, a Greek *polis* (city-state) grew largely from local customs or the customs of a colony's mother city, not from conscious design, and many of its constitutional provisions remained implicit, unwritten and customary.[4] Greek thinkers had understood a constitution—a *politeia*—to be the organization of a *polis*,[5] founded on the ethical nature of its citizens; the *polis* functioned according to the conception of justice that dominated it.[6] Aristotle developed a concept of *epieikeia* (roughly, "fairness" or "equity") to account for the influence of unwritten norms on the judgments of magistrates, which affirmed the moral foundations of the *polis*.[7] He wrote: "The goodness or badness, justice or injustice, of laws varies of necessity with the constitution of states. This, however, is clear, that the laws must be adapted to the constitutions (*politeiai*)."[8] The Greek conception of a constitution is an ethical conception, in which justice guides the development and use of laws, but in which there is no written constitution to serve as a fundamental law of the land.

Despite this disjunction with modern constitutional thought, ancient Athens offers an important lesson about the relationship between constitutions, laws, and political decision-making. During the fifth century B.C., Athens—the most culturally elevated of the Greek city-states—was brought

[4] Extant Greek "constitutions" are descriptive studies, not prescriptive plans; see, e.g., the Aristotelian *Constitution of the Athenians*; the *Constitution of the Theban Federation*; and the pseudo-Xenophonic *Constitution of the Athenians*, in J. M. Moore, trans., *Aristotle and Xenophon on Democracy and Oligarchy* (London: Chatto and Windus, 1983). See also Polybius, *Rise of the Roman Empire*, trans. Ian Scott-Kilvert (New York: Penguin, 1979), book 6. A few Greek constitutional laws are extant, e.g., the law code of Dreros, which set term limits for officials; and Chios, which established a council. "Foundation" documents for colonies, such as for Cyrene, do not specify a political system. See Charles Fornara, *Archaic Times to the Peloponnesian War* (Cambridge: Cambridge University Press, 1988), #11, 19, 18; and Michael Gagarin, *Early Greek Law* (Berkeley: University of California Press, 1989), 81–91. The seventh-century Constitution of Medina is a list of laws governing relations between groups: http://www.constitution.org/cons/medina/macharter.htm.

[5] The *politeia* is the *taxis* (arrangement or organization) of the *polis*, specifically its offices: see Aristotle, *Politics* 1289a15; *Constitution* 3.1, 4.1, 41.2, in *The Complete Works of Aristotle*, ed. Jonathan Barnes (Princeton, NJ: Princeton University Press, 1984).

[6] In cases where a *polis* did change its fundamental character, the early Greeks often relied upon the wisdom of a single lawgiver. See Gagarin, *Early Greek Law*, 51–80; and John David Lewis, *Early Greek Lawgivers* (London: Duckworth, 2007). The reforms of Solon (c. 594 B.C.) and of Cleisthenes (512–508 B.C.) involved major social and institutional changes. The constitution of Athens changed to a democracy in the middle of the fifth century, under the leadership of Ephialtes and others; a group of Athenians changed their constitution to an oligarchy in 411 B.C., probably with a written document, before turning back to democracy: see Aristotle, *Constitution* 21, 30. In *Federalist No. 38*, Madison wonders how "a people, jealous as the Greeks were of their liberty, should so far abandon the rules of caution as to place their destiny in the hands of a single citizen?" (Pole, ed., *The Federalist*, p. 200).

[7] For Aristotle on unwritten *nomos*, see *Rhetoric* 1374a17–20. He explains this as a matter of the generality of laws at *Nicomachean Ethics* 1137b26, and *Rhetoric* 1354a32–b22. The Spartans took this literally, and created an oral society in which it was unlawful to write the laws: see Plutarch, *Lycurgus* 13.1, in Plutarch, *Lives*, trans. John Dryden (New York: Modern Library, undated).

[8] Aristotle, *Politics* 1282b6–10; see also *Rhetoric* 1360a31–37 (knowledge of constitutions is good for lawmakers).

into grave crisis by a democratic government that had abandoned its laws in favor of unrestrained popular rule. At the depths of the crisis, however, the people of Athens rose past the strictures of tradition and faction to develop a unique solution, which allowed them to control their political decision-making without reverting to tyranny, to define their laws hierarchically, and to subordinate the decrees of the citizen Assembly to fundamental laws. The Athenian people faced a number of crucial questions. What is the nature of these fundamental laws? Should the laws remain immutable, legitimated by claims to divine sanction and the authority of their ancestors—or should the laws be open to the changes desired by people living now? How far should those changes be allowed to go? In answering such questions, the Athenians developed a constitutional solution, with precise conceptual terminology and highly refined procedures, to a grave moral-political-legal problem.

II. The Athenian Crisis of the Late Fifth Century b.c.

In the aftermath of the Peloponnesian War with Sparta (431–403 b.c.), Athens was defeated, garrisoned by a foreign army, and brutalized by a ruthless dictatorship—the so-called "Thirty Tyrants"—that was imposed by the Spartans. Although this crisis threatened the very existence of Athens as a democratic *polis*, the Spartans were not the major problem; a group of Athenian democrats overthrew the dictatorship and restored citizen government in a few months. The deeper and longer-term problem was internal, political, and, in modern terms, constitutional. This problem struck to the very core of the reasons for Athens's ignoble defeat.

Over the three generations prior to the war, the people of Athens had instituted unprecedented political changes, in which property qualifications for offices were eliminated, the power of the established nobility was undercut, and political power was placed directly into the hands of the entire body of male citizens.[9] This development included a series of challenges to the traditional authority of the long-standing aristocratic Council of the Areopagus. In the last decade of the previous century, around 512 b.c., the lawgiver Cleisthenes had reformed Athens's traditional *politeia* (the so-called "ancestral constitution") by creating a new Council of 500, selected by lot from the entire citizen body, which, over several decades, assumed many of the powers of the Areopagus.[10] The

---

[9] Citizenship was limited to males born of two Athenian-born parents; women, slaves, and foreign workers did not participate. Pericles' citizenship law of 451 made this official; the law was reenacted in 403 when the Athenians reinscribed their laws: see Aristotle, *Constitution* 26.4; discussed by Peter J. Rhodes, "The Athenian Revolution," and John K. Davies, "Society and Economy," both in *The Cambridge Ancient History*, vol. 5, 2d ed., ed. David M. Lewis et al. (Cambridge: Cambridge University Press, 1992), 76–77, 299–300.

[10] Aristotle, *Constitution* 20. Herodotus, *The Histories*, rev. ed., trans. Aubrey de Sélincourt (New York: Penguin, 1996), 5.66–70, 6.131. See Josiah Ober, *The Athenian Revolution* (Princeton, NJ: Princeton University Press, 1996), on the rise of Cleisthenes as an assertion of the

result was a growing sense of confidence and efficacy among the citizens, who began to assert themselves directly in the running of the city. Athens's creation of a navy—and the success of the navy in repelling the Persian invasion in 480 B.C.—allowed the poor citizens to claim pride of place as rowers who defended Athens, which bolstered their political strength. In the decades after the Persian Wars, a nonviolent political struggle between the Areopagus and the citizen Assembly had led to the political ascendancy of the Assembly.[11] The Council of 500 became probouleutic—meaning it reviewed Assembly proposals prior to an Assembly vote—but the final decision lay with the citizens, gathered in their Assembly.

At the outbreak of the Peloponnesian War in 431, Athens was a radical democracy. This was democracy in its most consistent form: the direct exercise of political power by the citizens, in which every male citizen had the right to speak, to make proposals, and to vote on matters of common import. The decisions of the Assembly could not be appealed—even though the Council of 500 had the authority to preview and approve proposals before an Assembly vote—and there were few effective limits to the Assembly's power. To use a modern term, the Assembly became sovereign over Athens.

This system was, up to 411 B.C., remarkably stable. We know of no civil wars and no prolonged violence in Attica from the traditional founding of the unwritten "ancestral constitution" by the lawgiver Solon in 594/93 B.C. up to the end of the Peloponnesian War in 403. But this does not mean that the Assembly always functioned according to law. Evidence suggests that the Assembly acted throughout the war with increasing arrogance, including heavy-handed treatment of allies that bred discontent and revolt.[12] The Assembly had become what Aristotle would later describe as a "composite tyranny."[13] Aristotle's analysis was based not on the numbers who participated in decision-making, but on whether the Assembly or the laws were the final authority.[14] The vital question concerned the relationship between the Assembly and the fundamental laws of Athens. It was, in modern terms, a constitutional question: Were there lawful limits to the popular power of the Assembly, or was this power unlimited?[15]

Athenian people. For a view more focused on the leadership, see Charles Fornara and Loren J. Samons, *Athens from Cleisthenes to Pericles* (Berkeley: University of California Press, 1991). On the period after the Persian wars, see Peter J. Rhodes, "The Athenian Revolution," in Lewis et al., eds., *The Cambridge Ancient History*, vol. 5, pp. 62–95.

[11] Aristotle, *Constitution* 27.

[12] See Thucydides, *History of the Peloponnesian War*, trans. Rex Warner (New York: Penguin, 1972), 1.97–101, on the Athenian use of force against recalcitrant allies.

[13] Aristotle, *Politics* 4.4, 1292a10–13. See Aristotle, *Constitution* 26, on demagogues and the loss of control in political life.

[14] Aristotle, *Politics* 4.4, 1292a4–7, finds a fifth form of *politeia* when the decrees of the Assembly and not the laws are authoritative.

[15] See Martin Ostwald, *From Popular Sovereignty to the Sovereignty of Law* (Berkeley: University of California, 1986), which hits the essence of the issue in its title.

It is difficult to discern what the Athenians thought this relationship should be. The fifth-century intellectual revolution has left us almost no democratic theory.[16] In essence, the Athenians thought that to elevate any person, or body of persons, over the Assembly (e.g., to establish a council with the power to veto a decision of the Assembly) was to usurp the democracy and to establish tyranny.[17] There was no institutional separation of powers, and no checks against a vote taken by the Assembly. There was a rudimentary functional separation of powers based on procedures; proposals had to be considered by the Council of 500 before being voted upon in the Assembly, but the Assembly, if swayed by orators, did at times overrule this custom.[18] The use of lots in selecting jurors and council members may have been intended to prevent manipulations such as bribery, and to forestall the factional problems that could arise from the popularity contest that is an election.[19] This was the Athenian answer to tyranny, but as events would show, this solution was incomplete at best.

From the very establishment of the Athenian democracy there had been warning signs of a problem. Throughout the fifth century, for instance, the Assembly had become a forum for ostracism, a political mechanism by which a quorum of citizens could vote once a year to exile any man suspected of gathering too much personal power.[20] Although ostracism was not used regularly—there was no reign of terror—it became a means to eliminate political rivals, and drained Athens of its most capable leaders. Those exiled included Miltiades, the hero of the Athenian victory over the Persians at Marathon, who was tried while gravely wounded; his son Cimon inherited his father's ruinous fine, defeated the Persians in 466, and was himself ostracized. Thucydides son of Melesias (not the

---

[16] The closest we have to such theory is in Herodotus's Persian constitutional debate (*The Histories* 3.80f.); the Pseudo-Xenophonic *Constitution of the Athenians*, an antidemocratic pamphlet; and the funeral oration of Pericles as reconstructed in Thucydides, *History* 2.35f. Aristotle's *Constitution* does not treat the Assembly as an institution of government. To most Greek intellectuals, the Assembly easily became "the mob" (*ochlos*), which acted by popular opinion rather than reason; see, e.g., Thucydides, *History* 7.8 (see note 29 below).

[17] To usurp the democracy was a serious crime. See the oath of Demophantos, in Andocides 1, *On the Mysteries* 96–98, in *Minor Attic Orators I: Antiphon, Andocides*, trans. K. J. Maidment (Cambridge, MA: Harvard University Press, 1982); and the Heliastic Oath, in Demosthenes 24, *Against Timocrates*, in *Demosthenes III*, trans. J. H. Vince (Cambridge, MA: Harvard University Press, 1986), 149–51. The Athenians passed a similar resolution after the defeat by the Macedonians in 338 B.C. See Ilias Arnaoutoglou, *Ancient Greek Laws* (London: Routledge, 1998), 74–77.

[18] See Aristotle, *Politics* 4.14, for functional distinctions between deliberative institutions, offices, and courts.

[19] The practice of Athenian law focused more on the integrity of the procedures than on substantive rules. Stephen C. Todd, *The Shape of Athenian Law* (Oxford: Clarendon Press, 1993), 70–71.

[20] Aristotle, *Constitution* 22.1, attributes the ostracism law to Cleisthenes c. 508 B.C., but the first recorded ostracism, of Hipparchus, probably occurred in 487 B.C. According to Plutarch, *Aristides* 7, the last was Hyperbolus, killed in 411. Plato, *Gorgias* 516 d–e, sees ostracism as silencing undesired voices; only a few officials prevented the Assembly from throwing Miltiades into the pit. See *Plato: Complete Works*, ed. John M. Cooper (Indianapolis, IN: Hackett, 1997). On the personal rivalries, see Rhodes, "The Athenian Revolution," 62–67.

historian), politically allied with Cimon, was ostracized by Pericles. The opponents of this group included men such as Xanthippus (father of Pericles) who prosecuted Miltiades and was himself exiled in 484; Pericles, who was not ostracized although he was fined; and the son of Pericles, who was later executed by the Assembly along with other generals after winning the sea battle at Arginusae in 406.[21] Themistocles, who built and commanded the navy that beat the Persians in 480, was ostracized and fled to Persia.[22] Thousands of pottery fragments, bearing the names of politicians facing ostracism, have been found by archaeologists in Athens. Hundreds had the name Themistocles written by a very few hands, which suggests that these ballots may have been distributed to the voters in order to rig the voting.[23]

The Assembly could also audit officials by demanding an account of their actions when their term came to an end.[24] This was an important way to control officials without infringing on an official's ability to conduct his office as he saw fit—but it became a forum for revenge. The citizens also maintained control over the military by electing generals to fixed terms. This, along with the threat of prosecution, prevented the growth of personal authority of the kind that brought civil war to Rome in the first century B.C.; no Athenian general ever marched on Athens to attempt a coup. But these generals were also at the mercy of the Assembly's whims, a situation that affected their ability to make proper decisions, and that could induce a climate of fear among the commanders.

The historian Thucydides—who had as much disdain for the mob as any other Greek intellectual—details many instances of the Assembly's irrationality during the war with Sparta.[25] The most ruinous was the Sicilian expedition. In 416 B.C., the Assembly voted to conquer Sicily, perhaps to disrupt Spartan trade with the west, even though the Athe-

---

[21] As a victim of such conflict one could name the democratic leader Ephialtes, an associate of Pericles, who was assassinated. But his killing was an anomaly—the only political assassination of which we know from fifth-century Athens prior to the end of the Peloponnesian War.

[22] Herodotus, *Histories* 6.136; Plutarch, *Themistocles* 22; Plutarch, *Cimon* 17; Demosthenes 23, *Against Aristocrates*, in Vince, trans., *Demosthenes III*, 205; *Diodorus of Sicily*, in *Library of History*, 12 vols., trans. C. H. Oldfather (Cambridge, MA: Harvard University Press, 1962), 12.55. See A. W. Gomme, et al., *A Historical Commentary on Thucydides* (Oxford: Clarendon Press, 1956–1981), comments to Thucydides 2.65.4, for a discussion of the prosecutions of Pericles and his associates. See also Aristotle, *Constitution* 22, 43.5; *Politics* 1284a17f.

[23] See Russell Meiggs and David Lewis, *Greek Historical Inscriptions to the End of the Fifth Century B.C.* (Oxford: Clarendon Press, 1980), #21, for inscriptional evidence.

[24] Aristotle, *Politics* 1274a15–18 and 1281b32–35, claims that Solon gave this power to the *demos*; *Politics* 1318b29 connects this to agrarian democracy. See Jennifer Tolbert Roberts, *Accountability in Athenian Government* (Madison: University of Wisconsin Press, 1982).

[25] In 429 B.C., the Athenian navy subdued Mytilene; the Assembly voted to kill all the men and sell the women and children into slavery. A ship was dispatched with the order—but the next day the Assembly repented and sent a ship to reverse the order. (The ship arrived in time.) Thucydides, *History* 3.36–49.

nians had no idea of the size of the island or the scope of the operation.[26] The general Nicias, who had opposed the invasion and only reluctantly agreed to it, was chosen to lead it.[27] After arriving in Sicily, his co-general Alcibiades—who had promoted the expedition—got word of his impending prosecution in Athens for religious crimes. This was the so-called Profanation of the Mysteries in 415 B.C., when rumors swept Athens that Alcibiades and his friends had mocked the sacred Eleusinian mysteries. The religious nature of the allegations made it likely that the Assembly would usurp the courts and try him directly, a situation that could result in his swift execution. He fled rather than face the charges.[28] According to Thucydides, when Nicias's military situation in Sicily became hopeless he refused to retreat, citing fear of retribution by the Assembly for cowardice.[29] In the end, the Athenians suffered perhaps the worst per-capita military defeat in history—and they blamed their leaders, "as if they had not voted for it themselves."[30]

In his famous evaluation of political affairs after the death of Pericles in 429, Thucydides wrote that what was nominally a democracy was in fact the rule of one; Pericles had controlled the Assembly through sound leadership: "he led it rather than being led by it." Because Thucydides accepted the Greek idea that politics was primarily a matter of "who shall rule," he failed to see that if the limits to the actions of a political institution are found not in law but in a leader's ability to restrain that institution, then the government is not one of laws but of men. After Pericles died, he was followed by populists who took advantage of the Assembly's authority by appealing to the emotions of the crowd.[31] The stage was set for the Assembly to disregard the limits of the law, and to demand the right to act as it desired because it desired to do so. One of the results was the defeat in Sicily.

In 411 B.C., an oligarchic faction, opposed to the excesses of the democracy, developed proposals to permanently reduce the power of the Assembly. To pass these measures, the oligarchs first had to limit participation to wealthy citizens, who would be amenable to the oligarchic proposals. The oligarchs convened the Assembly at Colonus, outside the walls of Athens. Sparta had a fort on Athenian soil, and the military danger limited participation in the Assembly to citizens able to afford armor. Meanwhile the Athenian navy, along with thousands of rowers, was at Samos in the Aegean Sea; this further weakened the

---

[26] Thucydides, *History* 6.1.

[27] Thucydides, *History* 6.8–25.

[28] Thucydides, *History* 6.60–61. I say more about the so-called Profanation of the Mysteries below.

[29] Thucydides, *History* 7.48. Mistrustful of oral reports "to the mob," Nicias sent a letter to Athens (ibid., 7.8–15). See ibid., 4.65, on the three generals punished in 424 B.C. for failing to conquer Sicily.

[30] Thucydides, *History* 8.1.

[31] Thucydides, *History* 2.65.

democratic voices in Athens. The oligarchs proposed nothing less than to do away with the Assembly and to establish a Council of 400 as the ruling authority in Athens.[32]

Paradoxically, the oligarchs were restrained by the one means that could prevent the Assembly from becoming a tyrant: a law that permitted any citizen to challenge the legality of an Assembly proposal prior to a vote. The *graphē paranomon*, a charge that a proposal was "contrary to law," was one of the central constitutional protections of the Athenian government.[33] Should any citizen challenge a proposal brought before the Assembly, a sworn jury would have to examine and accept the legality of the proposal before the Assembly could vote on it. The legality of the proposal was considered to be distinct from the question of its adoption, and this legality could be challenged even after the passage of the proposal. In principle, this allowed any citizen to act as a dampening force upon the Assembly, and to subject the Assembly to the limitations of law, as determined by a jury.

Under this law, any citizen, now or in the future, could challenge the proceedings taken at Colonus by bringing a *graphē paranomon* charge against the decision. This would force the Athenians to convene a jury to examine the decision. So when the Assembly was convened, among the first orders of business was to repeal the *graphē paranomon*. The Assembly voted to repeal this safeguard in order to eliminate legal challenges to the oligarchic clique.[34] Constitutional protections were eviscerated, dissent was stifled, and the Assembly turned Athens over to a council dominated by wealthy, armored citizens.

Among the other paradoxes of the so-called oligarchic counterrevolution of 411 were its attempt to limit the power of the Assembly by calling an Assembly to vote itself out of existence, and its attempt to reestablish the ancestral laws of Athens by eliminating the means by which Athenian citizens could challenge proposals on the basis of those laws. The resultant oligarchic government—the so-called Four Hundred—governed nonviolently, but the desire for democracy in Athens was too strong, and within months the Athenians reestablished the *graphē paranomon* and citizen government. But the fact that the Assembly had been able to repeal the *graphē paranomon* shows that, ultimately, there was no law above the Assembly. This was the constitutional flaw that had yet to be corrected.

---

[32] On the events of 411 B.C., see Thucydides, *History* 8.47–50, 53–54, 63–98. See also Aristotle, *Constitution* 29–33; *Diodorus of Sicily* 13.34–38. See also Gomme, *Commentary on Thucydides*, 5:184–256, along with Peter J. Rhodes, *A Commentary on the Aristotelian Athenaion Politeia* (Oxford: Clarendon Press, 1993), sections 29–33.

[33] On *paranomos* as "illegal," see Plato, *Apology* 31e, where Socrates claims to be preventing illegal happenings in Athens, as he had done at the trial of the generals (see note 35 below).

[34] Thucydides, *History* 8.67.2. Aeschines, *Against Ctesiphon* 3.191, reminisces that "in those days the *graphē* had to be put away to overthrow the democracy." See *The Speeches of Aeschines*, trans. Charles Darwin Adams (Cambridge, MA: Harvard University Press, 1988).

A few years later another event occurred that showed even more starkly the constitutional problem that bedeviled Athens. By 406 B.C., Athens was losing the war in the Aegean Sea. The Athenian navy was blockaded on the island of Lesbos, and Sparta was about to cut Athens's jugular vein, the grain routes to the Black Sea. In a state of desperation, the Assembly appointed ten new generals, who manned the last of the city's ships and rowers, won the battle against Sparta, relieved the blockaded navy, and secured the grain routes.

The response of the Assembly was to recall the generals on the charge of failing to pick up dead sailors in the water, to try them as a group, and to execute the six who returned.[35] This violated at least three Athenian legal customs: that trials had to be before sworn jurors and not the Assembly; that each individual had a right to a separate trial; and that each had the right to speak in his own defense.[36] The writer Xenophon claims that a *graphē paranomon* challenge was raised, but that voices in the Assembly threatened to try anyone who challenged the charges along with the generals. A voice rose from the back of the crowd: "it is monstrous if the people cannot do whatever they wish."[37] The right to challenge a proposal legally was not officially repealed; it was simply shouted down, by a mob that accepted no limits to its power.[38]

After two contentious meetings of the Assembly, in which opposing voices could not prevail, the six generals, including Pericles' son, were condemned and executed. With the best of her commanders destroyed, no ships left, and her treasury bankrupt, Athens was at the end of her resources. Within two years she starved and surrendered.

III. The Deeper Cause of the Crisis

The political context for the crisis in Athens had been established decades earlier, with the assertion of unlimited authority by the assembled citizens over long-standing aristocratic institutions and standards. But the intellectual cause was rooted in a certain attitude toward ideas, expressed in rhetorical arguments in which ethical and political concepts were disconnected from fixed principles. *Nomos*—a singular noun meaning the customs and norms of Athens as well as its laws—was increasingly seen

---

[35] This affair is narrated by Xenophon, *A History of My Times*, trans. Rex Warner (New York: Penguin, 1979), 1.7. Plato, *Apology* 32b, has Socrates recall his opposition to the trial.

[36] Xenophon, *History* 1.7.5, says the generals were not given the time allowed by law. The connection of group trials to tyranny may also be seen in the trial of Charias and three accomplices a century later, c. 300 B.C. See Christian Habicht, *Athens from Alexander to Antony*, trans. Deborah Lucas Schneider (Cambridge, MA: Harvard University Press, 1997), 84.

[37] Xenophon, *History* 1.7.10.

[38] Xenophon wrote that the citizens later regretted their actions, and shunned one of the prosecutors, who starved to death—an instance of the Assembly acting irresponsibly and then denying its own responsibility.

as a set of human conventions, with no basis in reality other than that which human beings asserted. In these terms, the decisions of the Assembly established what was proper—and those decisions were the product of rhetoric, the art of public speaking for persuasive purposes.

During the war with Sparta, rhetoric was studied and taught in Athens by a loosely connected group of thinkers known to us as the sophists. The sophists were united not by a single content to their teachings—there is no "sophistic" school of philosophy—but rather by a common concern for rhetoric, and by a willingness to teach for a fee. At the foundation of their thought they rejected absolute principles of morality and politics, and accepted that all principles were relative to a particular situation, malleable by the skillful use of language, and dependent on the particulars of the moment. A successful argument was not a true one that proved a case logically, but rather one that used words in a crafty way to create an image of reality, in order to induce an audience to make the desired decision.

The triumph of the demagogues during the war with Sparta and the resulting actions of the Assembly were contemporaneous with the rise of rhetoric as an art in Athens. The sophist Protagoras of Abdera was likely in Athens by 443 B.C.; and by 427 B.C. rhetorical teaching had been imported from Sicily, by Gorgias and perhaps by Thrasymachus of Chalcedon.[39] In the political speeches recreated in the *History* of Thucydides, in the surviving fragments of fifth-century forensic oratory, and in the scraps of rhetorical handbooks, we find the idea that right and wrong have no fixed meaning, but can be understood only in terms of probabilities, determined by the expediency of the moment. Antiphon's *Tetralogies*—twelve speeches, arranged in three groups of four—are rhetorical exercises that argued opposite sides of the same case, in terms of probabilities rather than truth.

Such argumentation is proper, sophists maintained, because there are no absolute standards in truth, morality, or law. In the words of one anonymous sophist, in the *Dissoi Logoi* or "Opposing Arguments," moral values are relative to any particular moment:

> Two-fold arguments are put forward in Greece by those who philosophize. Some say that the good is one thing and the bad another, but others say that they are the same, and that a thing might be good for some persons but bad for others, or at one time good and another time bad for the same person. I myself side with those who hold the latter opinion.[40]

[39] On Gorgias, see Thucydides, *History* 4.86.3; *Diodorus of Sicily* 12.53.2. See also Martin Ostwald, "Athens as a Cultural Center," in Lewis et al., eds., *The Cambridge Ancient History*, vol. 5, pp., 341–69.

[40] Rosamond Kent Sprague, *The Older Sophists* (Indianapolis, IN: Hackett, 2001), 279.

For those who accepted these views, all standards and all conclusions were left without anchor, as floating products of whim. Having rejected divine inspiration as the source of such standards, they took the first steps toward skepticism: the idea that there is no knowledge, only opinion, and that an idea is true only in relation to a person who accepts it. Aristotle described the views of the sophist Protagoras in this way:

> Protagoras said that man is the measure of all things, meaning that what appears to each person also *is* positively the case. But once this is taken to be so, the same thing turns out both to be and not to be, and to be bad as well as good, not to mention other opposites, since often what seems noble to this group of people will seem opposite to that group, and since what appears to each man is taken to be the measure.[41]

According to Protagoras as he is portrayed in Plato's work, these moral views are based on a dichotomy between experience and being, which requires the manipulation of appearances as a means to establish validity:

> But the man whom I call wise is the man who can change appearances—the man who in any case where bad things both appear and are for one of us, works a change and makes good things appear and be for him.[42]

These are the kinds of ideas that gained prevalence in Athens during the war with Sparta. The orator's job—and the specialty of the sophists—was the ability to change appearances in order to win an argument. In his play *The Clouds*, a biting satire directed at such teachings, the Athenian comic playwright Aristophanes dramatized the sophistic method of arguing with his allegorical characters "Good Argument" and "Bad Argument." Bad Argument can prevail over Good Argument by slippery forms of persuasion that can make the worse case look better, and thus allow the bad to triumph over the better.[43] In his *Rhetoric*, Aristotle attributed such argumentation to Protagoras, and noted many critical objections to the training the sophist had offered.[44]

In the sophists' view, social, political, and legal principles, which most Greeks understood to be aspects of ethical thought, are arbitrary human constructs that cannot be derived from the facts of nature. Because the sophists could not find immutable moral standards in nature (*phusis*),

[41] Aristotle, *Metaphysics* 1062b13.
[42] Plato, *Theaetetus* 166d.
[43] Aristophanes, *The Clouds* 1039–40, 1075–78, in Aristophanes, *Lysistrata and Other Plays*, trans. Alan H. Sommerstein (New York: Penguin, 1973).
[44] Aristotle, *Rhetoric* 1402a22–28.

many decided that such standards were a mere convention (*nomos*). Given this view, there is no way to judge the truth of an argument, only its effectiveness, and a method of reasoning will be judged as appropriate if it is convincing.[45] Such views were strengthened and complicated by an influx of philosophical ideas into fifth-century Athens. Archelaus, for instance—the earliest philosopher of whom we know in Athens—merged early physical theories with social theories, in an attempt to bring *phusis*— concerned with natural phenomena—into line with *nomos*, the humanly created customs and laws that vary with particular times and localities.[46]

The orators who were trained in such theories were concerned less with the truth of their arguments than with their ability to sway the audience. Thus, the historian Thucydides, in the introduction to his *History*, bases his reconstruction of political speeches on *ta deonta*—the things necessary for each speaker to make his case. In doing so, Thucydides shows that the cause of the Peloponnesian War was to be found in certain matters of human nature—a desire for security, honor, and interest—which allowed the Athenian Assembly and other bodies to be led by cunning speakers.[47] Thucydides was describing the unalterable *phusis* of men, in a world of political interactions defined by the shifting standards of *nomos*.

All of this was immediately and directly applicable to matters of law. The Greek word for a law or custom is also "*nomos*"—the same word used to describe the norms that many sophists saw as arbitrary. In the view of the sophists, the laws are also subjective human constructs that are not better or worse in any absolute sense, but can be manipulated to bring a desired result. In such a climate, the arguments presented to juries became increasingly bent on success rather than truth, and it became acceptable to twist the laws if necessary to prevail. Logic often gave way to arbitrary arguments and appeals to character. The standard for rhetorical excellence was not truth; it was effectiveness at inducing a decision by the crowd.[48]

The sophists' concern for rhetoric implied active engagement with political affairs, not philosophical withdrawal for the sake of contemplation. The democracy of Athens allowed aspiring political actors to bring their rhetorical skills directly into political discourse before the Assembly and the courts. The major sophists were legal orators as well as political speakers and actors. Major political figures—including those connected to the regime of "The Thirty Tyrants" imposed by Sparta after the defeat of Athens—were associated with the sophists, as teachers or as students,

[45] See Plato, *Protagoras* 337d, on *phusis* and *nomos*. Aristotle, *Sophistic Refutations* 173a7–19, understands *nomos* as the opinions of the many, and *phusis* as the truth according to the wise.
[46] Reported anecdotally in Diogenes Laertius 2.16. See Ostwald, "Athens as a Cultural Center," 340, 352.
[47] Thucydides, *History* 1.22–23.
[48] Aristotle, in his *Rhetoric*, later offered a corrective, distinguishing a rhetorician—one skilled at rhetoric—from a sophist, on the basis of the latter's choices. The difference is between the real, and the apparent, means of persuasion: *Rhetoric* 1355b15–22.

including Callicles, Theramenes, Charmides, Critias, and Alcibiades. They practiced their methods, and conveyed their ideas, directly before the Assembly.

In the end, the turn away from the ancestral laws by the Assembly was part and parcel of the turn away from the traditional moral standards by the sophists and their students. As the sophists thought that such norms were the product of arbitrary conventions, so the Assembly acted as if whatever the people decided for the moment defined what was right— and as if the decision-making capacity of the assembled citizens should be unlimited. On one level, the sophists identified a philosophical basis for this development, in the form of subjective moral theories that denied absolute moral standards. On another level, the formation of these theories strengthened the underlying subjectivism that was influencing many of those speaking before the Assembly. The change in Athens's unwritten ethical constitution had warped its legal constitution, and had brought the *polis* to the brink of political and military disaster.

IV. THE ATHENIAN RESPONSE TO THE CRISIS

The defeat of Athens brought to a climax a powerful two-pronged reaction against such ideas, a reaction that had begun two decades earlier. The first reaction was by those associated with traditional religious cults, who were appalled at the challenge to the gods posed by the sophists and other intellectuals. A fragment by the playwright Euripides—or perhaps by the political leader and student of the sophists, Critias—claims that the gods were invented by men to induce fear and obedience.[49] The three best symbols of the reaction to such thinking may be (1) the recall of Alcibiades from the Sicilian expedition in 415 B.C.; (2) the exile of Diagoras of Miletus, who was likely prosecuted for questioning religion, although his reputation as an atheist is probably overblown; and (3) the execution of Socrates, ostensibly for teaching the youth in ways that denied the existence of the gods accepted in Athens.[50] These attacks on religion were connected to criticisms of scientific thinking, and were parodied in

---

[49] For the Euripides "Sisyphus" fragment, see the English text in Richard Winton, "Herodotus, Thucydides, and the Sophists," in Christopher Rowe and Malcolm Schofield, eds., *The Cambridge History of Greek and Roman Political Thought* (Cambridge: Cambridge University Press, 2000), 89–90. See also Sprague, *The Older Sophists*, 259–60; and Ostwald, "Athens as a Cultural Center," 357.

[50] Diagoras is alluded to in Aristophanes' *Clouds*, 830, perhaps to tarnish Socrates with atheism. Aristophanes' *Birds* 1071–75, has a price on Diagoras's head. The date of his exile was likely c. 431 B.C., or c. 415, after the massacre of Melos; see Leonard Woodbury, "The Date and Atheism of Diagoras of Melos," *Phoenix* 19 (1965): 178–211. For other reactions to science and philosophy, see John Lewis, "Oh Mist! Science, Religion, and History in Aristophanes' *Clouds*," in *Themes in European History: Essays from the Second International Conference on European History*, ed. Michael Aradas and Nicholas C. J. Pappas (Athens: The Athens Institute for Education and Research, 2005), 33–47. Aristophanes, *The Birds and Other Plays*, trans. David Barrett (New York: Penguin, 1986).

Aristophanes' *Clouds*, where the existence of justice is denied, the gods are reduced to physical principles, and philosophical education is a means to subvert justice in the law courts.

The second reaction was constitutional and began with the commitment to rediscover, and to reinscribe, the ancestral laws of Athens.[51] These were the norms and principles, embodied in laws, that could set proper limits to the actions of the Assembly, but would not require the establishment of a political body superior to the Assembly. Athens had fallen into problems, many could have claimed, because the Assembly had failed to follow the traditional laws established by Solon and other lawgivers. This was, in the minds of many "conservatives," connected to the rejection of the gods, whom they considered to provide both sanctions for the ancestral laws and moral points of focus for the Athenians. In the late fifth century, the laws had fallen out of use, and had become scattered and disorganized, a process that had begun with the Persian sack of Athens in 480, when the laws, arranged in public displays, may have been destroyed.[52]

Under the oligarchic government of the Four Hundred in 411 B.C., a board of lawmakers (*thesmothetai*) had been charged with researching these traditional laws and with reinscribing them into stone for public viewing. The very approach was legalistic and intellectual in nature; rather than electing new officials and hoping for a good man to lead them, the Athenians opted for a solution in law, which required public knowledge of the laws.[53] Nearly a decade later, after their defeat by the Spartans in 403, the Athenians continued to grapple with how to maintain their laws, in a tense atmosphere that came at times close to violence. Exiles and others who had fled Athens were trying to return, and whether and how they could regain their citizenship was a hot issue. Tensions were high between supporters of the democracy—who established a fortress on the Munychia, a hill near the Peiraeus—and those who had aided "The Thirty" (the despotic clique, first installed after the Spartan victory, that had waged a campaign of terror that killed some fifteen hundred Athenians). In a battle at the Munychia, the oligarchs were defeated and fled; the democracy was restored. But the desire for vengeance was high, and the Athenians had to decide how far the law could be used to avenge past crimes.

To end the vengeance, the restored democracy would ultimately enact, as law, an *amnēsia* (a "forgetting-ness") that made it illegal to prosecute political enemies for past grievances. In addition, the traditional laws of

---

[51] Draco's homicide law was reinscribed in 409/8: Meiggs and Lewis, *Greek Historical Inscriptions*, #86.

[52] Herodotus, *History* 8.51–54 (on the sack of the Acropolis).

[53] Hedrick thinks the Athenian epigraphy was intended to make knowledge available. See Charles W. Hedrick, "Democracy and the Athenian Epigraphic Habit," *Hesperia* 68, no. 3 (1999): 387–439.

Solon were reinscribed, and applied only to crimes after 403 B.C.[54] This task, which took years, may have culminated under the leadership of Euclides, in 403/402 B.C., when the Ionic alphabet was made the standard for official communication. A distinct office, the *nomothesia*, was created, and the *nomothetai* were the officials responsible for preserving the integrity of the publicly inscribed laws. Procedures to maintain the authority of the laws were introduced.[55]

Along with the standardized alphabet, the reinscribed laws, and the new offices, the Athenians reinforced a conceptual and procedural distinction between a written law (*nomos*) and a decree of the Assembly (*psēphisma*).[56] *Nomos* meant custom and law, but after 402 B.C. the term came to mean a *fundamental* law that was inscribed in public view.[57] A *nomos* was understood to be a stable standard that was, ideally at least, not subject to the shifting arguments of orators. In contrast, a *psēphisma* was a decree passed by a vote of the Assembly, directed against a particular situation.

Evidence strongly suggests that Athenians were conceptually precise about the distinction between a decree of the assembly (a *psēphisma*) and a written law (a *nomos*). Mogens Herman Hansen supports this contention first with fourth-century epigraphic evidence: some five hundred inscriptions refer to *psēphismata*, and some six refer to *nomoi*. Despite the disparity in the amount of evidence, Hansen observes the strict institutional distribution between the two political acts: "There is no example of a *nomos* passed by the *demos* [the Assembly] or of a *psēphisma* passed by the *nomothetai* [the officials charged with maintaining the written laws]." Literary sources are also consistent; of some two hundred *psēphismata* passed by the Assembly that are cited in the work of orators and historians, there are only five cases in which an enactment by the Assembly is

---

[54] Christopher J. Joyce, "The Athenian Amnesty and Scrutiny of 403," *Classical Quarterly* 58, no. 2 (2008): 507–18.

[55] Thucydides, *History* 8.97.2 (on the *nomothetai* of 409 B.C.); Demosthenes 24, *Against Timocrates* 21–30 (on the "legislative committee"). Andocides 1, *On the Mysteries* 81–87, claims that laws before the archonship of Euclides were invalid. K. Clinton, "The Nature of the Late Fifth Century Revision of the Athenian Law Code," *Hesperia* Supplement 19 (1982): 27–37, challenges the idea that laws before 410 were invalid. F. B. Tarbell, "The Relation of ΨΗΦΙΣΜΑΤΑ to NOMOI at Athens in the Fifth and Fourth Centuries B.C.," *American Journal of Philology* 10 (1889): 79–83, stresses that with the institution of the *nomothesia*, the Assembly "was deprived of its sovereign character and became, to speak in modern terms, subject to a written constitution." On Euclides as archon, see *Diodorus of Sicily* 14.12.1.

[56] Hansen has offered the strongest arguments supporting this distinction. See Mogens Herman Hansen, "Graphē Paranomon Against Psēphismata Not Yet Passed by the Ecclesia," in Hansen, *The Athenian Ecclesia II* (Copenhagen: Museum Tusculanum, 1989), 271–81; Hansen "Nomos and Psēphisma in Fourth-Century Athens," in Hansen, *The Athenian Ecclesia I* (Copenhagen: Museum Tusculanum, 1983), 161–76; and Hansen, *The Sovereignty of the People's Court in the Fourth Century B.C. and the Public Action Against Unconstitutional Proposals* (Odense: Odense University Press, 1974).

[57] Martin Ostwald, *Nomos and the Beginnings of Athenian Democracy* (Oxford: Oxford University Press, 1969), traces the concept of *nomos* through the fifth century.

referred to as a *nomos*.[58] Nor is any measure referred to by both terms. Given the looseness with facts for which the orators are famous, this distribution of terminology is evidence for a strong conceptual distinction between the two terms, as well as for a strong distinction between the institutions responsible for each type of enactment.

One essential attribute of a *nomos* was to be written. The Athenians understood that to write a law is to preserve it in a way that is not subject to the vagaries of memory. Because a *nomos* was written and carried the force of tradition, it was more stable than a decree, and less susceptible to the winds of whim that blew through the Assembly and its votes. The Assembly could break a written law if it wished—there was no institutional authority above it—but the written laws were available for all to see. A person making proposals before the Assembly who tried to undermine the written laws would face opposition from those who valued the laws. Although the legal orators of the fourth century were notorious for inventing laws—not everything was written—there is good reason to think that the original laws of Solon, written in the first two decades of the sixth century and lost after the sack of Athens by the Persians in 480 B.C., had regained their moral and legal force. The mere mention of Solon's name in fourth-century Attic law speeches was a powerful claim to legitimacy.[59]

A *nomos* was also more general than a *psēphisma*: a written law was a generalization of wider scope than an Assembly decree. Like a law-court, a meeting of the Assembly generally dealt with particular issues. Should we go to war against Chios? Should we send aid to the Corcyraeans? Should we make friends with the Thebans? Who should fund the next tragic chorus? Should we build a new building? Assembly decrees (*psēphismata*) passed for such purposes could have far-reaching effects, as did the decision in the 480s to build a navy rather than distribute the wealth of the Laurion silver mines, but the decisions were for the most part *conceptually* less general than *nomoi*. A *nomos* was of wider application than a *psēphisma;* the former applied to more particular cases than the latter.[60] It is important, however, not to elevate the issue of generality to a position of fundamental importance; decrees of the Assembly could be

[58] Hansen, *Ecclesia I*, 163–67, shows that the five exceptions were all in the fifth century. He finds no exceptions after 400 B.C. Hansen also shows that, with one exception, the *"demos"* is never credited with passing a *nomos* in the fourth century. The sole exception, Demosthenes 59, *Against Neara* 88f., may hinge on the sense in which *"demos"* is used, and is not sufficient reason to consider the pattern broken.

[59] On Solon in fourth-century speeches as a moral reproach, see, e.g., Demosthenes 19, *On the False Legation* 256, in *Demosthenes II*, trans. C. A. Vince and J. H. Vince (Cambridge, MA: Harvard University Press, 1999).

[60] This was also understood by Aristotle; see *Nicomachean Ethics* 5.10, 1137b11–32 (a *nomos* is a general, standing rule; a *psēphisma* applies to the facts of the moment). In my view, the "open texture" of Athenian law is the use of generalizations applied to particular cases, and the issue turns on this philosophical point. "Open texture" is a phrase from Herbert Lionel Adolphus Hart, *The Concept of Law* (Oxford: Oxford University Press, 1961). On the application to Athens, see Robin Osborne, "The Law in Classical Athens," *Journal of Hellenic*

quite general. The basic issue at stake is not the degree of generality of a decree, but rather the requirement that it be consistent with the written laws; that is, the basic issue is its constitutionality.[61]

Most important to preventing the usurpation of the laws, the Athenians established a legal hierarchy between *nomos* and *psēphisma*. In essence, a *psēphisma* was never to be more authoritative than a *nomos*. In any discrepancy between a *psēphisma* and a *nomos*, the *nomos* had precedence. This served to set limits on the Assembly; it could not pass decrees that countermanded written laws. This rule is cited in the speech of the orator Andocides (*On the Mysteries*), where he states that *psēphismata* must accord with *nomoi*:

> In no case shall a magistrate enforce a law that is unwritten. No decree of the council or of the Assembly shall override a law. No decree shall be imposed on an individual that does not apply to all the Athenians, unless an Assembly of 6,000 shall so vote in a secret ballot.[62]

To further place the written laws outside the reach of the Assembly, the authority to change a *nomos* was made procedurally, institutionally, and conceptually distinct from the procedure used to enact a *psēphisma*.[63] In a direct parallel to the process for amending the American Constitution, which cannot be done by an act of the legislative or executive branches, the procedures for passing an Assembly decree were different from those required to change the written laws. In essence, the fundamental laws of Athens—its written *nomoi*—were placed beyond the reach of the Assembly. All changes to the written laws were subject to legal review by a jury sworn to uphold the laws. Any citizen could initiate a challenge to any proposal.

The law courts are the key to understanding how the Assembly was brought under the control of the laws. An Athenian jury was a group of several hundred citizens selected by lot, who heard two sides of a case and then decided without deliberation by a vote. The fundamental difference between the Assembly and the jury was a juror's sworn obligation to judge a case according to law. The so-called Heliastic oath reads, in part:

> I will give verdict in accordance with the statutes [written laws] and decrees of the people of Athens [the Assembly] and the Council of

---

Studies 105 (1985): 40–58; and Edward Harris, "Open Texture in Athenian Law," *Dike* 3 (2000): 27–79.

[61] This was noted by Tarbell, "The Relation," in 1889.

[62] Andocides 1, *On the Mysteries* 87.

[63] For a description of passing a *nomos*, see Demosthenes 24, *Against Timocrates* 20–23.

500. . . . I will not allow private debts to be cancelled, nor land nor houses belonging to Athenian citizens to be redistributed. . . . I will give impartial hearing to prosecutor and defendant alike, and I will give my verdict strictly on the charge named in the prosecution.[64]

Juries did not, of course, always function legally—but the Assembly was not limited by such an oath, and could, on principle, pass any measure at any time. The lack of a law that was firmly authoritative over the Assembly is the factor that Aristotle identified as having allowed the democracy to become a composite monarchy, and a tyranny.[65]

Should any citizen challenge an Assembly proposal with a *graphē paranomon*—literally, a charge that a proposal was "beside the law" or "illegal"—debate in the Assembly would stop, and the case would be transferred to a jury, which would be sworn to consider the legality of the proposal. If an existing *psēphisma* were found to be in conflict with a new *nomos*, or a new *psēphisma* with an existing *nomos*, then the *psēphisma* was repealed. The jury had to agree that the proposal was not contrary to the laws.[66] Thus, the written laws—the *nomoi*—became the authority against which the decrees of the Assembly were measured, and such a written standard provided a check against attempts to manipulate the decisions of the Assembly using emotional appeals.[67]

To further protect the *nomoi*, the Athenians also had a way for any citizen to challenge proposed changes to the *nomoi*. This was expressed in the descriptive phrase *graphē nomon mē epitedeion theinai*, a charge (*graphē*) that an unfit written law (*nomos*) had been proposed.[68] The ability of any citizen to charge that a speaker had proposed an unfit *nomos* was similar to the *graphē paranomon* for a *psēphisma*. Procedurally, however, a *psēphisma* was turned over to legal review only if challenged; a proposed *nomos* required a legal review in every case. The standard by which the sworn jury considered the fitness of the proposed *nomos* was the existing written laws, as well as the general fitness and consistency with accepted standards that a law must possess.

The procedure to change a law worked something like this: at the start of the year the people in Assembly would consider whether they wished

---

[64] Demosthenes 24, *Against Timocrates* 149–51, dated 355 B.C. The oath was dramatized a century earlier in Aeschylus's *Eumenides*. See Todd, *The Shape of Athenian Law*, 54–55, for sources.

[65] Aristotle, *Politics* 1292a11–12; 1305a7–9 (popular leaders became tyrants).

[66] See Hansen, "*Nomos* and *Psēphisma*," 170, for six examples. Hansen notes as "astonishing" the idea that a new *nomos* would repeal existing *psēphismata*, but this is what Demosthenes 20, *Against Leptines* 44, states, and it is supported by a law on silver coinage. *Demosthenes III*, trans. J. H. Vince (Cambridge, MA: Harvard University Press, 1998). Ronald S. Stroud, "An Athenian Law on Silver Coinage," *Hesperia* 43 (1974): 157–88.

[67] Aristotle, *Rhetoric* 1354a24–25.

[68] For citations of this or a similar phrase, see Aristotle, *Constitution* 59.2; Demosthenes 24, *Against Timocrates* 1.

to permit the introduction of new laws that year. If they agreed, then a citizen could propose to change a *nomos*, which required the introduction of a new *nomos* to take its place. No *nomos* could be repealed without a new *nomos* to replace it. If such proposals came forth, they were posted in public. A board was appointed, along with a commission of jurymen, to conduct a trial of the proposal. The commission indicted the law, and a jury heard arguments for and against it in the light of existing laws, which were defended by chosen advocates. The point is that the legality of the law had to be examined and cleared before the Assembly could even consider whether the law was desirable. The legal question was to be largely separated from the political question—and the *nomos* was off-limits to changes by the Assembly without legal review.[69]

Orators who argued cases before Athenian juries were not legalistic as in a modern courtroom; their citations of laws and of earlier law-givers (especially Solon) were often intended to smear their opponents morally. Epichares is "one most debased of all" (*ponērotatos pantōn*), said Andocides of an opponent, "and desiring to be that way."[70] But a city is like a man, thought Demosthenes, who said that "debased laws" (*hoi ponēroi nomoi*) injure a community.[71] This again suggests the strong connection between moral values and laws. The standardization of the laws, and their inscription in a central place in the *polis*, amounted to a rejection of the sophistic approach to moral standards, as applied to the rhetorical approaches of public speakers. This rejection was not complete, of course; there was still great latitude for argument, and speeches preserved from the next century are full of obfuscations and rhetorical ambiguities. But the Assembly did not again take the city over the cliff as it had during the war with Sparta—and the sophists did not regain the kind of intellectual or political strength they had held in the late fifth century.

Ultimately, the integrity of the fundamental laws—the anchors for Athenian political life—depended upon the commitment of individual Athenian citizens to those laws, and their willingness to take self-motivated, self-generated action to challenge attempts to violate those laws. The beauty of the system was that it took a jury review as well as a majority vote in the Assembly to pass a proposal, but any citizen could stop the voting with a legal challenge. One rational man could bring the issue to legal review, while no one person or group could pass a proposal. The all-too-frequent examples of the Assembly taking an action and then regretting it later were, to some extent, alleviated by these challenges and the closer, more deliberate, examination afforded to any particular issue.

---

[69] Demosthenes 20, *Against Leptines*, offers evidence about how a challenge to a law would work.

[70] Andocides 1, *On the Mysteries* 95.

[71] Demosthenes 20, *Against Leptines* 49.

V. Fundamental Law, Ancient and Modern

The Athenian reforms provide a series of parallels to the American Founding, as well as to our own day. The parallels begin with the recognition of the need for fundamental laws, to which political institutions must conform. In *Federalist No. 78*, Alexander Hamilton defined the American conception of a constitution as embodying fundamental laws that are enforceable by an independent judiciary:

> The interpretation of the laws is the proper and peculiar province of the courts. A constitution is, in fact, and must be regarded by the judges as, a fundamental law. It therefore belongs to them to ascertain its meaning as well as the meaning of any particular act proceeding from the legislative body. If there should happen to be an irreconcilable variance between the two, that which has the superior obligation and validity ought, of course, to be preferred; or, in other words, the Constitution ought to be preferred to the statute, the intention of the people to the intention of their agents.[72]

The American Founders understood the need to resolve potential conflicts between the legislators and the political principles on which the nation was founded, even though they left open the specific means to accomplish this. They also had to define the terms of popular consent, in order to prevent inappropriate attempts by the people to tamper with the principles of the constitution. The "intention of the people" does not mean the people's agreement with the *particular* acts of the legislature as determined by regular popularity contests, but rather the original consent to fundamental principles—the *fundamental* laws upon which political action is founded.[73] The so-called supremacy clause in the Constitution itself (Article VI) establishes the Constitution as the "supreme Law of the Land," and binds the judges in every state to the Constitution. The courts have assumed the authority to define and protect those principles, through judicial review of legislation.[74] Although the Founders did not define the procedures for federal judicial review of state legislation, they did establish a conceptual, political, and legal hierarchy to govern the relationships between legislation and the fundamental laws. In their late-fifth-century reforms, the Athenians recognized all of these hierarchies, as they applied to their *nomoi*.

The central lesson from the Athenians as to what a constitution should do is that it should stand above the popular and legislative winds of the

---

[72] Hamilton, *Federalist No. 78*, in Pole, ed., *The Federalist*, 415. See *Federalist Nos. 78–83* for Hamilton's ideas concerning the role of the judiciary.

[73] *Federalist No. 49* speaks against too often referring to the decisions of the people, and *Federalist No. 50* rejects both periodic and particular appeals to the people.

[74] See *Marbury v. Madison*, 5 U.S. 137 (1803).

moment and hold firm to its principles. One essential similarity between the Athenian and American systems, as each developed over time, is that the *particular* enactments of the popular institutions must not be allowed to supersede the *fundamental* principles written into the laws. Should legislation—or popular referenda—contradict the constitution, those enactments are invalid.

In other words, the Athenians tell us that the whims of popular opinion— either in public assembly or through the decisions of legislators—must not be made superior to the fundamental laws. In a similar vein, Hamilton continues his discussion of the judiciary in *Federalist No. 78*, explaining both the nature of the people's consent and how legislative acts are to be evaluated:

> [W]here the will of the legislature, declared in its statutes, stands in opposition to that of the people declared in the constitution, the judges ought to be governed by the latter, rather than the former. They ought to regulate their decisions by the fundamental laws rather than by those that are not fundamental.[75]

This statement establishes a hierarchy between the fundamental laws, written in the Constitution, and the nonfundamental laws enacted by the legislature. By urging judges to follow the fundamental laws, the statement implies that legislative acts that are contrary to the fundamental laws ought not be enforced. The Athenians offer a lesson here as well. In Athens, the citizen Assembly, the council, and the juries were the same people—every citizen was eligible for all—and (despite political machinations) they all had to accept the objective supremacy of the laws to some degree, or face a legal challenge from any concerned citizen. It was in the Assembly that decrees could be passed to handle particular cases not addressed by the laws—and those decrees had to be consistent with the generalized laws. Such an approach is inconsistent with the modern claim that "the Constitution is what the judges say it is," just as it is inconsistent with any shout from the Assembly that the people may do whatever they wish and call it lawful.[76]

The Americans and the Athenians attempted to preserve their fundamental laws in different ways. The American system upholds a separation of powers by granting the courts no role in passing legislation, and allowing the legislature no power to intervene in legal judgments.[77] Yet

---

[75] Hamilton, *Federalist No. 78*, 415.

[76] David J. Danelski and Joseph S. Tulchin, *The Autobiographical Notes of Charles Evans Hughes* (Cambridge, MA: Harvard University Press, 1973), 143. The shout from the crowd was recorded by Xenophon at the trial of the Arginusae generals: Xenophon, *History*, 1.7.12. (See note 36 above.)

[77] Although the line has blurred in the past century—for example, through the regulatory powers delegated by Congress to administrative bureaucracies of the executive branch.

the system allows judicial review of laws in particular cases, in which the courts may rule a law unconstitutional if it contradicts the Constitution. In contrast, the Athenians interjected judicial review at the level of legislation, allowing any citizen to initiate a review of any proposal prior to passage. American judges always hear particular cases, which can reveal contradictions between a provision of the law and the Constitution. The Athenians put the proposed law itself on trial, subjecting it to prosecution and defense before a sworn jury. The American Constitution forbids bills of attainder—legislative acts that single out individuals or groups—as well as *ex post facto* laws.[78] The Athenians forbade decrees that did not apply to all, and, in crisis, stopped *ex post facto* decrees and trials against supporters of the former government (the *amnēsia*).[79]

The Athenians and the American Founders also recognized that their fundamental laws had to be written by a few select men, and then accepted by the people as written. The early Athenian lawgivers Solon and Draco were models for the establishment of the many offices, boards, and commissions established in the fifth and fourth centuries to study, define, and inscribe the laws. The moral sanction of the early lawgivers provided an important source of legitimacy for the laws. In *Federalist No. 43*, James Madison observed that one of the defects in the original Articles of Confederation was that "in many of the States it had received no higher sanction than a mere legislative ratification." Not only did the Articles fail to meet the standards for popular consent (thereby failing to rise above the status of treaties), but they were open to legislative and popular manipulations. To remedy this flaw and to place the nation's fundamental laws and principles off-limits to popular and legislative fiat, the American Founders designed specific and distinct procedures for constitutional ratification and amendment. The Constitutional Convention of 1787, the state ratifying conventions, and the processes of constitutional amendment were the processes by which the original Constitution was to be formulated and debated. The supreme authority of the Constitution—the standard against which other laws would be evaluated—provided ongoing legal checks against the state and federal legislatures. The parallel in Athens was in the use of jurors, sworn to follow the written laws, to evaluate Assembly proposals.

The Athenians of the late fifth century and the Americans of the twentieth century were both societies in which certain philosophical positions shaped political practice and the interpretation of the laws. The various American progressive and populist movements suggest parallels to both the democratic and sophistic movements in Athens.

---

[78] U.S. Constitution, Article I, section 9. See Madison, *Federalist No. 44*: "Bills of attainder, ex post facto laws, and laws impairing the obligations of contracts, are contrary to the first principles of the social compact, and to every principle of sound legislation" (in Pole, ed., *The Federalist*, 244).

[79] Andocides 1, *On the Mysteries* 87. I discussed the *amnēsia* in Section IV above.

Politically, the progressives—like the Athenian democrats—lobbied for greater direct exercise of power by the people, through, for instance, the direct election of senators, and the primary system that has largely replaced the party conventions. The idea that the United States is a federal republic is largely lost today amid the triumph of the populist agenda. In Athens, the Assembly arrogated to itself the function of legislature, ratifier of the popular will, and even judge—the latter when it assumed the functions of the courts, dispensed with the need for oaths, and tried the six generals after they had won a naval battle against the Spartans at Arginusae (discussed above in Section II).

Intellectually, the Greek sophists were counterparts to the modern subjectivists, who rejected religious dogmatism and supernatural morality, but replaced them with skepticism and moral relativism. The political manifestation of such views is pragmatism, which considers every issue to be an isolated particular case, finds normative standards only in relation to particular situations, and eschews the use of firm principles. The legal counterpart to pragmatism is in the philosophy of Oliver Wendell Holmes, who sought to balance various claims rather than to evaluate them using principles in the law. He wrote famously, "All my life I have sneered at the natural rights of man."[80] Value choices, he wrote, are "more or less arbitrary. . . . Do you like sugar in your coffee or don't you? . . . So as to truth."[81] "[A] thing might be good for some persons but bad for others, or at one time good and another time bad," said the anonymous sophist twenty-four hundred years earlier. Each took his views into the interpretation of the law, and each then saw fit to determine that the law was what he said it was.

In classical Athens—as today—there were many who opposed such subjectivism. Seeing the sophists as destroyers of the moral foundations of society, they demanded a return to the standards associated with the traditional gods. The characters in Aristophanes' *Clouds* react against sophistic thought by burning down Socrates' school—a chilling presage to the historical death of Socrates. He remains the preeminent symbol of those who investigate matters in heaven and earth, question the gods, and purport to teach—and then fall victim to those who see such actions as crimes. The reactionaries in Athens also have counterparts today: the conservatives of the religious right, who decry the loss of moral standards among the modern sophists, and call for a return to religious standards— replacing skepticism with tradition and divine moral commandments, and wanting law and order over mob rule. A similar desire motivated some who favored the reinscription of the ancestral laws of Athens. But this approach threatens to leave the laws subordinated to tradition—a

---

[80] Oliver Wendell Holmes, letter to Harold Laski, September 15, 1916. See First Amendment Center website, http://www.firstamendmentcenter.org/analysis.aspx?id=20074.
[81] Oliver Wendell Holmes, letter to Lady Pollock, September 6, 1902. See ibid.

primitive form of "original intent" that depends upon some view, drawn from tradition, of what that "intent" might have been.

Throughout history intense debates have often raged between traditionalists and those who challenge tradition by thinking independently — debates over the ethical foundations of a nation's political health and the relationship between ethics, law, and the exercise of power. In Rome during the second century B.C., for instance, the conservative Cato the Censor was appalled by the openly skeptical method of argument used by visiting Greek philosophers, and the implications this kind of thinking had for the survival of the republic.[82] Philosophers such as Carneades had adopted a relativistic approach to moral questions, with striking similarities to certain "living constitution" views today.[83] The story is that Carneades argued one side of a case and won; then he took the other side and won again. In Cato's vision, such arguments could undercut the authority of Roman laws by elevating political expediency over adherence to fundamental truths; as the Roman youth abandoned the certainties of the past, the Roman political order would be vulnerable to potentially fatal changes. By inducing the Senate to order the philosophers out of Rome, Cato could claim to have saved the republic, by rescuing its moral character and its constitutional foundations from such skeptical assaults.

Aristotle came closest to providing an alternative to the skeptics and the sophists, as well as to religious traditions. He viewed laws neither as dogmas inherited from a divinely inspired past nor as subjective constructs, but rather as objective generalizations by which jurors judge particular cases. This approach starts with facts, since "the underlying facts do not lend themselves equally well to the contrary views."[84] The jurors should be concerned with the facts, and the laws should provide the means to evaluate those facts: "Properly formulated laws should define as much of a case as they can, and leave as little as possible for the jurors to decide."[85] As well as reducing the influence of passions and individual interests on judgment, Aristotle's claim reflects the nature of the lawmaking process — to produce general rules without knowing the particular facts of the future — and the process of judgment, which has evidence but needs rules about how to judge the facts. Laws are objective principles that can be used to guide our decisions about particular matters. This is all the more true in matters of constitutional interpretation, which deals

---

[82] Carneades (214–129 B.C.), head of Plato's Academy, visited Rome in 155 B.C., along with Critolaus (a Peripatetic) and Diogenes (a Stoic). See Plutarch, *Marcus Cato* 22. This does not imply that Carneades was a sophist.

[83] See William H. Rehnquist, "The Notion of a Living Constitution," in Arthur and Shaw, eds., *Readings in the Philosophy of Law*, 520–25.

[84] Aristotle, *Rhetoric* 1355a36–37.

[85] Aristotle, *Rhetoric* 1354a32–b22. Aristotle, *Constitution* 9.2, defends Solon's laws by noting the difficulty involved in formulating general principles applicable to particular cases. *Politics* 1272b5–7 is clear that the rule of good laws is superior to the rule of men. Aristotle says that passion warps the decisions of kings at *Politics* 1286a17–20.

with the most abstract and general rules for a nation, and which serves to guide lower levels of legislation. At the level of constitutional interpretation, the issue of rule by laws versus men is of greatest importance.

VI. Conclusion

It would be improper to exaggerate the institutional and conceptual precision of the classical Athenians in solving their problems. They were certainly not aware of a need for a written plan of their government, and no ancient prescriptive "constitution" as detailed as that of the United States has ever been found. But the essential identification the Athenians made—the need for a law that is superior to the actions of the people and their agents, and which can be changed only by a procedure that differs from routine political actions—is essentially the same as the identification made by the American Founders. What constitutions should do must be determined within the broader identification of a constitution as the fundamental law of the land.

Philosophy, Politics, and Economics Program, Duke University

CONTRACT, COVENANT, CONSTITUTION*

By Loren E. Lomasky

I. Introduction

The authority that states claim for themselves is so sweeping and unaccommodating to challengers that, absent a compelling justificatory account, it verges on despotism. An imaginative story offering a less heavy-handed representation of the state will, therefore, be welcome. In the liberal tradition, the protagonist of that story has usually been *social contract*. There are, of course, numerous variations on the contract narrative, but in each the state is deemed to be not the master but rather the creation of individual citizens. More precisely, to the extent that the state does exercise mastery, it does so in virtue of a status freely conferred on it by those over whom rule is exercised.

The social contract story yields several morals. First, it implies that private citizens are not the mere chattels of their rulers; they are not slaves or unemancipated minors or inferiors by nature. Rather, they are self-determining agents who have exited the state of nature and formed a civil order through an exercise of their own wills. Second, the state is in the service of its citizens. It owes them those performances for the sake of which it was created. Third, the bounds of obedience are not without limit. Should the regime fail to uphold the terms of the social contract, it can justifiably be cashiered.[1] Running through the narrative, then, is a commitment to the dignity of ordinary human beings. The ruled possess a moral status that entitles them to respect even from the most elevated of their rulers (who are, strictly speaking, not rulers but rather those who serve the ruled by exercising power on their behalf). To be a party to the enabling contract is to be an author of one's own political fate; it is to be not merely a subject but a citizen.

* I am indebted to Stewart Braun, Noah Greenfield, and Louis Lomasky for critiques of a previous draft. They are not, of course, responsible for errors of fact or interpretation offered herein. Ellen Paul's nonpareil editorial services have once again gently guided me across the compositional Red Sea and into the Promised Land of a finished manuscript. To her I owe thanks and probably also a few sets of tennis.

[1] That is so even for Thomas Hobbes, the most absolutist of the contract theorists. Once the state is unable to provide security for its citizens, the obligations they owe to their sovereign are rendered null and void: "The Obligation of Subjects to the Soveraign, is understood to last as long, and no longer, than the power lasteth, by which he is able to protect them. For the right men have by Nature to protect themselves, when none else can protect them, can by no Covenant be relinquished." Thomas Hobbes, *Leviathan*, chap. 21, "The Liberty of Subjects," ed. Richard Tuck (New York: Cambridge University Press, 1991), 153.

© 2011 Social Philosophy & Policy Foundation. Printed in the USA.

Even beginning philosophy students are aware that the great founding theorists of liberalism differ sharply among themselves concerning the framework of the contract that undergirds the state. I hereby nod at these issues but mostly ignore them in what follows. The essay aims to set out what contract theories share in virtue of being contract theories, not what distinguishes them one from another. In particular, it aims to display the weaknesses of social contract as a basis for grounding a tolerable political order. Five reasons are set out in Section II for maintaining that contractarianism is unable to ground the authority that state institutions are routinely deemed to enjoy. If anarchism is to be avoided, some alternative strategy is needed. Section III resurrects one such strategy: *covenant*. I don't mean covenant as a synonym for contract; that would be too slender a circle to be worth traversing. Rather, I mean covenant as paradigmatically enacted at Sinai between Israel and its god and subsequently reinterpreted for purposes both religious and political. (The "new covenant" of Christianity is one but not the only instance of reinterpretation.) Section IV argues that *constitution* can usefully be understood as something of a hybrid between contract and covenant, and that it thereby acquires some of the advantages of each. Section V sums up. Quite unimaginatively, the constitution that takes pride of place in the discussion is the American constitution drafted in Philadelphia. Is that special pleading? Of course it is. Political justification does not come easily, and not every document that can be identified as a constitution plausibly supplies it. The interesting question is what constitution, at its best, can contribute to strong political foundations.

II. What's Wrong with Contract?

Here is how vintage social contract theory proceeds: In a prepolitical condition, also known as the "state of nature," life is precarious. The sorts of disagreements that regularly present themselves in a world of scarcity and partiality are apt to escalate into rampant violence. Life is hard enough when it is only sabertooth tigers that need to be fended off, let alone one's fellow men, so sooner or later people have the wit to appoint a common judge over themselves in order to secure the peace. If that original compact does not constitute a civil order, then another step or two of institution-creation does. The result is government by the consent of the governed. The story is enormously edifying. It is also dubious.

A. It never was

If I have agreed to supply you with apples in exchange for your oranges, then there is a moral onus on me to be forthcoming with the apples (especially if you have already transferred the oranges). But if we never actually agreed to exchange apples for oranges, however appealing that exchange might be in principle, then no such obligation obtains. Contracts that we *could have* made or even those that we *would have* made under various specified circumstances lack the force of promissory performances. Hypothetical consent may have normative significance as a heuristic for ascertaining achievable reciprocal benefit, but what it cannot do is ground obligation in performance.

One liability of contractarianism, then, is that the primordial compact establishing a civil order never occurred. None of the classical theorists of liberalism is of a mind to declare otherwise. At best, they are vague about the particulars of egress from the state of nature. No hypothesis is hazarded concerning the place or date of the epochal transition; the contractors themselves are bathed in anonymity. Once human beings lived without benefit of political institutions, and then in the foggy past of the species, political structures emerged. In the telling of this story, contract is a black box hypothesized to account for the transition. The only indispensable content of the box is that the changeover was *voluntary*, an act of men rather than an act of God or of unthinking nature. So, for example, John Locke argues against Sir Robert Filmer at stupefying length in the *First Treatise of Government* that no divine proclamation subsequent to the creation of Adam establishes any one man as rightful ruler over his fellows. In the *Second Treatise*, Locke observes that human beings are so similar one to another in mind and body that there can be no assumption that they are sorted into exclusive classes of natural rulers and ruled.[2] The only remaining explanation of the fact that people in every civilized realm are united under institutions of government is that states originated as products of free choice.

Perhaps the most noteworthy fact about the inference to contract is its fragility. At least one other potential origin of states presents itself as no less plausible a mechanism: subjugation of the weak by the strong. That is a dynamic that can be observed in the present, in both private and public realms, so only a very gentle extrapolation is needed to make it the founding motif of states. Thomas Hobbes acknowledges that force majeure is often the means by which individuals are made subjects. In his account, however, forceful subjugation is not an alternative to contract but a version of it.[3] Contract so understood includes offers one cannot (reasonably)

---

[2] "[The state of nature is] a state also of equality, wherein all the power and jurisdiction is reciprocal, no one having more than another; there being nothing more evident, than that creatures of the same species and rank, promiscuously born to all the same advantages of nature, and the use of the same faculties, should also be equal one amongst another without subordination or subjection." John Locke, *Second Treatise*, in Locke, *Two Treatises of Government* (1689), ed. Peter Laslett (New York: New American Library, 1963), sec. 4.

[3] "*A Commonwealth by Acquisition* is that, where the Sovereign Power is acquired by Force; And it is acquired by force, when men singly, or many together by plurality of voyces, for fear of death, or bonds, do authorizse all the actions of that Man, or Assembly, that hath their lives and liberty in his Power." Hobbes, *Leviathan*, chap. 20, "Of Dominion Paternall, and Despoticall," 138.

refuse. Not many will want to follow Hobbes down this particular road. It is questionable whether genuine consent can be elicited at the point of a sword, and it is more questionable still whether, once the imminent peril has passed, individuals should consider themselves constrained by terms thereby extracted. Liberals, as opposed to Hobbesian absolutists, will be disinclined to establish political legitimacy on foundations of acquiescence born of intimidation.

B. Terms of consent

Set aside the problem of whether any credence can be given to the story of a founding contract. There remains the question of what it is to which the contractors agreed. The story told by theorists is that the state of nature is intolerable.[4] Because insecurities are everywhere, exit is much to be desired. But exit to what? The indicated answer is: to whatever alternative is achievable. Leaping out of the frying pan is a remarkably attractive idea if there is so much as a lively possibility that one isn't thereby leaping into the fire. To put it another way, even morally mediocre states are preferable to unpredictable anarchy. That is not to maintain that all states offer better prospects to the representative citizen than statelessness. Cambodia under the Khmer Rouge did not. Arguably, neither do contemporary North Korea or Zimbabwe. (I say "arguably" because whether life prospects there are inferior to those, say, in anarchic Somalia[5] is hard to determine.) The point is that a vast range of political forms can reasonably be judged superior to a state of nature and, therefore, contractors would rationally choose any one of these if it was the indicated alternative to anarchy.[6] Even granted the premise that some social contract obtains, that tells us almost nothing about what the terms of the contract are.

Hobbes aside, however, the classical theorists contend that a useful degree of specificity can be attributed to the articles of agreement. In return for citizens' pledges of loyalty and obedience, government is obliged to protect the preexisting natural rights of the ruled. Minimally, government will not itself be a violator of those rights. States that are either ineffectual or predatory lack legitimacy. Additionally, some sort of attentiveness to the will of the governed may be said to be part of the package, including representative institutions and occasions for voting.[7] Hobbes would object that

---

[4] Jean-Jacques Rousseau is the conspicuous exception.

[5] Those who believe that Somalia's collection of assorted warlords and puppets constitute the government of a state are invited to choose some other example.

[6] That is more or less Hobbes's argument. The choice boils down to Sovereignty or Savagery, and so it is clear-cut. One may be luckier or unluckier with the quality of the rulers and institutions one gets, but that is not relevant to regime legitimacy.

[7] Locke, for example, declares, "For when any number of Men have, by the consent of every individual, made a *Community*, they have thereby made that *Community* one Body, with a Power to Act as one Body, which is only by the will and determination of the *majority*.

this is wishful thinking, and he would have a strong case. A compromise position is that contract strips justification from especially unresponsive and horrific regime forms but is otherwise open-ended. Because anarchy is almost always more threatening to the well-being of individuals than civil society, contractors will accept whatever state is on offer.

Contract might instead be understood in an idealized form as choice under epistemically favorable conditions of the *best* regime type. I call this "idealized" because the suggestion that any such construction would be feasible with the ravening predators of the state of nature licking at one's heels is far-fetched. Construed as the outcome of an idealized process of deliberative choice, the bargain is far removed from any realizable grounding political scenario. It will instead be posed in the form of a hypothetical choice scenario, so as to do service as a heuristic for eliciting principles of justice that meet demands of impartiality and mutual benefit. This is, of course, the strategy of John Rawls in *A Theory of Justice*.[8] Because the return to fashion of social contract theory is almost entirely due to Rawls's efforts, it would, perhaps, be presumptuous to dismiss the Rawlsian strategy as not being genuinely contractarian. What is clear, though, is that the hypothesized agreement by contractors in the original position to Rawlsian principles of justice does not lend those principles any additional justificatory force beyond their putative status as the uniquely rational solution to choice under extreme uncertainty. Whatever function contract may serve in Rawls's framework, it does not ground obligation on actual freely tendered consent. Thus, if the question at issue is what citizens are obligated to comply with and why, idealized contract of the Rawlsian sort is irrelevant.

C. *How stringent are the obligations established by consent?*

Even if it is the case that nothing but consent suffices to ground citizens' obligations to obey, it does not follow that those who have given their consent are obligated to anything approaching the extent that classical liberal theory supposes. Without denying that agreement to perform some activity carries normative weight (else the practice of giving and accepting commitments would have no point), we can yet deny that this weight is infinite—or even, in the usual case, especially large.

Suppose you and I have agreed to meet at 2:00 to play tennis. At noon I call you and say, "I'm running behind with the paper I've got to submit this week. Would it be okay if I take a rain check?" The proper response is, "Of course." It would be distinctly odd for anyone who is not either under

---

For that which acts any Community, being only the consent of the individuals of it, and it being necessary to that which is one body to move one way; it is necessary the Body should move that way whither the greater force carries it, which is the *consent of the majority*." Locke, *Second Treatise*, sec. 96.

[8] John Rawls, *A Theory of Justice* (Cambridge, MA: Harvard University Press, 1971).

the age of eight or Immanuel Kant to protest instead, "But you *promised!*" Conventions of promising are useless if they carry no binding force, but they are suffocating if they mandate compliance on all occasions. This is something that we all recognize in ordinary life, but theorists often feign that promises are sacrosanct simply in virtue of being promises. A more reasonable approach is to acknowledge that some promises are enormously committal, to be set aside only in the most extreme situations, if at all, while other promises lack stringency altogether. The central question for social contract theory is: On which end of this spectrum does enlistment in a civil order lie?

I don't believe that the answer is clear-cut. On the one hand, the reliance interests of those seeking to exit the state of nature and its concomitant perils can be literally a matter life and death. The perils of anarchy are not to be underestimated. On the other hand, the extent of the demands that states make on the citizenry are so far-reaching that denial of any option of exit from the state is draconian. What if the state should turn out to tax more and provide less security than one had anticipated? What if rulers at some point in the state's history show themselves to be as predatory as the denizens of the state of nature? Doesn't that experience provide one reason to say, "Look, this relationship really isn't working out; I think we should just be friends"?

Hobbes would have one believe that this is an impossibility, that civil dissolution is equivalent to civil war. This is not very plausible. States may be a technology necessary for the maintenance of peace, but it does not follow that all juggling of their components is a mortal threat to security. Whether borders expand or contract does not speak to the issue of whether law is satisfactorily upheld within those borders. Indeed, the existence of lively exit options for citizens is apt to have a salutary influence on the behavior of their governors. Emigration is not an adequate check insofar as it deprives the state only of continued control of one's person but not of one's property. No doubt these are complicated issues, and absent a well-worked-out theory of optimal secession it is impossible to speak confidently on the issue. But that is no less true for those who espouse the orthodox theory of irrevocable social contract than for those who see the attractions of opting out. Locke, for example, maintains that individuals are not obliged to depart from the state of nature and enter a civil order, but that once one has brought his person and property into political society, he may never then withdraw them. Why not? I cannot see that Locke provides any substantive argument for that conclusion. It is question-begging to maintain that the contractors have undertaken a perpetual obligation. Perpetuity is a very long time, and risk-averse persons will be loath to tie themselves down to that extent, especially if they enjoy some prescience concerning the inefficiencies and moral obtuseness that states regularly display. They might very well instead build into the original compact a requirement of periodic reaffirmation. But who knows?

That is to return to the previous section's examination of the uncertainty of the social contract's terms. It also leads into the next section's examination of consent and future generations.

D. Transgenerational consent

Contract would have value as a *descriptive theory* if there were reasons to believe that states come into the world on the back of consent. Alas, such reasons are scant. Contract has value as a *prescriptive theory* of political obligation if those who have consented (or are deemed to have consented) are held to account as a result of their free assent. That, though, is not the normative significance attributed to contract by the canonical liberal theorists. Rather, *primordial assent* is invoked to justify ascription of duties to *citizens here and now*. It is unclear how this is supposed to work. A fixed point of our moral conceptions is that people can bind themselves via their own free acts, but cannot so bind unrelated others.[9] Allegiances sworn long ago or far away do not travel well.

Locke is acutely aware of this problem and turns to a consent that is ongoing and *tacit* to ground political duties. An extensive literature, much of it highly critical, addresses this aspect of the Lockean theory. Tacit consent as it presents itself in the *Second Treatise* bears an uncomfortably close resemblance to Hobbes's coerced consent. If the only alternative to obedience one has is to flee the sovereign's domain, thereby forfeiting property and valued personal associations, the alleged voluntariness of acquiescence is dubious. There may be ample reasons to comply with governors' commands, but these will be reasons of self-interest under duress.[10] Sometimes, though, one might be able to avoid the reach of the rulers. To get away with evading onerous demands is not the same as faithlessness to a freely assumed loyalty. So-called tacit consent should be understood as the midwife of tacit resistance, not of political duty.

Autonomy is the privilege of every generation. "The earth belongs in usufruct to the living," Thomas Jefferson famously wrote to James Madison in a letter dated September 6, 1789, going on to declare, "Every constitution, then, and every law, naturally expires at the end of nineteen years. If it be enforced longer, it is an act of force and not of right."[11] Practicality was not Jefferson's greatest strength, and as a piece of constructive political engineering, the nineteen-year sunset provision can seem bizarre. (Madison seems to have so regarded it.) No less bizarre, however, is an assumption

---

[9] I say "unrelated" because liability for debts or specific performances can extend to spouses or business partners. Note that these relationships are themselves voluntarily assumed.

[10] A plausible alternative is that there exists a general moral duty to obey lawful political authorities, but that would render contract theory redundant.

[11] Julian P. Boyd and William H. Gaines, Jr., eds., *The Papers of Thomas Jefferson*, vol. 15 (Princeton, NJ: Princeton University Press, 1958), 392–97.

that ancestral acts of agreement are transmitted through the national DNA to generation after generation of citizens. If consent is even in the ballpark as an answer to the question of how political obligation is incurred, then it must be *one's own consent* that does the work. Jefferson is simply working out the implications of that moral datum for the new American experiment. Now that the experiment is well into its third century, whatever normative impetus it may have received from voluntary subscription by the former colonists is long used up.

E. Interpreting obligation

Locke is something of an optimist concerning the moral infrastructure of the state of nature. (Of course, compared to Hobbes, it's hard not to seem optimistic.) There is built into the state of nature a natural law that commands self-preservation and requires that one not "harm another in his Life, Health, Liberty, or Possessions."[12] This precept is not the dictate of an artificial sovereign[13] but rather is an imperative of natural reason. That is why constraining oneself so as not to encroach on others is not intrinsically self-sacrificial. The law of nature is not the exclusive precinct of savants or paragons; all men insofar as they are rational enjoy access to it. Most of them can be expected to observe its ordinances most of the time. If my self-restraint with regard to your life, liberty, and property is likely to be met by concomitant restraint on your part rather than predation, then I shall find it both just and prudent to exercise that restraint. Moreover, because everyone in the state of nature possesses an executive right to punish transgressions of natural law, intrusion on the proper domain of others is neither just nor usually prudent. Because states are not needed to invent basic precepts of justice, why does Locke briskly proceed to their contractual derivation?

It is because laws are neither self-enforcing nor self-interpreting. Even if one assumes good will among all interacting persons—an assumption more heroic than prudent—individuals will nonetheless view questions of rights and duties from their own epistemically and morally circumscribed perspectives. You will know circumstances that I do not; I will be partial to various persons and principles that leave you unmoved. The inevitable result will be tensions that often escalate into violence. "I easily grant," says Locke, "that *Civil Government* is the proper Remedy for the Inconveniences of the State of Nature, which must certainly be Great, where Men may be

---

[12] Locke, *Second Treatise*, sec. 6. Locke appends to this negative admonition the further stricture that one must, when one's own preservation is not in question, act (positively) to preserve the rest of mankind.

[13] It is, though, the product of the absolute Sovereign of Heaven and Earth. Because the theological postulates on which Locke relies have fallen out of favor in contemporary political philosophy, latter-day Lockeans look elsewhere for moral foundations. For example, Robert Nozick, in *Anarchy, State, and Utopia* (New York: Basic Books, 1973), sedulously excises any theological appurtenances from his "Lockean" account of political legitimacy.

Judges in their own Case." [14] States are justified insofar as they constitute a common judge to contain and adjudicate disputes.

Unfortunately, while Lockean contract dampens conflict-generating actions *within the state,* it is of little help with regard to actions *by the state.* Should parliaments overreach or executives oppress, there is no recourse except the "appeal to Heaven." That is because over private individuals and the common judge there stands no meta-common judge. The same binary choice, either to acquiesce or to fight, that one confronts in the state of nature vis-à-vis other individuals presents itself again, but with an antagonist far more formidable. The inconveniences of the state of nature have not been eliminated but merely repositioned.

Political justification takes place on two levels. The ground floor is justification of a state, the campaign against anarchy (and anarchism). The upper level comprises justification of particular actions and omissions by the state. It is the campaign against despotism and corruption. Contractarianism speaks more emphatically to the former than to the latter. That is in part because of the lack of specificity of contract terms discussed above in Section II.B. However, even if it is entirely clear in some particular case that the governors are overstepping the limits of the authority ceded to them, the moral fallout remains unclear. It would be entirely extravagant to maintain that any single failing automatically dissolves the bonds tying rulers to ruled, yet it is supine to acknowledge as justified every policy up to whatever it is that triggers a latent right to revolution. That which is not strictly speaking intolerable may nonetheless be unjustifiable, and a duty to obey the law is not a duty *always* to obey the law. Traditional contract theory is less than helpful in sketching out these distinctions.

III. Covenant

Social contract grounds the legitimacy of authoritative institutions on the consent of the governed. It is not the first theory to do so. Long before Hobbes and Locke began to ply their trade, chroniclers of the polity of ancient Israel also conceived its foundation as crucially incorporating the consent of citizens. The term employed for these primal foundations is *covenant* (in Hebrew, *b'rit*). A covenant is a binding agreement among all parties, so it is linguistically proper to speak of it as "contract." Doing so would, however, be misleading. Not all contracts are created equal, and the one constitutive of the institutional structure of Israel is strikingly unlike those hypothesized by modern liberal theory. Sketching out the differences is the task of this section.

Numerous covenants are adduced in the Hebrew scriptures. God makes a covenant with Noah in the aftermath of the great flood (Genesis 9:9), and with Abram/Abraham (Genesis 17:4–14). The prophet Jeremiah

---

[14] Locke, *Second Treatise,* sec. 13.

announces the imminence of a new, improved version, a Covenant 2.0, if you will (Jeremiah 31:31–34). That idea is taken up with gusto by an early Christianity that proclaims possession of its own new covenant, also known as "new testament." As interesting as these many variations on a theme are to students of the concept, the paradigmatic covenant in Israel's self-consciousness, and the one on which its offices and legal structure are grounded, is the covenant enacted at Sinai. Prior to assembling at the mountain, the people who had recently escaped from Egyptian bondage are not exactly in a state of nature—they have in Moses an acknowledged, if not always well-heeded, leader—but they are a rabble without either land or law. Afterward, they still have some decades to wait before taking possession of the land (a possession that remains problematic in the twenty-first century), but they possess the framework of what will become their commonwealth.

The essence of the Sinai story is conveyed in Exodus 19–20. Israel is only two months removed from captivity and has recently been delivered at the Red Sea from what seemed to be well-nigh certain destruction. But yet more momentous events await. God commands Moses to tell the people that he is prepared to offer them his laws on condition that they swear allegiance to his rule: "Moses came and summoned the elders of the people and set before them all these commands which the LORD had laid upon him. The people all answered together, 'Whatever the LORD has said, we will do.' Moses brought this answer back to the LORD." [15] This is the covenant in embryo: the parties to the agreement are identified, the free assent of each is confirmed, and quid pro quos are outlined. The remainder of the Pentateuch is largely given over to specifying in minute detail the legal obligations of the governed and, incidentally, telling some good stories.

There is one obvious difficulty with establishing institutional structures on a covenantal foundation: God might choose not to be as obliging to other would-be partners as he is to the Children of Israel. The extreme of not being obliging is not existing, and for many contemporaries this is the most plausible theological proposition there is. They attach no credibility to a theistically-based social design. (Even a creche in a public building may be seen as too much religion in the public square.) Nonetheless, a brief examination of covenantal theory is worthwhile even for committed secular moderns because it reveals possible avenues of authority via assent that traditional contract theory lacks.

A. Actuality of covenant

A number of tales in scripture are just that: inspiring or hortatory narratives that make no pretense of historical verisimilitude. The book of

---

[15] Exodus 19:7–8. All scriptural citations are from the New English Bible.

Job is one example. A righteous man who suffers grievously yet endures
is a story for every place and time. It is an archetype of which there is an
indefinite number of tokens. That is not, however, the way Israel recounts
its covenantal origins. Rather, the event is specified as to year and month
of its occurrence, the particular mountain in the particular wilderness
where it is initiated, and the parties to it—identified en masse (the "house
of Jacob," the "seventy elders") and, for the central figures, by name and
title (Moses; Aaron the priest; "the LORD your God who brought you out
of Egypt, out of the land of slavery"). That it is truly a covenant rather
than a unilateral command by a sovereign authority (who is, after all,
irresistible) is underscored by the explicit statement that the people one
and all freely agree to accept the law that is on offer to them.[16] They have
good reason to do so, because of the enormous benefits that are consequent on taking it up. These are spelled out most eloquently in the "blessings" specified in Deuteronomy 28:1-14. These are not to be regarded,
however, as unconditional gifts. Deuteronomy 28 goes on to specify in
horrific accents the penalties that will befall Israel if it fails to uphold its
obligations. The relationship, then, is held to be genuinely mutual, incorporating specific performances from both parties. Moreover, in the immediate aftermath of the initial giving of the law, an example is related
(Exodus 32) of a particular transgression by Israel (the molding of the
Golden Calf) and the concomitant penalty (three thousand wrongdoers
executed).

This could, of course, be a fiction replete with realistic details. It is not
my intention here to argue on behalf of the historicity of the scriptural
account—or to argue against it. Rather, my intention is to suggest that the
biblical authors have little truck with what might be called Hypothetical
Covenant Theory. The authority ascribed to the covenant at Sinai[17] is the
authority stemming from an actual undertaking by just those parties who
are specified in the account and no others. Unlike the contracts of liberal
theory, it is not indefinitely repeatable. If it did not happen as related,
then no substitute covenant is on offer.

B. Terms of covenant

No one can complain that Torah lacks specificity with regard to the
provisions of Israel's covenant with God. The edicts are spelled out in

[16] The question can legitimately be raised concerning just how voluntary an agreement
can be with a deity who has just shown his power by drowning the Egyptian hosts under
a wall of water. Indeed, the rabbis themselves raise it in the Babylonian Talmud (Tractate
Shabbat 88a), where they play on the wording of Exodus 19:17 so as to read it as "Israel
stood under the mountain," i.e., God suspended the mountain over their heads and then
"offered" them the covenant.

[17] Strictly, the covenantal terms are not presented as being revealed all at once at Sinai but
are instead handed down throughout Israel's extended sojourn in the wilderness. "Covenant at Sinai" is a synecdoche. I owe this reminder to Noah Greenfield.

mind-numbing—others would say mind-elevating—detail throughout the remainder of Exodus and on into Leviticus and Numbers. Just in case that might not provide quite enough information, Deuteronomy repeats the instructions while providing further bits and pieces. The best known of the covenantal requirements are those stipulated in the Ten Commandments, but these do not come close to exhausting the obligations taken on by Israel. The latter are traditionally numbered as 613 distinct laws,[18] but this is somewhat arbitrary as provisions incorporate subprovisions which themselves breed an indefinite range of rules of application.

Nor are the injunctions all of the simple "thou shalt" and "thou shalt not" variety. Rather, some are constitutive of offices and practices that are meant to carry authority in the ongoing political and legal life of the nation. A hereditary *priesthood* is established that will do for Israel roughly what Washington bureaucrats, the Centers for Disease Control, and Oprah Winfrey do for Americans. They are not, however, Israel's only functionaries. *Prophets* play a pivotal role at most of the critical junctures of the nation's history. The office of prophet is not constituted by an enabling act of Torah—various instances of prophecy precede the existence of the nation—but the text does address the issue of how to distinguish between a true prophet and an imposter. Because the former possesses an imposing authority that the nation disregards at its great peril, while false prophets corrupt the people and lead them into sin, the concern is of no little urgency for Israel. A solution of sorts is proffered in Deuteronomy 18.[19] Duties attaching to the office of the *king* are specified even though it will be many generations before one is appointed.[20] And so on. This is clearly a document intent on establishing an authoritative institutional structure for the polity, not simply on preaching ritual and ethics.[21]

C. Stringency of covenant

That many precepts of Israel's covenant are of utmost urgency is not controversial. "Thou shalt not kill" is one example. Its urgency, however, does not arise from being a provision of the covenant; just the reverse. Prohibition of murder is a conclusion of natural human reason that is brought to positive law rather than originating from it. A rule that pork not be eaten is different. It carries no intrinsic normative weight. If there

[18] The origin of the tradition is the Babylonian Talmud (Makkot 23b), where it is disputed. From this emerges an extensive literature to which Maimonides is perhaps the most definitive contributor. I owe this observation to Noah Greenfield.

[19] Subsequent narratives of scripture indicate that Israel's success in employing the criteria is decidedly mixed.

[20] Deuteronomy 17:14–20. Modern biblical scholarship explains this remarkable foresight by suggesting that Deuteronomy reads back into the time in the desert various practices and problems that emerge much later in the history of the nation.

[21] I concede that this conceptual distinction is anachronistic, but I use it to underscore the avowedly political aspirations of the Hebrew scriptures.

is reason to eschew pork, it is because pork happens to be prohibited. That reason will be weighty if the way in which the prohibition takes place generates obligations that are stringent. Israel's understanding of covenant is that all of its permissions, prohibitions, and requirements are highly significant. Violations of some commandments carry heavier penalties than do violations of others, but the mere fact of being a provision of the covenant guarantees a strong incentive to comply. That is so for several reasons.

First, when the other party to the covenant happens to be Master of the Universe, heeding his injunctions presents itself as a very good policy to someone who wishes to stay out of trouble. Torah's narratives display many instances of transgressors against Yahweh meeting a dreadful fate. Fear is not, however, the essence of the driving force of the covenant; almost any two-bit earthly sovereign can unleash a lot of pain on those who displease. A second reason why the precepts of the covenant are authoritative is that they are prescribed under optimal epistemic conditions. No requirement is the product of ignorance, prejudice, lack of imagination, or miscalculation. Those who live under the rules need harbor no concern that they are being led into a cul-de-sac by a deficient commander. Rather, they maintain every confidence that the law incorporates not only power but also wisdom.[22]

Third, the yoke of the law is not onerous—or at least not *only* onerous. Rather, according to scripture, the requirements imposed on Israel are a source of joy and peace.[23] That is, of course, not an impartial viewpoint, but it receives support both from the phenomenology of obedience and from the foundational postulate that Israel's God is loving and merciful. Even if the rationale for some decree is not apparent, even if the penalties consequent on violation seem draconian, there nonetheless is overriding reason to believe that the system of law taken as a whole cannot be improved upon as a structure for human flourishing.

Fourth, the covenant is not in the first instance between God and each individual taken singly but rather between God and the collectivity of

---

[22] That is not to maintain that in every instance where p is commanded, there exists a balance of reasons on behalf of p rather than any alternative and, furthermore, that is why God commands p. For example, there may be no rationale whatsoever for disallowing pork chops rather than lamb chops. Perhaps, though, it is a useful discipline to have some food or other off-limits, and so the covenantal precepts include a food prohibition that is in itself arbitrary. If so, it is the prohibition that makes eating pork bad and not vice versa. The underlying theological jurisprudence of Torah does not provide a univocal answer to the Euthyphro question. Maimonides' *Guide for the Perplexed* is not the last word on the logic of that jurisprudence, but it is a necessary word.

[23] A representative passage is Psalms 19:7-10: "The law of the LORD is perfect and revives the soul. The LORD's instruction never fails, and makes the simple wise. The precepts of the LORD are right and rejoice the heart. The commandment of the LORD shines clear and gives light to the eyes. The fear of the LORD is pure and abides for ever. The LORD's decrees are true and righteous every one, more to be desired than gold, pure gold in plenty, sweeter than syrup or honey from the comb." No late-night infomercial endorses its product so fulsomely.

Israel. Not just the nation's well-being but its very existence are a function of the Sinai undertaking. Covenant informs them what to do but also how to be. It means that Israel will thenceforth not only have a collection of biographies but a history. The covenant is a charter for communal achievement. Insofar as individuals have concern not only for their own self-serving ends but also for their kin, their neighbors, and their posterity, they possess additional bases to value that covenant.

Taken together, these constitute compelling reason to observe commands both major and minor. Provenance in covenant is itself reason-conferring. At least that is so when the covenantal partner is of uniquely sterling quality.

D. Transgenerational covenant

The covenant at Sinai was made with the living but clearly was not intended for them alone. Indeed, scripture emphasizes that the generation of those who received the law at the mountain was deficient. They are described as neglectful, rebellious, "stiffnecked." These failings count against their piety quotient. In addition, they exhibit distinctively political shortcomings. In every time and place, people need courage if they are to maintain the institutions of a free polity. The escapees from Egypt, however, are portrayed as excessively timorous. The spies who return from scouting out the land Israel is to occupy are dispiritingly negative, and their interlocutors almost swoon with fear (Numbers 13). Because they lack heart, they are disqualified from entering the land. Only Caleb and Joshua, the two men of courage and conviction, are granted an exception. If the covenant were, then, exclusively or primarily for the living, it would be stillborn. But that does not address the question of how the consent of the original generation can bind those who come later.

Part of the answer, as noted above, is that the covenant is conceived not just as enabling relationships with individuals but also as communal. Israel is a nonderivative party to it, both as beneficiary and giver of commitments.[24] At the very least, this means that the covenant is not rendered null and void by the demise of the last person to have been present at Sinai. So long as the collectivity identified as Israel continues to endure, both it and its members remain bound by a network of privileges and obligations. That, though, pushes the question back: How do those who have not chosen to join with the nation, but are simply born into it, inherit duties they did not voluntarily assume?

---

[24] The nature and extent of interconnectedness in scripture between individual and communal responsibility pose difficult interpretive problems. In the space of just one chapter God declares to Moses, "I have considered this people, and I see that they are a stubborn people. Now let me alone to vent my anger upon them, so that I may put an end to them," and then, "It is the man who has sinned against me that I will blot out from my book" (Exodus 32:9–10; 33).

Membership status in Israel is primarily opt-out rather than opt-in. If one is born to parents who are citizens of the nation, then one inherits that status. (If the parents are of mixed citizenship, then, according to most traditions of interpretation, it is the status of the mother that is determinative.) Birth, however, is not destiny. Those who enter the world lacking an Israelite identity can go through a process of naturalization (i.e., conversion) that brings them into the fold. Joining up is difficult, opting out more so. If, however, one knowingly and deliberately forsakes the old covenant for a new covenant, membership in Israel is thereby surrendered.[25] It would be an exaggeration to say that the process is painless and free of recrimination—but sundering loyalties is rarely frictionless.

One problem with the normative standing of opt-out rules is that they often trade on inertia. People who find themselves enrolled in some association without having done anything whatsoever to bring about that connection, perhaps without knowing how they got there or what they would have to do in order to extricate themselves, cannot be said to have *chosen* their status. This is not to say that the status is unmerited— criminals may merit punishment, for example, even though they do not choose it—but whatever justification the status possesses does not derive from consent. Under an opt-out system, genuine voluntariness depends on people being afforded knowledge of the conditions of membership and the location of the exit door. They must also be able to leave without suffering drastic penalties.[26]

For a young Israelite, instruction in the conditions of membership begins shortly after birth, and culminates with coming-of-age in early adolescence, when assumption of the full range of adult duties takes effect.[27] Scripture also mandates public instruction at regular intervals: "At the end of every seven years, at the appointed time for the year of remission, at the pilgrim-feast of Tabernacles, when all Israel comes to enter the presence of the LORD your God in the place which he will choose, you shall read this law [Torah] publicly in the hearing of all Israel" (Deuteronomy 31:10).[28] The last thing that Joshua, the successor of Moses, did after the people had

[25] The paradigmatic example is conversion to Christianity.

[26] An interesting recent examination of the advantages of opt-out over opt-in rules is Richard Thaler and Cass Sunstein, *Nudge: Improving Decisions about Health, Wealth, and Happiness* (New Haven, CT: Yale University Press, 2008).

[27] The ceremonial celebration of *Bar Mitzvah* is of relatively late origin, sometime in the Middle Ages. The female equivalent, *Bat Mitzvah*, is much later still. Because these rites only underscore a change in legal status that occurs independently of the ceremony, they are of no relevance to association membership and are only peripherally relevant to the communication of its significance. See Ivan G. Marcus, *The Jewish Life Cycle: Rites of Passage from Biblical to Modern Times* (Seattle: University of Washington Press, 2004), esp. 84–85 and 106.

[28] To ensure that the requirement is interpreted in the broadest possible way such that no affected party will be able to claim lack of notification, the text goes on to specify: "Assemble the people, men, women, and dependants, together with the aliens who live in your settlements, so that they may listen and learn to fear the LORD your God and observe all these laws with care. Their children, too, who do not know them, shall hear them, and learn to fear the LORD your God" (Deuteronomy 31:12–13).

taken possession of the promised land was to restate the covenant in front of all the people and set up a megalith as a continual reminder of their assent.[29] The law, then, is not to be an antiquarian relic or the arcane possession of a coterie of savants. Rather, it is everyone's possession, everyone's business.

Are individuals afforded permission to withdraw without penalty from the covenant? In a word, no. Great opprobrium is held out for any Israelite who would abandon the yoke of Torah. When Zimri of the tribe of Simeon took up against orders with a foreign woman named Cozbi, they were both neatly skewered on a spear cast by Phinehas, the son of the son of Moses' brother, Aaron. The summary execution was not disavowed; rather, it earned Phinehas great credit (Numbers 25:6–15). The only safe way to resign affiliation was to flee.

From Phinehas to *Fiddler on the Roof*, assent is much applauded, but in one direction only: the covenant may freely be taken on but not cast off. Israel's theory of consent is not liberal. This is not a surprising conclusion.[30]

E. Covenant interpretation

Laws, whether natural or positive, human or divine, are not self-interpreting. Their application in a given situation is a matter of judgment. High stakes often hinge on determinations of legality, so it can be expected that people will not routinely agree concerning whose conduct is innocent and whose is culpable, who owes damages to whom. Absent an authoritative system of adjudication, we remain locked in the "inconveniences" that Locke attributes to the state of nature.

Quite possibly there is no people in the history of the world that has labored under a greater horror of lawlessness or lack of legal uniformity than Israel.[31] Israel not only takes on for itself an intricate and demanding legal code that is held to issue from the highest quarters, but it also includes within that code extended instructions concerning the code's own interpretation. Various offices with power of investigation, adjudication, and punishment are specified in the text of scripture. A remarkably small area of judicial interpretation is handed over to the *king*; much more is reserved for the *priests* and their adjunct functionaries, the *levites*. The *judges* sometimes do operate as judges, but more often in capacities we would identify as distinctly nonjudicial (for examples, see the eponymous biblical book).

---

[29] Joshua 24:25–28. The text is unclear as to whether the covenant there enacted is identical to the Mosaic one or is revised by Joshua.

[30] The rupture of associational ties paradigmatic for liberalism (insofar as it speaks to the priority of the individual over the community of origin) is the so-called excommunication of Spinoza from the Amsterdam Jewish community. I say "so-called" because it is unclear from the record who dumped whom.

[31] "In those days there was no king in Israel and every man did what was right in his own eyes" (Judges 21:25). There is no libertarian jubilation in the pronouncement.

Somewhere along the way, *scribes* come on the scene as privileged in virtue of their command of documents. Running through the story and grabbing a prominent role at crucial junctures are *prophets*.

Whenever disputes arose concerning who was the authentic inheritor of covenant, the issue was phrased in terms of competing legal interpretations. Prophets quarreled with priests concerning what was or was not proclaimed by Moses in the wilderness.[32] According to both Josephus and the New Testament book of Acts, Pharisees differed from Sadducees concerning the authority of the Oral Law (and who possesses it). The Dead Sea community at Qumran has left us documents setting out its own legal understandings in opposition to the corrupt establishment in Jerusalem. Nearly all of the post-biblical history of Israel up until the modern era spotlights attempts to establish rabbinic hegemony against competing interpretive tendencies (e.g., Karaites, Sabbatians, and that most obstreperous of offshoots, Christianity). It is not for this essay to offer an opinion concerning how successful these attempts to establish authoritative practices of legal adjudication have been, but it would be hard to deny that covenant displays reflexive self-awareness of its own interpretive dimensions.

IV. CONSTITUTION

Constitution, like social contract and covenant, is a mechanism for generating political outcomes on consensual foundations. Variety among constitutions is great. To the confusion of generations of schoolchildren, a few are characterized as unwritten. Some, most notably the Soviet 1936 constitution, are not worth the paper they're written on. Others are worthy but obscure. (I have not read the constitution of Luxembourg and predict that I am unlikely to do so.) But just as the covenant at Sinai is the gold standard of covenants, the Constitution of the United States of America is the gold standard of constitutionalism. In the remainder of this discussion, unless explicitly stipulated otherwise, this is the constitution to which I refer. I believe that some of the results elicited in what follows apply to other constitutions,[33] but that argument will not be pursued here.

Constitutions can evolve as the unintended and unforeseen result of a process of social development (e.g., the constitution of the United Kingdom), but the one that emerged in Philadelphia in September 1787 was as deliberate a product of design as a foundational political charter can be.

---

[32] For example: "Add whole-offerings to sacrifices and eat the flesh if you will. But when I brought your forefathers out of Egypt, I gave them no commands about whole offerings and sacrifice; I said not a word about them" (Jeremiah 7:21–22).

[33] Australia's constitution would be a good candidate for analysis in this framework, especially because it was largely modeled on the U.S. Constitution, constitutes a new commonwealth, and has had a successful run.

Its drafting and adoption were preceded by extended debate among the delegates to the Constitutional Convention and prompted heated advocacy and counteradvocacy by federalists and antifederalists, and its provisions were debated anew in ratifying conventions in each of the thirteen sovereign states. On numerous levels and including numerous parties, then, the U.S. Constitution incorporates and derives its authority from acts of consent.

It is not mistaken to think of the constitutional founding as putting flesh on the theoretical bones of contract theory. The Constitution's liberal provenance is undeniable, especially when the Bill of Rights is also taken into account. The Constitution is not, however, the child of only one parent. In important respects it also descends from covenant theory. That other heritage goes a long way toward explaining, I believe, both its sturdiness and the esteem in which it continues to be held.

In one respect, the American Constitution is the antithesis of Israel's covenant: it displays itself as an entirely human contrivance. Indeed, its thoroughly secular character bears remarking. Should we imagine the United States preparing a similar document in the early twenty-first century, we would expect it to contain somewhere an effusive peroration to a benign providence or a plea for divine guidance. Their absence in the eighteenth-century document is a function of the uniquely rationalistic character of that phase of the American experience.[34] In other respects, however, the Constitution bears more resemblance to the Sinai story than it does to Lockean contract.

Most obviously, the agreement is neither hypothetical nor indefinite. The manner in which its terms are debated and approved is a matter of public record, and all parties to it are identifiable. Among them are the thirty-nine signers, but they are not proceeding on their own authority. Rather, they act on behalf of the states for which they are delegates. This constitution is a compact uniting those states, but, as the preamble makes explicit, it is not the states as such but rather the totality of *the people* who "ordain and establish" the union.

A people is, of course, too numerous and dispersed for each citizen to be active in designing and approving the instruments of a new government. There could be grounds for suspicion, then, that their imprimatur is being invoked as cover for the real actors. Allaying this concern are several related factors. First, the people are represented by the most respected and distinguished of their compatriots, arguably the most accomplished assemblage of Americans ever to occupy a room together. Their probity is exceptional. If these men cannot be trusted to transact the public business, it is hard to see who could be. Second, the Constitutional Convention's product is then taken back to the several states for ratifica-

---

[34] Not only chronologically is it maximally distant from the Mayflower Compact on one end and Billy Graham's revival meetings on the other.

tion. It is discussed at a higher level of sophistication—most notably in the *Federalist Papers*—than political discourse has ever subsequently been afforded on the continent. Citizens know what they are being offered and have access to illuminating and principled arguments for and against. The state conventions in which the ratification question is debated are responsive to the citizenry they represent. Approval is not by the unanimity that Israel allegedly offered up at Sinai, but it comprehensively engages public reason. This is indeed a mechanism of translating private opinion into public assent that justifies identification of the new polity's enabler as "the people."[35]

Writing constitutions is easy; some countries have gone through dozens.[36] Generating one that possesses stability and normative authority is more difficult. In this regard, the United States Constitution is a standout. With remarkably few modifications, it has served as the national charter from the first term of President Washington until the present. Americans do not always agree concerning what the Constitution forbids or requires, but with near-unanimity they accept constitutionality as the final authority for political warrant. It is held in a quasi-scriptural veneration. That calls for explanation.

An experience of recent escape from tyranny concentrates the mind. People who have taken drastic measures to shed oppressive structures will be especially keen to establish for themselves fair and effective alternatives. These are conditions in which politics will be taken *seriously*. Even more so will that be the case in the aftermath of an initial attempt that proves misbegotten. Compared with Israel's unfortunate flirtation with the Golden Calf, America's meandering under the provisions of the Articles of Confederation was benign. Nonetheless, the malaise of that period sufficed to underscore the costs of inadequate associational engineering. Young America was strongly motivated to construct and swear allegiance to a structure that enabled cooperation without oppression. Whether the proposals that emerged from Philadelphia in 1787 were likely to provide such a structure was an open question to contemporaries, but there was a strong presumption in favor of giving it a chance.

First impressions are important. Sometimes they are enduring. The functionaries of the new republic were a glittering lot, comparable in distinction to the framers. *Primus inter pares* was Washington himself. The

---

[35] It must be conceded that this people was almost entirely white, male, and propertied. Is that a blot on the popular authority claimed for the document? Undoubtedly. But rather than arbitrary exclusion undermining the normative status of the Constitution, over time the constitutional logic undermined policies of exclusion.

[36] Whether that numeration is strictly accurate depends on criteria for individuation of constitutions: When is it the old constitution substantially modified, and when is it, instead, a genuinely new framework? However one comes down on constitutional metaphysics, the variability of constitutions is undeniable. See Robert L. Maddex, *Constitutions of the World*, 3d ed. (Washington, DC: CQ Press, 2008); and Rudiger Wolfrum and Rainer Grote, eds., *Constitutions of the World* (New York: Oxford University Press, 2008).

nation's deliverer in time of war, he had earned the trust of an admiring citizenry. Indeed, there was less controversy in the new republic concerning whether he or someone else should be at the nation's helm than there was in the wilderness over Moses' leadership.[37] The cabinet Washington assembled was exemplary, crossing geographical and ideological lines. (Congress was less uniformly distinguished, but that became the norm for Congress.) Natural opponents such as Jefferson and Hamilton would disagree ferociously, but in doing so they established the precedent of fighting it out *within the parameters of constitutional governance* rather than extramurally. That precedent was strengthened by changes of administrations, with the losers accepting, however grudgingly, the verdicts of electorates acting under decision procedures established by the Constitution. Over time, the prestige of the initial generation grew. We now call them the "Founders," but the (politically incorrect) term "Founding Fathers" serves better to express the filial piety accorded them by subsequent generations.[38] Constitutional authority, in that sense, combines admiration for the excellence of the design with the personal authority of those who have accepted and acted in an official capacity under it.

This is not the occasion for a close examination of that design, so I content myself with an observation that the nation's early experience demonstrated the resilience of its constitution when subjected to stress. Increasing prosperity and expansion across half a continent proved, with one exception, to be compatible with maintenance of the "empire of liberty." The exception is the sanction afforded to slavery, and that grievous flaw proved almost fatal. In a roundabout way, however, that breakdown of the original constitutional design paid it a supreme tribute. The oceans of blood shed for the sake of preserving the Union testified to its more than quotidian significance. Especially in Lincoln's soaring rhetoric at Gettysburg and in the Second Inaugural, it assumed transcendent significance. When victory was finally secured and the primal blot on the nation's charter was written over by the post–Civil War amendments, the worthiness of the Constitution was burnished with a sacral patina.[39]

This provides a partial response to Jefferson's worries about domination of the living by the dead hand of the past. If the living have been confirmed in the faith of their fathers, then they are not conscripts but willing participants in the continuing association. Constitutional structures are capital goods that provide a flow of ongoing dividends. Disassembling them every nineteen years would be like blowing up a productive

---

[37] For the rebellion of Korah, see Numbers 16.

[38] I am not aware of a revisionary movement to eulogize George Washington as "Parent of his Country" but would not be surprised by its emergence.

[39] Redemption of a nation by blood has at most a marginal role in Israel's covenant but is central to Christianity's. At the risk of over-theologizing, Washington plays the role of Moses/Joshua in the American mythology, while the role of Jesus is taken by Lincoln (and reprised in a fashion by the Kennedys and Martin Luther King).

factory or chopping down an orchard. Inheritance of valuable properties is not a cause for regret, although it very well could be if the capital asset were immutable. (Even Henry Ford knew that his factories had to be retooled from time to time.) However, the constitution handed down by the Founders contains provision for amendment. This is not an easy process to carry out, but neither was its original design. Reasonable people can disagree concerning optimal constitutional malleability, but it must be acknowledged that each generation enjoys some prerogative of altering the document that it has received—and also a prerogative to enjoy its benefits unchanged.

A further respect in which the current generation is master rather than servant of the Constitution is that the job of interpretation is in its hands. The Supreme Court is the interpretive agency par excellence, but applying the Constitution to contemporary realities is also a task for the lower courts, the executive, and the legislature. The term "living constitution" is highly charged, but taken in the most literal sense, it could not be otherwise. The dead are beyond being either rulers or ruled. In a constitutional order, though, their influence remains profound because insofar as contemporaries see themselves as interpreting or reinterpreting the Constitution, they take themselves to be in a dialectical relationship with the entire history extending back to Philadelphia. They are free to apply the Constitution in novel ways, but they are not at liberty to substitute creation for interpretation. Such, at any rate, is the theory of constitutionalism.

The rabbinic theory of faithful allegiance to covenant was similar. A scholar suitably qualified by virtue of office and ingenuity could twist the precepts of scripture like a birthday entertainer does party balloons, but the grounding postulates must in one way or another always be affirmed. Nor was amendment allowed, at least not officially. In that respect, the purity of the founding document is preserved to the greatest possible extent. Whether that provided not enough, just the right amount, or too much scope to a "living covenant" has been the crux of debate in Israel's history from antiquity to the present. Mutatis mutandis, it is the central ongoing American jurisprudential debate.

V. Conclusion

Let me close by trying to be clear about the significance of covenant for understanding the functionality of constitutionalism. It has often been observed that Americans treat their founding documents[40] as having quasi-religious status. An important book-length development of this theme

---

[40] This discussion has focused exclusively on the Constitution, but a comprehensive examination of the country's testamentary inheritance would offer equal attention to the Declaration of Independence.

is Sanford Levinson's *Constitutional Faith*.[41] As I understand Levinson's thesis, he argues that Americans have come to view their constitution less and less as an ordinary legal-political document and more as a sacred text. This essay does not dispute that claim but aims to offer a complementary one. I have argued that the biblical narrative of covenant is undeniably theological but also intrinsically political. It presents a theory of institutional justification for which consent is a necessary condition. Unlike the thought experiments of the social contract philosophers, biblical covenant sees fit to supply matters of time, place, and circumstance of its own origin; spells out in considerable specificity its various provisions; makes a strong case for its own stringency; takes the issue of transgenerational consent seriously; and provides within itself a means of ongoing interpretive development. That renders it uniquely suitable as an alternative to social contract for modeling a polity of citizens who are bound by foundational law yet also free.

Philosophy, University of Virginia

---

[41] Sanford Levinson, *Constitutional Faith* (Princeton, NJ: Princeton University Press, 1988).

CONSTITUTIONALISM IN THE AGE OF TERROR

By Michael Zuckert and Felix Valenzuela

I. Introduction

What should constitutions do? To answer this question, we must begin with a prior one: What is a constitution? The idea of a constitution is very old, roughly as old as systematic thinking about politics. It was a central idea in the thinking of the Greeks, the first systematic political scientists. But if we go to Plato or Aristotle expecting to find the concept of constitution we deploy when we speak of "constitution," we will be surprised and perhaps disappointed. They use the term in the primordial sense of the word that we still readily recognize when we speak of someone as having a strong constitution. "Constitution," as used here and by the older political writers, means primarily the makeup of something—in the political case, the structure and arrangement of political offices. In the first instance, "constitution" was a descriptive term, but the Greeks also regularly asked: What is the best constitution?—a variant of the question we are asking, "What should constitutions do?"

In the United States and many other places, our usage of the term "constitution" does indeed still contain some of this earlier meaning, for when we think of the Constitution we also think of the layout of the offices of governance. But we think of other things as well. In particular, the Constitution for us is a document, a written legal text, able to be adjudicated in court. The Constitution not only specifies the offices of governance, but also attempts to define, channel, and limit the powers of the government. These limits can be defined in any number of ways, but in general there is an effort to define *what* may be done, and what may not be done (for example, some constitutions, though not the U.S. Constitution, prohibit capital punishment). Constitutions also say *how* things may be done: for example, at the discretion of the accused, individuals may be convicted of serious crimes only via a jury trial. And finally, constitutions specify *who* may do what may be done: for example, the U.S. president is commander-in-chief of the nation's armed forces. Thus, constitutions limit and channel power by specifying what may or may not be done, how it may be done, and who may do it. Constitutions that do all these things in a written text are what we will call "modern constitutions," to distinguish them from the older notion of constitution found in the work of Plato or Aristotle. We will call political systems that operate according to these features "constitutionalist."

Several of the crucial elements of this modern idea of constitutionalism arose in eighteenth-century America, which saw the birth of the idea of a constitution as a written and legally binding text under custody of a court.[1] But other elements, such as the idea of separation of powers, arose earlier, probably first in seventeenth-century England. This is a fact of great subsequent importance, for those who emigrated from England to America brought with them the English ideas of constitutionalism that arose in the seventeenth century and then, ironically, applied them against the British in the years leading up to the American Revolution.

The U.S. Constitution is perhaps the finest fruit of the American effort to apply these ideas to political practice. The Constitution is thoroughly marked by the *aspiration* to constitutionalism. One can find evidence of this throughout the document, but we will mention just three particularly important instances here. First, it is a document—a written text—which proclaims itself to be "the supreme law of the land," that is, law, and a special kind of law at that. Second, in both the Fifth Amendment and the Fourteenth Amendment (both added after the original document was ratified) the Constitution affirms that no person shall be deprived of life, liberty, or property without due process of law. Neither the states under the Fourteenth Amendment nor the federal government under the Fifth may so deprive persons. This is a particularly important provision of constitutional aspiration, for it throws the cloak of law around all persons— not just citizens—on whom government may attempt to act. Government may do so only with "due process of law." This clause, in effect, recognizes all human persons as rights-bearers, possessing the famous triad of rights to life, liberty, and property; government may treat persons and their property only in morally or legally permissible ways.[2]

A third part of the Constitution that reveals an aspiration to constitutionalism is the Tenth Amendment (added in 1791 as part of the so-called Bill of Rights): "The powers not delegated to the United States by the Constitution, nor prohibited by it to the States, are reserved to the States respectively, or to the people." This provision too is animated by an underlying principle, or perhaps two principles. First, the people are the ultimate source of political powers; government does not have inherent powers of its own, but only those delegated to it in the Constitution. This is the principle of popular sovereignty. Second, the Tenth Amendment

---

[1] See, e.g., Gordon Wood, *The Creation of the American Republic* (Chapel Hill: University of North Carolina Press, 1969), 259–344. As Wood and others make clear, the idea that courts may enforce constitutions against legislatures and executives arose well before *Marbury v Madison*, 1 Cranch 137 (1803). On the basis for judicial review in the U.S. Constitution, see Michael P. Zuckert, "Judicial Review and the Incomplete Constitution," in Steven Kautz et al., eds., *The Supreme Court and the Idea of Constitutionalism* (Philadelphia: University of Pennsylvania Press, 2009), 53–77.

[2] We speak of "aspiration" rather than of constitutionalism simply because the American political system, like all such systems, sometimes falls short of the operational reality affirmed or aimed at in the Constitution.

indicates that the limitations on the power of the government of the United States derive from the fact that people have reserved some powers to themselves; that is, they have not delegated the full sum of power, and, moreover, they have delegated power to two levels of government—the government of the Union and the governments of the states. Finally, we might notice the care with which the branches of the federal government are granted power. There is an enumeration of the powers of each branch, indicating that each branch has limitations on its powers imposed by the Constitution.

It is striking, then, that modern constitutionalism, the kind of constitutionalism we now take for granted, was so late in coming; it was roughly two thousand years from Plato to seventeenth-century England and eighteenth-century America. Why did it take so long for this now almost self-evident idea to appear? No doubt a full answer to that question would have to be a very long one, but one aspect of an answer stands out: the idea of constitutionalism is a truly daring one, perhaps even an insane one. As we said, constitutionalism represents the attempt to set limits on government—on what it can do, how it can act, and who can act. But is it safe or sensible to set such limits, especially to set such limits as legally binding norms? The political world is a tough one—as the saying goes: "politics ain't bean bag." The common good may at times require actions of the sorts meant to be limited in one of the various ways we have mentioned. Often constitutionalism is the attempt to limit the actions of the executive branch, as the most dangerous agency of government, the one in control of the organized force of the community. But the executive is also the agency of government most able to act quickly, decisively, and effectively in the face of new threats and dangers. Does it, therefore, make sense to limit the executive? Moreover, almost any substantive limitation one can have might at some times need to be violated in order for the community to successfully confront dangers. For example, we constitutionally reject coerced confessions, but might there not be occasions when coercing a prisoner might be necessary? There are well-known hypothetical cases often raised in this context: Let us say that a captured terrorist knows where a nuclear device is hidden, a device which is scheduled to explode within twenty-four hours. Given that millions might die if the bomb does explode, would it not be acceptable, or even desirable and morally obligatory, for the FBI to deploy coercion (i.e., torture) to extract the information, if there appears to be no other way to get it? And so on. It is relatively easy to think of examples where limitations of the sort constitutionalism attempts to implement are potentially disarming and therefore very dangerous for the community that adopts them. It is easy to understand why modern constitutionalism was slow to appear. Nonetheless, it had a sparkling future.

We have now provided a preliminary answer to our question "What should constitutions do?" Constitutions should limit and channel power and at the same time should somehow permit and foster those actions required to achieve the common good, actions that are sometimes quite different from what ordinary times require.

There are those who say that the aspiration to constitutionalism as sketched above is impossible to fulfill. Historically, perhaps the most famous such person is Thomas Hobbes, who made a dual case (in advance, so to speak) against constitutionalism as now understood. One side of his case was purely juridical: he began from the idea of a state of nature, a condition in which there is no government, but in which everyone possesses what he called the right of nature. This right in the first instance is a right to preserve oneself, which implies a right to take whatever action is needful in order to do so. It is a right, Hobbes argued, which expands under conditions of the anarchic state of nature into a right to everything, including the possessions (and even the bodies) of others. Hobbes wished to give an account of how political power, the power to coerce, arises as a matter of right. His argument is familiar: the equal possession of the right of nature in the state of nature produces a condition of war of all against all, a condition quite intolerable and ultimately at odds with the self-preservation to which all men have a right. The natural playing out of their rights to self-preservation leads to a situation where self-preservation is, in a severe understatement, "very insecure." In order to remedy that situation, men contract with each other to cede their right of nature to an individual or group, who either receives their rights or retains his (their) own. The juridical result is that the citizen/subject has no rights but what the positive law (or silence of the law) of the sovereign allows him, with the exception of a narrow right to preserve himself from immediate violence. There can be no idea of a constitution in the modern sense because all right, all power to act, must be surrendered to the sovereign individual or body. Any attempt to divide or limit authority is a mere illusion: there must always be some body that decrees and enforces the limitations, and that body, according to Hobbes, is sovereign. Sovereignty can be hidden but not evaded.[3]

In addition to his juridical argument, Hobbes had another, different kind of argument, which perfectly reinforced the juridical argument. Not only do human beings have the right to harm each other in the state of nature, but they have the ability and the desire to do so. That they have the ability to do so Hobbes took to be the basis for his claim that all men are equal, that is, equally able to harm or (more accurately) equally vulnerable to harm. "All men are mortal"—and all men's lives are contained in a more or less fragile body that must at some time sleep. Even the weakest can harm or kill the strongest one-on-one.

Moreover, human psychology being what it is, men add to their natural vulnerability a natural desire to harm each other. The result at the level of

---

[3] See Michael Zuckert, "Hobbes, Locke, and the Problem of the Rule of Law," in *The Rule of Law*, ed. Ian Shapiro (New York: New York University Press, 1994); and Jean Hampton, "Democracy and the Rule of Law," in ibid.

empirical reality is conflict and violence. So rooted in the nature of man is the propensity to conflict that only a very powerful state, only the sovereign state outlined in Hobbes's juridical theory, can keep the peace and secure for men what they rationally desire—peace as a means to self-preservation. The threats to civil peace are so extensive that it makes no empirical sense to limit or divide powers. The sovereign ruler is the only logically and juridically possible political arrangement. Openly sovereign absolutism is the only right order.

Hobbes was one of the targets against whom modern constitutionalism was aimed, but the Hobbesian argument was never simply defeated. In the twentieth century, for example, the German jurist and philosopher of law Carl Schmitt revived a Hobbes-like position in his now well-known doctrine of the "exception."[4] According to Schmitt, the "liberal constitutional state," what we are calling modern constitutionalism, attempts to "repress the question of sovereignty by a division and mutual control of competences."[5] It is that possibility of repression of sovereignty that Schmitt denies.

The "exception" is the basis for his affirmation of the concept (or rather the necessary fact) of sovereignty. Many political societies make explicit provisions for the exception in their constitutions by specifying a condition called a "state of emergency," or some equivalent. As was the case in the Weimar Republic, the constitution may specify who may decree the emergency and thus the suspension of ordinary law; Schmitt insists, however, that "the precise details of an emergency cannot be anticipated, nor can one spell out what may take place in such a case, especially when it is truly a matter of an extreme emergency and of how it is to be eliminated."[6] Neither the "preconditions" nor the extent of emergency powers can be specified in advance, and that means that the state of emergency remains a true exception, an exception to ordinary constitutionalism as it regulates and channels the flow of power.[7] In the moment when the decision about the exception must be made, the underlying fact of sovereignty is exposed in the person who declares the "exception." Liberal constitutionalism, Schmitt concludes, fails to achieve its aims.

Is the failure of modern or liberal constitutionalism inevitable? Must political societies experience and then recognize the state of emergency

---

[4] Schmitt defines the question about the "exception" as "who decides in a situation of conflict what constitutes the public interest or interest of the state, public safety and order, *le salut public*, and so on. The exception, which is not codified in the existing legal order, can at best be characterized as a case of extreme peril, a danger to the existence of the state, or the like. But it cannot be circumscribed factually and made to conform to a preformed law." Carl Schmitt, *Political Theology* (1922), trans. George Schwab (Chicago: University of Chicago Press, 1985), 6.

[5] Ibid., 11. Schmitt is of course well known for his Nazi connections, but these do not detract from the force of his argument.

[6] Ibid., 6–7.

[7] Ibid., 7.

that Schmitt speaks of? He apparently kept an open mind on that question: "but whether the extreme exception can be banished from the world is not a juristic question. Whether one has confidence and hope that it can be eliminated depends on philosophical, especially on philosophical-historical or metaphysical, convictions."[8] But as one suspects from the discussion in his *Political Theology* (1922), from which we have been quoting, Schmitt is not so open-minded here as he may seem to be. In his book *The Concept of the Political* (1932), Schmitt elucidated the grounds for his implicit belief that "the exception is more interesting than the rule. The rule proves nothing; the exception proves everything."[9] The political, which Schmitt finds to be the most fundamental category of human social life, is constituted by the distinction between friend and enemy. Every political society (an assemblage of "friends," or "we") is faced by and defined over and against other communities (assemblages of potential or actual "enemies," or "theys"). Actual or theoretical war is the central fact of political life and thus of human life. One can see here Schmitt's Hobbesian roots, or rather his "hyper-Hobbesianism"—for even more than Hobbes, Schmitt sees the state of war intruding into and defining the state of civil society. With war always a possibility, the state of emergency is always hovering on the edge of politics as usual.

Hobbes and Schmitt together raise a great challenge to modern constitutionalism: Can constitutions do what they should? Can they channel and control power and at the same time provide for all the needs a political community may face? Although Schmitt is quite contemptuous of liberal constitutions for their blindness to the need for and the real meaning of "the exception," we maintain that whatever may have been the character of nineteenth and early twentieth century constitutional thinking in Germany, the American founding generation pondered deeply and well the problems that Hobbes had raised (and that Schmitt would later raise). Specifically, the American founders developed three different models of constitutionalism, which gave three somewhat different answers to the questions of what constitutions should do and how they should do it. These models dealt, in different ways, with the problem of the "exception" as Schmitt would later develop it.

Perhaps the most revealing way to classify these different answers is by locating them in relation to two fundamental questions: (1) Can or should the constitution be written and/or interpreted so as to include the (extraordinary) powers that may be needed for extraordinary or emergency circumstances? (2) Which agency of governance should have constitutional or extraconstitutional responsibility for dealing with extraordinary situations? In particular, should the executive have such responsibility? Sim-

---

[8] Ibid.

[9] Carl Schmitt, *The Concept of the Political* (1932), trans. George Schwab (Chicago: University of Chicago Press, 1996). The quotation is from Schmitt, *Political Theology*, 15.

plifying a great deal from real-world possibilities and activities, we can develop different models of constitutionalism by setting up a two-by-two table along the dimensions suggested by our questions (see table 1). A constitution may attempt to contain extraordinary powers within it, or it may not. A constitution also may look to the executive as the agency of action, or it may not. The result is four different models of constitutionalism, three of which were developed and affirmed by one or another member of the American founding generation.

Although we will later attach historical names to these models, for the moment we will leave them abstract so as to briefly describe their generic character. Model I rejects the idea of encompassing extraordinary powers inside the ordinary law and also rejects executive-centeredness. It is the most restrictive of the four models and corresponds most closely to what Schmitt rejects as "liberal constitutionalism." Its insistence on limits may be based on an overriding fear of governmental power, especially executive power, or it may be based on an overriding commitment to the rights of citizens.

Model II rejects the inclusion of emergency powers within the constitution but countenances going outside the constitution via executive action in cases of real necessity. It is inspired by suspicion of the effects on normal law of provision for extraordinary situations, and thus it commits to the notion that it is safer in the long run to go entirely outside the constitution in order to meet extraordinary needs.

Model III shares with Model II an executive-centeredness, but opts for the inclusion of extraordinary powers within the ordinary constitutional order. Model IV shares with Model III the commitment to include extraordinary powers in the ordinary constitution, but for the most part locates these powers outside the executive branch. Generally speaking, that means looking to the legislature as standing in more continuity with ordinary, democratic legitimacy than the executive.

Our aim in this essay is to develop in more historical and conceptual detail these four models of what constitutions should do, and to make some tentative judgments as to which of the four is best overall.

TABLE 1. *Four models of constitutionalism*

		Constitution is executive-centered	
		No	Yes
Constitution contains	No	Model I	Model II
extraordinary powers	Yes	Model IV	Model III

II. MODELS OF CONSTITUTIONALISM

A. Model I: Whig constitutionalism

Having sketched the four models in the abstract, let us turn to more historically concrete versions of the models as they emerged in the theory of particular thinkers and actual practice. The first proto-modern constitutionalists, the English Whigs, arose in England in the seventeenth century as part of the massive political conflicts that followed in the wake of the Reformation. The Whigs emerged in the context of a struggle with the reigning English kings—the Stuart line of kings—over the nature of the constitution. The Whigs thought the Stuarts were attempting to transform what had been a limited monarchy into an absolutist one on the model of France under Louis XIV. The Whigs rose up to defend traditional limitations but ended up transforming them into something like modern constitutionalism. The traditional limits on the monarchy had existed, for the most part, as matters of custom. Accordingly, the exact character of the limits was unclear. The source or authority of the limits was equally unclear, allowing the kings to declare that the limits were merely self-imposed by the monarchy and thus could be disregarded by the monarchs as well.

The Whigs, centered in Parliament, tried to make the limits more explicit, concrete, and secure. They promulgated various written statements containing limitations on the crown. Their notion of constitutional limitations was very rigid and directed exclusively against the monarchy. They tried to set out stringent limitations from which there were to be no exceptions. This line of constitutionalism was carried over into America by the enemies of the proposed U.S. Constitution, the Antifederalists, who feared and distrusted executive power as the earlier Whigs had, and thus sought a constitution with greatly truncated powers, especially with respect to the executive. The Whigs and the Antifederalists, however, were not alert to the dangers posed by the very idea of constitutionalism.

In the case of the English Whigs, the commitment to Model I constitutionalism was probably facilitated by the continued presence of the king in the constitution, whose powers remained substantial, despite Whig efforts to limit them. In the case of the American Antifederalists, the commitment to Model I constitutionalism sprang from a number of articles of faith flowing from the American experiment in republicanism. Republican government, the Antifederalists tended to believe, would be mild and pacific. Republican political orders would pacify the domestic scene, and the distance of America from Europe, along with the military capacity of citizen militias, would suffice to keep Americans safe from foreign threats.

In any case, the Antifederalists clearly (and the Whigs somewhat more ambiguously) were instances of Model I constitutionalism. They favored strictly defined limitations on all governmental power and were particularly hostile to executive power. Adherents of the other three models saw them as "naïve constitutionalists," for they did not provide for the kinds of emergencies that cannot be definitively abolished from political life.

B. Model II: Lockean and Jeffersonian constitutionalism

The American Founders, those who framed the Constitution, were not "naïve constitutionalists" of the Model I type. They were heavily influenced in their constitutionalisms by theoretical and practical developments in Europe, only one of which we can pause to discuss. It is well known that John Locke was an immense influence on American political thought and action leading up to the American Revolution. His constitutional theorizing, though to some degree superseded for the Americans by that of the French philosopher Montesquieu in his *On the Spirit of the Laws* (1748), was also an important influence on the body of thought in which Model II constitutional theory first arose.

Locke's version of constitutionalism contained many of the elements we associate with the earlier Whig constitutionalism: concern to limit the ends and powers of government; an attempt especially to limit the monarchy; and a parallel concern to elevate the legislative assembly to a position of preeminence. Thus, for Locke, the monarch becomes merely "the executive head," that is, the wielder of something called the executive power. The king is thus not sovereign. Supremacy belongs more to the legislature, and the executive is only the agency that executes the laws made by the legislature.[10]

Locke, moreover, strengthened the Whig position by attaching it to a new philosophy of politics, according to which human beings start out with rights in a state of equality with each other and institute government (via a social contract or via consent) in order to protect their preexisting rights. In this way, Locke made the notion of *limited government* much more coherent than the naïve Whig constitutionalists had done.

Although Locke incorporated many of the concerns of Whig constitutionalism, he also went substantially beyond and against the Whigs.[11] This further dimension of Locke's constitutionalism is especially visible in two places in his political philosophy where the executive—the transformed version of the king, who is to be limited and made subordinate to the legislature—escapes from his limits and, like Clark Kent in the fabled telephone booth, bursts forth from his trammeled role into a far more powerful and thus formidable figure.

---

[10] John Locke, *Two Treatises of Government*, ed. Peter Laslett (Cambridge: Cambridge University Press, 2005), II.145–48.

[11] For a good account of ways in which Locke goes beyond the Whigs and republicans of the seventeenth century, see Clement Fatovic, "Constitutionalism and Contingency: Locke's Theory of Prerogative." *History of Political Thought* 25, no. 2 (Summer 2004): 276–97.

The first place where the Super-executive appears in Locke is in his treatment of the differences between governmental powers exercised *within* a society and powers exercised *outside* it or vis-à-vis other states. This latter power he calls the "federative power," and it includes such things as "the power of war and peace, leagues and alliances, and all the transactions with all persons and communities [outside] the commonwealth." [12] The federative power, unlike the executive power, is not derived from a transfer of the rights and powers of the subjects and citizens, but inheres in the state as a state—existing in a state of nature with other states. That means that juridically the federative power is not subject to the same limitations as the executive power. Yet the two powers, different in origin and nature as they are, must be united in the same hands. Moreover, Locke says portentously that "though the well or ill management of [the federative power] be of great moment to the commonwealth, yet it is much less capable to be directed by antecedent, standing positive laws, than the executive [power]; and so must necessarily be left to the prudence and wisdom of those in whose hands it is in, to be managed [by them] for the public good." [13] That is to say, the federative power rightly escapes whatever legal or constitutional limits a constitutionalist order would seek to impose on the executive. The federative power is, in effect, outside the constitution.

A second place where the Super-executive appears in Locke is in his recognition of "prerogative," an executive power that can be used even in domestic affairs. Prerogative is a power "to act according to discretion, for the public good." [14] This power is necessary because emergencies or unexpected circumstances arise, requiring rapid response, and the legislature, being large and often not in session, cannot respond with the necessary "dispatch." [15] Locke understood that this prerogative power was both necessary and dangerous.

Locke thus stands as a paradigmatic Model II constitutionalist. He clearly recognizes that foreign relations require something other than stringent legalism, and, moreover, that emergency or extraordinary situations arise, which tend to escape the boundaries of ordinary law. It is the executive, acting outside and even at times against the law, who is to cope with foreign affairs and emergencies. Despite Schmitt's attempt to brand Locke as the father of the liberal constitutionalism that he (Schmitt) rejected, it is clear that this is not an accurate picture of Locke's own constitutional theory. Locke, of course, did not mean to make a simple assertion of extraconstitutional executive supremacy. Ultimately, the legislature has the right, he says, to reassert its supremacy and to judge whether the executive has indeed used his extraconstitutional power for the public

---

[12] Locke, *Two Treatises*, II.145.
[13] Ibid., II.145–48.
[14] Ibid., II.160.
[15] Ibid.

good. If the legislative and the executive powers disagree, Locke concludes that "the people shall be judge"—that in the final analysis there is indeed no legal rule that can be relied on to settle public life once and for all. In opening up the appeal to the sovereign people, Locke is, at the end of the day, recognizing something like what Schmitt does in his argument for the "exception": the appeal to the sovereign.[16] Yet Locke, more than Schmitt, attempts to maintain the commitment to constitutionalism despite the incompleteness of all constitutions.

Locke was a great inspiration for the American founders, but by the time they made their constitution, the idea of modern constitutionalism had evolved beyond him in two important respects. First, the American Constitution was the kind of written document we now think of. Second, the Americans had dropped the distinction between executive and federative powers, and had in fact allocated elsewhere some of the powers Locke identified as federative. Thus, most importantly, the power of war and peace was granted to Congress. Moreover, the treaty power was shared between the executive and the Senate.

Despite these changes, one of the American constitutional models— Jeffersonian constitutionalism—remained quite close to the Lockean prototype. Model II constitutionalism, it will be recalled, combines strict-construction constitutionalism with extraconstitutional appeals to the executive to meet needs that transcend the constitution. In order to systematize the comparison of the different constitutional models, one might identify a number of variables common to each to see where and how they differ from each other. Thus, Thomas Jefferson's constitutional model has six features: (1) strict construction of the constitutional powers; (2) the affirmation of firm modes of enforcement of strictly construed constitutional powers; (3) legalized rights protections; (4) means to enforce rights protections; (5) extraconstitutional power to deal with special situations; and (6) an executive-centered model of action in extraordinary situations.

Some of the best known elements of Jeffersonian constitutionalism relate to his concern to keep the powers of government limited, and especially to resist efforts to see them increase via constitutional construction. Thus, in his draft of the Kentucky Resolutions of 1798,[17] Jefferson affirmed that "the construction" of the "necessary and proper clause"[18] in the U.S.

---

[16] For a careful and probing examination of this aspect of Locke's theory, see Benjamin A. Kleinerman, "Can the Prince Really Be Tamed? Executive Prerogative, Popular Apathy, and the Constitutional Frame in Locke's *Second Treatise*," *American Political Science Review* 101, no. 2 (May 2007): 209–22.

[17] The Kentucky Resolutions, drafted by Jefferson, were adopted by the Kentucky legislature in response to the Alien and Sedition Acts of 1798. The resolutions laid out a case for the unconstitutionality of the acts and proposed a method of responding to that unconstitutionality.

[18] The "necessary and proper" clause is part of the U.S. Constitution's Article I, section 8, which specifies the powers granted to Congress. It specifies that "Congress shall have

Constitution, as promoted by the Federalist party, "goes to the destruction of all limits prescribed to their power [i.e., the power of Congress] by the Constitution." He thought the Hamiltonian interpretation of the clause (see below) distorted the Constitution and indeed was contrary to the nature of constitutions altogether: "words meant by the instrument to be subsidiary only to the execution of limited powers, ought not to be so construed as themselves to give unlimited powers." [19]

Jefferson provided a yet fuller account of his theory of strict construction in his opinion on the constitutionality of a national bank. Early in 1791, Jefferson responded to President Washington's request for an opinion on the constitutional legitimacy of the proposal by his Secretary of the Treasury, Alexander Hamilton, to charter a national bank. In response, Jefferson affirmed that the constitutional system was grounded on the principle laid out in the Tenth Amendment to the Constitution: "I consider the foundation of the Constitution as laid on this ground: that 'all powers not delegated to the United States by the constitution, nor prohibited by it to the States, are reserved to the States or to the people.'" [20] Jefferson's rationale for this principle of resistance to any kind of expansive reading of the powers under the Constitution was based, in turn, on his judgment that "To take a single step beyond the boundaries thus specially drawn around the powers of Congress, is to take possession of a boundless field of power no longer susceptible of any definition." [21] If the Constitution allows room for moving beyond the strict enumeration of powers, then, Jefferson feared, the entire aspiration to limit and control power that constitutes the constitutionalist impulse is mooted. Note that it is constitutionalism and not states' rights, as is often thought, that is the core of Jefferson's concern for strict construction. In the Kentucky Resolutions, he expressed his conviction that the strict boundaries of constitutional powers must be maintained through "the chains of the Constitution." [22]

Jefferson would not leave constitutional limitations as mere declarations of principle. He also affirmed concrete constitutional mechanisms for enforcing the constitutional limitations of power. Thus, in his opinion on the constitutionality of a national bank, he appealed to "the negative [veto] of the President" as "the shield provided by the Constitution to protect against the invasions of the legislature" on the powers and rights

---

power . . . to make all laws which shall be necessary and proper for carrying into execution the foregoing powers, and all other Powers vested by this Constitution in the Government of the United States or in any Department or Officer thereof."

[19] Thomas Jefferson, "Draft of Kentucky Resolutions," in Lance Banning, ed., *Liberty and Order: The First American Party Struggle* (Indianapolis, IN: Liberty Fund, 2004), 235.

[20] Thomas Jefferson, "Opinion on the Constitutionality of the Bill for Establishing a National Bank," in ibid., 78.

[21] Jefferson, "Opinion on the Constitutionality of a National Bank," February 1791, in Banning, ed., *Liberty and Order*, 78.

[22] Jefferson, "Draft of Kentucky Resolutions," 236.

of others.[23] President Washington failed to follow his advice in this case and signed legislation that Jefferson believed went well beyond the bounds of the Constitution. Later, President Adams went along with the even more despised Alien and Sedition Acts of 1798. Over time, Jefferson was thus led to seek an additional check on congressional power, one that might prove more reliable than the presidential veto. By the time of the Kentucky Resolutions, he had developed his theory of state nullification. As he put it, "every state has a natural right in cases not within the compact . . . to nullify of their own authority all assumptions of power by others within their limits."[24]

Jefferson would limit powers of government not only through his strict constructionism but also though explicit protections of individual rights. Thus, in the debate over ratification of the Constitution, he favored the inclusion of a Bill of Rights, influencing his friend James Madison to take a more positive stand on the issue. Madison, in turn, was the leading figure in pushing the Bill of Rights through Congress en route to establishing it as a series of amendments to the Constitution. As Jefferson said in one of his letters to Madison: "A bill of rights is what the people are entitled to against every government on earth . . . and what no government should refuse, or rest on inference."[25] A bill of rights is a commitment to limit governmental power on behalf of the rights of individuals.

The protections of individual rights that Jefferson wished to incorporate in the Constitution via the Bill of Rights would also have an explicit means of enforcement. Perhaps surprisingly, given his well-known doubts about judicial review (and, at times, his hostility toward the concept), it was to the judiciary that Jefferson looked for the concrete protection of rights.[26]

In his concern that the government not step into that "boundless sea of power," he was especially worried about the executive branch. For example, he wrote in a 1787 letter to Madison that he was opposed to the absence of a limit on the number of terms a president could serve under the proposed Constitution, because he was "not a friend to a very energetic government," which, he thought, was "always oppressive."[27] As James Read well said, "Jefferson was faithful to the fear-of-power element in the English oppositional Whig tradition."[28]

[23] Jefferson, "Opinion on the Constitutionality of a National Bank," 80.

[24] Jefferson, "Draft of Kentucky Resolutions," 235.

[25] Thomas Jefferson to James Madison, December 20, 1787, in Thomas Jefferson, *The Papers of Thomas Jefferson*, ed. Julian P. Boyd (Princeton, NJ: Princeton University Press, 1955), 440.

[26] Thomas Jefferson to James Madison, March 15, 1789, in Merrill Peterson, ed., *Jefferson: Writings* (New York: Library of America, 1984), 943.

[27] Thomas Jefferson to James Madison, December 20, 1787, in *The Papers of Thomas Jefferson: The Retirement Series*, ed. J. Jefferson Looney (Princeton, NJ: Princeton University Press, 2006), 12:442.

[28] James H. Read, *Power Versus Liberty* (Charlottesville: University Press of Virginia, 2000), 121.

Yet Jefferson was not a Model I constitutionalist. As Jeremy Bailey shows very clearly in his thorough survey of Jefferson's thoughts about executive power and his actions as governor of Virginia and then president of the United States: "Throughout his career, he attempted to preserve the law by interpreting it strictly while at the same time explaining that a strict construction of the law would require that the law be set aside during times of necessity or emergency on the condition that the executive submit to the political judgment by announcing his extralegal activity."[29] It is the space that Jefferson regularly made for action outside the law and the Constitution that makes him a Model II constitutionalist like Locke, and not a Model I constitutionalist like the Whigs.

One of the major trials—and achievements—of Jefferson's presidency was the Louisiana Purchase of 1803, about which he had many constitutional qualms: "Our peculiar security is in possession of a written Constitution. Let us not make it a blank paper by construction." Of two possible interpretations of the text, he said, he would always "prefer that which is safe and precise."[30] Thus, Jefferson reaffirmed his commitment to stringent and narrow interpretations of the grants of power in the Constitution, especially of grants to the executive. At first he even thought that a constitutional amendment would be required to allow the Louisiana Purchase, but when he became convinced that delay might endanger the transaction, he decided to forgo the amendment and instead proceed as necessity seemed to him to dictate. He looked to Senate ratification and House appropriation of the funds for the purchase as legislative ratifications of the extraconstitutional action.

He stated his general principles of action later when an admirer wrote to him in the years immediately following his presidency wishing to know "whether circumstances do not sometimes occur, which make it a duty" to go beyond the law of the Constitution. Jefferson thought the answer easy in principle, though sometimes "embarrassing" in practice. It is a high duty for officials to obey the law, but it is not their highest duty: "the laws of necessity, of self-preservation, of saving our country when in danger, are of higher obligation. To lose our country by a scrupulous adherence to written law, would be to lose the law itself, with life, liberty, property and all those who are enjoying them with us: thus absurdly sacrificing the end to the means."[31] This "higher law" is not for everyone, however. It is not for persons charged with "petty duties," but for those with great duties, especially the president. Jefferson's position is thus

---

[29] Jeremy D. Bailey, *Thomas Jefferson and Executive Power* (Cambridge: Cambridge University Press, 2007), 171.

[30] Thomas Jefferson to Wilson C. Nicholas, September 7, 1803, in Thomas Jefferson, *The Writings of Thomas Jefferson*, ed. Andrew A. Lipscomb (Washington, DC: Thomas Jefferson Memorial Association, 1930), 10:418.

[31] Thomas Jefferson to John B. Colvin, September 20, 1810, in Looney, ed., *The Papers of Thomas Jefferson: The Retirement Series*, 3:99.

very close to Locke's: the Constitution should be written for safe times and ordinary circumstances. It should bind power closely. But Jefferson knew that what works in ordinary times may not suffice for extraordinary times. Nevertheless, extraordinary needs should not infect the principles of governance for ordinary times. Yet when the extraordinary did occur, Jefferson believed it had to be met—by recourse to extralegal action by the agent best able to so act: the president.

C. Model III: Hamiltonian constitutionalism

Models III and IV differ from Models I and II in rejecting the strict constructionism of the latter two. They also differ from Jefferson's Model II constitutionalism in rejecting his willingness to supplement a strictly construed constitution with extraconstitutional action.

We can define Hamiltonian constitutionalism along the same set of six variables that we have used for Jefferson, but in this case it is best to begin with the Jeffersonian affirmation of a strong extraconstitutional dimension, for Model III constitutionalism is shaped to a very significant extent by the rejection of that Lockean-Jeffersonian feature of Model II. Hamilton thought Model II made no sense: it violated "axioms as simple as they are universal: the means ought to be proportioned to the end; the persons from whose agency the attainment of any end is expected, ought to possess the means by which it is to be attained."[32] Jefferson himself conceded that the ends of political life outstripped the constitutional means of his brand of constitutionalism. On Hamilton's view, the powers required to deal with the kinds of extraordinary necessities Jefferson conceded could arise must be contained in the Constitution itself, not in some extraconstitutional no-man's land, where every use of them is an action against the Constitution. Thus, Hamilton necessarily developed an approach to constitutional construction very different from Jefferson's.

Hamilton's principle was intended to obviate the need implied by Jefferson's principle: the need to go outside the Constitution. If one is to remain within the Constitution, then the Constitution must be capable of being read capaciously in order to find within it the extraordinary powers that the "state of exception" may require. Thus, Hamilton rejected Jefferson's strict constructionism. He voiced his theory, as had Jefferson, in the context of the debate over the establishment of a national bank, and on other occasions as well.

He took a much a larger view of the Constitution than Jefferson did. Although the constitutional debate was complicated, we may safely focus attention on the way Hamilton read the "necessary and proper" clause of Article I, section 8: "Congress shall have the power . . . to make all laws

---

[32] Hamilton, *Federalist No. 23*, in Alexander Hamilton, James Madison, and John Jay, *The Federalist*, ed. Jacob Cooke (Middletown, CT: Wesleyan University Press, 1961), 147.

necessary and proper for carrying into execution the foregoing powers, and all other powers vested in the government of the United States, or in any department thereof." Here clearly is an explicit grant of power to go beyond the explicitly granted powers. But how far beyond? In keeping with his understanding of the character of constitutionalism, Jefferson nearly read this clause out of the Constitution—for, as he saw it, a broader reading threatened to propel the government out into that "boundless sea of power" he so feared. "Necessary," he concluded, must mean something stricter than *convenient* or *conducive to,* "for there is not one [non-enumerated power] which ingenuity may not torture into a convenience in some instance or other to some one of so long a list of enumerated powers. It would swallow up all the delegated powers, and reduce the whole to one power ... of instituting a Congress with power to do whatever would be for the public good of the United States; and as they would be the sole judge of the good or evil it would be also a power to do whatever evil they please." [33] Jefferson rejected "convenient" and like terms and instead interpreted "necessary" very strictly: "Nothing but a necessity invincible by any other means." Seldom can a constructed power meet a test of that stringency.

Hamilton's view paralleled a famous remark Chief Justice John Marshall would make later, in *McCulloch v. Maryland* (1819): "We must never forget that it is a *constitution* we are expounding." [34] Accordingly, Hamilton read "necessary" much more loosely than Jefferson had done: "necessary often means no more than *needful, requisite, incidental, useful,* or *conducive* to." As a matter of dictionary definition, perhaps Hamilton's reading of the word is too loose, but that is not where the crux of his case lies. Jefferson's "restrictive interpretation of the word *necessary* is," according to Hamilton, "also contrary to this sound maxim of construction: namely that powers contained in a constitution of government, especially those which concern the general administration of the affairs of a country, its finances, trade, defence, etc. ought to be construed liberally in advancement of the public good." This, Hamilton believed, is a universal rule, depending not at all on "the particular form of a government or on the particular demarcation of the boundaries of its powers, but on the nature and objects of government itself." Hamilton restated with great concision the reservation against constitutionalism that we have already seen expressed by others before him. "The means, by which national exigencies are to be provided for, national inconveniences obviated, national prosperity promoted, are of such infinite variety, extent and complexity, that there must, of necessity, be great latitude of discretion in the selection and application of those means." [35] If the needs are so variable and unpre-

---

[33] Jefferson, "Opinion on the Constitutionality of a National Bank," 80.
[34] *McCulloch v. Maryland,* 4 Wheat. 316, 407 (1819) (emphasis in the original).
[35] Hamilton, "Opinion on the Bank," in Banning, ed., *Liberty and Order,* 82, 83.

dictable, then the aspiration to constitutionalism must itself be of questionable validity. Hamilton's doctrine of "necessary and proper" is an attempt to enshrine the extraconstitutional within the Constitution. It is easy to see in Hamilton's reading of the constitutional text that "boundless sea of power" that Jefferson feared. Yes, Hamilton would say, but that is the nature of the political beast. Better to incorporate all necessary power in the Constitution than to face the need for more or less regular violations of the Constitution, or more or less regular failures to respond to the genuine needs of the community.

Hamilton's development of Model III constitutionalism depends very little on standard modes of constitutional interpretation. He puts no weight on original intent and very little on text or original meaning. Rather, he engages in very abstract reasoning about the nature of government and of governmental powers. The core of his argument is contained in the following passage: "[E]very power vested in a government is in its nature *sovereign* and includes by *force* of the *term* a right to employ all the *means* requisite and fairly *applicable* to the attainment of the ends of such power; and which are not precluded by restrictions and exceptions specified in the Constitution, or not immoral, or not contrary to the essential ends of political society." [36] For our purposes, the essential points here are Hamilton's claims (1) that all vested powers imply an end for the sake of which the power is vested, and (2) that the end of the vested power implies further powers as means toward attaining the end. Armed with this general construct, Hamilton reads the "necessary and proper" clause in the loose sense of "convenient" or "conducive to," as we have noted above. This is the reading of the constitutional language that allows it to cohere with the general principle that governs all governmental power.

Hamilton has a plausible theory. Powers are granted for the sake of some end in view, and they are but means for the attainment of the end. [37] Not all the powers or means that may conduce to a given end may be specified. No legislator is prescient enough to name all needed powers. Only the large powers pointing toward the large ends can be identified in a constitution. Moreover, the Hamiltonian principle almost guarantees that the Constitution contains within its four corners all the powers that may prove necessary for it to face the challenges that political life throws in its path. If some powers are granted to deal with the major political ends or political needs—the sort of ends that are identified in the preamble to the U.S. Constitution—then the Constitution will carry within it all the powers it requires to deal with extraordinary as well as ordinary circumstances. Hamilton's constitution contains all that Schmitt would require of it (and perhaps more). In effect, Hamilton's Model III consti-

---

[36] Ibid., 84.
[37] See Sotirios Barber, *Welfare and the Constitution* (Princeton, NJ: Princeton University Press, 2003), 92–96.

tution affirms empowerment as the rule, and limitation or absence of power as the exception.

Thus, Hamilton laid much less stress on power-limiting enforcement mechanisms than Jefferson did, but this is not to say that he ignored them entirely. Like Jefferson, he saw the executive veto as such a mechanism. More clearly than Jefferson, he saw the role of the courts as legitimately power-limiting. Where Jefferson seems to have seen judicial enforcement of the Constitution as particularly suited to the protection of individual rights, Hamilton in his well-known argument in *Federalist No. 78* made a case for a more extensive power of judicial review. "No legislative act . . . contrary to the Constitution can be valid." [38] Of course, Hamilton's very broad principles for construing the constitutional powers of the government imply that the courts would seldom have occasion to invalidate laws on the basis of their exceeding the delegated legislative authority. Nonetheless, in his opinion on the bill to establish a national bank, Hamilton did identify some instances of legislation that would outstrip even his capacious reading of congressional power.[39]

He was also much less enthusiastic than Jefferson about adding a Bill of Rights to the Constitution and thus adding explicit protection for the rights of individuals. Indeed, Hamilton's *Federalist No. 84* is one of the classic statements against the need for a Bill of Rights in the Constitution. Although he tended to oppose the addition of new rights protections, he did take note of protections in the original constitutional draft—for example, the protection of the right of *habeas corpus*, and the prohibitions against *ex post facto* laws and bills of attainder. "Limitations of this kind can be preserved in practice no other way than through the medium of the courts of justice; whose duty it must be to declare all acts contrary to the manifest tenor of the Constitution void. Without this, all the reservations of particular rights and privileges would amount to nothing." [40] Thus, while Hamilton, compared to Jefferson, would downplay legalized protections of rights, he would not reject them altogether, nor did his Model III constitutionalism lack enforcement mechanisms for such rights as were protected.

Moreover, Hamilton favored the notion that the power to respond to extraordinary circumstances resided chiefly in the executive. In this respect, he moved back toward Locke's idea of the federative power, although he did not use that term and spoke of Locke's federative powers as powers of the executive. Hamilton noted that the very important part of Locke's federative power—the power of war and peace—had been granted to Congress by the Constitution, but he insisted that this, like foreign-affairs powers in general, is *inherently* an executive power. The Constitution had

[38] Hamilton, *Federalist No. 78*, in Cooke, ed., *The Federalist*, 524.
[39] See, e.g., Hamilton, "Opinion on the Bank," 84.
[40] Hamilton, *Federalist No. 78*, p. 524.

carved it out of the core of executive powers and given it to the legislature. The grant of power to the executive contains everything executive except what is explicitly given to the legislature. Nonetheless, the power of war and peace needs to be seen as an exception to the broad array of powers given to the president when Article II of the Constitution says: "The executive power shall be vested in a President of the United States of America." And all exceptions should be read narrowly.[41] Hamilton so favored the executive not only because the text of the Constitution read as it did, but, again, for theoretical reasons. On his view, the executive possesses the institutional means to best respond to the extraordinary needs that may arise. It has unity, which allows secrecy, dispatch, and decision.[42] Thus, whereas Jefferson would deny legal power and go outside the Constitution to find it in the executive, Hamilton would find it in the Constitution, and particularly in the general grant of the executive power.

D. Model IV: Madisonian constitutionalism

James Madison, the reputed "father of the Constitution," had collaborated with Hamilton in writing *The Federalist Papers*, a defense of the Constitution during the debate over whether to ratify it. Beginning in the 1790s, however, he also collaborated with Jefferson in resisting and opposing Hamilton's expansive executive-centered reading of the Constitution. These two facts serve to suggest that he was somewhere between the two poles, and that would be a perfectly correct inference. Like Hamilton, Madison rejected the Jeffersonian model, in particular the core combination of very strict construction and extraconstitutional appeals for extraordinary powers for emergency situations. But Madison's main line of argument against Jefferson was somewhat different from Hamilton's. In *Federalist No. 49*, Madison responded to a scheme proposed by Jefferson to deal with constitutional disagreements or perceived constitutional imperfections. The proposal went as follows: "Whenever any two of the three branches of government shall concur in opinion, each by the voices of two thirds of their whole number, that a convention is necessary for altering the Constitution or correcting breaches of it, a convention shall be called for that purpose."[43] This scheme is consistent with Jefferson's Model II constitutionalism: when constitutional issues arise, one should return to the source of constitutional authority, the people as represented in special conventions. Madison thought otherwise.

Although he agreed with Jefferson that the people were the ultimate source of constitutional authority, Madison did not think that regular or

---

[41] Alexander Hamilton, "Pacificus Number I," in *The Pacificus-Helvidius Debates of 1793–1794*, ed. Morton J. Frisch (Indianapolis, IN: Liberty Fund, 2006).

[42] Hamilton, *Federalist No. 70*, in Cooke, ed., *The Federalist*, 472.

[43] Quoted in Madison, *Federalist No. 49*, in Cooke, ed., *The Federalist*, 339 (emphasis omitted).

frequent "recurrence to the people" was a wise idea. One of his strongest objections is particularly relevant to Jefferson's attachment to supplementary extraconstitutional action. To appeal to the people "would carry an implication of some defect in the government, frequent appeals would in great measure deprive the government of that veneration, which time bestows on every thing, and without which perhaps the wisest and freest governments would not possess the requisite stability." The same could be said of extraconstitutional but necessary actions: every such act "would carry an implication of some defect in the government." Madison was particularly sensitive to the need for "veneration" toward government:

> If it be true that all governments rest on opinion, it is no less true that the strength of opinion in each individual, and its practical influence on his conduct, depend much on the number which he supposes to have entertained the same opinion. . . . When the examples, which fortify opinion, are *antient* as well as *numerous*, they are known to have a double effect. In a nation of philosophers, this consideration ought to be disregarded. A reverence for the laws, would be sufficiently inculcated by the voice of an enlightened reason. But a nation of philosophers is as little to be expected as the philosophical race of kings wished for by Plato. And in every other nation, the most rational government will not find it a superfluous advantage, to have the prejudices of the community on its side.[44]

Every government, no matter how rational in itself, depends on "prejudices" that breed "reverence for the laws." The Model II tendency to concede (more or less regularly) the inadequacy of the laws undermines that veneration, and for that reason, if no other, Madison held that it was not a good approach to constitutionalism.

On the broad question of constitutional interpretation, Madison was neither quite a strict nor a loose constructionist—he was looser than Jefferson, but stricter than Hamilton. Madison was serving in the House of Representatives when the debate over Hamilton's proposal for a national bank erupted. He led the opposition in the House. With great insight, he zeroed in on the theme that would be the centerpiece of Hamilton's expansive reading of implied powers. "Whatever meaning the [necessary and proper] clause may have," Madison argued, "none can be admitted that would give an unlimited discretion to Congress."[45] Agreeing this far with Jefferson, he had his doubts about the language used by the bank's proponents to bring it within the scope of the constitutional clause; he did not think "conducive" and related terms carried at all the same meaning as "necessary." He also called attention to the form of reasoning evoked

[44] Madison, *Federalist No. 49*, p. 340.
[45] James Madison, "Speech on the Bank Bill," in Banning, ed., *Liberty and Order*, 75.

by the bank's supporters. "To borrow money is made the end and the accumulation of capitals implied as means. The accumulation of capitals is then the end and a bank implied as the means. The bank is then the end and a charter of incorporation, a monopoly, capital punishments, etc. implied as means."[46] Madison saw, in other words, the escalator-like character of Hamiltonian reasoning.

In particular, he saw that the Hamiltonian reading modified the language and, he thought, the logic of the constitutional delegated powers:

> [There is] a distinction which had not been sufficiently kept in view, between a power necessary and proper for the government or union and a power necessary and proper for executing the enumerated powers. In the latter case, the powers included in each of the enumerated powers were not expressed, but to be drawn from the nature of each. In the former the powers composing the government were expressly enumerated. This constituted the peculiar nature of the government; no power therefore not enumerated could be inferred from the general nature of government.[47]

In this paragraph lies the core of the Madisonian alternative to Hamiltonian loose construction. Although he shared Jefferson's concern that the logic of the constitutional powers as enumerated (and therefore, in principle, limited and controlled) not be lost, Madison did not agree that even one step beyond the enumerated powers opened up that "boundless sea of power" upon which Jefferson did not wish to embark. He saw a way — and indeed affirmed it as logically necessary to any government — to draw implied powers out of the Constitution while maintaining boundaries around those powers.

That way is not the Hamiltonian way, however. Madison called attention to powers that were implied as means to ends implied by the enumerated powers. He thus differed from Jefferson in downplaying "necessity" as the standard to be applied when judging constitutional powers, and instead emphasizing that the implied powers must be seen as means to the enumerated powers. He differed from Hamilton in denying that the implied powers are means to ends implied by the enumerated powers; instead, Madison held that they are only means to the enumerated powers themselves.

Madison was equally firm in rejecting Jefferson's version of strict construction. Jefferson had begun his opinion on the bill to establish a national bank by listing all the laws of the states that the bill would contravene. He seemed to believe that the conceded powers of the states must signal a limitation of some kind on Congress. Early in his speech on the bank,

[46] Ibid., 75.
[47] Ibid., 76.

Madison explicitly denied this part of Jefferson's position: "Interference with the power of the states was no constitutional criterion of the power of Congress. If the power was not given, Congress could not exercise it; if given, they might exercise it although it should interfere with the laws or even the constitutions of the states." [48] Madison was not, as some would say, endorsing the same position as Jefferson.

Although Madison, arguing against the constitutionality of the bank, emphasized the limits of the "necessary and proper" clause, it is nonetheless clear that he saw it in a much more capacious way than Jefferson did: "The clause is in fact merely declaratory of what would have resulted by unavoidable implication, as the appropriate, and as it were, technical means of executing those [enumerated] powers." [49] Madison recognized the dangers of the "doctrine of implication" for a government "composed of limited and enumerated powers," but he still affirmed that powers are implied. He differed from Jefferson in so affirming; he differed from Hamilton with respect to the "rule of interpretation" that he thought properly governed this clause. Madison did not adhere to Jefferson's "absolutely necessary" criterion; he did accept implied powers that are "necessary and proper for executing the enumerated powers." [50] Accordingly, Madison never shared Jefferson's constitutional qualms about the Louisiana Purchase. He did understand the Constitution to impose limits on the powers of government, but he did not rule out constitutional construction, nor did he advocate rigid and fixed limits as Jefferson did. As Madison said in *Federalist No. 51*: "You must first enable the government to controul the governed; and in the next place, oblige it to controul itself." [51] Since the first task in constitution-making is enabling the government to control the governed (and, as Madison would no doubt add, enabling it to do all the other things governments must do), empowering government is the primary task; controls on government are important, but secondary. In *Federalist No. 51*, Madison expressed another point that he and Hamilton agreed on: one must properly "contrive the interior structure of the government, as that its several constituent parts may, by their mutual relations, be the means of keeping each other in their proper places." [52] The structure of the institutions was to be the chief reliance for securing effective and safe government, and in this Madison differed from Jefferson, who would have relied on limitations implicit in the grants of power in the Constitution. Madison and Hamilton agreed, up to a point, in rejecting Jefferson's strict constructionism and his willingness to go outside the Constitution to do what the Constitution did not provide for.

[48] Ibid., 74.
[49] Ibid., 75.
[50] Ibid., 76.
[51] Madison, *Federalist No. 51*, in Cooke, ed., *The Federalist*, 349.
[52] Ibid., 347–48.

In addition to affirming the enumerated powers and a limited theory of implied powers, Madison also affirmed limits on the powers of government deriving from explicit protections of rights in the Constitution. Thus, although he was an early skeptic, Madison came around to the idea of a Bill of Rights; he not only drafted the first ten amendments in a form close to the one in which they entered the Constitution, but pressed unrelentingly for their adoption. He did this in the face of (perhaps surprising) indifference on the part of the Antifederalists, who had originally pressed for a Bill of Rights, and in the face of often open opposition from Federalists. Moreover, at the time of the debate over the 1798 Alien and Sedition Acts, Madison wrote the first real manifesto of First Amendment freedom of speech in his Virginia Report, a document written in defense of the Virginia Resolutions he had authored earlier against the Alien and Sedition Acts. Although he had come around to Jefferson's commitment to a Bill of Rights somewhat reluctantly, Madison came to see that the rights guaranteed in the Constitution's first ten amendments were an essential part of constitutionalism.

Like Jefferson, Madison was concerned that the rights protections not be mere "parchment barriers." He wanted to insure that they had some teeth, that is to say, some enforcement mechanisms. In his major speech in Congress defending the adoption of a Bill of Rights, he followed Jefferson in appealing to the "independent tribunals of justice" as "the guardians of those rights."[53] In the same speech he also expressed his belief that the state legislatures would keep a watchful eye on the legislation of the United States, testing the latter against standards explicitly contained in the U.S. Constitution. In his Virginia Resolutions of 1798, he followed up on that suggestion by calling on the states to "interpose" themselves in order to resist the Alien and Sedition Acts. Of course, just what he meant by "interposition" has been a subject of controversy ever since; for present purposes, we need not settle that difficult question.[54]

Madison was also in the middle between Jefferson and Hamilton on the issue of the executive power. He took great exception to Hamilton's theory that the power of war and peace was inherently an executive power, and thus he disagreed with all the inferences that Hamilton drew from that theory. Madison never downplayed the importance of the executive, but he tended toward a view like that of Locke, who held that the legislature (especially in a republic) had a certain supremacy. Madison argued that the delegation of the power of war and peace to Congress represented a recognition that a power of such importance belonged to the most supreme and republican agency of government, the legislature. He conceded that in emergencies (e.g., surprise attack) the executive must act without con-

---

[53] James Madison, "Speech in House of Representatives, June 8, 1789," in Banning, ed., *Liberty and Order*, 28.

[54] See James Madison, "Virginia Resolutions," in Banning, ed., *Liberty and Order*, 237. See also Madison, "Virginia Report," in Banning, ed., *Liberty and Order*, 259.

gressional authorization, but he saw the need to repair to the legislature for authorization at the earliest possible moment. Madison thus rejected Hamilton's version of what has come to be called the theory of the "unitary executive," a theory that puts great weight on the vesting clause of Article II of the Constitution: "The executive power shall be vested in a President of the United States." Hamilton took that clause to be more than the identification of an office within the separated-powers scheme: it was, he thought, a grant of substantive power, the "executive power," over and above the presidential powers enumerated in the subsequent clauses of Article II. On Hamilton's view, the "executive power" thus had a kind of essence or fixed character. Hamilton did not go into detail regarding how or where one ascertains the powers of the executive, but his implicit procedure suggests that he used the powers of the British king as the template for powers that were, in their nature, executive. This was a move already made by the great English jurist William Blackstone: in his *Commentaries on the Laws of England* (1765–1769), he had reinterpreted the powers of the king as executive powers, employing the conceptual apparatus suggested by Locke's and Montesquieu's constitutional theories.[55]

Hamilton noticed, of course, that some powers held by the king in England were explicitly given to the legislature in the American Constitution, and this led him to affirm as "the general doctrine of our Constitution" the notion that "the EXECUTIVE POWER of the Nation is vested in the President, subject only to the *exceptions* and *qualifications* which are expressed in the instrument."[56] As we have already noted, the exceptions are to be taken narrowly, leaving to the president most of the power over foreign relations that the English king possessed (indeed, in this respect, the Hamiltonian president exercises something close to prerogative power).

Despite the fact that he and Hamilton later clashed over the nature of executive power, Madison apparently was the first to call attention to the difference in wording between the vesting clauses of Article I ("All legislative Powers herein granted . . .") and Article II ("The executive Power shall be vested . . ."). On Madison's view, the difference pointed to the existence and possession by the president of something like an executive-power-in-itself. But Madison's notion of this power was more like Locke's notion of the executive per se; that is, it was a power to see to the execution of the laws as contained in the president's Article II duty to "take care that the laws be faithfully executed." Hamilton added to the executive power per se the powers Locke had identified as federative and prerogative, and dubbed the whole "executive." Madison held that these meta-executive powers did not belong by nature to any branch of government, and that the actual constitutional distribution must be followed.

---

[55] William Blackstone, *Commentaries on the Laws of England* (Chicago: University of Chicago Press, 1979), vol. I, chaps. 3–7.
[56] Hamilton, "Pacificus Number I."

E. *Summary*

To summarize, then, Jefferson, Hamilton, and Madison differ from each other along two dimensions: first, regarding whether all necessary power is or should be in the Constitution; and second, regarding who should exercise the powers to deal with extraordinary circumstances. We are left with a crucial question: How do the Jeffersonian, Hamiltonian, and Madisonian models of constitutionalism bear on our main question, "What should constitutions do?" In particular, what should they do in an age of terror? The three models might be compared and assessed on at least two different dimensions:

(1) As construals of the American Constitution: Here, as a reading of the text, Madison's model seems best, an unsurprising conclusion given his role as "father of the Constitution." The constitutional doctrines of Jefferson and Hamilton reveal in their different ways the misgivings their authors had about the Constitution as adopted.

(2) As responses to the problem of the "exception" as identified by Schmitt: Perhaps the first thing that must be said is that neither Jefferson's Model II nor Hamilton's Model III are anything like Schmitt's polemical vision of liberal constitutionalism. In their different ways, both models are capable of coping with the extraordinary or emergency situations on which Schmitt places so much emphasis. Madison's Model IV comes closest to Schmitt's "liberal constitutionalism," for Madison rejects the chief means by which Jefferson and Hamilton open the legal order out to the extraordinary. Like Hamilton, he commits to remaining within rather than going outside the law; like Jefferson, he rejects the extremely elastic Constitution that Hamilton affirms in order to remain within the legal order. Madison's Constitution is not so restrictive as Jefferson's, but Madison still affirms real limits that, in theory, could hamper the government from dealing with emergencies. For example, in his rejection of the Hamiltonian doctrine of implied powers, he says: "Had the power of making treaties ... been omitted, however necessary it might have been, the defect could only have been lamented or supplied by an amendment of the Constitution." [57] Of course, that power was not omitted, and Madison can argue that his doctrine of implied powers is adequate, for the Constitution grants all major powers necessary to meet the real needs of governance—even emerging and unexpected needs.

In any case, we can recognize Madison's Model IV constitutionalism as the most balanced of the models we have discussed, in terms of its attempt to fulfill the complex mandate supplied by our preliminary answer to the question of what constitutions should do. (Recall that in Section I we suggested that constitutions should limit and channel power and at the same time should permit and foster those actions required to achieve the com-

[57] Madison, "Speech on the Bank Bill," 76–77.

mon good.) But Model IV also has some obviously problematic features and leaves some open questions: (a) Can we plausibly say of the American Constitution, or of any effort to draw up a Model IV constitution, that it contains all the large grants of power that would be necessary? (b) Is a fundamentally legislature-centered model sufficient to meet the emergency or extraordinary needs that Schmitt points to and that the threat of terrorism regularly poses? (c) Is the Madisonian Model IV constitution as we have so far discussed it actually sufficient to meet the aim of setting limits of various sorts on governmental power in the name of individual rights? And to the extent that it can set such limits, does this tend to prevent it from meeting the needs posed by extraordinary circumstances?

These questions are perhaps best considered in light of the concrete possibilities and needs raised in our contemporary discussions of constitutionalism in the face of the challenge of terrorism. In what follows, we hope to accomplish two things. First, we hope to show that our four constitutional models serve as useful paradigms for organizing, classifying, and understanding the various positions taken by commentators and official decision-makers in recent discussions. Second, we hope to use the current discussions to examine further the relative merits of the models, with an eye to concluding whether constitutionalism is viable in difficult times, or whether Schmitt is essentially correct.

III. Contemporary Perspectives

How then do these alternate versions of constitutionalism relate to the War on Terror? Remarkably well, as it turns out. For the main positions that were taken by spokespersons for the administration of George W. Bush, by its critics, by the Supreme Court, and by scholars are much the same as (or close variants of) the constitutional models we have sketched. For example, the Bush administration took a Hamiltonian Model III view (or even a hyper-Hamiltonian one); the critics took a Whig Model I or (more often) Jeffersonian Model II view; and the Supreme Court has, for the most part, taken the Madisonian Model IV position.

A. Model I: Contemporary Whigs

The Whig position begins by arguing that executive power ought to be constrained through strict construction of relevant constitutional provisions, implying that the executive should not have plenary prerogative power. Pushing the traditional Whig position further, the contemporary Whigs argue against the prerogative power by explaining that it is nothing more than a myth.[58] They argue that America's political heritage and

---

[58] See, most explicitly, Raoul Berger, *Executive Privilege: A Constitutional Myth* (Cambridge, MA: Harvard University Press, 1974), 1. See also Louis Fisher, "Lost Constitutional Moor-

its centuries-old constitutional system explicitly reject presidential prerogative. Although they recognize that many past presidents have exercised the prerogative power, these Whigs argue, just as John Marshall did, that "[t]he peculiar circumstances of the moment may render a measure more or less wise, but cannot render it more or less constitutional."[59] In order to establish the unconstitutionality and illegitimacy of the presidential prerogative, contemporary Whigs stake their argument on three primary grounds. First, they argue that the American Constitution presupposes a constrained executive, departing from the historical British model. This departure leads to their second argument, which reasons that the Framers feared concentration of power in the executive branch due to the potential dangers it posed. Third, they argue that the provisions of the constitutional text, as well as the arguments of the drafters, exhibit an explicit intention to prioritize Congress over the executive.

We turn first to the contemporary Whigs' argument that the American Constitution presupposes a complete break from the British model of executive power. Most indicative of this break is the fact that the British model concentrated the war power in the king.[60] Whereas the British king had the entire war power, contemporary Whigs argue that the United States Constitution instead vests this power in Congress. They point to Article II and argue that it only gives the president charge over the military "when called into the actual Service of the United States."[61] Article I, they explain, invokes the war power when it allots Congress the power to "declare War [and] grant Letters of Marque and Reprisal."[62] Even if one merely grants that the Constitution does not vest all war power in the executive, this would provide enough ground for contemporary Whigs to conclude that the American model breaks from the executive-centered British war powers model. Decades before the current War on Terror, Raoul Berger took this argument a step further in his book *Executive Privilege: A Constitutional Myth* (1974) and explained that not only does the Constitution break from the British model, but the American Framers "purposely cut all roots to the royal prerogative.... A supraconstitutional residuum of powers not granted expressly or by necessary implication was not only furthest from their thoughts, but avowal

---

ings: Recovering the War Power," *Indiana Law Journal* 81 (2005): 1202, where he writes, "Scrutinize the U.S. Constitution as carefully as you like and you will not find a single one of Blackstone's prerogatives assigned to the President."

[59] John Marshall, "A Friend of the Constitution V," in *John Marshall's Defense of McCulloch v. Maryland*, ed. Gerald Gunther (Stanford, CA: Stanford University Press, 1969), 190–91; quoted in Berger, *Executive Privilege*, 10.

[60] Blackstone, *Commentaries*, 1:249. Blackstone explains: "[T]he king has also the sole prerogative of making war and peace."

[61] U.S. Constitution, Article II, section 2.

[62] Letters of marque are specific authorizations that allow the holder to search, seize, and/or destroy possessions of another person outside of the issuing nation's borders. Letters of reprisal authorize the holder to retaliate against an individual who has broken the laws of war; they permit the holder also to ignore the laws of war during the retaliation.

of such a residuum would have affrighted them and barred adoption of the Constitution."[63] Following Berger's reasoning, Arthur Schlesinger commented in 1989 that Madison's *Helvidius* "denied that the powers of making wars and treaties were inherently executive. This 'vicious' doctrine obviously had been 'borrowed' from Britain. The fact that these were royal prerogatives in Britain did not make them presidential prerogatives in the United States."[64]

Instead, the contemporary Whigs maintain that the executive must be constrained by the rule of law. Legal scholar David Luban points out that this rule of law is in direct opposition to the model of war, which provides "much freer rein than that of law. . . ."[65] The model of war gives the executive more prerogative power since it does not impose the same stringent procedural standards, the same protection of human rights, the same evidentiary guidelines, or the same presumption of innocence that the rule of law requires. Luban contends that the executive *must* abide by the rule of law, which places legal limits on presidential action. This stance against the routinization of the war model is a stance against the normalization of prerogative power, leaving the executive to act inside— and only inside—the explicit legal code. Since the U.S. Constitution presupposes a stark break from the British model and the war model, the contemporary Whigs argue that the American executive cannot claim the prerogative power *sua sponte*.

On the view of the contemporary Whigs, it is precisely this *sua sponte* concentrated power that the American Founders feared. For this line of argument, they begin with the framing debates and argue that "[a] close look at the Founders' conception of the executive power will disclose its meager scope."[66] The primary reason why the Founders limited executive power was that they wanted to counter presidential ambition, presidential glory-seeking, presidential quests for immortal fame.[67] Berger explains that in order to limit presidential ambition the Founders carefully defined and confined executive powers by including various enumerated powers in Article II. Since these enumerated powers trump the vesting clause's vague grant of executive power, Berger maintains that interpretations that prioritize the vesting clause "pervert the design of the Framers. . . ." He explains that the function of the vesting clause is merely transitional, providing "no more than a label designed to differentiate

---

[63] Berger, *Executive Privilege*, 107–8.

[64] Arthur Schlesinger, *The Imperial Presidency* (Boston: Houghton Mifflin Company, 1989), 19. The *Helvidius* letters were a series of essays by Madison attacking Hamilton's theory of executive power at the time of President Washington's Neutrality Proclamation in 1793. See note 41 above.

[65] David Luban, "The War on Terrorism and the End of Human Rights," in *The Constitution in Wartime*, ed. Mark Tushnet (Durham, NC: Duke University Press, 2005), 219.

[66] Berger, *Executive Privilege*, 52.

[67] See Fisher, "Lost Constitutional Moorings," 1204; and Michael Treanor, "Fame, the Founding, and the Power to Declare War," *Cornell Law Review* 82 (1997): 605.

presidential from legislative functions. . . ."[68] The clause does not imply a radical shift to extensive executive powers, Berger concludes.

This Whig reading of Article II renders the vesting clause not only unnecessary, but also trivial. If this reading is correct, then it does not explain how the Whigs can simultaneously maintain that the drafters of the U.S. Constitution were careful with their language but careless with their vesting clauses—or so devotees of Model III constitutionalism would argue.

In her amicus brief in the 2004 *Rumsfeld v. Padilla* case, former Attorney General Janet Reno follows Berger's lines of reasoning and counters the argument that the president has the prerogative power to detain American citizens without the benefit of the criminal justice system. Reno denies that the executive has this prerogative power and argues that such a power is not only illegitimate but also unnecessary. She argues that both the Constitution and congressional legislation provide the president with myriad resources to combat domestic terrorism, eliminating the need to "resort to the extraordinary power claimed . . . by the President."[69] Even though this framework may prevent the president from efficiently responding to novel emergencies, Reno explains, "this is an inherent consequence of the limitation of Executive power."[70] That is, Reno acknowledges that domestic terrorism may create difficulties, yet these pale in comparison to the dark possibilities created by overly concentrating power in the executive.

The contemporary Whigs take issue with Alexander Hamilton's executive-empowering argument in his letters from *Pacificus*. Berger argues that Hamilton's interpretation "does violence to the . . . clear intention to create an Executive of rigorously limited powers."[71] Further, Berger argues that this position is dissonant with Hamilton's arguments in the Constitutional Convention of 1787 and during ratification. Schlesinger goes so far as to appeal to the authority of an earlier Hamilton against the later Hamilton, explaining that during the Constitutional Convention, Hamilton argued in favor of vesting the war powers in the Senate, with the executive only having war powers *after* a war had been authorized or begun.[72] Moreover, during the ratification process, Hamilton argued that executive power ought to be confined,

[68] Berger, *Executive Privilege*, 55.

[69] *Rumsfeld v. Padilla*, 542 U.S. 426 (2004), Janet Reno Amicus Brief, 24. In this case, the Supreme Court was asked to decide whether the president could militarily detain American citizens without benefit of civilian procedural rights, so long as he determined that they were enemy combatants. The Court sidestepped the issue here by deciding that the complaint had been improperly filed, thus failing to resolve the question of the limits of the president's power.

[70] Ibid., 29.

[71] Berger, *Executive Privilege*, 57. The *Pacificus* letters were written by Hamilton in defense of President Washington's Neutrality Proclamation in 1793. See note 41 above.

[72] Arthur Schlesinger, *The Imperial Presidency* (Boston: Houghton Mifflin Company, 1973), 3.

defined, and limited.[73] Berger eventually concludes, "It is the unmistakable lesson of history that the President was intentionally given a few enumerated powers, no more."[74]

Additionally, contemporary Whigs maintain that the executive's role is a limited one, because according to the constitutional text, the executive's role is secondary to that of the Congress. The Constitution's longest section is devoted to the Congress. The section on the executive branch follows the one on Congress, both in constitutional structure and power. Therefore, explains the legal scholar Louis Henkin, the executive's powers are "more modest than those bestowed upon Congress," making the president the *executive-agent* of Congress.[75] Berger utilizes a similar structural priority to argue that Hamilton's *Pacificus* argument was backward: congressional power is not carved out of executive power, but executive power derogates from congressional power "eked out slowly, reluctantly, and not without limitations and safeguards."[76] Since the Constitution grants immense power to Congress, the president is "severely limited ... designedly subordinate to Congress. ..."[77] These contemporary Whigs conclude, then, that the Constitution presupposes congressional priority in order to forestall concentrated power in the president.

Other latter-day adherents of Model I, like the American Civil Liberties Union (ACLU), focus their attention on governmental limitations on behalf of the rights of individuals, rather than on separation-of-powers concerns. They sometimes treat rights as "absolutes" and are unwilling to weigh and balance the goods to be achieved by limiting rights against the cost to liberty of these limitations. They tend not to be pragmatists. They would treat terrorists and other enemies as criminals, to whom all the normal constitutional safeguards apply. As they see it, all the rights and protections specified in the Constitution apply with equal force in time of war as in time of peace.[78]

B. Model II: Contemporary Jeffersonians

The Jeffersonian position has a more relaxed grip on executive power than the Whig position. It allots the executive prerogative power in order to meet unforeseen threats to the civil order, while also limiting the executive through a strict adherence to the explicit legal order. Contemporary Jeffersonians follow their classical counterparts due to an overwhelming

[73] Berger, *Executive Privilege*, 58.
[74] Ibid., 138.
[75] Louis Henkin, *Foreign Affairs and the Constitution* (Mineola, NY: Transnational Pub., 1972), 33.
[76] Berger, *Executive Privilege*, 50.
[77] Ibid., 13.
[78] See Richard Posner, *Not a Suicide Pact* (Oxford: Oxford University Press, 2006).

fear of excessive power located in the executive. They argue that if the president may constitutionally use the prerogative power, then the president has the incentive and ability to normalize broad grants of power. Yet they disagree among themselves about how the executive's extraordinary uses of power are to be checked or monitored. Some look mainly to Congress, others to the people.

The foundational motive for the contemporary Jeffersonians lies in a fear of trivializing emergency power. That is, once an executive uses emergency power, which substantially enlarges executive power, that executive will look for additional emergencies in order to wield the power again. However, emergencies are few, which implies that the executive might feign emergencies in order to exercise additional power. When the emergency becomes normalized and integrated into the rule of law, contemporary Jeffersonians argue, the executive ceases to be a democratic leader and instead becomes a monarchical dictator. Therefore, normalizing emergency power would lead to a reprehensible and unstable legal order.

In order to deal with these theoretical possibilities, legal scholar Mark Tushnet, in his essay "Emergencies and the Idea of Constitutionalism," creates a conceptual framework for dealing with emergency power through an analysis of the incorporation of the war power. He argues that the best way to meet wartime needs is to recognize that war creates a fundamental shift, requiring extraordinary exercises of power by governmental actors. Therefore, war suspends the normal rule of law. Without the technical requirements of the legal order, the government can efficiently respond to grave threats and deploy military forces without the technical delay imposed by law's procedural requirements.

Tushnet wants to separate executive war powers from the executive's day-to-day powers, since normalizing war powers will make war a normal activity. He explains that if the executive's extraordinary powers are read into the Constitution, then the extraordinary power becomes ordinary and governmental actors will push for even greater grants of extraordinary power. He cautions: "The temporary will be made permanent, threatening civil liberties well beyond the period of the emergency."[79] Therefore, Tushnet argues that war requires a fundamental shift in the distribution of power. By permitting the executive to exercise power outside of the Constitution, the hope is that the power will remain extraconstitutional, and therefore extraordinary.

Yet this is precisely where Tushnet parts ways with other Jeffersonians. In order to keep the extraordinary emergency power out of the normal lawmaking sphere, Tushnet relies on a mobilized citizenry. He explains that alarmists will continually decry the executive's use of the prerogative

---

[79] Mark Tushnet, "Emergencies and the Idea of Constitutionalism," in Tushnet, ed., *The Constitution in Wartime*, 44.

power, forcing other citizens to closely monitor governmental actions.[80] This continual monitoring will frustrate executive power grabbing such that the executive will seek other nonemergency means, which are guarded by the separation of powers and federalism.

Other contemporary Jeffersonians do not rely as exclusively on the will of the people. Instead, they look to the other branches to check the abuse of emergency power. For example, Mark Brandon argues that Congress ought to be far more diligent in protecting its powers from executive overreaching. He takes very seriously the fact that the United States has been in a war or warlike conflict for more than 80 percent of its existence, making the United States a warrior state where foreign wars occur while domestic conditions are relatively normal.[81] Since the warrior state implies extensive executive power, Brandon argues that Congress ought to take an affirmative role in defending its constitutional power. Should the executive push to increase his power, Congress ought to reply by passing legislation that counters the executive's play for power. Yet Brandon laments that Congress has failed to live up to this adversarial role, and has instead conceded power to the executive, making future contestations of power far more difficult to win.

One of the most prominent voices in the current discussion is also very close to Jefferson. We refer to Judge Richard Posner of the Seventh Circuit Court of Appeals, whose 2006 book *Not a Suicide Pact* recognizes that extraordinary times may call for extraordinary actions, which should not be enshrined in the ordinary law. Posner would countenance some of the more controversial aspects of the War on Terror— coercive interrogation, rendition, intrusive surveillance—but he would, for the most part, cordon these things off from the ordinary law. In effect, they would be allowed, but not endorsed. He thus calls for a very restrained role for courts in these matters, for courts find themselves having to say yea or nay to the legality of the practices that come before them, and that is what Posner does not want them to say. He does not dwell on the issue of who is to check extraordinary power; rather, as a jurist, he stresses the inadvisability of the judiciary injecting itself into the issue on either side.

In the end, the contemporary Jeffersonians agree that ordinary presidential power needs to be understood in a limited way; yet, at the same time, they acknowledge that the executive may require powers that were unforeseeable at the time of the Constitution's drafting, and thus they would create a prerogative power that intentionally stands outside the normalized legal order. By keeping this prerogative power outside of the normal, peaceful operation of government, these Jef-

---

[80] It may be noted, however, that in looking to the people Tushnet is closer to the original Jeffersonian model than are many other contemporary devotees of Model II.

[81] Mark Brandon, "War and the American Constitutional Order," in Tushnet, ed., *The Constitution in Wartime*, 11.

fersonians attempt to separate normal governmental power from exceptional power.

C. Model III: Contemporary Hamiltonians

Unlike the Jeffersonians, modern-day Hamiltonians worry more about the existence and security of the nation than about executive overreaching. They argue that the government, and especially the executive, ought to have substantial power to stop potentially deadly attacks while they are still inchoate. In effect, contemporary Hamiltonians argue that the Whigs and Jeffersonians have priorities that are pathologically inverted. They hold that these alternate visions of constitutionalism set day-to-day lawmaking above the higher law of national survival; these visions value constitutional means above constitutional ends.

Contemporary Hamiltonians focus on the vast grant of power in the vesting clause of Article II. Joseph Bessette and Gary Schmitt argue, for example, that the Framers carefully created the vesting clause in order to bind the chief executive to fulfill various important duties. Bessette and Schmitt develop their creative hermeneutic by closely reading Madison's notes on the Constitutional Convention and attending to Gouverneur Morris's role in drafting the vesting clause. They argue that Morris explicitly changed the language of Article II from powers to duties, in order to differentiate discretionary powers from affirmative duties and thus to strengthen the executive by making his tasks obligatory rather than discretionary. For example, they explain that Morris insisted on changing a draft clause that stated that the executive "may recommend to [the legislature] . . . such measures as he shall judge necessary, and expedient." Morris wanted to replace "may" with "shall," in order to "make it the *duty* of the President to recommend, [and] thence prevent umbrage or cavil at his doing it."[82] They argue that Morris's action here "is an explicit recognition of the difference between a discretionary power and a positive duty."[83] Capitalizing on Morris's argument, Bessette and Schmitt emphasize the duties imposed by Article II rather than the powers conferred by it, and they conclude that the duties of the executive "lie at the heart of the constitutional presidency."[84]

This interpretation of Article II is not merely a change in semantics, but a fundamental shift in conceptualizing executive power. Not only do the duties take priority and convey a certain necessity for the executive to exercise vigorously the granted powers, but once Article II is read as consisting primarily of duties, the duties become the grounds for the

---

[82] Joseph Bessette and Gary Schmitt, "The Powers and Duties of the President: Recovering the Logic and Meaning of Article II," in *The Constitutional Presidency*, ed. Joseph Bessette and Jeffrey Tulis (Baltimore, MD: Johns Hopkins University Press, 2009), 10.

[83] Ibid.

[84] Ibid., 2.

powers granted and for any other powers that may be necessary or suitable for fulfilling the duties. The duties set the ends, and the powers, granted and implied, are conceived as means. Bessette and Schmitt thus interpret Article II much as Hamilton interpreted the "necessary and proper" clause.

Their interpretive principle implies that the explicit powers in the Constitution are merely examples of powers that the executive has, rather than comprising a comprehensive list of such powers. If this reading is accurate, then the executive may utilize almost any conceivable power to discharge effectively the duties incumbent upon his office. At the same time, however, this creative interpretation implies that the power-conferring provisions of Article II are redundant, merely detailing some possibilities of what the executive might do to uphold the laws of the land.

Another neo-Hamiltonian is John Yoo, now a law professor at UC Berkeley, but formerly a Justice Department official heavily involved in developing the Bush administration's doctrine on the War on Terror. Yoo goes beyond Hamilton, who saw war-making as an inherently executive function, but conceded that important parts of the war power had been given to Congress, thus carving out exceptions from essentially executive powers. In particular, the power "to declare war" was given to Congress, and Hamilton admitted that this set a definite limit on executive powers. Scholars tell us that even at the time of the founding, the practice of issuing formal declarations of war was becoming far less common, but what was then only a nascent trend of using force without declaration of war has since become almost a matter of course. The last time the United States actually declared war was World War II, and since then the U.S. has used military force in Korea, Vietnam, Grenada, Haiti, Iraq (twice), Kosovo, Afghanistan, and elsewhere — all without declarations of war. This nonuse of the declaration of war, with Congress's explicit or implicit approval most of the time, led the Bush administration to its ultra-Hamiltonian approach: its belief that the president, through his executive and commander-in-chief powers and because of his institutional competence, has the power to commit to the use of force on his own authority and to determine what is necessary to the effective use of force. In his 2005 book *The Powers of War and Peace*, Yoo argues that the power to declare war is not actually a power to commit to the use of force, but merely a power to change the nation's official legal status both externally and internally.[85] Such a change in status has many legal consequences, but is not necessary for the use of troops, which the president may initiate on his own authority. This is not to say that Yoo defends completely unchecked presidential power. Congress has the power of the purse and can use it to assert itself against unilateral presidential actions if it so desires. The

[85] John Yoo, *The Powers of War and Peace* (Chicago: University of Chicago Press, 2005).

Constitution Yoo outlines is beyond Hamiltonianism in that it gives the president more independent authority than Hamilton did, and it reads the Constitution as mandating a pervasive "struggle for control" of foreign and military policy between the president and Congress. In this struggle, as developed by Yoo, the executive branch has a great structural advantage, for it can act with a kind of dispatch and decisiveness that it is very hard for Congress to match. Thus, the executive can commit military forces to the field, and it is up to Congress to decommit them—a very difficult thing for Congress to do, as the debate on the Iraq military surge showed.

Yoo's position is one that pays great attention to one half of the issues raised by the problem of constitutionalism—the need for extraordinary powers to deal with extraordinary circumstances, and like Hamilton and Madison, Yoo seeks to incorporate those powers inside the Constitution. But he almost totally depreciates the other half—the aspiration to constitutionalism itself, the sober caution the American Founders exercised when they set out to build in safeguards against extraordinary executive powers. As John Locke once said, good and wise kings do not themselves require to be checked, but their extralegal activities are precedents and dangers in the hands of the less-good and less-wise rulers who will almost certainly follow them. Thus, even if one is inclined to empower a particular president, as Professor Yoo was when he credited George W. Bush as a good and wise ruler, we still need to be cautious in arming a president with tools that can be badly misused by a future president in other circumstances.

Many of the contemporary Model III constitutionalists go to great lengths in attempting to allay the fears of those less sanguine about the misuses of executive power. Law professors Eric Posner and Adrian Vermeule argue, for example, that executive decisions rendered in the heat of the moment do not always have negative precedential effects. They hold that anti-Hamiltonians (Jeffersonians and Whigs) argue against broad grants of executive power for two reasons: ratcheting and fear. First, anti-Hamiltonians argue against even small grants of emergency executive power because they assume that the executive will exploit such a grant and use it to expand his power by artificially creating new emergencies. Then, when the executive has attained more power, he will repel calls for diminishing his power and will instead seek to increase his power even further. Posner and Vermeule label this situation a "ratcheting effect," indicating unidirectional and irreversible change. They argue that ratcheting is improbable due to a status quo bias in the legal system, which will tend to work against a ratcheting effect because there are institutional mechanisms that can insert sunset provisions into emergency actions.

Posner and Vermeule next attack anti-Hamiltonian arguments concerned about the clouding effect fear has on executive judgment, which they refer to as the "panic thesis." This thesis states that "because of the danger of panic, constitutional constraints should not be relaxed during emergencies."[86] Advocates of this thesis argue that institutions should be structured to manage effectively the panic that is sure to arise during emergencies, and to prevent governmental actors from acting irrationally due to fear. Posner and Vermeule argue that this position is counterhistorical because the executive and legislative branches have been the rational, active "champions of civil liberties during emergencies in American history. . . ." Even during times of panic, the executive and the legislature act rationally, not impetuously as the panic thesis proponents claim. Therefore, Posner and Vermeule imply, emergency restrictions should not limit presidential and legislative actions but empower them.

While Posner and Vermeule argue that emergency-induced fear does not produce irrational decisions, other contemporary Hamiltonians argue that fear actually produces *very* rational decisions. In his 2007 book *The Terror Presidency*, Jack Goldsmith, former United States Assistant Attorney General for the Office of Legal Counsel in the Department of Justice, describes various circumstances where executive officials operated under two types of fear: the fear of not doing enough and the fear of doing too much.[87] In the aftermath of terrorist attacks, decision-makers fear that their decisions will be insufficient to prevent future attacks, and that they consequently will be blamed for future catastrophes. Conversely, they fear that their proactive decisions will go further than necessary and will needlessly infringe on civil liberties. Goldsmith's account swings back and forth between these two poles, portraying the fear that undergirds everyday operations in the executive branch.

Goldsmith argues that fear inside the executive branch also leads actors to be overly legalistic. Fear of future prosecution for inaction or overreaction forces executive officials to comply, as rigorously as possible, with the technical details of the law. However, since it is inevitable that the law will not prefigure all of the executive's desired actions, there is a strong incentive to read the law as creatively as possible, in an attempt to move desired actions under the legal umbrella. This kind of creative legal reasoning, which Goldsmith accuses Yoo of having practiced, produces a very ambiguous situation: the impression of lawfulness that may rest on a greater or lesser distortion of the law.

Although Goldsmith voices reservations about the ideas of other contemporary Hamiltonians and hyper-Hamiltonians like Yoo, he nonetheless remains firmly in the camp of Model III constitutionalism, for he argues that the executive ought to have vast powers to deal with the daily threats to the safety of the nation. Further, he agrees that extraordinary executive power ought to be vested in the ordinary Constitution. He

---

[86] Eric Posner and Adrian Vermeule, "Accommodating Exceptions," in Tushnet, ed., *The Constitution in Wartime*, 80.

[87] Jack Goldsmith, *The Terror Presidency* (New York: W.W. Norton, 2007), 12.

points out that past executive actions by respected presidents like Franklin D. Roosevelt have been extraordinary, though legally approved; indeed, such decisions have often been made behind closed doors, with little information provided to the public. In order to temper executive overreaching, Goldsmith, like Hamilton himself, looks to the political process as a source of safety from too much power.

D. Model IV: Contemporary Madisonians

Contemporary Madisonians fear future dangers as much as Hamiltonians do. Therefore, they condone extensive governmental power to deter, prevent, and repel attacks against the country. At the same time, however, they also fear executive usurpation of broad powers, as do the contemporary Whigs. This leads Madisonians to deny that the president has *sua sponte* prerogative power. In order to accommodate both of these inclinations, modern-day Madisonians look to the legislature as the seat of authorization and control of extraordinary power. In his 2006 book *Before the Next Attack*, Bruce Ackerman, one of the most active contemporary Madisonians, looks specifically to Congress for approval of emergency powers; he displays his Madisonian hesitations about an infinitely flexible Constitution by constructing a complicated system to prevent a ratcheting of power through long-term use.

Unlike the Jeffersonians, Ackerman finds within the Constitution implied power for Congress to declare emergencies and authorize the executive to exercise extraordinary powers. His framework begins with a decision to utilize emergency powers, requiring at first only a regular majority of Congress. After this initial grant of power, Congress must reauthorize the emergency powers every two months, but must do so via an ever-larger majority each time: after two months, 60 percent of the Congress must approve; after four months, 70 percent. Finally, after six months, 80 percent of Congress must agree, and must continue to do so every two months thereafter. Ackerman's reason for proposing the escalating threshold is to forestall the routinization of extensive executive power. Additionally, the two-month hiatus between approval votes encourages members of Congress to quell their passions and base future votes on reason, rather than passionately acceding to presidential or popular demands. Ackerman believes that the cooling-off period will make it very difficult, if not impossible, to retain supermajorities after the immediacy of an emergency has vanished. The representatives will eventually push for a return to normalcy.[88] And if they do not, that must signify that there are persuasive grounds for remaining in emergency mode.

---

[88] Bruce Ackerman, *Before the Next Attack* (New Haven, CT: Yale University Press, 2006), 82.

Although there are many details to quibble about in Ackerman's proposal, its most deeply rooted problem threatens to throw it completely off-track. Ackerman anticipates his plan being adopted as a piece of regular legislation, mostly because he does not imagine that it could survive the constitutional amendment gauntlet. He hopes that it will or can achieve something like unofficial constitutional status by being accepted by the nation as "higher law" rather than ordinary legislation. Ackerman requires, but cannot guarantee, such a status for it. Otherwise, Congress can, by a simple majority, override any law it has made requiring a special majority. The fact that one Congress cannot bind a future Congress (or even itself at a later time) by ordinary legislation means that there is no way to enforce the escalator provision against a simple majority that believes in what it wants to do (for example, maintaining emergency powers, detaining prisoners without *habeas corpus*, or engaging in otherwise illegal surveillance).

Ackerman's plan is not workable, but it admirably displays many of the features of Madisonian Model IV constitutionalism. It affirms the expansive character of the Constitution and its reservoir of power to deal with emergencies. It puts the power and the onus for authorizing extraordinary action on Congress, and it seeks to promote a periodic, deliberate, and cool-headed reconsideration of extraordinary powers and actions.

Probably the most significant Madisonian voices in recent constitutional thinking, however, have been those coming from the Supreme Court. By saying that these voices are Madisonian, we are affirming that they find the necessary powers in the Constitution, but hold Congress to be the main body to authorize policy on emergencies and the president to be the agent to execute the policy. The line between policy and execution is, of course, never quite a bright and shining one, but the disagreements that have emerged among the justices of the Supreme Court have largely been ones of interpreting congressional statutes. They have accepted Congress as the voice that must be deferred to. We will not dwell on these disagreements—they are technical and would be very tedious to dissect.

The disagreements among the Madisonians raise a very pointed question, however: What does it signify that justices using the Madisonian paradigm come to different conclusions—such as that the original Bush military tribunals were—or were not—legal? A candid reading of the various opinions, such as in *Hamdi* (2004),[89] *Hamdan* (2006),[90] and *Boumediene* (2008),[91] leads to the suspicion that the different justices are interpreting the var-

[89] *Hamdi v. Rumsfeld*, 542 U.S. 507 (2004). Here the Court ruled that although the executive has the constitutional power to detain enemy combatants, detained U.S. citizens must be provided the ability to challenge their detention in front of an impartial judge.

[90] *Hamdan v. Rumsfeld*, 548 U.S. 557 (2006). In *Hamdan*, the Court concluded that the Bush administration military commissions violated the Uniform Code of Military Justice and the Geneva Conventions of 1949.

[91] *Boumediene v. Bush*, 553 U.S. 723 (2008). Here the Court ruled that foreign nationals, held as military enemy combatants, have a constitutional right to a *habeas corpus* hearing.

ious statutory provisions in light of some ulterior or additional considerations beyond the mere legal text. The Court split 5-3 in *Hamdan* over
whether the military tribunals meet the process requirements contained
in congressional legislation. The split between the five justice *Hamdan*
majority and the *Hamdan* dissenters indicates that there are, in fact, two
variants of Madisonian constitutionalism.

The *Hamdan* dissenters, Justices Scalia, Thomas, and Alito, accept the
basic Madisonian position that Congress must be the body to set broad
policy on war and peace. But the *Hamdan* majority[92] goes beyond that
and notices that American constitutionalism not only distributes authority among different ruling bodies, but also contains a pledge to treat *all*
persons as rights-bearers—it makes a promise not to deprive persons of
life, liberty, or property without due process of law. The *Hamdan* majority,
even when it does not invoke this constitutional provision, is moved by
sensitivity to this pledge. Thus, they have extended the *habeas corpus*
right, they have rejected tribunals where due process rights are denied,
and they have insisted that detainees have a right to a hearing before a
neutral party.

Does this insistence on honoring the due process commitment make the
members of the *Hamdan* majority naïve constitutionalists, on the order of
the Whigs? The answer, we think, is no. The first thing that must be said
of the majority's concern for due process is that it *is* in the Constitution—
twice. Due process is part of the law the courts—and Congress and the
president—are to adhere to. The commitment to due process does not
mean, however, that the government is required to adhere to the very
strict procedural requirements laid out in the Bill of Rights. Due process
is looser and more flexible than that. As the Supreme Court said in a 1909
case: "What is due process of law depends on circumstances. It varies
with the subject-matter and the necessities of the situation."[93] The Court
majority has treated due process accordingly. It requires a hearing before
a neutral officer, but it does not require a jury trial, for example.

This approach is full-blown Madisonian constitutionalism, that is, a
constitutionalism that looks to Congress as the main bearer of extraordinary powers and holds the government to be committed to recognizing
all persons it deals with as rights-bearers. It contains the main elements of
Madison's own position on implied powers as developed in his speech on
the bank bill, his position on executive power as developed in *Helvidius*,
and his position on rights as developed in the Virginia Report.

IV. Conclusion

As is probably clear from our discussion of the various models, we lean
toward Madisonian constitutionalism as the model of what constitutions

---

[92] Justices Stevens, Souter, Ginsburg, Breyer, and Kennedy formed the majority.
[93] *Moyer v. Peabody,* 212 U.S. 78 (1909).

should do. We do not deny that there is much to be said for the Hamiltonian and Jeffersonian models. They are both efforts to combine the competing requirements of constitutionalism—to channel, control, and limit political power most of the time, and to allow action necessary to the preservation and security of the society in extraordinary times. Nonetheless, the Madisonian model does this to a greater degree than the other two.

Jeffersonian Model II constitutionalism has the disadvantage that the narrowly constrained everyday Constitution may frequently prove incapable of responding to political needs, and thus may require (if it is to succeed) relatively frequent actions by the executive that go beyond the Constitution. Admittedly, Jeffersonian executive action is subject to *ex post facto* ratification or rejection by the legislature or the people, but it runs the dual but opposite dangers of either inuring the people to constitutional violations or setting them so firmly against constitutional violations that necessary action will be hindered or made impossible. These dual dangers suggest the wisdom of Hamilton's concern that powers required to deal with extraordinary situations be located within the Constitution. Model II constitutionalism would seem well-equipped to respond to one half of the tasks of constitutionalism—to control and contain power. But in its failure to cope well with the other half, Model II runs the risk of not even dealing well with the half it is specially designed for.

Hamiltonian Model III constitutionalism is nearly the mirror image of Model II, and its deficiencies are the obverse. With its extremely elastic reading of constitutional powers under Article I's "necessary and proper" clause and Article II's vesting clause, it risks losing sight of one of the central tasks of constitutions: to limit and constrain power. This deficiency of Model III was visible in many of the actions (and arguments) of the Bush administration.

Thus, Madisonian Model IV constitutionalism is evidently the model that best combines the disparate requirements of constitutionalism. It better balances the needs of the quotidian and the needs of the extraordinary in a variety of respects: in its controlled reading of implied powers; in its attempt to control power in the name of rights; in its flexibility with regard to rule-of-law claims (as in the due process requirements enforced by the Supreme Court); and in its emphasis on the legislature and not the executive as the seat of the authority to define emergency powers. And, as we argued in Section II, the Madisonian Model is the one most in accord with the Constitution we do have. But our claim is more than this. The Madisonian Model IV is the Constitution that we (and others) should have.

It is difficult to be quite so categorical here, however. Let us close by raising a few questions to challenge Madisonian constitutionalism. First, is a legislature-centered model adequate to the exigencies of the Age of Terror? The Bush administration acted on the theory that an executive-centered response is necessary to deal with the threats we face. Yet the strongest case for the executive, it seems, is in those situations where an instant and decisive response is needed. One wonders how well this rationale fits the present situation. The War on Terror, President Bush told us, is not a matter of a month or a year, but a matter of a generation or more. One would think that a long-term threat and a long-term policy to deal with that threat takes us out of the realm of emergency and into the realm of policy that requires and benefits from acquiring regular legal status (i.e., adoption by the lawmaking body). It behooves us to plan for the long haul and to do so in a way that is most likely to consolidate public support behind the policy. As the Bush administration's policy demonstrated, policy imposed by the executive, often in secret, does not sustain public support if and when it becomes known.

Thus, Madisonian constitutionalism can and should defer to the president in an emergency of the kind requiring instantaneous action, and to Congress in setting longer-term policy in the sphere of war and peace, but it does not give to either a blank check of the sort that ultra-Hamiltonianism would give to the president.

Not only is the legislature the better locus for policy adoption, but Model IV is also the wisest and most prudential model. For there are good reasons, which Madison well articulated, not to give this kind of power to the president:

> In no part of the Constitution is more wisdom to be found than in the clause which confides the question of war or peace to the legislature, and not to the executive department. The trust and temptation would be too great for any one man. It is in war, finally, that laurels are to be gathered, and it is the executive whose brow they are to encircle. The strongest passions, and the most dangerous weaknesses of the human breast; ambition, avarice, vanity, the honorable or dishonorable love of fame, are all in conspiracy against the desire and duty of peace.[94]

The Madisonian model would look to Congress as the policymaking body for emergencies, but under this model does Congress have enough power and are the limits imposed on congressional power too extensive? The Madisonian model stands between the Hamiltonian and the Jeffersonian on legislative implied powers under the "necessary and proper" clause. The Madisonian model recognizes implied powers as means to the enumerated powers. It is not as open-ended as the Hamiltonian model—but does it recognize capacious enough powers to do what needs to be done in emergency situations? Unfortunately, we cannot say for certain.

---

[94] James Madison, "Helvidius Number IV," in *The Pacificus-Helvidius Debates of 1793–1794*, ed. Morton J. Frisch (Indianapolis, IN: Liberty Fund, 2006), 87.

But it surely seems likely. Congress is granted the war-making power, the power to suspend *habeas corpus* (and thus to institute martial law), the power to set the terms of due process, the power to raise and appropriate money. These powers and the powers that can be inferred as means to their effectuation (e.g., the power to define crimes against the United States) appear to be sufficient, in principle, to deal with war-like extraordinary circumstances.

But under Madisonian Model IV constitutionalism even Congress is not free to do whatever it likes in the sphere of its enumerated and implied powers. There are limits on congressional powers derived from rights protections in the Constitution. The full-blown Madisonianism of the Supreme Court majority in recent detainee cases is evident in its propensity to give due weight to those limits.[95] Thus, after the *Hamdan* decision, Congress adopted legislation establishing military tribunals, and in the process denied to detainees the right to file for writs of *habeas corpus*. The Court in the *Boumediene* case rejected this legislation as not adequately supplying rights protection to alleged enemy combatants. This decision is generally in accord with the mandates of Madisonian constitutionalism. It is not at all evident that giving detainees greater rights to challenge their detention will set back governmental efforts to supply safety and security to Americans citizens. If we recall that due process requirements are flexible and depend a great deal on circumstances, there is no reason why Congress and the Courts could not fashion procedures that honor the due process rights of detainees. (The due process clause applies to all "persons," not only citizens; it sets a standard of action for the U.S. government, not merely for action on U.S. soil.)

Treaties, congressional law, and perhaps even the Constitution itself (Amendments V and VIII together) prohibit torture.[96] Can we live with such consequences of Model IV constitutionalism? In a recent *New York Times* opinion piece, Charles Fried (a former solicitor general and now a Harvard law professor) ventured an answer to this question:

> Some argue that torture is justified if our survival is threatened; but even apart from the elasticity of this justification, it is flawed because it depends on an equivocation. Our physical survival is not what is of overriding moral importance (people give up their lives all the time for some higher value) but our survival as decent human beings acting for a decent society. And we cannot authorize indecency without jeopardizing our survival as a decent society.[97]

---

[95] See, for example, *Hamdi, Hamdan,* and *Boumediene,* cited in notes 89, 90, and 91.

[96] Amendment V reads, in relevant part, "No person shall be . . . deprived of life, liberty, or property, without due process of law. . ." and Amendment VIII prohibits "cruel and unusual punishments."

[97] Charles Fried, "History's Verdict," *New York Times,* January 10, 2009, 11.

Madisonian constitutionalism aims at being expansive and adaptive enough to meet extreme cases, without having that expansiveness infect day-to-day life and without throwing to the winds our aspirations to constitutionalism. In other words, it recognizes limits of various sorts on the powers of both the executive and the legislature. The reality of those limits implies that there is a role for the courts beyond what Madison himself perhaps favored. Locke and Jefferson look ultimately to the people to ratify or reject extraconstitutional action in extreme cases. In the final analysis, that must be the ultimate appeal of Madisonian constitutionalism as well. That this appeal is not empty is confirmed by the results of the 2008 U.S. presidential election. Both parties nominated candidates who turned their backs on administration policies like torture. But the ultimate appeal to the people does not imply the sort of minimal role for the courts that Judge Posner would favor. Courts are the first line of enforcement for the various constitutional limits that Madisonian constitutionalism recognizes. In checking even Congress, the courts do not necessarily counter popular will, for, as happened in the detention cases of the Bush years, the courts are able to help focus public awareness on what policy is and where constitutional values point. The people shall be—and can be—judge, as Locke puts it, but the people's judgment tends to be crude—a hammer, not a scalpel. The courts can be much more fine-tuned in their efforts to enforce the Madisonian constitution; thus, despite Madison's own reservations about judicial review, they have a valuable role to play in a Model IV constitution. For the most part, the Supreme Court has in fact played that role well during the Bush years. Indeed, we would say that while the executive and Congress have (mostly) acted as parts of a Hamiltonian constitution, the Supreme Court has acted as a guardian of the Madisonian constitution.

Political Science, University of Notre Dame

THE LIBERAL CONSTITUTION AND FOREIGN AFFAIRS*

By Fernando R. Tesón

I. Introduction

The law of foreign relations as a constitutional discipline in the United States has grown considerably in recent years.[1] While people have debated the meaning of the American Constitution's foreign-relations clauses since the beginning of the Republic, in recent years scholars, judges, and politicians have increasingly clashed over what the Constitution says. The acrimonious contenders are the internationalists and the exceptionalists.[2] Internationalists would like to see the Constitution adapt to the evolving strictures of international law and politics. They generally favor three policies: a robust incorporation of international norms into the American constitutional system;[3] more congressional and judicial control of the president's conduct of foreign policy;[4] and a limited role for federalism and the states in international affairs.[5] Exceptionalists claim either that the original understanding of the U.S. Constitution does not sit well with the internationalist view, or that the United States should follow its own course free of most international constraints, or both. To them, international norms may not be entirely compatible with the Constitution or the values and interests of the United States. According to exceptionalists, constitutional interpretation should reflect those differences. They

* I thank Ellen Frankel Paul for her excellent editorial comments.

[1] For a survey of the voluminous literature, see Curtis Bradley and Jack Goldsmith, *Foreign Relations Law: Cases and Materials*, 3rd ed. (New York: Aspen Publishers, 2009).

[2] Internationalists include almost all of the practitioners in the field until recently. See esp. Louis Henkin, *Foreign Affairs and the Constitution* (Oxford: Oxford University Press, 1996); Harold Koh, *The National Security Constitution: Sharing Power after the Iran-Contra Affair* (New Haven, CT: Yale University Press, 1990); and Peter J. Spiro, "The New Sovereigntists: American Exceptionalism and Its False Prophets," *Foreign Affairs* 79, no. 6 (2000): 9. The exceptionalist position can be found in the following works: Curtis A. Bradley and Jack Goldsmith, "Customary International Law as Federal Common Law: A Critique of the Modern Position," *Harvard Law Review* 110 (1997): 815; Curtis Bradley, "A New American Foreign Affairs Law?" *University of Colorado Law Review* 70 (1999): 1089; Saikrishna B. Prakash and Michael D. Ramsey, "The President's Power over Foreign Affairs," *Yale Law Journal* 111 (2001): 231; and John C. Yoo, "Globalism and the Constitution: Treaties, Non-Self-Execution, and the Original Understanding," *Columbia Law Review* 99 (1999): 1955. Needless to say, there are differences within each group.

[3] See, e.g., Gerald D. Neuman, "The Uses of International Law in Constitutional Interpretation," *American Journal of International Law* 98 (2004): 82.

[4] See, e.g., Michael Van Alstine, "Executive Aggrandizement in Foreign Affairs Lawmaking," *UCLA Law Review* 54 (2006): 309.

[5] See, e.g., Edward T. Swaine, "Negotiating Federalism: State Bargaining and the Dormant Treaty Power," *Duke Law Journal* 49 (2000): 1127.

generally favor policies that are the opposite of those favored by internationalists: limited foreign influence on the American constitutional system;[6] a strong role for the executive in the conduct of foreign policy and
a correspondingly limited role for Congress and the courts;[7] and a revival
of principles of federalism in foreign affairs.[8] As the newcomers to the
foreign policy scene, exceptionalists have challenged the internationalist
orthodoxy that dominated the discipline since the end of the Second
World War.

The contenders in this debate appeal to constitutional text, history, and
structure.[9] For the exceptionalists, the drafters of the U.S. Constitution
were weary of foreign entanglements and set up rules that reflected that
concern. Constitutional interpreters should respect that understanding.
On the exceptionalist view, the preeminence of the executive in foreign
affairs is supported by a combination of historical, textual, and functional
arguments. People at the time widely agreed that the executive was supposed to be in charge of foreign relations, and that is why the Constitution
remained silent on many of those issues. Functional reasons—reasons of
coordination—suggest that the executive must control foreign policy: deliberative bodies are too slow and cumbersome to manage decisions on war
and peace. Internationalists challenge these views on several grounds. To
them, text and history are not as clear as the exceptionalists claim. The
Founders were by and large neophytes in foreign policy, and, in part for
that reason, they expected the gaps in the constitutional text to be resolved
through custom.[10] And with respect to constitutional structure, the internationalists dispute the view that an all-powerful executive better serves
the foreign policy needs of the Republic. To them, the need to curb an
imperial president is as important as the need to have optimal coordination, at least in the long run.

I propose a fresh approach to this foreign policy debate. For the most
part, I will set aside the arguments from text, history, and structure,
and ask a more abstract question: How should one *ideally* design the
foreign-relations clauses of a liberal constitution? Given liberal values
and what we know about the world, what *should* the constitution say
about the conduct of foreign relations? The question is not merely aca-

[6] See Roger P. Alford, "Misusing International Sources to Interpret the Constitution,"
American Journal of International Law 98 (2004): 57.

[7] For a defense of executive power, see Michael D. Ramsey, *The Constitution's Text in Foreign Affairs* (Cambridge, MA: Harvard University Press, 2007), 49–131. There are unexplained
tensions within these views: For the exceptionalists, promoting a greater role for the states is
at odds with strong presidential powers. Conversely, for the internationalists, opposing a
greater role for the states seems at odds with their desire to curb an "imperial" presidency.

[8] See, e.g., Jack Goldsmith, "Statutory Foreign Affairs Preemption," *Supreme Court Review*
(2001): 175.

[9] For a summary of these arguments, see Martin S. Flaherty, "Case Studies in Conservative and Progressive Legal Orders: The Future and Past of U.S. Foreign Relations Law,"
Law and Contemporary Problems 67 (2004): 169.

[10] See ibid.

demic, for several reasons. A number of new nations have emerged in the last twenty years or so, some of which purport to embody liberal values. Fresh institutional design is obviously called for in their case, since their emergence is a clean break with their (usually) illiberal traditions. Moreover, focusing on ideal theory may help us to interpret the U.S. Constitution in a philosophically sound way, and to perceive more clearly the differences between what we have and what would be optimal. Last but not least, ideal design has a liberating effect because it steers constitutional debate away from original intent and actual constitutional practice—in particular, judicial precedent. We are forced to think about what the Constitution would look like if it were possible for us to ignore two hundred years of constitutional practice. I hasten to say that I do not mean to imply that standard constitutional arguments are unimportant or irrelevant. On the contrary, a plausible theory of law should give pride of place to such arguments. Yet the goal of this essay is different. I am not interested in the correct interpretation of the foreign-affairs clauses of the U.S. Constitution as a matter of law. Rather, my goal is to imagine what an ideal liberal constitution *should* do with respect to foreign affairs. Put differently: I will assess the claims of internationalists, exceptionalists, and others, not in terms of constitutional history, text, or structure, as they do, but in terms of political theory and social science. Hopefully I will show that philosophy and social science have something to say about the appropriate foreign policy arrangements for a liberal republic. Having said that, I will often refer to the foreign-relations clauses of the United States Constitution for expository convenience.

I argue that a liberal constitution must enable the republic to implement a morally defensible foreign policy in the light of available knowledge. In Section II, I examine the implications of the first pillar of a liberal foreign policy: the defense of liberty. I claim that the defense of liberty indicates not only national self-defense—defense of persons, territory, and institutions—but also, with due caution, the promotion of liberty abroad. Section III argues that a liberal foreign policy should enable people to pursue prosperity. To that end, the liberal constitution must foster free trade at home and abroad. In Section IV, I apply these principles to institutional design. I argue first that the liberal constitution's war provisions must facilitate the defense of liberty by securing combat readiness above all. This requires a flexible executive to respond promptly to threats. However, in line with most theorists, I recommend a democratic check on war whenever possible. I then address the question of the incorporation of international law into domestic law. I suggest that the approval of treaties should follow the same procedure used for domestic lawmaking, and recommend that treaties be generally self-executing. I then discuss customary law in detail. I propose a test to determine the quality of customary law that, in my view, can make that law eligible for use in domestic courts. I conclude Section IV by proposing that, in the light of well-known pathologies in the political process, the liberal constitution ought to prohibit the government from erecting protectionist barriers. In Section V, I propose some concrete constitutional clauses. Section VI sets forth some conclusions.

II. The Foreign Policy of a Liberal Republic: Liberty

A. What is a liberal constitution?

In this essay, I argue that a constitution should enable the government of a liberal state to defend its society and institutions—to defend the freedom of its people. This argument assumes that the justified constitution is the liberal constitution, that is, the set of basic rules that define the workings of a liberal society. This assumption, in turn, requires that I clarify what I understand by a liberal state. My definition here is simple and quite unsophisticated: a liberal state is a state that has two features. First, it protects individual freedom in the form of a bill of rights or similar legal device, conjoined with an effective (and not just rhetorical) institutional commitment to the rule of law and an independent judiciary. Second, it is ruled by democratically elected leaders who rotate periodically. To anticipate obvious objections, I hasten to say that the first feature is by far the most important. The second condition (the democratic credentials of the government) cannot alone rescue a society from tyranny, as the experiences in Nazi Germany and present-day Venezuela show. But the condition is still important for a number of reasons that have been amply discussed in the literature. In foreign affairs, the government is supposed to *represent* the people, and universal adult suffrage seems to be the least imperfect tool to establish that representation.

Someone may contest my assumption that the liberal constitution is the *only* justified constitution. For example, John Rawls has argued that the world contains regimes that, while illiberal, can still be seen as justified: they are "decent." [11] If so, I may be unduly biased in my analysis. If there is more than one justified constitution, then the analysis of the optimal foreign-relations clauses should reflect that diversity of (justified) regimes. For reasons I have presented elsewhere,[12] I disagree with Rawls—I do claim that the liberal constitution is the only one that can be justified philosophically—but here I do not need to substantiate that position. For Rawls's problem was different from the problem I tackle here. Rawls was concerned with devising a system of *international law* that would take account of the many inconsistent yet reasonable *existing* political and

---

[11] See John Rawls, *The Law of Peoples* (Cambridge, MA: Harvard University Press, 1999), 59–78.

[12] See Fernando R. Tesón, *A Philosophy of International Law* (Boulder, CO: Westview Press, 1998), 105–22.

religious systems of belief around the world. He would accept illiberal regimes (as long as they were not *tyrannical*) for the purpose of peaceful coexistence, as it were. For Rawls, if illiberal regimes are not tyrannical, liberal governments should treat them as members in good standing of the international community.

My goal is different. I am not trying to propose the best system of international law given the diversity of comprehensive conceptions of the good upheld by nations in the world (although, as I said, I have rejected Rawls's proposal). I am instead trying to imagine what the foreign-relations clauses of a *liberal constitution* should look like. This does not prejudge the *international* status of the many illiberal states in the world, nor does it prejudge what the foreign-relation clauses of an illiberal state should look like. I assume the moral superiority of the liberal constitution for all the standard reasons given by political philosophers, yet I need not assume that a system of international law (which I am not discussing here) should or should not welcome illiberal regimes.

B. Defense of liberty

An ideal constitution should enable the government to implement a morally justified foreign policy. Thus, I reject the view, anticipated by John Locke and sometimes endorsed by others, that while it is appropriate for constitutions to establish limits on governmental power *domestically*, foreign policy should largely be left to the government's (usually the executive's) unrestrained discretion.[13] There are a number of reasons for rejecting this view. First, establishing constitutional restraints on the government's conduct of foreign affairs does not mean depriving the government of the resources to confront foreign threats. Second, in a globalized world it makes sense to design institutions so that the citizens of the liberal state will see their rights protected, not only by their government's internal actions, but by its external actions as well.[14] If the main reason to have a constitution is to limit the power of government so that our rights will be protected, there is no reason to exempt foreign policy from this stricture. Finally, foreigners have rights too. They possess these rights by being persons. In this sense, basic human rights are not dependent on tradition and culture, and even less on citizenship. Rights come with personhood and are in this sense natural rights; in addition, they have

[13] Locke writes: "[W]hat is to be done in reference to foreigners, depending much upon their actions, and the variations of designs and interests, must be left in great part to the prudence of those who have this power committed to them, to be managed by the best of their skill, for the advantage of the Commonwealth." John Locke, *Two Treatises of Civil Government* (1690), ed. Peter Laslett (Cambridge: Cambridge University Press, 1960), *Second Treatise*, chapter 12, sec. 147.

[14] See Ernst-Ulrich Petersmann, "National Constitutions, Foreign Trade Policy, and European Community Law," *European Journal of International Law* 3 (1992): 1–3.

been partially embodied in international law.[15] The liberal constitution ought not to allow the violation of the basic human rights of foreigners (with some exceptions in cases of urgent threats to domestic liberty).

A precautionary warning is in order: A constitution cannot contemplate everything that might arise in the diplomatic arena. A solution that may seem justified in the abstract may not look so good once non-ideal conditions are specified. Institutional design must be consistent with what we know about the world and must take into account the incentives that constitutional norms create for domestic and foreign actors. So philosophy here is not pure critical philosophy: it is philosophy coupled with the best empirical theories and knowledge available. What's more, constitutional designers should realize that second-best solutions may be all that is possible in an imperfect world, especially because, hard as institutional designers may try, they cannot control future behavior—in particular, the future behavior of foreign governments and their citizens.

With this caveat, I start by outlining the legitimate goals of foreign policy. Assuming a reasonably well-functioning liberal state and the existence of foreign enemies, foreign policy should aim at *defending* the republic. This goal, in turn, has two related aspects. The more immediate goal of the government is to physically defend its citizens' lives and property and the state's territory against foreign aggression. This is one of the *raisons d'être* of governments. Moreover, the government must defend liberal institutions against enemies bent on destroying those institutions. The war against fascism and the current war against terrorism are examples of this dual aspect of the defense of liberty. A liberal government is not pacifist: it responds to foreign aggression against its citizens, and it likewise responds to foreign attempts to undermine or destroy its liberal institutions.

Someone may object that foreign policy should aim at defending the nation, its citizens, and its territory, regardless of the quality of its institutions. Let us call this view *patriotism*. On this view, defending liberty is not as important as defending persons and property. Rulers of unfree societies also have the power to defend their people and territory against aggression, so whether the constitution is liberal or illiberal is irrelevant to this aspect of foreign policy.

I have two answers. First, this essay focuses on the ideal constitution. If one assumes, as I do, that the optimal constitution is the liberal con-

---

[15] For the argument against relativism in international law, see Fernando R. Tesón, *Humanitarian Intervention: An Inquiry into Law and Morality*, 3d ed. (Ardsley, NY: Transnational Publishers, 2005), 36–55. For a typical list of international human rights, see the International Covenant of Civil and Political Rights (1966). I am aware of the controversy surrounding just which human rights are basic or natural. I cannot pursue the matter here; suffice it to say that they include the traditional liberal rights of life, personal security, and property (the latter for reasons that will become apparent in the text). The point is that we are not entitled to "use and consume" foreigners at will (to use Kant's phrase) just because they are not members of our political community.

stitution, it follows that the foreign policy of a liberal constitution must enable government to defend the justified institutions of the liberal state, in addition to the government's obvious job of defending its citizens and territory. Determining the justified foreign policy of illiberal states—that part of the self-defense rationale which is equally applicable to liberal and illiberal states—is beyond the scope of this essay. Suffice it to say that a liberal constitution must provide for the defense of persons *and* the defense of institutions. A liberal government is morally entitled to defend the country against enemies *because* its institutions are worth defending, not because they are *its* institutions.

Second, leaving aside the fact that this is an essay about liberal constitutions, I would point out that as a general proposition patriotism is only partially correct. It is true that a dictator has the power to defend the state against an unjustified attack even if he is illegitimate and even if the state's institutions are illiberal. A dictator has caretaker responsibilities notwithstanding the fact that he does not represent anyone, because he is the only person who can *in fact* command the state's resources and thus prevent a foreign aggressor from subjugating people. However, dictators do not have a right of self-defense against actions directed at ending *their* tyranny—that is, against justified humanitarian interventions. Thus, for example, Saddam Hussein's Revolutionary Guards were not morally entitled to confront the troops liberating Iraq. This is so, even if the intervention in Iraq was objectionable on some other ground, and even if members of the Revolutionary Guard could be morally excused for bearing arms in defense of a tyrant. So dictators have a provisional right to defend persons and territory against attack, but they do not have a right to defend illiberal institutions, including their own positions of power.

The goal of defending liberty suggests the desirability (and perhaps the obligation) for a liberal republic to secure alliances with other liberal republics. The justification for this is manifold. A liberal alliance secures the gains of cooperation by virtually eliminating the dangers of war among its members. According to the "liberal peace" thesis, war is highly unlikely among liberal nations. This thesis holds that there is a robust causal link between domestic liberal institutions and international peace. It was advanced first by Immanuel Kant, and revived after the Cold War by political scientists.[16] Kant's original idea was that democracies ("republics," in Kant's parlance) are less inclined to war because in a democracy the people know they will bear its burdens. Citizens internalize the costs of war. In a dictatorship, in

---

[16] Kant's argument is set forth in Immanuel Kant, *To Perpetual Peace: A Philosophical Sketch* (1795), trans. Ted Humphrey (Indianapolis, IN: Hackett, 1983). Leading modern proponents include Michael Doyle, "Kant, Liberal Legacies, and Foreign Affairs, Part 1," *Philosophy and Public Affairs* 12 (1983): 205–35; John M. Owen, "How Liberalism Produces Democratic Peace," *International Security* 19 (1994): 7–125; and Bruce Russett, *Grasping the Democratic Peace: Principles for a Post-Cold War World* (Princeton, NJ: Princeton University Press, 1993). For a rather optimistic endorsement of the theory, see Tesón, *A Philosophy of International Law*, 9–14.

contrast, the despot sends *others* to fight: his perks and riches remain largely intact.[17] He externalizes the costs of war. But history has shown that Kant's thesis is too strong, because democracies frequently go to war against nondemocracies. So "democratic peace" scholars have reformulated the Kantian thesis thus: democracies do not go to war with each other; however, they often go to war against illiberal states. And of course, illiberal states fight one another frequently. This reformulation has been dubbed the *separate* liberal peace, and it better fits the empirical evidence.[18] Democratic peace theory has provided support for the American (and perhaps European) policy of promoting liberal institutions overseas. The thesis has attracted vigorous criticism, but it is far from being refuted.[19]

Moreover, a liberal alliance is a bulwark against illiberal foreign threats. NATO was formed with this goal in mind (and not just to reap the benefits of liberal cooperation), and it served this function well during the Cold War. The nature of regimes, therefore, is important when forging alliances. Both moral and prudential reasons should incline liberal governments to create robust alliances with fellow democracies. The opposite view, that the moral credentials of allies are unimportant and that a liberal state should be free to secure alliances with whomever helps pursue that state's national interest (a view that has been historically popular, and is popular even today), is objectionable for moral and prudential reasons. Morally, freedom-loving governments should not cooperate with tyrants. Prudentially, there is always the danger that the illiberal ally will defect at crucial moments (precisely because, by definition, the tyrant is not interested in defending liberty), and that sooner or later the illiberal ally will blight the liberal values of the alliance (the Trojan Horse problem).

Finally, liberal governments have an obligation not to cooperate with tyranny.[20] By forming alliances with tyrants, liberal governments enable them to oppress their subjects. The obligation not to cooperate with tyranny is relatively weak. It does not necessarily entail a positive duty to depose the tyrant. But it does mean that a liberal regime should refrain from gestures toward the tyrant that enable him to persist in tyrannical practices. Of course, this is easier said than done. Often the liberal state has urgent security interests[21] that force it to forge provisional alliances with questionable regimes.[22] In addition, regimes are

---

[17] See Kant, *Perpetual Peace.*

[18] See Russett, *Grasping the Democratic Peace*, 30.

[19] Among the critics, see Christopher Layne, "Kant or Cant: The Myth of Democratic Peace," *International Security* 19 (1994): 5; David Spiro, "The Insignificance of the Liberal Peace," *International Security* 19 (1994): 50; and Sebastian Rosato, "The Flawed Logic of Democratic Peace Theory," *American Political Science Review* 97 (2003): 585.

[20] Here I follow Loren Lomasky, "Liberalism Beyond Borders," *Social Philosophy and Policy* 24, no. 1 (2007): 206–33.

[21] I treat the concept of "security interests" as coextensive with "defense-of-liberty interests."

[22] Two notorious examples are America's cooperation with the USSR during World War II and America's (less egregious) cooperation with Pakistan at present.

often hard to classify along this stark liberal-illiberal dichotomy. Latin America, for example, abounds in "kleptocracies": democratic governments which by-and-large respect fundamental freedoms but which prey on their citizens by stealing from them. These regimes perpetuate the subordination of the citizen to the government and prevent the achievement of general prosperity—usually for the sake of the politicians' own power and enrichment. It is unclear how a well-functioning liberal republic should deal with them.[23]

Not cooperating with tyrants is the right position to take in an ideal world. However, the real world is not so simple. I indicated at the outset that in foreign relations one must sometimes settle for the second-best solution. If making an alliance with a tyrannical regime is the only or the quickest way to defeat an implacable enemy, as it was in World War II, then it is morally permissible for a liberal government (reluctantly) to do so. But notice that this position—that a liberal state may ally itself with a tyrannical state if the alliance is indispensable for the successful defense of freedom (often not only the freedom of its own citizens but the freedom of millions of others)—is very different from the standard *realpolitik* view. According to the latter, a liberal government should be free to forge alliances with tyrants *whenever* such alliances advance the liberal state's national interest. This is a much more relaxed standard than the one I accept here, and I believe it should be rejected. Alliances with tyrants should be the exception, not the rule. In normal times, the liberal state should build alliances with fellow democracies, but this requirement is relaxed when survival is at stake.

C. Promoting liberty globally

A secondary goal of liberal foreign policy is to promote liberty worldwide. This goal is surely more controversial than the first, but I believe that, properly qualified, it follows from a commitment to liberal principles. The argument starts from the premise of the equal moral worth of all persons. I do not conceive this moral equality in the strong sense that we owe the same duties of justice to all persons around the globe.[24] Rather, for purposes of this essay, I endorse a weaker form of cosmopolitanism: every human being is entitled to live under just institutions regardless of

[23] The argument for an obligation not to cooperate with tyranny only shows that it is wrong to form alliances with tyrants, but does not show that there is a positive obligation to have any allies. It does not refute isolationism. The arguments for the liberal alliance, in contrast, do challenge isolationism.

[24] In particular, the debate in the global justice literature centers on whether people in rich countries owe duties of distributive justice to people in poor countries. I do not address the question here because I do not think it is relevant to constitutional design. For contrasting views, see Thomas Nagel, "The Problems of Global Justice," *Philosophy and Public Affairs* 33 (2005): 113; Joshua Cohen and Charles Stable, "Extra Republicam Nulla Iustitia?" *Philosophy and Public Affairs* 34 (2006): 147; and A. J. Julius, "Nagel's Atlas," *Philosophy and Public Affairs* 34 (2006): 176.

history and tradition.[25] This means that every person has basic rights
against others, and especially against the government. As I indicated
earlier, by "basic rights" I mean the traditional rights recognized by classical liberalism: rights to life, security, speech, property, and the like.[26] If
this assumption is accepted, liberal governments have a conditional duty
to promote liberty globally.

One needs to tread with care, however (which is why I use the word
"conditional"). A main objection to my suggestion that the liberal state
has a (conditional) duty to promote liberty globally is that a liberal society
is the result of consent in some form or other, the outcome of a social
contract.[27] The social contract determines the governing principles of a
liberal society and empowers the government to protect and implement
those principles, and (perhaps) to solve genuine market failures that
unrestricted voluntary relations may yield. Like all contracts, the social
contract binds only the parties, and the government's fiduciary duty is to
protect and implement liberty for its own citizens. On this view, a liberal
government has no business promoting the freedoms of persons who are
not parties to the contract. It must devote its energies and resources to its
domestic mission. Notice that this view (call it "contractarian") is stronger
than it seems at first blush. It coheres with the cosmopolitan assumption
of the equal worth of all human beings. Contractarians may agree that
every human being is entitled to liberty, but will point out that it is
someone else's duty to secure it. A foreigner is entitled to liberty, but the
obligated party is his own government. Moreover, the contractarian view
sits well with the liberal commitment to limited government. A government has no independent moral standing; it is a mere agent of the people.
Just as I expect my lawyer to defend me and not go around implementing
justice for everyone, so we expect our government to promote our freedom and not go around promoting the freedom of others to whom it has
no fiduciary obligations.

Contractarianism is certainly appealing and correct as far as it goes.
However, not all our moral obligations flow from the social contract. This
is a foundational issue in moral philosophy, and I cannot address it fully
here. But I will say this much. In addition to contractual obligations, we
sometimes may have obligations that stem from the role or position we

---

[25] See Allen Buchanan, *Justice, Legitimacy, and Self-Determination: Moral Foundations for
International Law* (Oxford: Oxford University Press, 2004), 73–111.

[26] I am aware that the universality of property rights is controversial these days. I specify
below why liberal constitutions must protect such rights.

[27] Perhaps in Edmund Burke's sense: "Society is indeed a contract. . . . It is a partnership
in all science; a partnership in all art; a partnership in every virtue, and in all perfection. As
the ends of such a partnership cannot be obtained in many generations, it becomes a
partnership not only between those who are living, but between those who are living, those
who are dead, and those who are to be born." Edmund Burke, *Reflections on the Revolution
in France*, in *Select Works of Edmund Burke* (Indianapolis, IN: Liberty Fund, 1999), vol. 2, para.
307; available online at http://oll.libertyfund.org/title/656/20374/1373287.

find ourselves in. If my assumption that all individuals around the globe have a right to live under just institutions is true, then I have an obligation (within reason, and conditioned on cost and on the fulfillment of other more pressing obligations) to make my small contribution to realizing that goal. Because isolated individuals cannot (or can hardly) act effectively in this regard, a liberal government seems to be a logical tool to help in the realization of universal freedom. This is true for both big and small governments. In other words, citizens in a liberal state delegate to their liberal government the responsibility to help achieve a more just world, to do the right thing internationally (with due caution and within the limits of the fiduciary relationship). In some extreme situations, one could also argue that the liberal government, which alone commands the resources of the state, has an obligation to stop genocide in a neighboring country, even if there is no evidence that the citizenry may have delegated such a power. This would be an obligation generated by the government's role, not by delegation: the government is the only entity in a position to stop the genocide.

Yet contractarian concerns are powerful enough to refute strong cosmopolitanism. The contractarian argument successfully blocks the view that we owe all persons around the globe the same duties and that there is no moral difference between compatriots and foreigners. It would be unacceptable, for example, to promote the freedom of foreigners at the expense of domestic freedom. However, I do not think the contractarian argument blocks the weaker cosmopolitan approach I endorse here. In most cases, my weak cosmopolitan approach is compatible with the contractarian conception of government, because the duty to promote liberty globally is a secondary duty. It takes a back seat to our duty, and the government's fiduciary duty, to defend liberty at home.

Here we may distinguish three scenarios. The first occurs when liberty at home is endangered. In that case, the liberal government has a quasi-absolute duty to protect liberty at home and defend it against foreign threats, even if doing so threatens the rights or interests of foreigners.[28] In this case, national defense—concern for the state's own citizens—displaces most (but not all)[29] concern for foreigners.

The second scenario arises when liberty at home is secure, yet many people abroad are unfree. In that case, the liberal government, I suggest, has a duty to help those persons, provided that the expenditure of resources and the costs to its own citizens are acceptable. Thus, for example, a liberal government may have the obligation to strengthen international institutions that will address the dire situation in Darfur, but perhaps it may not permissibly use military force to liberate the people there if the

---

[28] I say "quasi-absolute" to leave open the possibility that there may be actions that the government is morally prohibited from taking against foreigners under any circumstances.

[29] Even here, the liberal state may not commit war crimes in repelling the aggressor.

cost of doing so is prohibitive. Promoting liberty abroad is a conditional duty. It is subject to the primacy of the government's first duty, to defend liberty, and it is conditioned on cost. Under normal circumstances,[30] liberal governments will discharge their obligation to promote liberty globally by diplomatic and other measures in support of liberal constitutions abroad and liberty-friendly international institutions.

The third scenario arises when domestic liberty is secured and the liberal government attempts to advance, internationally, the interests of its citizens. Surely it can do so, even if the action does not improve the liberty of foreigners. Advancing the interests of its citizens is, of course, a major permissible goal of government. This the liberal state normally does through international competition for resources: competitive harm to foreigners does not give rise to legitimate grievances. But suppose that actions taken in the national interest significantly undermine the freedom of foreigners. Imagine that a liberal government wants to import good, inexpensive coffee in order to improve the welfare of its coffee-loving citizenry. This requires securing arrangements with an oppressive regime that enslaves its own people to produce cheap coffee. While the welfare of the citizens in the liberal state improves, I think the arrangement is morally impermissible. A liberal government should not enable a tyrant and contribute to the oppression of his subjects merely to increase the welfare of its population. This is a corollary of the general obligation not to cooperate with tyranny mentioned above. This may be a genuine difference between the contractarian approach and the cosmopolitan approach suggested in this essay. Contractarians are right that liberal governments should not try to remedy every wrong in the world, but cosmopolitans are right that a liberal government should not cooperate in the violation of the liberty of others unless this is necessary to protect its citizens and institutions against aggression.

Here, as elsewhere, it is crucial to be attentive to consequences and incentives. The duty to promote global freedom should not be discharged using counterproductive foreign policy tools. All too often, liberal governments understand their global mission in symbolic terms. Those in government are politicians, and foreign policy rhetoric suffers from the well-known pathologies of political rhetoric. Government officials will often *say* things that will advance their electoral goals even if *doing* those things would be ineffectual or counterproductive. Yet symbolic behavior and cheap talk are not good substitutes for actual results. Consider economic sanctions. It is an entirely empirical matter whether or not an economic boycott will promote liberty in the target country or elsewhere. For the politician interested in electoral success, however, it is important to *appear* to be doing the right thing. For example, when the U.S. president

---

[30] The exception to this is military humanitarian intervention, which I think is warranted in some cases. See Tesón, *Humanitarian Intervention*.

imposes an embargo on a dictatorial regime, he appears to be "tough" on the regime, even if, as an empirical matter, the embargo *worsens* the situation of the regime's victims.[31]

D. The defense of liberty must not be self-defeating

Because the paramount foreign policy goal of a liberal republic is the defense of liberty, a liberal government may not defend liberty against foreign aggression in a way that destroys or seriously impairs the very liberty that it aims to preserve. This means that restrictions on *domestic* liberty are justified only for the sake of preserving liberty itself. This may sound obvious; however, the issue has been obscured by recent debates in connection with the war against terrorism. Many people have posed a dichotomy between liberty and security, thus suggesting that these are different, competing values. An increase in security may lead to a decrease in liberty and vice versa, so the solution, it is thought, is to strike the right balance between these competing values. As I have argued elsewhere, this dichotomy is misleading.[32] The security measures in a liberal republic must themselves be liberty-enhancing. The purpose of increased security measures (such as wiretapping) can only be the protection of our liberty and liberal institutions. It follows that restrictions on liberty that do not make liberty more secure are unjustified. To be sure, we sometimes cannot tell whether a particular security measure is or is not justified as a liberty-enhancing measure. Is the suspension of *habeas corpus* for Guantanamo detainees justified? Does it really help the government prevent future terrorist attacks? Or are losses of liberty and losses of faith in institutions too great to justify the intelligence gains? The answers to these questions depend entirely on the facts.[33] From the standpoint of principle, whether or not a particular measure meets the test depends on whether or not there are absolute moral restraints on government action, regardless of consequences. For example, all liberals will quickly agree that the liberal state must *never* torture prisoners, including war enemies.[34] Yet even here people disagree about what torture is, not to mention the possibility that in extreme situations, as moral philosophers well know, the absolute prohibition may break down. (For example, is torture prohibited even if not torturing a prisoner will bring

---

[31] The Cuban embargo may be an example of this.

[32] See Fernando R. Tesón, "Liberal Security," in Richard Wilson, ed., *Human Rights in the 'War on Terror'* (Cambridge: Cambridge University Press, 2005), 57–77.

[33] Thus, if I had to guess, I would say that the procedures established after 9/11 to deal with detainees have not met the test. It does not seem to me that the gains in liberty obtained by these procedures have justified the loss of global prestige and standing by the United States (factors which also enhance liberty in the long run). But this is a guess: I lack the information to assert this confidently.

[34] As provided in the pertinent international instruments. See, e.g., U.N. Convention Against Torture and Other Cruel, Inhuman, and Degrading Treatment or Punishment (1975), http://www.hrweb.org/legal/cat.html.

about total annihilation?)[35] So the initial "never" turns out to be not so emphatic. I do not think the disciplines of law or philosophy have an answer for this, and I don't have one either. Perhaps all we can say is that the liberal constitution should not authorize torture, ever, and that whatever departures may occur in times of supreme emergency belong to the realm of moral necessity (or moral tragedy), not the realm of law. Torture, in other words, can never be *legally* protected. Be that as it may, my point is conceptual: security is *liberal* security. Only the need to protect liberty justifies restrictions on liberty. If those restrictions reduce liberty overall, then they are impermissible.

III. The Foreign Policy of a Liberal Republic: Prosperity

Another legitimate goal of a liberal foreign policy should be to enable citizens to seek material prosperity. This means that constitutions should have the tools to enable market agents to engage in voluntary transactions for mutual benefit and thus prosper. Domestic economic policy is centrally important here. A liberal constitution should protect robust rights of property and freedom of contract mainly (though not only) for empirical reasons: property rights and freedom of contract are the engine of material prosperity. Reliable economic research shows a strong correlation between robust property rights and the absence of poverty. Conversely, nations where property and contract are unprotected are much more likely to be poor. The ideal constitution must be consistent with these findings and must establish strong protections for property rights and freedom of contract.[36]

In foreign affairs, this means that the constitution must facilitate free trade. The law of comparative advantage is the most reliable analytical tool to ascertain the effects of trade. While not a sufficient condition for material prosperity, free trade is likely to be a necessary condition. Thus, constitutional rules must enable the government to open domestic markets and promote the opening of foreign markets. In particular, constitutional norms should prevent special interest groups from using the political process for protectionist rent-seeking. Each economic agent has an incentive to capture the power of government to shield him

---

[35] See the discussions in Alan Dershowitz, *Why Terrorism Works: Understanding the Threat, Responding to the Challenge* (New Haven, CT: Yale University Press, 2002), 142–62, 250–54; and Jeremy Waldron, "Torture and Positive Law: Jurisprudence for the White House," *Columbia Law Review* 105 (2005): 1681.

[36] The economic literature on the importance of market-friendly institutions for economic development is extensive. See, e.g., Douglass C. North, *Institutions, Institutional Change, and Economic Performance* (Cambridge: Cambridge University Press, 1990); Hernando De Soto, *The Other Path: The Invisible Revolution in the Third World* (New York: Harper and Row, 1989), esp. chap. 5; and Daron Acemoglu, Simon Johnson, and James Robinson, "The Colonial Origins of Comparative Development: An Empirical Investigation," *American Economic Review* 91 (2001): 1369–1401.

from competition, foreign or domestic.[37] This political pathology impairs prosperity in the name of (at best) false mercantilist assumptions.[38] It follows that the conventional view that constitutions should be neutral with respect to economic policy is mistaken.[39] Sound economics shows that a market-friendly economic policy is necessary for the prosperity of the citizens in a liberal democracy. Just as the constitution should protect citizens against government abuses by having a robust bill of rights, so should the constitution protect citizens against this other form of governmental abuse: the capture of the government by special interests seeking a shield against competition. Protectionist policies demonstrably harm domestic consumers, that is, the citizens of the state at large. The constitution should protect consumers because their organizational costs are too high, and thus they are likely to lose systematically in the political process.

My approach avoids the American debate about whether economic policy should abide by the classical-liberal beliefs of the Framers of the Constitution—the so-called *Lochner* debate.[40] Classical-liberal constitutional writers emphasize the fact that the United States was founded in accordance with classical-liberal convictions—most notably, commitments to strong property rights and freedom of contract. In their view, the modern administrative state violates this original intent.[41] Supporters of economic regulation either contest this historical account or claim that it is irrelevant in modern times. I do not pass judgment on the strength of the historical argument. My view here is simpler and (I would hope) less controversial. As such, it should be able to persuade those who deny or eschew original intent, as long as they are sensitive to empirical arguments: a liberal constitution should protect economic liberties *because* reliable economic theory and empirical studies show that economic lib-

[37] See Gene Grossman and Elhanan Helpman, "Protection for Sale," *American Economic Review* 84, no. 4 (1994): 833–50.

[38] Mercantilism views trade as a zero-sum game: one country's gains come at the expense of other countries. This view rests on the false assumption that a surplus in international trade must be a deficit for other countries. In fact, national well-being is based on present and future increased consumption. The importance of exports is only indirect: they provide the income to buy products to consume. As Thomas Pugel and Peter Lindert write: "[I]mports are part of the expanding national consumption that a nation seeks, not an evil to be suppressed." Thomas Pugel and Peter Lindert, *International Economics*, 11th ed. (New York: Irwin-McGraw-Hill, 1999), 33.

[39] The view that the U.S. Constitution should be neutral toward economic policy was stated by Justice Oliver Wendell Holmes in his famous dissent in the *Lochner* case, and endorsed ever since by courts and most commentators. See *Lochner v. New York*, 198 U.S. 45 (1905). I discuss *Lochner* more fully below; see notes 40 and 86.

[40] On the *Lochner* debate, see, e.g., Symposium: *Lochner* Centennial Conference, *Boston University Law Review* 85 (2005). For a vindication of *Lochner*, see David Bernstein, *Only One Place of Redress: African Americans, Labor Regulations, and the Courts from Reconstruction to the New Deal* (Durham, NC: Duke University Press, 2001).

[41] See Richard Epstein, *How Progressives Rewrote the Constitution* (Washington, DC: Cato Institute, 2007); and Randy Barnett, *Restoring the Lost Constitution: The Presumption of Liberty* (Princeton, NJ: Princeton University Press, 2005).

erties are conducive to prosperity. The evidence on this is overwhelming.[42] Thus, someone who does not care for original intent, yet believes that economic prosperity and the reduction of poverty are worthy goals,[43] and honestly pays attention to plausible empirical facts and theories, should be sympathetic to my argument. If she is not, she has the burden of challenging the empirical theories on which my argument rests. Moreover, originalism applies by definition to a historical, actual constitution. In this essay, I am concerned instead with constitutional *design*, that is, with writing a constitution from scratch, given liberal values and what we know about the world.

IV. From Principles to Constitutional Norms:
The Law of Foreign Relations

A. War powers

Assuming, then, that the defense of liberty and the promotion of prosperity are the proper goals of foreign policy, what are the consequences for the foreign-relations provisions of the liberal constitution? Given the priority of defending liberty, the constitutional norms of foreign relations should facilitate combat readiness while remaining consistent with basic liberal political principles. The standard position in American constitutional law is that Congress authorizes war, while the president conducts war.[44] Article I, section 8 of the U.S. Constitution empowers Congress to authorize war,[45] while Article II, section 2 empowers the president, as commander-in-chief, to conduct war. According to conventional doctrine, this commander-in-chief power comprises both

---

[42] See the works cited in note 36. I believe property rights are supported by moral considerations as well. For a Kantian argument to that effect, see B. Sharon Byrd and Joachim Hruschka, "The Natural Law Duty to Recognize Private Property Ownership: Kant's Theory of Property in His *Doctrine of Right*," *University of Toronto Law Journal* 56 (2006): 217.

[43] For a full development of the argument that free trade helps the poor, and a rejection of putative moral arguments opposing free trade, see Fernando R. Tesón and Jonathan Klick, "Global Justice and Trade," in *Distributive Justice and International Economic Law*, ed. C. Carmody, F. Garcia, and J. Linarelli (Cambridge: Cambridge University Press, forthcoming).

[44] The relevant provisions of the U.S. Constitution are Article I, section 8: "The Congress shall have the power . . . to declare war"; and Article II, section 2: "The President shall be Commander in Chief of the Army and Navy of the United States. . . ." Not every constitution establishes congressional-presidential war powers. In other liberal constitutions, the president both declares and conducts war. Examples of nations with exclusive executive war powers are the United Kingdom, Sweden, and Belgium. See EurActiv, "On A European War Powers Act," http://www.euractiv.com/en/security/european-war-powers-act/article. See also article 15 of the French Constitution.

[45] In U.S. constitutional law, the role of Congress has evolved from the power to *declare* war into the power to *authorize* war. See generally John Hart Ely, *War and Responsibility: Constitutional Lessons from Vietnam and Its Aftermath* (Princeton, NJ: Princeton University Press, 1993), 3-10; and Curtis Bradley and Jack Goldsmith, "Congressional Authorization and the War on Terrorism," *Harvard Law Review* 118 (2005): 2047.

the power to *direct* the conduct of war and to *repel* sudden attacks.[46]
There is considerable scholarly controversy on a number of points. First,
short of an official declaration of war, it is uncertain what actions undertaken by Congress constitute an authorization of war. Second, it is
unclear whether military commitments short of war require congressional authorization. Third, the line between the *initiation* of military action
and the *direction* of military action is blurred. Finally, it is uncertain
whether or not the use of military force to defend an ally who is
attacked requires congressional authorization. Here practical reasons of
combat readiness are crucial. It stands to reason that the ideal constitution should facilitate the effective use of force, one that is optimally
likely to lead to military success. But the constitution cannot decide in
advance the *merits* of any particular military commitment. All it can do
is to establish a process by which the government can effectively implement a morally justified foreign policy. Thus, if defending an ally is
justified under the defense-of-liberty rationale, the constitution should
make that military commitment easier, not harder. If the suddenness of
the attack (e.g., against the U.S. or an ally) requires immediate response,
then the executive branch should be able to act on its own.

Nonetheless, in cases where there is time for deliberation, there are
powerful reasons to require the participation of the people's elected
representatives. It may be thought that this concurrent war power can
be inferred from the general doctrine of separation of powers, an essential component of the liberal constitution. In the oft-quoted words of
Montesquieu: "When the legislative and executive powers are united in
the same person, or in the same body of magistrates, there can be no
liberty; because apprehensions may arise, lest the same monarch or
senate should enact tyrannical laws, to execute them in a tyrannical
manner."[47] The justification for the separation of powers into distinct
branches, then, is to maximize liberty by having the person who makes
the law be someone other than the person who executes the law. But
does this justification carry over to war? Authorizing war is not *exactly*
like legislating, and making war is not *exactly* like executing the law. In
spite of this asymmetry, I think that Montesquieu's point applies to
war as well: A tyrannical prince may declare an unjust war and then
wage it in an immoral manner. Moreover, the liberal constitution must
restraint a president who might lead the nation to war for his own
political gain and self-aggrandizement. This adventurism is more likely
to occur if there is no legislative control over the decision to wage war.
The usual checks-and-balances rationale for the separation of powers
applies to war as well, provided the constitution establishes a mecha-

---

[46] See the *Prize* cases, 67 U.S. 635 (1863).
[47] Baron de Montesquieu, *The Spirit of the Laws* (1748) (Amherst, NY: Prometheus, 2002),
151–52.

nism to respond to threats when there is no time for deliberation.[48] As Immanuel Kant suggested, the people should decide whether or not they want to incur the costs of war,[49] and this is best achieved by placing the decision with the legislature rather than with the executive. To be sure, legislatures will often make mistakes, but the democratic process, imperfect and flawed as it is, is preferable to the unilateral decision of the president. Finally, a successful war requires popular support, as Americans well know, so congressional approval (assuming, again, that events allow the time to seek it) will not only lend legitimacy to the war effort, but will also enhance the chances of victory.

The paramount goal of the constitutional regulation of war and the armed forces, then, is the defense of liberty. This means that this goal takes precedence over other worthy goals. For example, on this view, whether gays or females are allowed in combat is *entirely* a function of combat readiness. If allowing gays or females in combat enhances combat readiness, then they should be allowed. If not, they should not. To use the armed forces as an arena for equality of treatment in disregard of combat readiness is a serious mistake, as it may lead to military defeat. Conversely, excluding gays or females from combat purely on the basis of prejudice without any attention to combat readiness is irrational and dangerous. The point here is that the proper balance of constitutional considerations should be tipped in favor of military efficiency *because* in these urgent situations only military efficiency serves liberty well. Once we shift our attention back to civilian life, the standard equal-protection principles will reemerge. The ideal constitution, therefore, should be designed to facilitate combat readiness as a priority over other goals, assuming of course that basic liberties are not undermined.[50]

[48] The importance of having concurrent war powers may be shown by the case of Imperial Germany's entry into World War I. Even though the Reichstag had broad *domestic* legislative powers, the Emperor was in complete control of foreign policy decisions, including the decision to go to war. See Doyle, "Kant, Liberal Legacies, and Foreign Affairs," 216–17, note 8.

[49] See Kant, *Perpetual Peace*, and the discussion in Tesón, *A Philosophy of International Law*, 1–26.

[50] I have left out an important question here: Can the liberal constitution allow military conscription? Mainstream political theorists think so. See John Rawls, *A Theory of Justice* (Cambridge, MA: Harvard University Press, 1971), 380. Many modern states, but not all, allow conscription. See the breakdown by states at http://www.nationmaster.com/graph/mil_con-military-conscription. I am skeptical, however. The defense of the liberal state should be entrusted to those who have comparative advantages in the military profession and who voluntarily enroll in the armed forces. A possible solution is to allow the military draft only for wars of self-defense, but not for other (justified) foreign wars, such as humanitarian interventions, on the grounds that national defense is a public good notoriously vulnerable to market failure. For other justified wars, the government may only use a voluntary army. I tentatively suggest this approach in Fernando R. Tesón, "The Liberal Case for Humanitarian Intervention," in J. L. Holzgrefe and Robert O. Keohane, eds., *Humanitarian Intervention: Ethical, Legal, and Political Dilemmas* (Cambridge: Cambridge University Press, 2003), 93.

B. The status of international law in domestic law

Another lively controversy among constitutional scholars concerns the proper status of international law in domestic law. Internationalists advocate a maximal incorporation of international law into the U.S. legal system. Exceptionalists, in contrast, are much more cautious and distrust this wholesale importation of international norms into the domestic system. What should an ideal constitution do? I will discuss treaties and customary law separately, because they raise different questions. On the one hand, treaties are written documents to which governments expressly consent. For that reason, they blend more easily into the constitutional structure. Customary international law, on the other hand, is unwritten and (at least in its classical version) formed over relatively long periods of time by convergent state behavior. Given its relatively amorphous nature, customary international law blends uneasily into the constitutional structure.

1. *Who should make treaties?* Treaties are an indispensable part of diplomacy. A liberal republic needs treaties for all the obvious reasons. Not even the most rabid isolationist would deny this, and most constitutions have mechanisms to incorporate treaties into domestic law. What should the ideal constitution say about treaties? An initial question is who should be empowered to make treaties. In the United States, the president makes treaties, subject to the approval of two-thirds of the Senate.[51] It may seem that this procedure is as good as any, but on further inspection this is not so. This peculiar provision means that the treaty-makers are different from the lawmakers. The lawmakers are the two chambers of Congress and the president (including the possibility of Congress's overriding a presidential veto). The treaty-makers are instead the president and the Senate; the House of Representatives does not participate in the treaty-making process. This divergence creates an anomaly: It makes the treaty process vulnerable to the charge that it may be used to bypass the legislative process. To the extent that the lower chamber of the legislature is essential to conferring legitimacy on the law, the American treaty-making process appears somewhat defective. Moreover, it is hard to see the rationale of this provision. There is no compelling reason why an ideal constitution should have a different procedure for treaty approval. If treaties are to be the law of the land, they should be approved by a procedure similar to the one used for ordinary legislation. In that way, debate about a particular treaty will be a debate on the merits, and not a debate about whether or not the government may change domestic law through treaty. The change of domestic law through treaty, then, should be subject to the same strictures as the change of law through legislation.

2. *Should treaties be self-executing?* American constitutional practice has established a distinction between self-executing and non-self-executing

---

[51] U.S. Constitution, Article II.

treaties.[52] A self-executing treaty is one that can be invoked by private parties in court. Such a treaty is operative without the need of legislative implementation. In contrast, when a treaty is non-self-executing, private parties may not invoke it in court. Non-self-executing treaties require further legislative implementation before they can be invoked by private parties in court. The issue is important in the United States because there are a number of treaties to which the United States is a party that are not available to litigants.[53] This creates an anomaly: the United States is bound *internationally* by the treaty, but its citizens cannot use it *domestically* to enforce whatever rights the treaty may grant them. How do we know when a treaty is or is not self-executing? There are some clear cases, as when the Senate declares the treaty to be non-self-executing.[54] But when the Senate is silent, courts have had some trouble making the distinction.[55]

Fortunately, our analysis here need not be embroiled in this characteristically American debate.[56] There is no reason why the ideal constitution should require an additional formal legislative implementation of treaties in order to make them the law of the land. In our ideal constitution, treaties are approved by both legislative chambers and thus have the same status as domestic legislation. Legislative approval of a treaty, then, *is* its implementation. As I have indicated, in the current American system the body that implements a treaty, Congress as a whole, is different from the body that approves the treaty (the Senate) and from the official who makes the treaty (the president). Thus, further implementation represents an affirmation of legislative will *beyond* the prior act of Senate approval. But if we get rid of the uniquely American method of Senate approval, the issue of self-execution becomes much less important: when Congress approves a treaty, it normally implements it. Now, although I have said that the issue of self-execution becomes less important with the procedure I have proposed, the issue is not dead. For, in my proposed system, the legislature, when approving a treaty, may decide (for whatever reason) that it should not be self-executing. That is, the legislature may want the treaty to bind the state internationally, yet may not want the treaty to be used by private litigants in domestic courts. (The legislature may not want to create a "cause of action," as lawyers say.) And finally, some

---

[52] See the recent decision in *Medellin v. Texas*, 128 S. Ct. 1346 (2008) (holding, *inter alia*, that the president cannot unilaterally implement a non-self-executing treaty).

[53] A prime example is the International Covenant on Civil and Political Rights (ICCPR).

[54] Examples are the ICCPR and the 1948 Genocide Convention.

[55] In comparative law, the practice is not uniform. Some states assimilate treaties automatically; others, such as the United Kingdom and the Nordic states, always require an incorporating statute; yet others fall in-between. For Europe, see Council of Europe, *Treaty Making: Expression of Consent by States to Be Bound by a Treaty* (The Hague: Kluwer, 2001), 88–96.

[56] The curious reader may compare the views of John C. Yoo, "Globalism and the Constitution: Treaties, Non-Self-Execution, and the Original Understanding," *Columbia Law Review* 99 (1999): 1955, with those of Carlos M. Vazquez, "Laughing at Treaties," *Columbia Law Review* 99 (1999): 2154.

treaties by their very nature do not lend themselves to application by courts, and in that sense they may be "naturally" non-self-executing: this may be true, for example, if the treaty, by its very terms, cannot possibly be understood to generate private rights that could be enforced in American courts. But a treaty consented to by a liberal government and approved by its legislature fulfills the condition of legitimacy required for all law-making. The treaty has been consented to by the representatives of the people, and there is no reason in principle why the treaty should not be operative as a matter of domestic law (unless the legislature expressly blocks this).[57]

There are some caveats, however. The liberal constitution prevails over any treaty.[58] Treaties may not violate the constitution. Consider human rights treaties. If the liberal government consents to a treaty that *restricts* constitutional rights, then the courts should declare the treaty provision unconstitutional. Judicial review is a proper safeguard against inappropriate "importation." For example, if a treaty obligates the liberal state to restrict speech in violation of the constitution, the courts should declare the treaty unconstitutional.[59] But there is no objection, in principle, to *expanding* liberty through treaty. Someone may object that the expansion of the freedom of some is always done at the expense of the freedom of others. Imagine, for example, that the government signs onto a treaty that establishes universal health care for all the parties to the treaty. This would surely be illegitimate, it may be argued, since the government would be bypassing the legislative process. But, again, this objection is entirely parasitic on the fact that in the United States, as we saw, the treaty-makers are the president and the Senate, to the exclusion of the House of Representatives. As I have argued, an ideal constitution establishes treaty approval by the whole legislature, so the law created by treaty would be as legitimate as a law created by legislation. This would avoid the objection we are considering. Objections to universal health care established by treaty would then be based on the merits, not on

---

[57] Again, let us keep in mind that I am considering an ideal constitution. There may be doctrinal and historical reasons to take a different view in the context of U.S. law.

[58] When the legislature incorporates a treaty into domestic law, the treaty morphs into a new rule belonging to a new legal system, even if its content remains unchanged. The reason is that a treaty in international law is not subservient to any national constitution, while in domestic law it is subservient to the national constitution. The "dualist" theory is thus correct: international law and national law are two different legal systems, even if some of their respective rules are identical. But I cannot pursue this matter here.

[59] An example may be article 20 of the International Covenant on Civil and Political Rights, which seems to obligate states to prohibit "hate" speech. When the United States ratified this treaty in 1992, it made an express reservation to this article on the grounds that it was inconsistent with the U.S. Constitution. The reservation reads: "That article 20 does not authorize or require legislation or other action by the United States that would restrict the right of free speech and association protected by the Constitution and laws of the United States." The list of U.S. reservations, understandings, and declarations to the ICCPR can be found at the University of Minnesota Human Rights Library, http://www1.umn.edu/humanrts/usdocs/civilres.htm.

considerations of process, since the process for treaty approval would be virtually the same as for legislative approval.

Of course, there is no way a liberal constitution can prevent a government from importing bad treaties, just as it cannot guarantee that the legislature will not enact bad laws. All we can hope is that the constitution will prevent the importation of *some* bad treaties and the enactment of *some* bad laws. The constitution can achieve this by establishing a robust bill of rights (including strong protection of property rights) and limits to governmental powers. In terms of importing international law, the doctrine of constitutional supremacy will hopefully block bad treaties in many cases.

3. Customary law. Customary international law is a different story. According to classical doctrine, international customary law has two components: state practice and *opinio juris*. State practice is the convergent behavior of governments over time. Repeated acts by governments that meet with acquiescence or approval by other governments may generate rules of behavior. After a certain time, the conduct in question (that is, the act performed plus the acceptance by others) may become customary law. However, not all practice ripens into law. According to traditional doctrine, state practice is a necessary but not a sufficient condition for the existence of a customary legal rule. There are certain practices that are considered merely optional, such as the rules of international etiquette. In order to distinguish nonbinding international practice from binding customary international law, lawyers have long required that, in order to be law, the practice must be accompanied by a *belief* by governments that the practice is required by law. This requirement, called *opinio juris*, has puzzled many commentators for a number of reasons, of which I shall mention only one. Must governments have *as a reason for their behavior* the belief that the behavior is required by law? This seems implausible, for governments act for all kinds of self-interested reasons—reasons of national interest—unrelated to their perception of the legal status of the act in question.[60] More plausible is the idea that at some point in the life of the practice, participants begin to insist on compliance. Practice becomes law when supported by social pressure.[61] This is a better view because it does not require that governments act on a sense of legal obligation but simply that governments publicly *articulate* the rule as a legal rule, thus insisting that all governments must comply with the rule.[62]

This is the *classical* definition of customary law, under which state practice is a necessary condition for the formation of a legal norm. Accord-

---

[60] See Jack Goldsmith and Eric Posner, *The Limits of International Law* (Oxford: Oxford University Press, 2005), 23–78.

[61] See H. L. A. Hart, *The Concept of Law* (Oxford: Oxford University Press, 1960), 91.

[62] See the seminal treatment by Anthony A. D'Amato, *The Concept of Custom in International Law* (Ithaca, NY: Cornell University Press, 1971), 73–102. My own account of customary law draws on game theory. See Tesón, *A Philosophy of International Law*, chap. 3.

ing to some scholars, however, *modern* customary law includes, in addition to the classical rules, rules derived from "soft" materials such as United Nations resolutions, provisions in unratified treaties, judicial decisions by national courts, statements made by governments at international conferences, and the writings of law professors.[63] On this view, state practice is *not* a necessary condition for the existence of a customary international rule: sometimes, depending on context, importance, and other factors, a norm may become part of international law even if it is unsupported by state practice. Typically—but not always—such norms will be supported by a wide international consensus.

Internationalists favor the incorporation of all customary law (classical and modern) into domestic law. To them, domestic courts may use customary law both to decide cases and to interpret domestic law.[64] Exceptionalists challenge this view. To them, customary law suffers from a variety of infirmities that should preclude its use by domestic courts in the absence of formal incorporation by the legislature.[65] John McGinnis and Ilya Somin have offered a forceful defense of the exceptionalist position.[66] They argue that U.S. courts should not treat "raw international law" as the law of the land. By "raw international law" they mean international law that has not been formally incorporated into domestic law by the authorities designated by the Constitution. A properly ratified treaty meets the condition of formal incorporation, because the Constitution prescribes a procedure for domestic assimilation. Likewise, Congress can enact laws implementing parts of customary law, as it did with the Torture Victim Protection Act (1992).[67] However, McGinnis and Somin argue that, aside from these cases of formal assimilation, customary international law should be kept out of domestic courts because it suffers from a crucial legitimacy deficit, which in turn causes a host of other problems. In particular, customary law, because it is unwritten, is particularly vulnerable to manipulation by advocates and other agents of special interests, such as law professors. Customary law

[63] The widely cited Article 38 of the Statute of the International Court of Justice lists as sources of international law (alongside treaty, custom, and general principles of law) "judicial decisions and the teachings of the most highly qualified publicists [i.e., international law experts] of the various nations, *as subsidiary means for the determination of rules of law*" (emphasis added). Thus, this article accepts judicial decisions and the writings of international law experts *only* as ways to determine or specify rules generated by "hard" sources, and not as independent, autonomous sources of law. Article 38, therefore, does not support the modern definition of custom. Of course, this is not dispositive.

[64] See, e.g., Louis Henkin, "International Law as Law in the United States," *Michigan Law Review* 82 (1984): 1555.

[65] The leading critics of the internationalist position with respect to custom are Bradley and Goldsmith, "Customary International Law as Federal Common Law"; and John O. McGinnis and Ilya Somin, "Should International Law Be Part of Our Law?" *Stanford Law Review* 59 (2007): 1175.

[66] McGinnis and Somin, "Should International Law Be Part of Our Law?" All further references to their views are to this article.

[67] Torture Victim Protection Act, Pub. L. No. 102-256 para. 2, 106 Stat. 73 (March 12, 1992).

is made, not by the people's representatives, but by others who do not represent the individuals against whom the law is domestically enforced. Customary law does not, therefore, satisfy a minimal pedigree condition: that the law, to be binding, must be created by the people in accordance with democratic constitutional procedures. McGinnis and Somin intend their argument to apply to the United States, but it can be generalized. The law in a liberal state is created by the people, who alone can delegate lawmaking power. To be binding, a law must not be merely *imposed* by persons who lack delegated lawmaking powers (whether they are domestic dictators or foreigners). Customary international law does not satisfy this condition; therefore, it is not binding on citizens.

The exceptionalist position is buttressed by a sobering fact: The world does not consist only of liberal states. The participation of many illiberal states in the international lawmaking process blights customary law. Not only do the lawmakers often lack proper democratic credentials, but also some customary rules are unfriendly to liberal principles.[68] Even if we think that the liberal state may have to live with some of those bad rules internationally, it would be an affront to justice for domestic courts to foist those rules on the liberal state's citizens. This is another reason—a substantive reason—to be wary of importing customary law. Customary law is always undemocratic and sometimes morally objectionable on the merits. It is procedurally and substantively deficient, and for that reason, exceptionalists argue, it should not become the law of the land.

There is much that is right about McGinnis and Somin's argument. If customary law were little more than an invention of partisan advocates and biased academics, then McGinnis and Somin's argument would be a powerful indictment of the attempt to import it into domestic law. I agree with them that much of what passes as customary law should be unmasked for what it is: manipulative advocacy. However, I think that with the appropriate guarantees, *some* rules of customary law can be imported by the courts of a liberal state in a way that assuages these authors' concerns.

I start by noting that what international lawyers present as customary law varies widely. One distinction, already anticipated, is between *classical* and *modern* customary law.[69] Classical customary law, as we saw, is supported by robust international practice. Diplomatic interaction has yielded a number of rules over a relatively long period of time. Those rules have emerged as the result of behavior aimed at solving various

---

[68] Examples, in addition to the hate speech provision mentioned above, may be the anti-market bias of many of the rules on "economic rights" and those pertaining to natural resources—if they are customary rules at all.

[69] Bradley and Goldsmith draw the distinction in *Foreign Relations Law*, 578. See also J. Patrick Kelly, "The Twilight of Customary International Law," *Virginia Journal of International Law* 40 (2000): 449.

coordination problems.[70] Once a practice has emerged, we may assume that it is irrational for participants to deviate from it. Opportunistic deviation is punished with criticism, ostracism, or stronger action. This pressure to conform characterizes *opinio juris*. Classical customary law, then, is characterized by robust interaction over relatively long periods of time, supported by pressure to conform.[71] Modern customary law, as I indicated, is characterized by the use of soft materials such as United Nations resolutions, provisions in unratified treaties, pronouncements by officials and nongovernmental organizations, and scholarly writings. Notably, the rules thus advocated lack the support of state practice. As a result, they are less certain and more vulnerable to manipulation than classical customary law. We might say that modern customary law is strong in the *opinio juris* department, but weak in the practice department. Norms of modern customary law may have strong support in the opinion of international actors, even if this support is not accompanied by a long history of practice. Some human rights norms belong to this group.[72]

McGinnis and Somin claim that neither kind of customary law should be eligible for judicial importation. To them, domestic courts should not use modern customary law because it is not supported by state practice. For that reason, and because (like any customary law) it is unwritten, it cannot be determined objectively and is especially subject to manipulation. While classical international law fares better (because it is supported by state practice), it still cannot be determined objectively because it is unwritten. As a result, law professors and others with no authority get to say what the law is. In either case, customary law suffers from a fatal legitimacy deficit, and domestic courts should not use it to determine their decisions.[73]

However, I think the classical/modern dichotomy, while helpful and accurate as far as it goes, still does not capture the diversity of what international lawyers consider customary law. I propose to classify (what international lawyers call) "customary law" into *genuine* customary law and *fake* customary law. Genuine customary law comprises two subcategories. First, genuine customary law includes classical international law as already defined: a robust practice supported by strong pressure to

---

[70] See Tesón, *A Philosophy of International Law*, 85–89.

[71] Examples are the rules of diplomatic immunity, state responsibility, treaties, and jurisdiction.

[72] For example, virtually everyone agrees that customary international law prohibits state torture and indefinite detention. Yet those rules are not supported by state practice. My own view is that the assertions that these rules are "custom" are moral assertions which, depending on one's jurisprudential preferences, may be considered as part of the law. In the text, less ambitiously, I say that such rules have been agreed upon by strong consensus.

[73] Academics are demonstrably biased to the left. See Guido Pincione and Fernando R. Tesón, *Rational Choice and Democratic Deliberation: A Theory of Discourse Failure* (Cambridge: Cambridge University Press, 2006), 53–64. For empirical evidence, see John O. McGinnis et al., "The Patterns and Implications of Political Contributions by Elite Law School Faculty," *Georgetown Law Journal* 93 (2005): 1167.

conform (*opinio juris*). Second, genuine customary law includes a *real, strong international consensus*, even if it is not supported by a robust practice.[74] This second subcategory corresponds to a genuine, nonmanipulated version of modern customary law. Genuine international law includes, then, classical international law plus those rules that have been universally agreed to by nations, that is, a subset of modern customary law.

Fake customary law, in contrast, consists of those putative rules that are put forth by international lawyers and others but lack the pedigree of genuine custom just described. They are rules that international lawyers would *like* to be genuine rules of law but that in reality are not. Lawyers (in good or bad faith) assert these rules as law, but they are just pieces of advocacy. A rule of fake customary law is characterized, not by state practice or strong consensus, but by advocacy, partisan rhetoric, and unsupported assertion. Unfortunately, this kind of bad legal reasoning is quite prevalent in international law circles. Practitioners of fake customary law label as "customary law" any rule they favor. Typically, they cite "soft" materials in support of the desired rule, in an effort to look like they are asserting a genuine rule. Moreover, they do not merely attempt to justify the rule on policy or moral grounds, while recognizing that it is not yet law. (This would be honest, but would deprive them of the rhetorical force inherent in legal language.) Fake customary law lacks the appeal of genuine law. Genuine customary law reflects the aggregate sense of right and wrong in the community that has been elaborated and developed over a relatively long period or embodied in a strong consensus. Genuine customary law embodies equilibrium of some sort. In contrast, the practice of fake customary law misses all that. It misses what is most important about custom: its ability to reflect institutional history and filtered state expectations about what is lawful, mutually beneficial, ethical, or efficient. The practice of fake customary law has unfortunately degraded international law in the eyes of the general public, the courts, and the conventional legal community. To make things worse, some international courts have spread fake customary law by accepting it in their decisions.[75] While it is unclear how this trend can be modified in the inter-

---

[74] To the examples discussed above, I would add the modern customary prohibition against the execution of juveniles for capital crimes. Such executions were recently declared unconstitutional (in part based on international consensus) by the U.S. Supreme Court. See *Roper v. Simmons*, 543 U.S. 551 (2005).

[75] The International Court of Justice (ICJ) frequently mentions "general practice" without bothering to point to any instances of state practice—much less analyze it. McGinnis and Somin mention the *Nicaragua* case (decided June 27, 1986) as an example. See McGinnis and Somin, "Should International Law Be Part of Our Law?" 1201. In that case, the ICJ asserted that *collective* self-defense (that is, the defense by a state of another state) is available only against a full-fledged armed attack, and not against minor uses of force. For this the ICJ cited no precedent whatsoever. I would also mention two more cases. In the *Case Concerning Armed Activities in the Territory of the Congo* (2005), the ICJ reiterated the groundless *Nicaragua* findings about use of force and invented some customary law of its own, such as the principle of "permanent sovereignty over natural resources," citing only a nonbinding (and

national arena, for our purposes fake customary law lacks the necessary pedigree to be considered international law at all—let alone to become part of domestic law in a liberal state. The domestic courts of the liberal state should firmly reject this practice.

My initial proposal, then, is that the courts of the liberal state should only import *genuine* customary law. Yet even genuine customary law might be problematic. The international community[76] may strongly agree on rules that are unacceptable to the liberal state, so the principle for importing customary law should be restricted further. My amended proposal is that the liberal constitution may allow courts to use rules of customary law as the law of the land, *provided* (i) that they are genuine and not fake, (ii) that they are consistent with the liberal constitution, and (iii) that they do not displace duly promulgated domestic laws. It is my hope that provisos (ii) and (iii) will assuage some of McGinnis and Somin's concerns. Customary international law would be operative domestically only where there is no constitutional, statutory, or precedential rule to the contrary—just as Justice Horace Gray said in the 1900 *Paquete Habana* case.[77] Moreover, these provisos will weed out genuine customary rules that are inconsistent with constitutional guarantees of individual rights. The imported rules of customary law cannot be illiberal rules; they cannot be rules unsupported by state practice or strong international consensus; and they cannot prevail against domestic legislation.

But someone may still ask why the courts of the liberal state should accept *any* customary rule, genuine or fake, that has not been formally incorporated. In other words, I have not yet given a reason in favor of domestic assimilation. I think, however, that with the foregoing guarantees in place, there are good reasons for treating genuine customary international law as part of the domestic law of the liberal state. Good customary rules—that is, those that are genuine and consistent with liberal principles and domestic legislation—permit international coexistence and thus

---

much challenged) U.N. General Assembly Resolution. See *Case Concerning Armed Activities in the Territory of the Congo* (Judgment of December 19, 2005), http://www.icj-cij.org/docket/index.php?p1=3&p2=3&k=51&case=116&code=co&p3=4, paragraph 244. In the *Arrest Warrant Case* (decided February 14, 2002), the ICJ concluded that customary international law afforded foreign ministers absolute immunity from criminal jurisdiction. However, one searches in vain for any citation of any international incident or precedent supporting that claim. See *Arrest Warrant Case*, http://www.icj-cij.org/docket/files/121/8126.pdf, paragraphs 52–54. My point here is not that the rules the ICJ applied are not law: they may or may not be. My point is rather one of method: the rules in question are not supported by the arguments the ICJ gives.

[76] I say "community" for convenience; nothing follows from this term.

[77] See *The Paquete Habana*, 175 U.S. 677 (1900). In that case, the U.S. Supreme Court applied a rule of customary law that exempted fishermen from capture in times of war. Writing for the Court, Justice Gray wrote: "International law is part of our law, and must be ascertained and administered by the courts of justice of appropriate jurisdiction, as often as questions of right depending upon it are duly presented for their determination. For this purpose, *where there is no treaty, and no controlling executive or legislative act or judicial decision, resort must be had to the customs and usages of civilized nations. . .*" (id., 328–29; emphasis added).

enable the liberal state to prosper in the global arena. A necessary condition to preserve a liberal society is having a reasonably peaceful coexistence with other nations of the world. This coexistence increases the chances that the liberal state will preserve and protect its liberal institutions. Genuine customary law is an important part of international law that contributes to this coexistence, precisely because the rules have withstood the test of time or consensus. Now, some of those rules are not the kind of rules that can be naturally assimilated into domestic law. Others, however, can be naturally assimilated. The courts in the liberal state can use well-developed doctrines of standing, cause-of-action, and the like, to determine which customary rules can naturally be used as rules of decision in domestic cases. Courts can, for example, allow customary rules that specify rights and duties of individuals, and disallow those that do not do this.[78]

Consider the customary rule of international law that exempts diplomats from local taxes. Imagine that the government of a liberal state tries to collect a tax and the diplomat argues in court that he is immune to taxes under customary international law.[79] McGinnis and Somin would deny this immunity, since the rule invoked is "raw" international law. It has not been enacted by the legitimate legislative process or by the process of treaty implementation. However, I think that a liberal state can accept the importation of the rule of diplomatic immunity, even if the rule lacks formal democratic credentials. This is the price that citizens pay to secure the coexistence that makes the flourishing of the liberal state possible in the global arena. A citizen in a liberal state understands that, in order to coexist peacefully, the state's government should not disregard genuine customary rules pertaining to diplomatic immunity. In this way, importation of genuine customary law is indirectly linked to the preservation of liberal institutions and thus substantively justified, even if not formally enacted by the legitimate domestic lawmaking bodies. In the example discussed, a customary rule affording diplomatic immunity *requires* domestic importation if it is to be effective. The alternative is for the liberal government to turn around and say to other nations that it cannot honor the rule because it has not been duly incorporated into domestic law. But doing this defeats the purpose of the rule and thus creates unnecessary costs for the liberal state in its international relations. Designers of the liberal constitution can anticipate that it will be in the interest of the liberal state to assimilate those rules of genuine customary law that are consistent with liberal principles and facilitate international

---

[78] As U.S. courts normally do. See the discussion of the *Sosa* case below.

[79] This is a hypothetical example: this customary rule has been codified in the 1961 Vienna Convention on Diplomatic Relations. The United States has ratified this convention and implemented it domestically through the 1978 Diplomatic Relations Act, 22 U.S.C. The *customary* rule governs diplomatic immunity among those countries who are not parties to the Vienna Convention.

interaction. Another way of looking at it is this: a rule's democratic pedigree, important as it is, is not the only reason for accepting the rule. Importing a limited number of customary rules that meet the stringent conditions mentioned above does not do great violence to the principle of democracy and contributes to the health of the liberal state. Finally, if we look at the experience in actual liberal democracies, the incorporation of customary law does not seem to have disrupted or threatened liberal institutions.

A 2004 decision of the United States Supreme Court, *Sosa v. Alvarez-Machain*, illustrates the approach I suggest here.[80] In that case, the Court wisely held that any use of the law of nations (i.e., customary international law) for purposes of domestic litigation under the Alien Tort Statute must meet two conditions. First, the law invoked must be sufficiently determinate; that is, it should not consist of vague generalities but should instead clearly specify the rights and duties asserted by the litigants (the Court requires "definite content"). Second, the invoked rule must be universally agreed upon by the nations of the world (in the Court's words, "acceptance by civilized nations"). Notice that the Court does not require that domestically acceptable customary law should be supported by *practice*, but rather that it should be widely agreed upon by the nations of the world. The *Sosa* Court thus accepted not only classical customary law, but also genuine *modern* customary international law, as I have suggested here. This important holding about customary law (if extended beyond the Alien Tort Statute) establishes a kind of quality control (in the Court's words, "vigilant door-keeping") for the domestic use of customary international law—a level of quality control that would exclude both fake customary law and genuine customary law inconsistent with domestic law or liberal principles.

To the extent that McGinnis and Somin's argument applies specifically to the United States, it has only a limited bearing on the topic of this essay, since my purpose here is to design ideal foreign-relations clauses. For example, McGinnis and Somin observe that the American public is rationally ignorant of international law, a fact which contributes to the democratic deficit. Yet that is an entirely contingent fact. The public in other liberal democracies seems to be better informed, and we should not assume ignorance of customary law in the design of ideal institutions. Moreover, the public is also rationally ignorant of domestic law, yet obviously this fact should not influence the courts' acceptance of that law. Also, McGinnis and Somin claim that American law might serve people (citizens and foreigners alike) better than international law, given the special position of the United States as a superpower. Yet that special position, important as it is, is also a matter of contingent fact. It is an open question whether or not the ideal constitutional rules should take into account superpower

---

[80] *Sosa v. Alvarez-Machain*, 542 U.S. 692 (2004).

status. We want rules for a liberal republic that will endure regardless of its relative position of power in the world. The liberal state has an obligation to defend and protect its liberal institutions and to promote similar institutions elsewhere, regardless of its relative power.[81]

Finally, I have suggested that customary rules that meet the proposed tests (i.e., that are genuine and consistent with domestic legislation and liberal principles) can safely be used by domestic courts. Does this mean that those customary rules should displace *state* laws in a federal system? Recall that my purpose is to explore ideal constitutional design for foreign relations. It is an open question whether liberal principles require a unitary constitution or a federal constitution. The arguments for and against federalism are well known: On the one hand, by diluting power geographically, the federal constitution maximizes liberty. On the other hand, local rulers can be oppressive, and if so, their victims could have a hard time finding relief in a federal state. At any rate, it seems to me that liberal principles do not mandate federalism. However, if the benefits of federalism are thought to outweigh its costs, then the issue of whether customary international law should displace state law will arise. It is well accepted in liberal states that properly ratified treaties prevail over state law. The reason for this is to ensure proper coordination in the conduct of foreign affairs. The same reasoning suggests that customary international law that meets the tests suggested here should generally preempt state law, unless the state law in question is securing a fundamental individual liberty in accordance with the federal structure.[82]

C. Foreign commerce

Virtually all liberal constitutions grant broad governmental powers to regulate commerce with other nations.[83] The U.S. Constitution is no exception: Article I, section 8, clause 3 grants Congress the power to "regulate Commerce with foreign Nations." It is undisputed that this constitutional

---

[81] McGinnis and Somin also suggest that the world might be better off if the United States exported its own superior law, rather than adopting the inferior customary international law. There is nothing wrong with exporting beneficial laws. But this does not mean that domestic courts should disregard good customary rules, that is, those meeting the quality conditions I have specified.

[82] For example, in the unlikely event that someone invokes a rule of customary law to invalidate a state law of fundamental importance, such as a law pertaining to the criminal process, or basic common law rules such as property or tort, then state law should prevail. The mainstream position in the United States on preemption is, in my judgment, too formalistic: if customary international law is federal law, then it preempts state law, period. I think a balancing test would be in order here. If the customary international rule offends liberty in some important sense, then it should not preempt state law.

[83] The members of the European Union have delegated the regulation of foreign commerce to the Union. See the discussion in the text. Other examples include the Brazilian Constitution, Article 22, section 8; the Australian Constitution, Article 51, section i; and the Mexican Constitution, Article 131.

provision allows Congress to erect trade barriers. This protectionist function was very much on the minds of the Founders. For example, Alexander Hamilton argued that the federal power to regulate commerce would allow the United States to use access to U.S. markets as "bargaining chips" to exact favorable commercial conditions. He wrote: "By prohibitory regulations, extending, at the same time, through the States, we may oblige foreign countries to bid against each other, for the privileges of our markets."[84] The United States Supreme Court has held that this power is very broad: "[N]o individual has a vested power to trade with foreign nations which is so broad in character as to limit and restrict the power of Congress to determine what articles of merchandise may be imported into this country and the terms upon which a right to import may be exercised."[85] Thus, in the modern post-*Lochner* era, free trade has suffered an even worse fate than property and contract.[86] On the view of the Supreme Court and mainstream constitutional scholars, just as in domestic cases "[t]he Fourteenth Amendment does not enact Mr. Herbert Spencer's Social Statics,"[87] so, it seems, the Constitution does not enact Mr. David Ricardo's theory of comparative advantage.[88]

U.S. citizens have a de facto right to trade freely across states, that is, within the United States. The constitutional structure generally favors *domestic* competition.[89] Europe has adopted a similar structure (domestic free trade and foreign protectionism) but has done so more directly. The

---

[84] Alexander Hamilton, *Federalist No. 11*, in *The Federalist Papers*, ed. Clinton Rossiter (New York: New American Library, 1961).

[85] *Buttfield v. Stranahan*, 192 U.S. 470 (1904).

[86] The "*Lochner* era" refers to a period in American history when the Supreme Court invalidated Progressive legislation on the grounds that it interfered with freedom of contract. Subsequently, the Supreme Court overruled *Lochner v. New York*, 198 U.S. 45 (1905) (the emblematic case of that era), thus allowing broad governmental regulation of economic activity. This began the post-*Lochner* era, which endures to this day. Paradoxically, the *Buttfield* case (cited in note 85) was decided at around the same time as *Lochner*, yet it is still good law today. This suggests, perhaps, that foreign trade has always been the stepsister of economic liberties: even the *Lochner* Court would not extend its defense of property rights and freedom of contract to foreign trade.

[87] *Lochner v. New York*, 198 U.S. 45 (1905) (Holmes, dissenting).

[88] Jon Klick and I discuss the place of trade in a theory of justice in Fernando R. Tesón and Jonathan Klick, "Global Justice and Trade," in Carmody, Garcia, and Linarelli, eds., *Distributive Justice and International Economic Law*.

[89] The actual structure of the U.S. Constitution is quite complicated, and a full account is beyond the scope of this essay. Article I, Section 8, para. 3 (the commerce clause) reads: "The Congress shall have Power . . . to regulate Commerce with foreign Nations, and among the Several States, and with the Indian Tribes." However, Article I, section 10, para. 2 expressly forbids states from unilaterally erecting trade barriers: "No State shall, *without the Consent of the Congress*, lay any Imposts or Duties on Imports or Exports . . ." (emphasis added). It is clear from these provisions that Congress has a vast power to intervene in markets, foreign or domestic. The Constitution does not guarantee citizens that their products will flow freely within the United States, since Congress may authorize states to impose interstate trade barriers. Given this, it is fortunate that Congress has had the good sense not to exercise this power domestically. But the *foreign* commerce power is "plenary," that is, unaffected by domestic concerns such as federalism or the Bill of Rights. And Congress (or the president using delegated power) routinely enacts restrictions on foreign trade.

European Union Treaty expressly recognizes freedom to trade *within the Union;* that is, neither governments nor European agencies may impede the freedom of trade among Members.[90] But the Union has an almost unlimited power to enact protectionist laws regarding trade with non-European Union members (witness the European Union's extensive agricultural protectionism). Both in the United States and in Europe, these protectionist powers are checked only by these countries' obligations toward the World Trade Organization. Citizens do not have a right against their governments to trade freely with outsiders.

Allowing the government to erect trade barriers is a major constitutional flaw. Luckily, this anti-trade precedent does not bind the ideal liberal constitution. Constitutional design must incorporate reliable economics. If we do so, we learn two things. First, we learn that, because of the principle of comparative advantage, free trade increases prosperity in the long run, nationally and globally (even though those persons who would be favored by the segmentation of markets will lose out). Second, we learn that governments, including (and, some would say, especially) liberal governments, are vulnerable to capture by special-interest groups who do not wish to compete with foreign producers. Governments harm their own citizens when they succumb to this pressure, because they deny citizens access to better and cheaper goods. Moreover, protectionist measures are morally objectionable because they redistribute wealth for private, not public, purposes. Yet political mechanisms make it quite easy for protectionist interests to succeed. In view of this grim reality, I propose that the liberal constitution *prohibit* government from erecting trade barriers. The writers of the constitution should anticipate the pathology just described and should ban the government from harming citizens in this way. An analogy with individual rights may help us see this. Why does the liberal constitution prohibit the government from censoring speech? There are, of course, several reasons, but one reason is the knowledge that governments, even decent ones, are prone to silence their critics. No one likes criticism, and politicians like it even less, because criticism interferes with the exercise of power. Similarly, constitutional designers should anticipate that governments are likely to be captured by protectionist interests if the constitution grants government the power to enact protectionist policies. Therefore, rulers should not have that power.[91]

---

[90] See Case 240/83, *Procureur de la Republique v. ADBHU,* [1985] ECR 531, 548 (1983).

[91] The view that national constitutions and international law should recognize a right to trade was pioneered by German scholar and European Commissioner Ernst-Ulrich Petersmann. In a series of articles, he argued that national constitutions and international law should recognize economic liberties, and in particular the individual right to trade freely, alongside the traditional human rights. See Petersmann, "National Constitutions, Foreign Trade Policy, and European Community Law"; and Ernst-Ulrich Petersmann, "Time for a United Nations Global Compact for Integrating Human Rights into the Law of Worldwide Organizations: Lessons from European Integration," *European Journal of International Law* 13 (2002): 621. Petersmann's suggestion has angered some human rights scholars. See, e.g.,

V. Concrete Suggestions

Can the proposals put forth in this essay be codified in a written constitution? Because my concern is with the design of an effective liberal constitution, I am neutral about the best way to implement the foreign-relations provisions that I recommend in this essay. Depending on history and context, perhaps it might sometimes be best to draft only a brief constitutional list of the various powers and rights, and to allow the courts to interpret them in the way I recommend. However, experience has shown that words alone, even words solemnly enshrined in revered constitutional documents, have failed to deter the enemies of freedom and those who seek to enlist the coercive power of the government for private gains. Time and again, governments and courts have ignored or mangled clear constitutional language, even in countries with the best constitutional traditions. I can offer no satisfactory solution to this,[92] except to say that mere pieces of paper, even venerable ones, cannot preserve free institutions: Men and women must be prepared to defend them.

With that caveat, here are my suggestions:

War Powers

1. The Legislature shall have the power to authorize all large-scale uses of force, subject to the following provisions.

2. The President shall be the Commander-in-Chief of the armed forces. This includes the power to direct combat and the power to repel attacks against the state's territory, the state's citizens, the state's institutions, and the state's foreign allies. In conducting hostilities, the President shall observe the relevant rules of domestic and international law pertaining to combat.

Philip Alston, "Resisting the Merger and Acquisition of Human Rights by Trade Law: A Reply to Petersmann," *European Journal of International Law* 13 (2002): 815. For Petersmann's reply, see Ernst-Ulrich Petersmann, "Taking Human Rights, Poverty, and Empowerment of Individuals More Seriously: Rejoinder to Alston," *European Journal of International Law* 13 (2002): 845. For reasons that are unclear, Alston's wrath reaches my own work (Tesón, *A Philosophy of International Law,* which Petersmann approvingly cites), although in that book I do not discuss international trade in any detail. Alston endorses the critique of my book by Patrick Capps, "The Kantian Project in Modern International Legal Theory," *European Journal of International Law* 12 (2001): 1003, without, it seems, having read either one, because Capps's critique has nothing to do with trade. (Rather, Capps thinks I have misread Kant.) Yet I would imagine that Alston should have been attracted to the views in my book, since there I suggest that human rights should be the basis of international law. On the merits, Alston's argument is weak. He thinks that Petersmann is wrong because international human rights have never included a right to trade freely. But of course, this begs the question, since the failure of international law to recognize a right to trade is precisely what Petersmann wants to change.

[92] Perhaps Guido Pincione is right: just give government the minimal power possible and forget about the Bill of Rights and other attempts to restrict the powers of the state. See his essay in this volume.

3. The President shall also have the authority to use force to stop a massive humanitarian catastrophe in another country, where there is no time to seek legislative approval.

Treaties and Customary Law
1. This Constitution, the laws made in pursuance thereof, and the treaties made by the President with approval by the Legislature by simple majority, are the law of the land.
    a. Treaties shall be self-executing unless: (i) the Legislature, when approving a treaty, expressly indicates that it is not self-executing; or (ii) by its very nature, the treaty does not recognize individual rights or claims that can be enforced in a court of law.
2. The law of nations is also the law of the land, provided:
    a. That it is consistent with the Constitution, laws, judicial precedents where applicable, treaties in force, and the principles of free government;
    b. That it is sufficiently precise; and
    c. That it is universally agreed upon by the community of nations.

Economic Liberties
1. Everyone has the right to private property and the right to contract freely with others, including the right to trade freely with foreigners.
2. The government shall not interfere with these rights except:
    a. In the interests of national security; or
    b. When their exercise significantly harms others. For the purposes of this provision, "harm" does not include competitive harm.

VI. Conclusion

Many have seen the foreign-relations clauses of the U.S. Constitution as primarily concerned with practical functionality: what is the distribution of powers that will assure an effective, smooth conduct of foreign relations? I concede that this is very important, and that we should always learn from the historical experience of the functioning of liberal constitutions. However, in this essay I have tried to show that the content and structure of the foreign-relations provisions of a constitution are connected to the philosophical principles that underlie a liberal society. I have suggested that, over a broad range of issues, the foreign-relations provisions of a constitution can channel the implementation of liberal ideals in different ways, and that some ways are better than others. My project here is tentative, to be sure, and there are many avenues for future research. One of them is to connect the principles for the conduct of foreign relations by the liberal state with the principles of global justice. For example, analyzing the war powers of a liberal state presupposes a theory of just war; and proposing a particular design for the regulation of foreign commerce presupposes a theory of economic justice across borders. Another avenue for future research is to connect this project with the literature on the incentives created by constitutional design. In this essay, I have made no more than an educated guess about those incentives. Finally, the discussion about incorporation of international law into domestic law must be connected to a general theory of international law.

Law, Florida State University

DO CONSTITUTIONS HAVE A POINT? REFLECTIONS ON "PARCHMENT BARRIERS" AND PREAMBLES

By Sanford Levinson

I. Introduction: Why Write Down Constitutional Understanding?

A basic question facing any student of constitutions is what accounts for the modern prevalence of *written* constitutions. Political scientists since Aristotle, after all, have understood that societies invariably have collective political understandings that can be called "constitutions," whether or not they are written down. What is the point of putting such understandings in writing? As we are often reminded, the United Kingdom—one of the world's great democracies, at least by conventional criteria—sustained itself over many centuries without such a constitution, even if one might well regard British membership in the European Union and its commitment to the European Convention on Human Rights as fatally weakening the conventional description of the country as lacking a written constitution. Moreover, that description is still accurate with regard to one of Britain's former colonies, New Zealand, which may have "superstatutes," such as the New Zealand Bill of Rights Act, but still functions without a canonical constitution. The same is true of Israel. Still, it is obvious that at least since the loss in 1783 of one of the major parts of the British colonial empire—in terms of subsequent history, it is perhaps not unduly chauvinistic to say *the* major part of that empire—the trend has been very much in favor of written constitutions. For this, one may presume, the United States bears some significant responsibility; it had, by 1787, become the home of a plethora of written constitutions.

As noted by the late Willi Paul Adams, one of the most distinguished European students of American constitutional practices, the United States Constitution of 1787–88 was preceded not only by the ineffective Articles of Confederation, but also, and far more importantly, by a host of state constitutions drafted in the immediate aftermath of the Declaration of Independence.[1] Many of the great issues that would be hashed out in Philadelphia in 1787 were first broached in state capitals—and, of course, James Madison, an assiduous student of comparative constitutionalism, was also well aware of constitutional debates ranging from ancient Rome to the Dutch Republic. What was written down was of obvious import.

[1] Willi Paul Adams, *The First American Constitutions: Republican Ideology and the Making of the State Constitutions in the Revolutionary Era* (Lanham, MD: Rowman and Littlefield, 2001).

After all, the people of Massachusetts had engaged in genuine collective discussion and then rejection in 1778 of the first draft of the proposed Massachusetts constitution; after modification, it was ratified in 1780, so that Massachusetts can legitimately claim to be governed by the oldest continuing constitution in the world.[2] And, of course, the Constitutional Convention in Philadelphia was triggered by widespread discontent over the revealed limitations of the first constitution of the United States, the Articles of Confederation, which had become operative in 1781. The moral of the Articles' failure was, obviously, not to reject the turn toward written constitutionalism, but rather to draft a new and better foundational agreement.

What might account for the undoubted triumph of written constitutions, at least if one puts to one side the important possibility of a "contagion effect," that is, the influence of both the American and the French revolutions on subsequent developments, culminating in the belief that truly respectable countries ought to have written constitutions? From a functionalist perspective, I have come to believe that the most important attribute of a written constitution is its setting down of clear rules, most of which are *not* open to serious interpretive dispute, about the most basic structures of government. These rules encompass such factors as establishing the institutional contexts for the making and enforcement of laws, including setting out the basic ground rules for the election (or appointment) of officials and the length of the terms of their offices. If, as is the case in all more-or-less democratic regimes, one can anticipate that those currently in power might be replaced in the future by people who are now in the opposition, then it is especially important to have clearly delineated rules setting out the mechanisms of election and replacement. One can easily believe that it is best to inscribe such rules in indelible ink rather than to rely on tacit understandings.

It is true, of course, as I have argued recently in my book *Our Undemocratic Constitution*,[3] that some of the specific rules of the U.S. Constitution, however much sense they might arguably have made at the time of initial adoption, may be significantly counterproductive today. My model example with regard to the U.S. Constitution is the Inauguration Day clause, set out in the Twentieth Amendment, which establishes January 20 of the year following elections as the date for inaugurating the winner.[4]

---

[2] See Oscar and Mary Handlin, eds., *The Popular Sources of Political Authority: Documents on the Massachusetts Constitution of 1780* (Cambridge, MA: Harvard University Press, 1966). See generally John Dinan, *The American State Constitutional Tradition* (Lawrence: University of Kansas Press, 2006), for a convincing argument that constitutional theorists have much to learn from the study of the many remarkably different American state constitutions.

[3] Sanford Levinson, *Our Undemocratic Constitution: Where the Constitution Goes Wrong (and How We the People Can Correct It)* (New York: Oxford University Press, 2008).

[4] U.S. Constitution, Amend. XX, section I: "The terms of the President and Vice President shall end at noon on the 20th day of January . . . and the terms of their successors shall then begin." The reason a constitutional amendment was necessary, incidentally, was not because

Given that elections (by statute) take place in early November, my own view is that this creates far too long a hiatus between the election and the inauguration of a new president and generates a problematic split between political and legal authority. This was vividly illustrated in December 2008, when participants at an international economic "summit" in the United States were far more eager to talk with President-Elect Barack Obama and his incoming team of economic advisers than with President George W. Bush (though Obama scrupulously avoided any encounters that might have called President Bush's authority into question). One might debate exactly when a new president should take office—only in a parliamentary system with "shadow governments" is it really possible to emulate the British practice of a new prime minister's taking office literally the day following election—but it is hard to believe that ten weeks is optimal, especially in a world where time is ever more compressed with regard to such issues as national security, economic crisis, or natural disasters. Still, at least there is no dispute about when the opposition is entitled to take over and, even more importantly, the political legitimacy of that takeover, even if it requires prevailing in an equally arcane and normatively indefensible electoral college.[5]

In focusing on the dominant importance of quite formal political structures, I am, to some extent at least, rejecting the pervasive contemporary view that the most important function of constitutions is to guarantee and then assure the implementation of important rights. Too often, I believe, people tend to yawn at discussions of such issues as unicameralism versus bicameralism or the precise number of votes it should take, in a presidential system, to override a presidential veto (assuming the president has a veto power at all, which is hardly a self-evident proposition). People become animated only when discussion turns to freedom of speech or religion, the rights of racial, ethnic, or gender groups, or, indeed, the protection accorded to private property. This is a profound error. I hasten to say that I do not believe that the latter debates are unimportant or the rights not worth cherishing, whether one is referring to the classic bundle

---

the original Constitution indicated a different date. No date at all was specified; March 4 became Inauguration Day because of an early act of Congress. But because the Constitution did specify that the president would have a four-year term, once the statute was passed and became operative, it became the equivalent of a hard-wired constitutional text, inasmuch as any change, by definition, would either reduce or lengthen the fixed four-year term. Thus, as a result of the Twentieth Amendment, ratified in 1933, Franklin D. Roosevelt's first term of office was in fact only three years and ten-and-a-half months, given that he was initially inaugurated on March 4, 1933, under the old regime, and then inaugurated for the second time on January 20, 1937.

[5] Americans do not vote "directly" for presidential candidates, but, rather, vote on a state-by-state basis for "electors" committed to the given candidates, who will then, as a result of arcane procedures set out in the Twelfth Amendment and subsequent legislation, meet to cast their votes for their particular choices. It is this feature of the Constitution that explains, for example, why the person who comes in second in the national popular vote can nonetheless win the electoral vote, as happened notably in 2000.

of liberal "negative rights" (perhaps best summarized by Justice Brandeis's famous reference to "the right to be left alone—the most comprehensive of rights, and the right most valued by a free people")[6]—or to more contemporary "affirmative rights," where one looks to the government for active succor against certain vicissitudes of life.[7]

Nonetheless, whatever the genuine ideological importance of written guarantees of rights, whether "negative" or "affirmative," I have become steadily more skeptical with regard to their practical importance. There is, of course, a rich tradition in American constitutional thinking of skepticism about mere "parchment barriers" against governmental overreaching. James Madison famously concluded *Federalist No. 48* by observing "that a mere demarkation [*sic*] on parchment of the constitutional limits of the several departments, is not a sufficient guard against those encroachments which lead to a tyrannical concentration of all the powers of government in the same hands."[8] Interestingly, the particular "parchment barriers" about which he was expressing his skepticism involved "separation of powers" concerns at the national level, and one might say the same about vertical separation of powers between the national and state governments. Surely the record of United States constitutional law in particular inspires no great confidence on either point, whether one applauds or is dismayed by the changes revealed by any survey of the record of "American constitutional development." (At the very least, this offers cautionary lessons about the genuine "stickiness" of all apparent settlements.) But skepticism about the ability of "parchment barriers" genuinely to protect the rights of vulnerable minorities is also amply justified. Anyone who believes that the simple language of the Constitution explains contemporary protections, say, of seditious speech has to explain why no such interpretation of the language was given earlier in our history. Perhaps the constitutional language has *some* explanatory force, but it seems foolhardy to

---

[6] *Olmstead v. U.S.*, 277 U.S. 438, 478 (1928) (Brandeis, J., dissenting).

[7] Whether ironically or not, given the failure of the United States Constitution to include any clear protections of such rights, at least some credit for the movement toward such guarantees in the rest of the world goes to President Franklin D. Roosevelt. His 1944 State of the Union message to Congress called for a "new Bill of Rights," on the basis of his belief that "individual freedom cannot exist without economic security and independence" and that it is a vital role of government to guarantee such security by recognizing rights "to a useful and remunerative job in the industries or shops or farms or mines of the nation; . . . to earn enough to provide adequate food and clothing and recreation; . . . to a decent home; . . . to adequate medical care and the opportunity to achieve and enjoy good health; . . . [and] to adequate protection from the economic fears of old age, sickness, accident, and unemployment." Although one might believe that a free-market system would often prove adequate to provide such "rights," it is clear that for Roosevelt and his followers, government would have both the authority and the duty to step in and fund such necessarily redistributive programs, should market solutions be perceived as inadequate.

[8] James Madison, *Federalist No. 48*, in Philip Kurland and Ralph Lerner, eds., *The Founder's Constitution* (Chicago: University of Chicago Press, 1987), vol. 1, chap. 10, doc. 15, available online at http://press-pubs.uchicago.edu/founders/documents/v1ch10s15.html.

privilege its importance over other developments in the general political culture. It is always foolhardy to confuse the "law on the books" (even if the "book" is an ostensibly revered constitution) with the "law in action" within a given society. (A side issue, which is not a central concern of this essay, is whether it is realistic to expect "independent" judiciaries to be effective guarantors of constitutional rights if such rights do not, in fact, have significant popular support. Like many political scientists—and even some lawyers—I am skeptical.)[9]

Even if we share some of Madison's skepticism about "parchment barriers," it is wise to recognize that many constitutions, including the U.S. Constitution, *do* include significant patches of text that are widely accepted as controlling and, therefore, impervious to change outside the authorized process of amendment (which, in the U.S. Constitution, establishes hurdles sufficient to make most amendment impossible). It is a mistake to overemphasize what I have elsewhere called the "narrative of change" with regard to understanding the realities of American constitutionalism; that narrative, however accurate and important, is nearly irrelevant with regard to "hardwired" institutional structures like Inauguration Day or bicameralism. It must be complemented with a "narrative of stasis."[10] One need not adopt a controversial theory of language with regard to texts establishing these structures. The point is pragmatic: For whatever reason, there is simply no public debate—or even debate among the most "creative" constitutional lawyers—about the constitutional legitimacy of Wyoming's having the same voting power in the U.S. Senate as does California, even if one believes, as I do, that this allocation is normatively indefensible. The absence of any such debate is surely as important as the pervasive controversy about, say, the legitimacy of affirmative action.

My discussion of the "point" of constitutions has thus far been cast in entirely functionalist terms: Any political system will presumably function better, at least most of the time, if it has reasonably ascertainable rules as to who is authorized to exercise (and to succeed to) political power. Such rules will not preserve a system if its rulers are perceived, whether by key elites (including the military) or the public at large, as exercising power tyrannically. At that point, as in America in 1776, it is possible that the voice of revolution will be heard throughout the land. Still, even if such rules are not sufficient to guarantee stability, one might well believe they are a necessary condition. (This is why customary conventions are of special importance, even in systems that lack canonical written constitutions.)

Thus, one way of analyzing constitutions is to identify two separate aspects of constitutional texts. On the one hand, there are provisions that

---

[9] The standard citation is surely Gerald Rosenberg, *The Hollow Hope: Can Courts Bring about Social Change?*, 2d ed. (Chicago: University of Chicago Press, 2008).

[10] See Sanford Levinson, "Our Schizoid Approach to the United States Constitution: Competing Narratives of Constitutional Dynamism and Stasis," *Indiana Law Review* 84 (2009): 1337.

genuinely *settle* certain important issues, such as the day on which a new president takes over legal authority, even if we happen to think that the particular rule established is open to serious criticism. On the other hand, there are those provisions that may be best viewed as *invitations to conversation*, where equally well-trained lawyers will offer sometimes dramatically different "interpretations" of constitutional texts. For examples of the latter sort within the American Constitution, one need look no further than the First Amendment's protection of "the freedom of speech" or the Fourteenth Amendment's guarantee of "equal protection of the laws"; and, indeed, similar interpretive controversies are easily attached to the assignment of power to Congress in Article I, section 8. Only the most ambitious, or delusional, constitutional designer could truly imagine that any given document would operate exclusively as a "constitution of settlement," but it should be just as obvious that a constitution that served *only* to generate conversations would itself be of limited utility. All constitutions feature both attributes and, therefore, have two distinctive (and sometimes contradictory) points: (1) to settle and make almost literally undebatable, at least in legal terms, certain fundamental features of the polity; and, at the same time, (2) to generate almost endless, and often acrimonious, debate about other fundamental features.

What I want to focus on in the rest of this essay is the particular problem posed by constitutional preambles, an extremely interesting, but relatively underanalyzed, feature of most constitutions. Relatively few of the drafters of the now hundreds of written constitutions that exist at both national and subnational levels were willing to stop simply with setting out the basic institutional structures or even including guarantees of rights to be protected in the new constitutional order. Instead, most constitutions have preambles.[11] Some of them are short and (relatively) easily memorizable, as is the case with the preamble to the U.S. Constitution: "We the People of the United States, in Order to form a more perfect Union, establish Justice, insure domestic Tranquility, provide for the common defence, promote the general Welfare, and secure the Blessings of Liberty to ourselves and our Posterity, do ordain and establish this Constitution for the United States of America."[12] Others may be consid-

---

[11] In a forthcoming essay, Liav Orgad notes that a "non-representative sample of fifty democratic countries" revealed that thirty-seven of them have preambles and only thirteen do not—and five of the latter have "introductory articles" that may be said to function as preambles. See Orgad, "The Preamble in Constitutional Interpretation," forthcoming in *I-CON* (2011), ms. p. 3 n. 4. Similarly, a more comprehensive survey of 578 of the 801 total constitutions written from 1789 to 2006 indicated that 79 percent of them included preambles. Indeed, not only are more-recent constitutions (those written since 1950) more likely to include preambles, but they are also likely to be considerably longer than were earlier preambles. See Zachary Elkins and Tom Ginsburg, "The Comparative Constitutions Project" (2010), available online at http://comparativeconstitutionsproject.org.

[12] Indeed, the preamble can even be put to music. See (or listen to) http://www.youtube.com/watch?v=aNb9AoY5XXE.

erably longer, as illustrated by the preamble to the aforementioned Massachusetts Constitution of 1780:

> The end of the institution, maintenance, and administration of government is to secure the existence of the body-politic, to protect it, and to furnish the individuals who compose it with the power of enjoying, in safety and tranquillity, their natural rights and the blessings of life; and whenever these great objects are not obtained the people have a right to alter the government, and to take measures necessary for their safety, prosperity, and happiness.
>
> The body politic is formed by a voluntary association of individuals; it is a social compact by which the whole people covenants with each citizen and each citizen with the whole people that all shall be governed by certain laws for the common good. It is the duty of the people, therefore, in framing a constitution of government, to provide for an equitable mode of making laws, as well as for an impartial interpretation and a faithful execution of them; that every man may, at all times, find his security in them.
>
> We, therefore, the people of Massachusetts, acknowledging, with grateful hearts, the goodness of the great Legislator of the universe, in affording us, in the course of His providence, an opportunity, deliberately and peaceably, without fraud, violence, or surprise, of entering into an original, explicit, and solemn compact with each other, and of forming a new constitution of civil government for ourselves and posterity; and devoutly imploring His direction in so interesting a design, do agree upon, ordain, and establish the following declaration of rights and frame of government as the constitution of the commonwealth of Massachusetts.

Just as we should ask why so many people think it is important to have written constitutions rather than relying on customary conventions, we should independently ask why so many people who engage in the enterprise of drafting constitutions believe that it is also important to include preambles. What is *their* point? With regard to written constitutions themselves, I have offered a basically functionalist explanation involving the clear social benefits of having clear-cut rules for the acquisition and maintenance (and loss) of political power. Moreover, with regard to the provisions of constitutions that invite conversations built around different interpretations of indeterminate texts, even those conversations are quintessentially "legal" inasmuch as they are instantiated in arguments directed, most obviously, to judges called upon to declare concrete winners and losers in particular controversies that turn on the meaning assigned to the text. Perhaps a functionalist account of the "constitution of conversation" would emphasize the social and political goods thought to be served by "legalizing" these controversial issues and establishing a social practice of looking to lawyers and judges to resolve such controversies (though, obviously, one can debate the normative desirability of such a practice).

Nonetheless, it is harder to come up with a functionalist account of preambles, not only because they most often feature glittering generalities (like "establishing justice"), but also because they generally do *not* serve as invitations to *legal* conversations. So we must explain why constitutional drafters would feel impelled to precede the identification of political officials and their powers—or even the delineation of protected rights—with the kinds of statements that are regularly found in preambles. Presumably, preambles have a point, but it really cannot be the same kind of point that would be attributed to the main body of a written constitution.

II. The (A)legal Status of Constitutional Preambles

The easiest way to demonstrate this difference, I suggest, is by reference to the very different *legal* status of a preamble from the rest of the constitution. The preamble to the U.S. Constitution is rarely cited—and even more rarely seriously discussed—by the United States Supreme Court. Ironically, perhaps, one of the earliest decisions of that Court, *Chisholm v. Georgia* (1793), in which the Court held that Georgia was liable to being sued in a federal court by a resident of South Carolina, *did* include a discussion of the preamble. The discussion appeared in the concurring opinion of Justice James Wilson, one of the primary figures involved in the Constitutional Convention of 1787, and in the Pennsylvania convention that ratified the U.S. Constitution thereafter. Wilson justified the decision in the *Chisholm* case on the basis of "the declared objects, and the general texture of the Constitution of the United States," including its commitment "to form an union more perfect, than, before that time, had been formed." Moreover, he noted, "Another declared object is, 'to establish justice.' This points, in a particular manner, to the Judicial authority. . . ."[13] It is also worth noting, though, that the Court's decision in *Chisholm* was met with a storm of protest from objecting states, and that the very first amendment to the Constitution following the Bill of Rights—the Eleventh Amendment—was explicitly designed to overrule the Court's decision. Citations to the preamble of the Constitution have been few and far between since then.[14] The most recent appears to be Chief Justice William Rehnquist's majority opinion involving claims of constitutional protection by a Mexican national whose property had been searched and seized by U.S. agents in Mexico in a manner that would have violated the

---

[13] *Chisholm v. Georgia*, 2 U.S. 419, 465 (1793).

[14] See Milton Handler, Brian Leiter, and Carole E. Handler, "A Reconsideration of the Relevance and Materiality of the Preamble in Constitutional Interpretation," *Cardozo Law Review* 12 (1990–1991): 117, 120–21 n. 14 (reporting a total of only twenty-four citations, over 80 percent of which occurred in dissenting opinions).

Constitution had it been done within our own borders. Rehnquist cited the preamble (and many other parts of the Constitution) to support the argument that the Constitution applies *only* to members of the American political community and, therefore, not to foreign nationals abroad.[15] Far more important, and basically dispositive for practicing lawyers, was the Court's comment over a hundred years ago: "Although th[e] preamble indicates the general purposes for which the people ordained and established the Constitution, it has never been regarded as the source of any substantive power conferred on the government of the United States, or on any of its departments."[16] Justice Oliver Wendell Holmes once (in)famously described the equal protection clause of the Fourteenth Amendment as "the usual last refuge of constitutional arguments,"[17] just before, as one might predict, dismissing the relevance of such an argument. One might offer the same comment about the preamble as a source of "constitutional arguments." Things might change in the future, as was most certainly the case for equal protection arguments, which have become almost ubiquitous in the modern, post-Holmesian world. But it remains true that no law professor teaches students that citing the preamble as a principal support for one's argument would be a smart move.

One reason for such reticence was well stated by the nation's first attorney general, Edmund Randolph, in his 1791 memorandum to George Washington concerning the constitutionality of the proposed Bank of the United States. Noting that some proponents of the bank relied on the preamble, he told Washington—who, of course, had been president of the Constitutional Convention itself—that "the Preamble if it be operative is a full constitution of itself; and the body of the Constitution is useless." After all, if it became sufficient to make direct appeals to "establishing justice" or "assuring domestic tranquility," then why bother demonstrating that Congress had been assigned such powers or, even more to the point, why pay any heed to barriers against government's achieving such happy goals? Thus, Randolph pronounced "the legitimate nature of preambles" to be "declarative only of the views of the convention, which they supposed would be best fulfilled by the powers delineated."[18]

III. Relationships Between a Constitution's Ends and Constitutionally Authorized Means

Preambles, more than any other parts of constitutions, make vivid the complex relationship between the presumptive ends underlying a given

---

[15] *United States v. Verdugo-Urquidez*, 494 U.S. 259, 265 (1990).

[16] *Jacobson v. Massachusetts*, 197 U.S. 111, 22 (1905).

[17] *Buck v. Bell*, 274 U.S. 200, 208 (1927).

[18] Memorandum from Edmund Randolph to George Washington, quoted in Paul Brest et al., *Processes of Constitutional Decisionmaking*, 5th ed. (New York: Aspen Publishers, 2006), 32.

constitution and the particular means that it authorizes to achieve those ends. Of course, in the case of the U.S. Constitution, one might argue that the views of the Constitutional Convention, which rest on empirical pre-dictions of what means would "best fulfill" the great ends set out in the preamble, might be subject to later disconfirmation; future interpreters should thus feel free to interpret the Constitution in a way that allows achievement of the ends. Why, after all, would one confine oneself to certain means to an end if one discovers that those means are counter-productive to achieving the specified end? As I have already suggested, that might well explain the decidedly checkered history of constitutional interpretation with regard to the initial view that the national government— and, in some respects, the state governments as well—were far more governments of "limited powers" than has turned out to be the case.

Here the canonical Supreme Court opinion is probably *Home Building and Loan Association v. Blaisdell* (1934),[19] a case that arose during the Great Depression. In this case, a sharply divided Court upheld the power of the Minnesota legislature, responding to the plight of impoverished home-owners faced with the loss of their homes, to suspend the duty of debtors to adhere to their specific contracts with creditor banks. To be sure, the "mortgage moratorium" was temporary, scheduled to expire in May 1935, and the debtors were obligated under its terms to pay banks a "fair" rental for the homes they continued to live in. At the time, mortgages were structured very differently from the system that now operates in the United States, where monthly payments are of a uniform amount. Instead, mortgages at the time typically included a "balloon payment" at the end of the mortgage term, so that, for example, fifty-nine monthly payments of $100 would be followed by the obligation to make a $5,000 payment. Typically, new mortgages would then be written, which would make it unnecessary actually to come up with the final payment; of course, this assumed the creditworthiness of the borrower, precisely what was negated by the Depression. Hence the perceived need for the moratorium and the suspension of contractual obligations, in spite of the seemingly clear pro-hibition by the contract clause of Article I, section 10 of the U.S. Consti-tution, which bars states from "pass[ing any] Law impairing the Obligation of Contracts."

This is the most dramatic evidence in the Constitution of a decided preference for creditors over debtors; indeed, many supporters of the new Constitution expressed hostility to debtor-relief legislation that had pre-viously been passed by Rhode Island and other states. The contract clause was seen as a decisive barrier against such legislation in the future. Thus, both textual absolutism—what part of "no state shall pass any law" does one not understand?—and historical understandings seem to invalidate legislation such as that passed by the Minnesota legislature, however

---

[19] *Home Building and Loan Association v. Blaisdell*, 290 U.S. 398 (1934).

understandable the pressures for such legislation might be. Nonetheless, Chief Justice Charles Evans Hughes, writing for the majority of the Supreme Court, upheld the legislation, demonstrating, for some, that the contract clause was indeed only a "parchment barrier" against legislation that was widely thought to be necessary to respond adequately to the exigencies of the day. In a key paragraph, Hughes wrote:

> It is no answer to say that this public need was not apprehended a century ago, or to insist that what the provision of the Constitution meant to the vision of that day it must mean to the vision of our time. If, by the statement that what the Constitution meant at the time of its adoption it means today, it is intended to say that the great clauses of the Constitution must be confined to the interpretation which the framers, with the conditions and outlook of their time, would have placed upon them, the statement carries its own refutation. It was to guard against such a narrow conception that Chief Justice Marshall uttered the memorable warning—"We must never forget that it is a *constitution* we are expounding" (*McCulloch v. Maryland*, 4 Wheat. 316, 407)—"a constitution intended to endure for ages to come, and, consequently, to be adapted to the various crises of human affairs." [20]

Why do I dwell on *Blaisdell*, given the central theme of this essay? The answer is simple: Hughes does not simply say that maintaining "domestic tranquility" or "establishing justice" is enough to validate Minnesota's actions. Instead, among other things, he goes through a painstaking doctrinal analysis to demonstrate that prior cases legitimate the legislature's actions.

To be sure, one might view John Marshall's comment as sufficiently open-ended to make any invocation of the generalities found in the preamble unnecessary. Yet we can be confident that Hughes would never have used the Marshall quotation to justify inaugurating Franklin D. Roosevelt on, say, January 20, 1933, instead of March 4 (prior to the proposal and ratification of the Twentieth Amendment, which indeed changed the established, and presumably constitutionally entrenched, date of March 4). Even though there is a broad scholarly consensus that the United States was significantly ill-served by the long hiatus between Roosevelt's trouncing of Herbert Hoover in November 1932 and his actually taking office four long months later, and even though there were those who encouraged Roosevelt in effect to declare himself a "dictator"

---

[20] Id. at 442–43. My colleague Scot Powe once suggested that anytime one sees a citation to these passages from *McCulloch*, readers should engage in the equivalent of holding onto their wallets, because the one certainty is that the most obvious construction of the Constitution is likely to fall by the wayside in favor of the upholding of highly controversial exertions of governmental power.

upon his inauguration,[21] Hoover's ability to stay in office until March 4, 1933, was never in doubt. This underscores my own distinction between the genuinely "hardwired" parts of the Constitution and those that, when all is said and done, serve more as "parchment barriers" than as necessarily effective constraints against actions, and "adaptations," that are thought to be required to meet "crises."

Thus, we can arrive at the following conclusion: To rely on the statements of purposes set out in the preamble in order to justify a strongly teleological approach to the U.S. Constitution would be to remove what many regard as the greatest benefit of written constitutionalism itself, which is precisely its mixture of *specification* and *limitation* of powers. Here another Marshallian chestnut might be invoked, this time from *Marbury v. Madison* (1803): "The powers of the legislature are defined, and limited; and that those limits may not be mistaken, or forgotten, the constitution is written." [22] (I will leave for another day the potential contradictions revealed when one juxtaposes the *Marbury* chestnut with the *McCulloch* one.)

Americans of all ideological persuasions are hesitant to support the proposition that those who hold political power should simply be able to do "whatever they think best for the country" or that the current oaths required of federal officials should be modified to require only fidelity to the Constitution's preamble and to let it go at that. Perhaps this is a mistake, especially given developments in the United States over the past seventy-five years that have transformed, if not eliminated, initial visions of limited government. Still, it is significant that the justifications for enhanced powers over this period have been found not in the preamble, but, with regard to Congress, in the "necessary and proper" clause that concludes the assignment of powers to the national legislature in Article I, section 8 of the Constitution, and, with regard to the president, in certain readings of Article II, dealing with presidential authority. Some analysts focus on Article II's very first sentence, which refers to "the Executive Power," unlike Article I, which specifies that Congress enjoys only those powers "herein granted." On the one hand, if powers have not been granted to Congress, one may well believe that Congress does not have them. On the other hand, if there is no such reference to the president, then one may feel free to argue that the chief executive enjoys, say, the "prerogative" powers articulated by John Locke in Chapter XIV of his *Second Treatise of Government*. Other analysts focus on the implications of assigning the president the power to serve as commander-in-chief of the armed forces. University of St. Thomas Law School professor Michael

---

[21] Walter Lippmann, one of the most widely respected newspaper columnists of the era, wrote in a pre-Inauguration column: "A mild species of dictatorship will help us over the road in the roughest months ahead." Quoted in Jonathan Alter, *The Defining Moment: FDR's Hundred Days and the Triumph of Hope* (New York: Simon and Schuster, 2007), 187.

[22] *Marbury v. Madison*, 5 U.S. (1 Cranch) 137, 176 (1803).

Stokes Paulsen emphasizes the importance of the "oath of office" clause as a justification for extraordinary action that many would view as stretching the Constitution to the breaking point.[23] Not even Paulsen, though, offers the preamble in support of his argument.

As for countries other than the United States, I know far more about the formal content of their constitutions than I do about their argumentative practices. And it is true that most (though certainly not all) constitutions include preambles. As political science professor Beau Breslin has noted in his recent study of written constitutions, preambles are the sites within constitutional texts "where constitutional framers proclaim their principal intentions, where they communicate their deepest aspirations for the newly created polity."[24] Given Breslin's elaboration of the multiple functions of contemporary preambles, it is perhaps all the more significant that he offers no examples in which a preamble has become an important part of a given country's professional legal tradition of argument and adjudication (although, as we will see shortly, there may in fact be some such examples).

Especially telling in this regard is latter-day South Africa, not least because its new 1996 Constitution was, by all accounts, intended to serve as a radical break with the past and a harbinger of a transformed future.[25] Anyone who doubts this must merely read its preamble:

> We, the people of South Africa,
> Recognise the injustices of our past;

[23] See Michael Stokes Paulsen, "The Constitution of Necessity," *Notre Dame Law Review* 79 (2004): 1257. The most obvious "extraordinary action" involves torture and other breaches of ordinary legal norms.

[24] Beau Breslin, *From Words to Worlds: Exploring Constitutional Functionality* (Baltimore, MD: The Johns Hopkins University Press, 2009), 50.

[25] The "transformationist" impulse behind the Constitution has been recognized by the South African Constitutional Court and plays some role in its jurisprudence. See, e.g., Justice Mahomed's opinion in *State v. Makwanyane*, which invalidated the death penalty in South Africa:

> In some countries the Constitution only formalizes, in a legal instrument, a historical consensus of values and aspirations evolved incrementally from a stable and unbroken past to accommodate the needs of the future. The South African Constitution is different: it retains from the past only what is defensible and represents a decisive break from, and ringing rejection of, that part of the past which is disgracefully racist, authoritarian, insular and repressive, and a vigorous identification of and commitment to a democratic, universalistic, caring and aspirationally egalitarian ethos expressly articulated in the Constitution.

State v. Makwanyane, 1995 (3) SA 391 (CC), 1995 (6) BCLR 665 (CC). See also *Soobramoney v. Minister of Health (SwaAulu-Natal)*, 1009 (1) SA 765 (CC), 1997 (12) BCLR 1696: "We live in a society in which there are great disparities in wealth. Millions of people are living in deplorable conditions and in great poverty. . . . [T]hese conditions already existed when the Constitution was adopted and a commitment to address them, and to transform our society into one in which there will be human dignity, freedom and equality, lies at the heart of our new constitutional order." See also Christopher Roederer, "Founding Provisions," in *Constitutional Law of South Africa*, 2d ed., ed. Stuart Woolman et al. (Cape Town: Juta, 2002), 13-4.

Honour those who suffered for justice and freedom in our land;
Respect those who have worked to build and develop our country; and
Believe that South Africa belongs to all who live in it, united in our diversity.
We therefore, through our freely elected representatives, adopt this Constitution as the supreme law of the Republic so as to

- Heal the divisions of the past and establish a society based on democratic values, social justice and fundamental human rights;
- Lay the foundations for a democratic and open society in which government is based on the will of the people and every citizen is equally protected by law;
- Improve the quality of life of all citizens and free the potential of each person; and
- Build a united and democratic South Africa able to take its rightful place as a sovereign state in the family of nations.

May God protect our people.
Nkosi Sikelel' iAfrika. Morena boloka setjhaba sa heso.
God seën Suid-Afrika. God bless South Africa.
Mudzimu fhatutshedza Afurika. Hosi katekisa Afrika.[26]

Interestingly enough, this preamble is immediately followed by several "founding provisions," the first of which states:

[Section] 1. *Republic of South Africa*
The Republic of South Africa is one, sovereign, democratic state founded on the following values:

a. Human dignity, the achievement of equality and the advancement of human rights and freedoms.
b. Non-racialism and non-sexism.
c. Supremacy of the constitution and the rule of law.
d. Universal adult suffrage, a national common voters roll, regular elections and a multi-party system of democratic government, to ensure accountability, responsiveness and openness.[27]

---

[26] South African Constitution, available online at http://www.info.gov.za/documents/constitution/1996/96preamble.htm. The final three lines of the preamble invoke God's blessings in several of the official languages of South Africa.
[27] Ibid., available online at http://www.info.gov.za/documents/constitution/1996/96cons1.htm.

Even if one regards the preamble, like Article I, as "foundational,"[28] they are both apparently treated as nonjusticiable,[29] that is, unsuitable for judicial enforcement. This means, practically speaking, that professional lawyers (and most legal academics) will simply tend to ignore such passages inasmuch as they presumably provide no "added value" to one's explicitly legal arguments—arguments that focus on clauses that courts *will* enforce. Thus, in an interesting case dealing with the voting rights of imprisoned felons, the Chief Justice of the South African Constitutional Court, Arthur Chaskalson, acknowledged that "[t]he values enunciated in section 1 of the Constitution are of fundamental importance" inasmuch as "[t]hey inform and give substance to" the Constitution in its entirety, but then went on to proclaim that "they do not, however, give rise to discrete and enforceable rights in themselves."[30] Still, there *are* cases in which the South African Court has looked to the preamble for interpretive guidance.[31]

A similar decision seems to have been reached by the Indian Supreme Court with regard to the preamble of that country's complex constitutional document: "Regarding the use which can be made of the preamble in interpreting an ordinary statute, there is no doubt that it cannot be used to modify the language if the language of the enactment is plain and clear. If the language is not plain and clear, then the preamble may have effect either to extend or restrict the language used in the body of an enactment." The Indian justice who authored this statement, interestingly enough, went on immediately to quote, among others, the nineteenth-century American justice Joseph Story, who had described the preamble of U.S. Constitution as only "a key to open the mind of the makers." According to Indian Chief Justice Sikiri, a preamble may "show the general purposes for which [those framing the constitution] made the several provisions in the Constitution; but nevertheless the preamble is not a part of the Constitution."[32]

It may be worth noting that Article 116 of the 1990 Nepalese Constitution (supplanted, apparently, by a new constitution in 2008) specified that "[a] bill to amend or repeal any Article of this Constitution, *without prejudicing the spirit of the Preamble of this Constitution*, may be introduced in either House of Parliament: Provided that this Article shall not be subject

[28] See G.E. Devenish, *A Commentary on the South African Constitution* (Durban, South Africa: Butterworths, 1998), 28–29.

[29] See Roederer, "Founding Provisions," 13-5 n. 1.

[30] *Minister of Home Affairs v. National Institute for Crime Prevention and the Re-Integration of Offenders (NICRO)*, Case No. CCT03/04 (2004).

[31] See, e.g., Liav Orgad, "The Preamble in Constitutional Interpretation," *I-CON* (forthcoming 2011).

[32] *Kesavananda Bharati v. The State of Kerala*, AIR 1973 SC 1461, available online at http://openarchive.in/newcases/29981.htm. See Joseph Story, *Commentaries on the Constitution of the United States*, ed. Ronald D. Rotunda and John E. Nowak (Durham, NC: Carolina Academic Press, 1987), 163.

to amendment."[33] Almost undoubtedly the most notable use of a preamble has occurred in France, where the Constitutional Council in 1971 invalidated a law passed by the French parliament in light of the "fundamental principles recognized by the laws of the Republic."[34] As a matter of fact, these "fundamental principles" are nowhere named in the 1958 constitution, but are in the preamble to the 1946 constitution. As Liav Orgad writes,

> In later decisions, the council held that the Preamble to the 1946 Constitution enjoys legal force and constitutes an independent source of rights.[35] Interestingly, at the time it was drafted, the 1946 Preamble did not enjoy any legal status. Thus, the Constitutional Council, through a reference to the 1946 Preamble in the 1958 Preamble, effec-

[33] Nepalese Constitution of 1990, Article 116 (emphasis added), available online at http://www.servat.unibe.ch/icl/np00000_.html.

[34] See Decision of the Constitutional Council No. 44-71 (1971).

[35] The preamble to the 1958 French Constitution begins as follows: "The French people hereby solemnly proclaim their dedication to the Rights of Man and the principle of national sovereignty as defined by the Declaration of 1789, reaffirmed and complemented by the Preamble to the 1946 Constitution." See http://www.servat.unibe.ch/icl/fr00000_.html. The 1946 preamble itself is considerably longer and more detailed:

> In the morrow of the victory achieved by the free peoples over the regimes that had sought to enslave and degrade humanity, the people of France proclaim anew that each human being, without distinction of race, religion or creed, possesses sacred and inalienable rights. They solemnly reaffirm the rights and freedoms of man and the citizen enshrined in the Declaration of Rights of 1789 and the fundamental principles acknowledged in the laws of the Republic.
>
> They further proclaim, as being especially necessary to our times, the political, economic and social principles enumerated below:
>
> - The law guarantees women equal rights to those of men in all spheres.
> - Any man persecuted in virtue of his actions in favour of liberty may claim the right of asylum upon the territories of the Republic.
> - Each person has the duty to work and the right to employment. No person may suffer prejudice in his work or employment by virtue of his origins, opinions or beliefs.
> - All men may defend their rights and interests through union action and may belong to the union of their choice.
> - The right to strike shall be exercised within the framework of the laws governing it.
> - All workers shall, through the intermediary of their representatives, participate in the collective determination of their conditions of work and in the management of the work place.
> - All property and all enterprises that have or that may acquire the character of a public service or de facto monopoly shall become the property of society.
> - The Nation shall provide the individual and the family with the conditions necessary to their development.
> - It shall guarantee to all, notably to children, mothers and elderly workers, protection of their health, material security, rest and leisure. All people who, by virtue of their age, physical or mental condition, or economic situation, are incapable of working, shall have the right to receive suitable means of existence from society.
> - The Nation proclaims the solidarity and equality of all French people in bearing the burden resulting from national calamities.

tively granted the 1946 Preamble a higher status than it had previously enjoyed.[36]

So perhaps it is fair to place the preamble of the United States Constitution at one end of a spectrum in being barely, if at all, "legalized," whereas the 1946 French preamble, whatever its initial status, has become strongly generative for modern French constitutional law.[37] Still, even taking into account such examples as South Africa, India, or France, I still think it safe to say that, generally speaking, the motive force behind writing a preamble is to serve some function(s) other than providing an additional patch of text for use in the standard arsenal of legal arguments. Let us turn now to what those functions might be.

IV. The "Nonlegal" Functions of Constitutional Preambles: Delineating the Nation

For better or worse, one important clue to the possible importance of preambles is provided by the German (and, one must always note, at least briefly Nazi) legal philosopher Carl Schmitt.[38] For Schmitt, the existence of a political nation (which, of course, may or may not have

---

- The Nation guarantees equal access for children and adults to instruction, vocational training and culture. The provision of free, public and secular education at all levels is a duty of the State.
- The French Republic, faithful to its traditions, shall conform to the rules of international public law. It shall undertake no war aimed at conquest, nor shall it ever employ force against the freedom of any people.
- Subject to reciprocity, France shall consent to the limitations upon its sovereignty necessary to the organization and preservation of peace.
- France shall form with its overseas peoples a Union founded upon equal rights and duties, without distinction of race or religion.
- The French Union shall be composed of nations and peoples who agree to pool or coordinate their resources and their efforts in order to develop their respective civilizations, increase their well-being, and ensure their security.
- Faithful to its traditional mission, France desires to guide the peoples under its responsibility towards the freedom to administer themselves and to manage their own affairs democratically; eschewing all systems of colonization founded upon arbitrary rule, it guarantees to all equal access to public office and the individual or collective exercise of the rights and freedoms proclaimed or confirmed herein.

Available online at http://www.elysee.fr/elysee/anglais/the_institutions/founding_texts/preambule_to_the_27th_of_october_1946_constitution/preambule_to_the_27th_of_october_1946_constitution.20243.html.

[36] Orgad, "The Preamble in Constitutional Interpretation," 12.

[37] See ibid., 13 n. 53, citing Alec Stone, *The Birth of Judicial Politics in France: The Constitutional Council in Comparative Perspective* (Oxford: Oxford University Press, 1992), 40–45, 66–78 (noting that seven of the sixteen annulments issued by the Council between 1971 and 1981 were based on interpretations of the 1958 preamble).

[38] See especially Carl Schmitt, *Constitutional Theory*, ed. and trans. Jeffrey Seitzer (Durham, NC: Duke University Press, 2008).

been organized into a political state) precedes the adoption of a constitution and, indeed, gives life to it. It is the unified political will of a people (as in "We the People") that creates a constitution—at least in those political orders that purport to rest on popular sovereignty.[39] And any constitution adopted by a national *volk* instantiates the particular perspectives of that discrete national entity, including, for Schmitt, the all-important division of the world into friends and potential enemies.[40] (Does any national constitution, for example, omit clauses dealing with the possibility of war?) We can speak, perhaps less freightedly, of a division of the world into the particular community included within the ambit of the constitution and the inevitably far larger group of others (or Others) who are excluded from it, even if one does not regard them as enemies. The Swiss Constitution, for example, seems altogether typical inasmuch as it ascribes to the Swiss Confederation "the intent of strengthening the alliance of the Confederates and of maintaining and furthering the unity, strength and honor of the Swiss nation."[41] Even if the Swiss do not look askance at the "unity, strength and honor" of other nations, that is clearly not a concern of those gathered together under the auspices of the Swiss Constitution. Nor, I presume, would anyone criticize the Swiss as being "parochial" for their lack of any such concern.

The South African Constitution may be remarkably universalist and cosmopolitan in some of its language, including the emphasis in the preamble on advancing presumably universal "human rights and freedoms." Still, no one reading the preamble would doubt that the constitution is aimed at residents of South Africa, perhaps even "citizens" of South Africa. Perhaps the best evidence is the concluding phrase, in which God's blessings are invoked in a plethora of the eleven official languages of South Africa (including, of course, English and Afrikaans).[42] Note, however, that the languages used are all "local." Arabic, for example, is *not* an official language of South Africa, nor are any of the other languages identified with other parts of Africa, such as Swahili. The South African Constitution is, in this sense, distinctly *not* "Pan-African."

One might notice similarly "localist" aspects in another preamble that appears to embrace universal values more than parochial ones, the pre-

---

[39] See, e.g., ibid., 65, 70.

[40] Carl Schmitt, *The Concept of the Political,* trans. George Schwab (Chicago: University of Chicago Press, 2007).

[41] Swiss Constitution, available online at http://servat.unibe.ch/icl/sz00000_.html.

[42] Thus, "Nkosi Sikelel' iAfrica," although isiZulu, works as well with isiXhosa because the languages are connected, and it might even evoke isiSwati and isiNdebele. "Morena boloka setjhaba sa heso" is Sesotho, but works also with Sepedi and Setswana. "Mudzimu fhatutshedza Afurika" is Tshivenda, while "Hosi katekisa Afrika" is Xitsonga. I am extremely grateful to Aifheli E. Tshivhase, a lecturer in the Faculty of Law at the University of Cape Town, for providing me with this information, and to Professor Christina Murray for putting me in touch with Mr. Tshivhase.

amble to the United States Constitution. It is ultimately "We the People of the United States," after all, who are to enjoy the full blessings of liberty or other goods protected by the Constitution, and not those who are not part of the American community. The most awful demonstration of this point, of course, is *Dred Scott v. Sandford*, an 1857 case in which the majority of the United States Supreme Court defined blacks, even if formally "free" rather than "slaves," as outside the American political community.[43] They were therefore left defenseless, as a matter of constitutional law, against being stripped of any rights that they might, as a matter of contingent fact, happen to possess as the result of the grace of their white rulers. To be sure, this aspect of *Dred Scott* was overruled after the Civil War by the first sentence of the Fourteenth Amendment, which established birthright citizenship for anyone born "within the territory" of the United States.[44] And the overruling of *Dred Scott* by the Fourteenth Amendment has not meant the elimination of the ability of the United States to distinguish between citizens and noncitizens, let alone residents and nonresidents, in structuring its actions.

But let us look at a number of other preambles from around the world and discern what they might be telling us about the visions of their authors (and the social groups they represent). One might, for example, wish to ascertain the relevance of *religion* to constitutional framers and to the communities for which they purport to speak. Although the South African Constitution would not strike most observers as religiously sectarian, it does, as already noted, acknowledge the community's presumptive belief in a God who is capable of "blessing" (or, presumably, otherwise judging) South Africa's new venture in democratic constitutionalism. The United States Constitution is widely viewed as among the most secular of national constitutions,[45] and the preamble certainly offers no succor to those who would challenge this. But one might consider the very last line of the Constitution, which, like the preamble, is presumably without litigative potential, but nonetheless of some import for those interested literally in every word of constitutions regardless of their interest to ordinary lawyers.

The U.S. Constitution concludes as follows: "Done in Convention by the Unanimous Consent of the States present the Seventeenth Day of September in the Year of *our* Lord one thousand seven hundred and

---

[43] *Dred Scott v. Sandford*, 60 U.S. (19 How) 393 (1857).

[44] It should be noted that this part of the Fourteenth Amendment was determined not to apply to American Indians, who were treated as part of separate, though distinctly subordinate, nations and, therefore, not entitled to birthright citizenship. American law with respect to the citizenship status of American Indians changed in 1924, but only because of the passage of a law by Congress. The Supreme Court has never overruled its decision in *Elk v. Wilkins*, 112 U.S. 94 (1884), which rejected birthright citizenship as a constitutional right.

[45] See, e.g., Isaac Kramnick and R. Laurence Moore, *Godless Constitution: A Moral Defense of the Secular State*, rev. ed. (New York: W. W. Norton, 2005).

Eighty seven and of the Independence of the United States of America the Twelfth."[46] To put it mildly, not everyone even at the time of the Constitutional Convention believed in a common "Lord" who was born (more-or-less), 1,787 years prior to the great events in Philadelphia.[47] Indeed, one might even suggest that any similar conclusion to a statute passed by Congress today would properly be found to violate the establishment clause of the First Amendment.

This controversial (and demonstrably false) claim to religious unity among the American people circa 1787, buried as it is in the Constitution's concluding line, is one that arguably needs to be teased out of the document. Yet the task of finding similar claims is scarcely so difficult with regard to many other constitutions around the world. Americans, for example, need only look to their north in order to find the opening words of the the constitution-like Canadian Charter of Rights and Freedoms: "Whereas Canada is founded upon principles that recognize the supremacy of God and the rule of law."[48] Switzerland begins its preamble by speaking "In the Name of God Almighty!"[49] And Germany's post–World War II framers were "Conscious of their responsibility before God and Men."[50] One might well regard these invocations of "God" as relatively nonsectarian, unless, of course, one does not believe in any god. Alternatively, one might be a religious believer who presumes that the "God" invoked by Canada, Switzerland, or Germany is some version of a Christian (or Judeo-Christian) god that one might not in fact believe in. There are, after all, said to be over three-quarters of a million Hindus in Canada,[51] and perhaps they could be forgiven for believing that the ostensible community that is organizing itself around the Charter of Rights and Freedoms, by referring only to "God" instead of multiple "gods," excludes them or, at best, merely "tolerates" their presence.

One cannot take refuge in some vague invocation of post–World War II Judeo-Christianity when reading some other preambles—even those of countries considered well within "the West." Thus, the preamble of the Greek Constitution consists in substance of "In the name of the Holy and Consubstantial and Indivisible Trinity."[52] (Not surprisingly, Article 3 establishes the Eastern Orthodox Church of Christ as the "prevailing religion"

---

[46] United States Constitution, available online at http://www.earlyamerica.com/earlyamerica/freedom/constitution/text.html (emphasis added).

[47] I was reminded to think about this passage of the Constitution by Ronald R. Garet, "With Radiant Countenance: Creation, Redemption, and Revelation," a paper prepared for delivery at the annual meeting of the American Association of Law Schools, January 2008.

[48] Canadian Charter of Rights and Freedoms, available online at http://www.efc.ca/pages/law/charter/charter.text.html.

[49] Swiss Constitution, available online at http://servat.unibe.ch/icl/sz00000_.html.

[50] German Constitution, available online at http://www.helplinelaw.com/law/germany/constitution/constitution01.php.

[51] See "Hinduism: The World's Third Largest Religion," http://www.religioustolerance.org/hinduism.htm.

[52] Greek Constitution, available online at http://www.hri.org/docs/syntagma/.

in the country.) The most remarkable of such preambles is almost certainly Ireland's:

> *In the Name of the Most Holy Trinity, from Whom is all authority and to Whom, as our final end, all actions both of men and States must be referred,*
>   We, the people of Éire,
>   Humbly acknowledging all our obligations to our Divine Lord, Jesus Christ, Who sustained our fathers through centuries of trial,
>   Gratefully remembering their heroic and unremitting struggle to regain the rightful independence of our Nation,
>   And seeking to promote the common good, with due observance of Prudence, Justice and Charity, so that the dignity and freedom of the individual may be assured, true social order attained, the unity of our country restored, and concord established with other nations,
>   Do hereby adopt, enact, and give to ourselves this Constitution.[53]

The naïve reader may well believe that a condition of membership within the "people of Eire" is "Humbly acknowledging all our obligations to our Divine Lord, Jesus Christ." One may wonder, of course, if this helps to explain anything interesting about Irish politics. After all, Dublin many years ago had a Jewish mayor, Robert Briscoe, who presumably acknowledged no such obligations. I have little doubt, moreover, that any attempt by contemporary Ireland to deny citizenship, say, to immigrants who do not acknowledge such obligations might well run afoul of the European Convention of Human Rights, but that is a matter for a different essay.

Perhaps the best non-Western analogue to Ireland's constitution is that of the Islamic Republic of Pakistan, whose preamble can, like Ireland's, be described as a form of political theology. It is also unusually long and, like the preambles of many contemporary constitutions, seems dedicated to telling the nation's story and placing its people in a given relationship with the universe.

> Whereas sovereignty over the entire Universe belongs to Almighty Allah alone, and the authority to be exercised by the people of Pakistan within the limits prescribed by Him is a sacred trust;
>   And whereas it is the will of the people of Pakistan to establish an order:
>   Wherein the State shall exercise its powers and authority through the chosen representatives of the people;
>   Wherein the principles of democracy, freedom, equality, tolerance and social justice, as enunciated by Islam, shall be fully observed;

---

[53] Irish Constitution, available online at http://www.taoiseach.gov.ie/attached_files/Pdf%20files/Constitution%20of%20IrelandNov2004.pdf (emphasis in the original).

Wherein the Muslims shall be enabled to order their lives in the individual and collective spheres in accordance with the teachings and requirements of Islam as set out in the Holy Quran and Sunnah;

Wherein adequate provision shall be made for the minorities freely to profess and practise their religions and develop their cultures;

Wherein the territories now included in or in accession with Pakistan and such other territories as may hereafter be included in or accede to Pakistan shall form a Federation wherein the units will be autonomous with such boundaries and limitations on their powers and authority as may be prescribed;

Wherein shall be guaranteed fundamental rights, including equality of status, of opportunity and before law, social, economic and political justice, and freedom of thought, expression, belief, faith, worship and association, subject to law and public morality;

Wherein adequate provision shall be made to safeguard the legitimate interests of minorities and backward and depressed classes;

Wherein the independence of the judiciary shall be fully secured;

Wherein the integrity of the territories of the Federation, its independence and all its rights, including its sovereign rights on land, sea and air, shall be safeguarded;

So that the people of Pakistan may prosper and attain their rightful and honoured place amongst the nations of the World and make their full contribution towards international peace and progress and happiness of humanity:

Now, therefore, we, the people of Pakistan,

Cognisant of our responsibility before Almighty Allah and men;

Cognisant of the sacrifices made by the people in the cause of Pakistan;

Faithful to the declaration made by the Founder of Pakistan, Quaid-i-Azam Mohammad Ali Jinnah, that Pakistan would be a democratic State based on Islamic principles of social justice;

Dedicated to the preservation of democracy achieved by the unremitting struggle of the people against oppression and tyranny;

Inspired by the resolve to protect our national and political unity and solidarity by creating an egalitarian society through a new order;

Do hereby, through our representatives in the National Assembly, adopt, enact and give to ourselves, this Constitution.[54]

Needless to say, not all countries wish to embrace such a sectarian self-understanding as do Greece, Ireland, or Pakistan (among many other examples that might be given). Thus, the preambles of at least some constitutions written in recent years, especially in Europe, seem to wish to

[54] Constitution of Pakistan, available online at http://www.pakistanconstitution-law.com/preamble.asp.

define the relevant political community—and its ostensible "unity"—in less religious terms. Especially interesting in this regard is Poland, not least because of its strong historical identification with Roman Catholicism, but also because its new constitutional self-understanding was developed during the reign of "the Polish Pope," John Paul II. The preamble to the Polish Constitution reads:

> Having regard for the existence and future of our Homeland,
>> Which recovered, in 1989, the possibility of a sovereign and democratic determination of its fate,
>> *We, the Polish Nation—all citizens of the Republic,*
>> *Both those who believe in God as the source of truth, justice, good and beauty,*
>> *As well as those not sharing such faith but respecting those universal values as arising from other sources,*
>> Equal in rights and obligations towards the common good—Poland,
>> Beholden to our ancestors for their labours, their struggle for independence achieved at great sacrifice, for our culture rooted in the Christian heritage of the Nation and in universal human values,
>> Recalling the best traditions of the First and the Second Republic,
>> Obliged to bequeath to future generations all that is valuable from our over one thousand years' heritage,
>> Bound in community with our compatriots dispersed throughout the world,
>> Aware of the need for cooperation with all countries for the good of the Human Family,
>> Mindful of the bitter experiences of the times when fundamental freedoms and human rights were violated in our Homeland,
>> Desiring to guarantee the rights of the citizens for all time, and to ensure diligence and efficiency in the work of public bodies,
>> Recognizing our responsibility before God or our own consciences,
>> Hereby establish this Constitution of the Republic of Poland as the basic law for the State, based on respect for freedom and justice, cooperation between the public powers, social dialogue as well as on the principle of aiding in the strengthening [of] the powers of citizens and their communities.[55]

Poland, obviously, tries to recognize the coexistence of religious and nonreligious elements of its heritage. But consider in this context the

---

[55] Polish Constitution, available online at http://servat.unibe.ch/icl/pl00000_.html (emphasis added). Consider also in this context the preamble to the 1998 Albanian constitution, which begins as follows: "We, the people of Albania, proud and aware of our history, with responsibility for the future, and with faith in God and/or other universal values, ... establish this Constitution." See http://www.ipls.org/services/kusht/intro.html. I am grateful to Zachary Elkins for informing me of this text.

preamble to the Spanish Constitution, which is striking in its failure to mention any aspect of Spain's equally notable religious history. The preamble calls upon the "Spanish Nation" "to establish justice, liberty, and security" and a panoply of other goods "in accordance with a just economic and social order." Moreover, "all Spaniards and peoples of Spain" will be protected "in the exercise of human rights, their cultures and traditions, languages, and institutions. . . ." But any acknowledgment that for many Spaniards, at least historically, these "cultures and traditions," not to mention "institutions," had anything to do with the Roman Catholic Church, is left between the lines, as it were. In its own way, the preamble to the Spanish Constitution seems comparable to that of the South African Constitution in distancing itself from what many would say is Spain's historical past.[56]

Almost certainly the most notable attempt of a preamble to establish a fully secular vision of its constituent people, at least when functioning as a polity, is that found in the constitution of modern Turkey:

> In line with the concept of nationalism outlined and the reforms and principles introduced by the founder of the Republic of Turkey, Atatürk, the immortal leader and the unrivaled hero, this Constitution, which affirms the eternal existence of the Turkish nation and motherland and the indivisible unity of the Turkish State, embodies;
>
> The determination to safeguard the everlasting existence, prosperity and material and spiritual well-being of the Republic of Turkey and to attain the standards of contemporary civilization as an honourable member with equal rights of the family of world nations;
>
> The understanding of the absolute supremacy of the will of the nation and of the fact that sovereignty is vested fully and unconditionally in the Turkish nation and that no individual or body empowered to exercise this sovereignty in the name of the nation shall deviate from liberal democracy and the legal system instituted according to its requirements;
>
> The principle of the separation of powers, which does not imply an order of precedence among the organs of State but refers solely to the exercising of certain State powers and discharging of duties which are limited to cooperation and division of functions, and which accepts the supremacy of the Constitution and the law;
>
> The recognition that no protection shall be accorded to an activity contrary to Turkish national interests, the principle of the indivisibility of the existence of Turkey with its State and territory, Turkish historical and moral values or the nationalism, principles, reforms and modernism of Atatürk and that, as required by the principle of

---

[56] See the Spanish Constitution, available online at http://servat.unibe.ch/icl/sp00000_.html.

secularism, there shall be no interference whatsoever by sacred religious feelings in State affairs and politics; . . .

This Constitution, which is to be embraced with the ideas, beliefs, and resolutions it embodies below [and] should be interpreted and implemented accordingly, thus commanding respect for, and absolute loyalty to, its letter and spirit,

Is entrusted by the Turkish nation to the patriotism and nationalism of its democracy-loving sons and daughters.[57]

One could write an entire essay on the Turkish preamble itself, since it raises so many questions beyond those of religion and secularism. It is obviously suffused with Turkish nationalism. It appears to require, for example, that all who wish to be deemed "good Turks" must recognize Atatürk as their "immortal leader" and "unrivaled hero," in spite of the fact that any multicultural society will feature a multiplicity of "heroes," some of whom will have been historical adversaries and, consequently, are unlikely to be the objects of universal admiration. (Consider, in the case of the U.S., Robert E. Lee and Ulysses S. Grant, or Abraham Lincoln and Jefferson Davis.) I have written elsewhere of the importance to any society of its public monuments, which are necessarily "tutelary" inasmuch as they attempt, with varying success, to shape the consciousness of the citizenry and of future generations and inculcate in them the norms of "political correctness."[58]

From this perspective, the opening paragraph of the Turkish preamble is a model example of this tutelary function, for good or (from the perspective of those less taken by Turkish nationalism) for ill. Few other preambles are as "personalistic" as the Turkish one, but many reflect the desire of their authors to model a history of the particular nation that is being given a certain form of political life to go with its preexisting social one.

Exemplary in this regard is the constitution of Croatia, written in the aftermath of the dissolution of the multiethnic state of Yugoslavia in 1992.[59] The Croatian preamble presents an extended history lesson, presumably part of an effort to educate the surrounding community and, perhaps, pay a "decent respect to the opinions of mankind,"[60] though one assumes that it will also play a role in the future civic education of young Croatians:

---

[57] Constitution of the Republic of Turkey, available online at http://www.servat.unibe.ch/icl/tu00000_.html.

[58] Sanford Levinson, *Written in Stone: Public Monuments in Changing Societies* (Durham, NC: Duke University Press, 1998).

[59] Constitution of Croatia, available online at http://www.servat.unibe.ch/law/icl/hr00000_.html.

[60] See the American Declaration of Independence: "When in the Course of human events it becomes necessary for one people to dissolve the political bands which have connected them with another . . . a decent respect to the opinions of mankind requires that they should declare the causes which impel them to the separation." Available online at http://www.ushistory.org/declaration/document/index.htm.

The millenary identity of the Croatian nation and the continuity of its statehood, confirmed by the course of its entire historical experience within different forms of states and by the preservation and growth of the idea of a national state, founded on the historical right of the Croatian nation to full sovereignty, manifested in [a series of specified historical events occurring in the seventh, ninth, and tenth centuries, as well as other events in 1527, 1712, 1848, 1868, 1918, and 1939].

[With the establishment of] the foundations of state sovereignty during the course of the Second World War, by the decisions of the Antifascist Council of National Liberation of Croatia (1943), as opposed to the proclamation of the Independent State of Croatia (1941), and subsequently in the Constitution of the People's Republic of Croatia (1947) and all later constitutions of the Socialist Republic of Croatia (1963–1990), on the threshold of the historical changes, marked by the collapse of the communist system and changes in the European international order, the Croatian nation by its freely expressed will at the first democratic elections (1990) reaffirmed its millenary statehood. By the new Constitution of the Republic of Croatia (1990) and the victory in the Homeland War (1991–1995), the Croatian nation demonstrated its will and determination to establish and defend the Republic of Croatia as a free, independent, sovereign and democratic state.

Considering the presented historical facts and universally accepted principles of the modern world, as well as the inalienable and indivisible, non-transferable and non-exhaustible right of the Croatian nation to self-determination and state sovereignty, including its fully maintained right to secession and association, as basic provisions for peace and stability of the international order, the Republic of Croatia is established as the national state of the Croatian nation and the state of the members of autochthonous national minorities: Serbs, Czechs, Slovaks, Italians, Hungarians, Jews, Germans, Austrians, Ukrainians and Ruthenians and the others who are citizens, and who are guaranteed equality with citizens of Croatian nationality and the realization of national rights in accordance with the democratic norms of the United Nations Organization and the countries of the free world.

Respecting the will of the Croatian nation and all citizens, resolutely expressed in the free elections, the Republic of Croatia is hereby founded and shall develop as a sovereign and democratic state in which equality, freedoms and human rights are guaranteed and ensured, and their economic and cultural progress and social welfare promoted.[61]

---

[61] Constitution of Croatia, available online at http://www.servat.unibe.ch/icl/hr00000_.html.

Similarly tutelary, one can be confident, is the preamble to the 1992 constitution of the Socialist Republic of Vietnam, which, after referring to the "millennia-old history" of "the Vietnamese people," goes on to offer a synopsis of developments "[s]tarting in 1930, under the leadership of the Communist Party of Vietnam formed and trained by President Ho Chi Minh." Needless to say, this includes reference to the 1945 Declaration of Independence by the Democratic Republic of Vietnam and the military victories over France and the United States that "reunified the mother-land, and brought to completion the people's national democratic revo-lution." Along the way, constitutions were adopted in 1946, 1959, and 1980.

> Starting in 1986, a comprehensive national renewal advocated by the 6th Congress of the Communist Party of Vietnam has achieved very important initial results. The National Assembly has decided to revise the 1980 Constitution in response to the requirements of the new situation and tasks.
>
> This Constitution establishes our political regime, economic sys-tem, social and cultural institutions; it deals with our national defence and security, the fundamental rights and duties of the citizen, the structure and principles regarding the organization and activity of State organs; it institutionalizes the relationship between the Party as leader, the people as master, and the State as administrator.
>
> In the light of Marxism-Leninism and Ho Chi Minh's thought, carrying into effect the Programme of national construction in the period of transition to socialism, the Vietnamese people vow to unite millions as one, uphold the spirit of self-reliance in building the country, carry out a foreign policy of independence, sovereignty, peace, friendship and cooperation with all nations, strictly abide by the Constitution, and win ever greater successes in their effort to renovate, build and defend their motherland.[62]

The Turkish, Croatian, and Vietnamese preambles test the reader not only by their length, but also by their invocation of either (or both) nineteenth-century-style organic nationalism or vanguards that claim to speak in the name of the entire social order. It is as if the Declaration of Independence—and not simply the preamble—appeared at the out-set of the United States Constitution and, after specifying the "long train of abuses" that justified American secession from the British Empire, went on to single out George Washington and those who rallied to his leadership as exemplary Americans.

---

[62] Constitution of Vietnam, available online at http://www.servat.unibe.ch/icl/vm00000_.html.

It is obvious that many more preambles could be analyzed in terms of the lessons their authors wished to convey to their readers, whether locals who would presumably be socialized into the understandings of the new constitution or foreign onlookers who might be reassured by references to the international community and the expressed desire to become a member in good standing of that community. Thus, as Breslin writes, a number of the constitutions drafted in Eastern Europe "have included language that not only articulates the distinctiveness of the particular regime but also includes statements acknowledging the place of the polity within the international community of sovereign states."[63] Nowhere, of course, have the ravages of organic nationalism been more virulent than in Eastern Europe, and one might see these national constitutions as way stations to a European Union that will, in time, establish its own strong identity. One should remember, however, that one of the most divisive issues in the creation of what many called a draft "constitution" for the European Union was precisely the language of the preamble and, more particularly, whether Europe's Christian heritage would be acknowledged. Largely because of France, apparently, there was no such reference.[64]

V. Conclusion: Unity, Multiplicity, and Preambles

We have seen that preambles serve far more what might be described as an "expressive" function than a "legal" one. What is being expressed is the ostensible "essence" of the people or nation in whose name the constitution has been drafted, whether defined in terms of religion, language, ethnicity, shared history of oppression, or even commitment to some scheme of universal values. This raises a final important question: Is there a perhaps fatal tension between (1) the constitutional drafters' aim of describing (or perhaps creating) national unity through the language of a preamble and (2) the reality that the societies being described are rarely so cohesive as certain preambles might suggest? Consider in this context the statement of the American Supreme Court justice Oliver Wendell Holmes in his dissenting opinion in the 1905 case of *Lochner v. New York*. There he famously proclaimed that the United States Constitution—and is there any reason to limit the force of his statement *only* to that constitution?—"is not intended to embody a particular economic theory, whether of paternalism and the organic relation of the citizen to the state or of laissez faire. *It is made for people of fundamentally differing views.*"[65] Holmes even wrote that "state laws may regulate life in many ways which we, as legislators, might think as injudicious, or, if you like, as tyrannical. . . ." It would make no difference

---

[63] Breslin, *From Words to Worlds*, 60.

[64] For an interesting overview of the controversy, see "Do 'God' and 'Christianity' Have a Place in the European Union Constitution?" http://www.religioustolerance.org/const_eu.htm.

[65] *Lochner v. New York*, 198 U.S. 45, 75 (1905) (Holmes, J., dissenting) (emphasis added).

with regard to his own duty to uphold those laws, so long as they represented majority sentiment. To be sure, Holmes also wrote, in the next paragraph, of the dispositive role of "fundamental principles as they have been understood by the traditions of our people and our law." So perhaps he saw the American people as deeply unified around certain "traditions" even as we are "fundamentally differing" in views concerning "economic theory," among other things. Holmes was the master of the aphorism or, as he called it, the *apercu*, nowhere more than in his short and question-begging *Lochner* dissent. Nonetheless, it is still reasonable to ask if anyone who agrees with Holmes's general perspective, captured far more in his initial comments than in his cryptic caveat, would agree as well with the suggestion that the writing of preambles is more a testament to a yearning for homogeneity (whether of religion, ethnicity, or political ideology) than a reflection of reality. Sometimes this yearning may be relatively innocent and, on occasion, even inspiring—if we happen to agree with the preambular aspirations. But if one does not share the visions instantiated in a particular preamble, then it is surely permissible to view it as exemplifying simply one more power play in the struggle to establish the legitimacy of institutions of coercion that we call "law."

When I teach courses on constitutional design, I ask my students to imagine themselves as "certified constitutional designers" who will be asked to provide counsel to constitutional framers near and far on the writing of constitutions. It is easy enough to suggest that they should begin by addressing those particular issues that demand settlement, given, as I argued at the outset, that settlement is surely one of the most important functions of any constitution. But it is also obvious that one cannot understand constitutions simply from the perspective of settlement. Constitutions also function to generate (perhaps endless) legal conversations, particularly about rights, through the litigation of disputes and the accompanying legal interpretations offered by those charged with adjudicating such disputes. But then there are constitutional preambles, which make little or no contribution to the settlement function and, because they are relatively rarely the focus of litigation, almost as little contribution to the legal-conversation function. So the best way of concluding this essay is simply to ask a question of those who are brave (or foolhardy) enough to offer themselves as consultants on constitutional design: How would they respond if their clients asked them for advice on whether to write a preamble to the new constitution? To be sure, there is no one-size-fits-all answer, but that simply forces us to ask many other questions about the society in question before we decide whether to write a preamble at all, what precisely to say, and even what language(s) to say it in.

Law, University of Texas at Austin

THE ORIGINS OF AN INDEPENDENT JUDICIARY IN
NEW YORK, 1621–1777*

By Scott D. Gerber

I. Introduction

An independent judiciary is an essential component of the American conception of separation of powers.[1] Not surprisingly, the framers who drafted the judicial article of the U.S. Constitution during the summer of 1787 were influenced, both positively and negatively, by the state practices of the day: they embraced some practices and rejected others. The result was a federal judiciary that forms a separate branch of the national government, judges who enjoy tenure during good behavior, and salaries that cannot be diminished while in office.[2] New York, among the most significant of the original thirteen states,[3] was prominent on the question of judicial independence. This essay explores the constitutional development of the judicial branch in New York and assesses the influence of New York's judiciary on the federal constitution that followed.[4] As will be

* I would like to thank Ohio Northern University for a summer research grant, Brian Haagensen and Larry Sunser for research assistance, and George Billias, Peter Galie, Dan Hulsebosch, Sandra McDonald, Ellen Frankel Paul, Steve Veltri, and Jim Viator for comments on drafts. This essay, which will appear as a chapter in my book *A Distinct Judicial Power: The Origins of an Independent Judiciary, 1606–1787* (Oxford University Press, forthcoming), is dedicated to the memory of Norman Barry.

[1] Scott D. Gerber, "The Court, the Constitution, and the History of Ideas," *Vanderbilt Law Review* 61, no. 4 (2008), 1067–1126.

[2] Article III, section 1, of the U.S. Constitution provides: "The judicial Power of the United States, shall be vested in one supreme Court, and in such inferior Courts as the Congress may from time to time ordain and establish. The Judges, both of the supreme and inferior Courts, shall hold their Offices during good Behaviour, and shall, at stated Times, receive for their Services, a Compensation, which shall not be diminished during their Continuance in Office."

[3] To mention the most famous example in support of this proposition, *The Federalist Papers*, a series of newspaper articles penned pseudonymously by Alexander Hamilton, James Madison, and John Jay that are almost universally regarded as the best guide to the framers' understanding of the Federal Constitution of 1787, were written to persuade the people of New York to ratify the U.S. Constitution. The fear was that, without New York's approval, the U.S. Constitution would not be enacted. See, for example, Jack N. Rakove, *Original Meanings: Politics and Ideas in the Making of the Constitution* (New York: Alfred A. Knopf, 1996). See generally *The Federalist Papers*, ed. Clinton Rossiter (New York: New American Library, 1961).

[4] Gordon S. Wood, the preeminent early American historian, has been calling for a study such as this for four decades. See, for example, Gordon S. Wood, *The Creation of the American Republic, 1776–1787* (Chapel Hill: University of North Carolina Press, 1969), 624; Gordon S. Wood, "The Origins of Judicial Review," *Suffolk University Law Review* 22, no. 4 (1988): 1293, 1304–5. Wood is a historian; I am a lawyer and a political scientist. He almost certainly would approach the subject differently than I do. I discuss the development of an indepen-

seen, New York provides a vivid case study of a state "groping" toward a new ideal that became a reality a decade after its own constitution was enacted in 1777 and at a different level of government.[5]

II. THE DUTCH PERIOD, 1621–1664

A. Charter of the Dutch West India Company of 1621

In 1609, Henry Hudson, an Englishman sailing under Dutch colors, was searching for the Northwest Passage to the Orient (now Asia). Instead, he found the river that bears his name. His discovery provided the Netherlands with a claim to territory—also claimed by England—that includes present-day New York, New Jersey, Delaware, and part of Connecticut. On June 3, 1621, the Dutch government—their "High Mightinesses the States-General of the Netherlands"—granted a charter to a group of Dutch merchants operating as the Dutch West India Company that conferred upon the company for twenty-four years exclusive rights to trade in what was called "New Netherland."[6]

Although the Dutch West India Company was inspired by the previous successes of several trading posts along the Hudson River Valley and motivated by commercial concerns,[7] the charter conferred by the Dutch government was as much an organic law—a constitution—as a trade agreement.[8] It authorized the company to maintain naval and military

---

dent judicial power in light of what Montesquieu famously identified as three separate types of government power. I also focus on constitutional texts, where ideas about political architecture are memorialized.

[5] E-mail to the author from Daniel J. Hulsebosch, Professor of Law, New York University (January 8, 2009).

[6] The 1621 charter is available online at http://www.yale.edu/lawweb/avalon/westind.htm.

[7] Michael G. Kammen, *Colonial New York: A History* (New York: Scribner, 1976), 19–20, 23–26. See also Alden Chester, *Courts and Lawyers of New York: A History, 1609–1925*, 3 vols. (New York: American Historical Society, 1925), 1:51 n. 1: "Adventure brought men to Virginia; politics and religion to New England; philanthropy to Georgia; but New York was founded by trade for trade and for nothing else." A 1614 charter issued to several Amsterdam merchants sought to encourage exploration of the territory by promising generous trade rights. The charter expired in 1618. James Sullivan, *The History of New York State*, book 1, chap. 3, part 7, available online at http://www.usgennet.org/usa/ny/state/his/bk1/ch3/pt7.html. In a bibliography of New York colonial legal research materials, law librarian Robert A. Emery observes that "writings on New York colonial law are voluminous, and it would be pointless to list them all." Robert A. Emery, "New York Prestatehood Legal Research Materials," in Michael Chiorazzi and Marguerite Most, eds., *Prestatehood Legal Materials: A Fifty-State Research Guide, Including New York City and the District of Columbia*, 2 vols. (New York: Hawthorne Information Press, 2005), 2:795, 809. I concur. I limit my citations in this essay to the most useful of the existing research related to my topic. Much of the secondary literature is repetitive. For a well received recent treatment, see Daniel J. Hulsebosch, *Constituting Empire: New York and the Transformation of Constitutionalism in the Atlantic World, 1664–1830* (Chapel Hill: University of North Carolina Press, 2005).

[8] Charles Z. Lincoln, *The Constitutional History of New York*, 5 vols. (Rochester, NY: The Lawyer's Cooperative Publishing Co., 1906), 1:5–6. Lincoln's treatise was the first constitutional history of New York.

forces, to exercise judicial and administrative powers, and to make war and peace with indigenous peoples.

The powers conferred upon the company were divided among five "chambers" representing the different cities of the Netherlands. These powers were then delegated to an "assembly of XIX" comprised of representatives from the constituent cities.[9] The charter authorized the company "to appoint and remove governors, officers of justice, and other public officers," and the powers delegated to the assembly of XIX were themselves delegated to a governor—known as the "director-general"—and a council residing in New Netherland.[10] All officers were required by the charter to swear an oath of allegiance to both the company and the Dutch government. The "will" of the company, expressed in its instructions to the director-general and his council, "was to be the law of New Netherland." There was no separation of powers: the director-general and council were to exercise all executive, legislative, and judicial authority.[11] The Amsterdam chamber, charged with the administration of the company's affairs in New Netherland, maintained supervisory control over the governmental decisions made in the province—a power delegated to it by the assembly of XIX.[12]

Attorney Charles Z. Lincoln concluded in his landmark treatise *The Constitutional History of New York* that because of the small number of settlers and the need to concentrate on sheer survival, there was likely "little, if any, occasion for organizing courts" during the first decade or so of New Netherland's existence.[13] The director-general and his council were the court, with a "schout-fiscal" (a sort of attorney general) added to the mix in or about 1626. Commencing in 1638 and continuing for the next nine years, the province was ruled by an autocratic director-general, William Kieft, who retained "in his own hands the sole administration of justice."[14] The people eventually demanded change, and, in 1647, Peter Stuyvesant, the most significant of New Netherland's directors-general,[15] established a court of justice—called the tribunal of the "Nine Men"—with plenary jurisdiction, subject, not surprisingly, to appeal to the director-general himself in certain situations.[16] This arrangement also proved

---

[9] Ibid., 412.

[10] Peter J. Galie, *Ordered Liberty: A Constitutional History of New York* (New York: Fordham University Press, 1996), 12.

[11] Lincoln, *Constitutional History*, 1:413. The commissions to the various directors-general echoed the charter's command regarding the government of the province. Ibid., 12–13.

[12] Ibid., 412–13.

[13] Ibid., 455.

[14] Ibid. However, in August 1641 Kieft called a meeting that became the first representative body in the province. Galie, *Ordered Liberty*, 12.

[15] Kammen, *Colonial New York*, 48–72. An earlier director-general, Peter Minuit, has attained mythical status for his purchase of Manhattan from Native Americans for goods valued at a mere sixty guilders. Chester, *Courts and Lawyers of New York*, 1:181–82.

[16] The tribunal of Nine Men was antedated by the boards of Twelve Men (1641) and of Eight Men (1643 and 1645), but these preceding boards did not exercise judicial power.

unsatisfactory to the people. After years of requests by the settlers, the governing officials of the Dutch West India Company agreed to establish a court composed of one "schout" (a combination district attorney and sheriff), two "burgomasters" (a kind of mayor), and five "schepen" (a sort of alderman) for each part of the province.[17] Director-General Stuyvesant did not like these courts, but was forced to tolerate them.[18] He retained appellate jurisdiction for himself and his council, with arbitration being the preferred method of dispute resolution.

B. Charter of Freedoms and Exemptions of 1629

The assembly of XIX issued a Charter of Freedoms and Exemptions on June 7, 1629, to speed the settlement of New Netherland. This charter awarded special privileges and powers to "patroons" (rough translation: patrons or participants) willing to relocate there. (The plan resembled that of the English commercial colonizers.)[19] Any patroon who brought to New Netherland during a four-year period fifty or more adults was given a twenty-five kilometer riverfront plot, exclusive hunting and fishing privileges within his estate, and judicial and administrative authority over it (subject, of course, to review by the Dutch government and the company).[20]

The charter mentioned "Courts of the patroons," but historians have concluded that it is doubtful they took the form of feudal courts baron and leet (manorial courts that date from the early Middle Ages). Instead, disputes between a patroon and persons living on his estate were likely resolved by the previously described courts.[21] Moreover, only one of the patroonships, that of the Van Rensselaers, was successful.[22]

In summary, what the framers of the U.S. Constitution would come to regard as constitutional government was subordinated throughout the administration of New Netherland to the commercial interests of the Dutch West India Company. Nonetheless, modest gestures were made in

---

Chester, *Courts and Lawyers of New York*, 1: chap. 15. The tribunal of Nine Men was the first inferior court established in what is now the state of New York. Ibid., 221.

[17] Lincoln, *Constitutional History*, 1:456–58. In 1653, New Amsterdam (present-day New York City) became the first locality to enjoy burgher government. Outlying settlements soon followed suit.

[18] Ibid., 457.

[19] Charles M. Andrews, *The Colonial Period of American History*, 4 vols. (New Haven, CT: Yale University Press, 1937), 3:82. The English commercial colonizers offered financial and political incentives to speed settlement of their provinces.

[20] Ibid.; Chester, *Courts and Lawyers of New York*, 1:79; Lincoln, *Constitutional History*, 1:413; Kammen, *Colonial New York*, 32.

[21] Andrews, *The Colonial Period*, 3:82 n. 3.

[22] Ibid., 83. See generally Chester, *Courts and Lawyers of New York*, 1: chap. 8. An amended Charter of Freedoms and Exemptions was issued in 1640. It reduced the number of adults a patroon was required to bring to New Netherland from fifty to five. Kammen, *Colonial New York*, 34. In 1650, the Charter of Freedoms and Exemptions was again amended, but not in any material respect. Lincoln, *Constitutional History*, 1:12.

the direction of constitutionalism. Two of these merit brief mention. One occurred in 1657 when the burgomasters of New Amsterdam (today, New York City) established separate meeting days for their judicial and legislative responsibilities and also requested permission from Director-General Stuyvesant that these two powers of government be exercised by two separate sets of men. Although Stuyvesant denied the request and the court of schout, burgomasters, and schepens continued as a mixed tribunal until the end of Dutch control of New Netherland, the request itself represented an important step in the constitutional development of New York's judiciary.[23]

The second gesture in the direction of constitutionalism arose from the contentious relationship between Adriaen Cornelissen van der Donck of the tribunal of Nine Men and Director-General Stuyvesant. Van der Donck was the author of two remonstrances condemning Stuyvesant's autocratic ways presented to the states-general in Holland. (Stuyvesant was accused of, among other abuses, governing as if his will was "law absolute.") In fact, Van der Donck was largely responsible for forcing Stuyvesant to institute burgher government in the province. Had war not broken out between England and Holland, and Stuyvesant's expertise as a military commander not been potentially necessary, Van der Donck almost certainly would have been successful in getting Stuyvesant dismissed from his director-generalship.[24]

III. The Ducal Proprietary Period, 1664–1685

A. Grant of the Province of Maine of 1663/64[25]

Two nations with competing claims to the same territory constitute a war waiting to happen. For England and the Netherlands, the war over New Netherland ended without a fight. On August 27, 1664, Director-General Stuyvesant acquiesced to Articles of Capitulation with the English, whose much stronger forces were anchored off the coast.[26] The articles did more than simply transfer control of the territory from the Dutch to the English: they "also suggested how deeply entrenched charters of governance and the protection of personal rights were."[27] The articles permitted all settlers — including those from the Netherlands — to continue to inhabit the province and to dispose of their property as they pleased. The articles also guaranteed liberty of conscience to the Dutch settlers.[28]

---

[23] See Chester, *Courts and Lawyers of New York*, 1:133–34 (describing the incident).
[24] Ibid., 235–44.
[25] The British American colonies did not adopt the Gregorian calendar until 1752. Pre-1752 Julian calendar dates between January 1 and March 25 necessitate reference to both the Gregorian and Julian years.
[26] Kammen, *Colonial New York*, 69–72.
[27] Galie, *Ordered Liberty*, 17.
[28] Ibid.

Several months earlier, on March 12, 1663/64, "Charles II gave to his brother, James Duke of York, quite a gift":[29] a grant of land that included, among other territory, "Hudsons River and all the land from the west side of Conecticutte River to ye east side of Delaware Bay."[30] New Netherland thus became "New York" (named for the duke). The charter was the "briefest and most hastily executed of all the seventeenth-century colonial charters, as well as the only one ever issued in behalf of a member of the royal family and to one who was also heir to the throne."[31]

The nature of the grant was "in ffree and common soccage and not in capite nor by Knight service," which meant it was unencumbered by the tenurial rights of a feudal overlord and awarded for honorable service. The duke and his heirs and assigns were to enjoy "full and absolute power and authority" over the province. This power specifically included—as if any specification were necessary following so comprehensive a grant—command of trade, land grants, and military matters. It also included, again by specification, the executive power (e.g., to "pardon governe"), the legislative power (to make "lawes orders ordinances direccons and instruments"), and the judicial power (over "all causes and matters capitall and criminall as civill both marine and others"). The duke and his heirs and assigns were empowered to appoint government officers, including judges, to help effectuate these powers. In fact, the only limitations on the duke's power over the proprietary were that (1) he was to deliver yearly forty beaver skins to the king upon the king's request (the king apparently never requested them),[32] (2) the laws he enacted were to be "as neare as conveniently may be agreeable to the lawes and statutes and government" of England, (3) the king retained appellate jurisdiction over judicial matters, (4) the colonists were to declare their allegiance directly to the king, and (5) all writs were to issue in the name of the king.

The Duke of York commissioned Colonel Richard Nicolls as his deputy governor, and vested in Nicolls the authority "to perform and exact all and every" of the powers granted to the duke by the king's patent.[33] These powers were codified in the famous Duke's Laws of March 1, 1664/65, an amalgam of the codes of Connecticut and Massachusetts and of English and Dutch law.[34] The Duke's Laws, which continued in force until 1683, represented both a digest of ordinances and a frame of government. With respect to governmental structure, no provision was made

---

[29] Kammen, *Colonial New York,* 71.

[30] The grant is available online at http://www.yale.edu/lawweb/avalon/states/me03.htm. The 1663/64 grant included what had been the province of Maine. It was incorporated into the province of New York, which had been surrendered by the Netherlands.

[31] Kammen, *Colonial New York,* 76.

[32] Andrews, *The Colonial Period,* 3:97.

[33] Chester, *Courts and Lawyers of New York,* 1:302 (quoting Nicolls's commission).

[34] My discussion of the Duke's Laws benefited from Chester, *Courts and Lawyers of New York,* 1: chap. 18.

for a provincial assembly. However, a judicial system was put in place. A court of assizes was to sit once a year as the supreme judicial tribunal of the province, and it was to consist of the governor, the governor's council, and two justices of each of the judicial districts (called "ridings"). The court of assizes heard appeals from lower courts. Acting with a jury, it also had original jurisdiction over criminal cases and, in both law and equity, over civil disputes in which more than twenty pounds was in controversy. Appeal could be made to the crown in council from the judgments of the court of assizes, and special courts of oyer and terminer (from the Law French, "to hear and determine") could be called by the governor and council to expedite the adjudication of criminal matters.

The court of sessions was next in rank, and it was divided into three districts, with each district manned by justices of the peace appointed by the governor and his council. The justices served at the governor's pleasure. The courts of sessions, sitting with a jury, were to meet three times (later twice) per year. They possessed civil jurisdiction over disputes involving five or more pounds and criminal jurisdiction over noncapital cases. They also sat as an orphans' court and performed many executive tasks for their particular districts. Appeals to the court of assizes were available in civil disputes in which twenty pounds or more was at issue and in criminal matters.

Town courts were also established. Each town had a board of eight (later four) overseers elected by the freemen, who governed the town, including as magistrates. One of the overseers was selected to serve as constable. The town courts had jurisdiction over civil matters in which less than five pounds was in dispute. In order to ease the transition to English control, Nicolls initially left the burgher government in place in distinctly Dutch towns such as Fort Orange (renamed Albany). By about 1674, these towns, with the notable exception of New York City, were integrated into the town court system. New York City retained the court of schout, burgomasters, and schepens, albeit operating under the appellation "mayor's court." [35]

B. Grant of the Province of Maine of 1674

New York changed dramatically in the decade following the 1663/64 grant. In 1665, the Duke of York awarded his friends Lord John Berkeley and Sir George Carteret the portion of his territory that is New Jersey today. In 1667, the western half of Connecticut was ceded to that colony. [36] And in 1673, the Dutch briefly recaptured New York. On June 24, 1674, following a second ouster by the English of Dutch control, King Charles issued to his brother James a second grant of the province of Maine. The

---

[35] Ibid., 305.
[36] Kammen, *Colonial New York*, 75.

1674 charter was "new only in time not in content."[37] The duke and his heirs and assigns were to enjoy the same "full and absolute power and authority" over the province that they had enjoyed under the 1663/64 grant. Neither grant contained a provision for a legislative assembly, and this omission, more than any other, became a source of great stress for the province.[38] As political scientist Peter J. Galie observes in his history of constitutionalism in New York, "James had created an absolutist state — government by a fixed code without an assembly."[39] Indeed, Edmund Andros, the experienced colonial administrator the duke had made his first governor under the 1674 grant, advised the duke to authorize an assembly. The duke refused, at least initially, apparently believing that the court of assizes was the assembly.[40] However, in January 1675/76, he wrote to Andros, "if you continue of [the] same opinion, I shall be ready to consider any proposalls you shall send to [that] purpose."[41]

On January 23, 1682/83, the duke finally relented to the people's continuing clamor for a legislative assembly. (All the other American colonies already had assemblies.) He instructed his new governor, Thomas Dongan, to summon one. Both the duke and the governor were to possess veto power over laws written by the assembly, but the duke promised that "if such laws shall be propounded as shall appear to me to be for the manifest good of the country in general, and not [prejudicial] to me, I will assent unto and confirm them."[42] Charles Lincoln concludes that these instructions marked "the dawn of a new era in the colony."[43] They said nothing about the judiciary, although they did commit the duke to abide by the terms of the Magna Carta, the so-called Great Charter of 1215 that required the English monarch to declare certain rights, respect certain procedures, and accept that his will could be bound by law.

C. Charter of Liberties and Privileges of 1683

On October 17, 1683, New York's first legislative assembly convened. The assembly enacted as its first order of business "The Charter of Libertyes and privileges granted by his Royall Highnesse to the Inhabitants of New Yorke and its dependencyes."[44] Its nearly thirty paragraphs contained a bill of rights and a frame of government for the colony. The bill of rights

[37] Andrews, *The Colonial Period*, 3:111. The 1674 grant was virtually a verbatim replication of the 1663/64 grant. The 1674 grant is available online at http://www.yale.edu/lawweb/avalon/states/me04.htm.

[38] Lincoln, *Constitutional History*, 1:425–27; Kammen, *Colonial New York*, 100.

[39] Galie, *Ordered Liberty*, 18.

[40] Chester, *Courts and Lawyers of New York*, 1:390.

[41] As quoted in Lincoln, *Constitutional History*, 1:427.

[42] As quoted in ibid., 430.

[43] Ibid., 429.

[44] The charter is available online at http://www.montauk.com/history/seeds/charter.htm.

was clearly modeled on the Magna Carta. For example, one provision of the Charter of Liberties and Privileges provided:

> THAT Noe freeman shall be taken and imprisoned or be disseized of his ffreehold or Libertye or ffree Customes or be outlawed or Exiled or any other wayes destroyed nor shall be passed upon adjudged or condemned But by the Law-full Judgment of his peers and by the Law of this province. Justice nor Right shall be neither sold, denied or deferred to any man within this province.

The frame of government detailed both the legislative and executive powers. With respect to the legislative power, the charter specified "THAT The Supreme Legislative Authority under his Majesty and Royall Highnesse James Duke of Yorke Albany &c Lord proprietor of the said province shall forever be and reside in a Governour, Councell, and the people mett in Generall Assembly." The charter addressed the executive power as follows: "THAT The Exercise of the Cheife Magistracy and Administracon of the Government over the said province shall bee in the said Governour assisted by a Councell with whose advice and Consent or with at least four of them he is to rule and Governe the same according to the Lawes thereof." There was no separation of powers: notwithstanding the duke's capitulation to the creation of a legislative assembly, the Charter of Liberties and Privileges specified that the governor and his council were to possess legislative power (along with the representatives of every "ffreeholder within this province and ffreeman in any Corporacon"), in addition to executive power. Nothing was provided in the charter about the judicial power. However, near the end of the ducal proprietary period, the provincial assembly modified the court system articulated in the Duke's Laws: the court of assizes was replaced by a court of chancery consisting of the governor and council; a permanent court of oyer and terminer was established; the jurisdictional amounts of the town courts were reduced; and the jurisdictional limits on the courts of sessions were eliminated altogether—all in an effort to improve the administration of justice.[45]

IV. THE ROYAL PERIOD, 1685–1776

The Duke of York signed the Charter of Liberties and Privileges on October 4, 1684. He never returned it to New York. On February 6, 1684/85, King Charles II died, and the duke became King James II. As king, James re-embraced his earlier view that parliamentary bodies were an "inconvenient adjunct of government" that interfered with the exercise of

---

[45] Julius Goebel, Jr., "The Courts and the Law in Colonial New York," in Alexander C. Flick, ed., *History of the State of New York*, 10 vols. (New York: Columbia University Press, 1933), 3:3, 18–21.

the royal prerogative. He therefore vetoed the charter on March 3, 1685/ 86.[46] New York was now a royal colony, rather than a proprietary one, and the government soon "reverted to a hierarchical pattern" of the governor and his council administering the executive, legislative, and judicial affairs of the colony, subject to the king's approval.[47] On April 7, 1688, New York, along with New Jersey, was annexed by royal decree to the Dominion of New England, a "megacolony" created by James II two years before. Edmund Andros served as governor of the megacolony.[48]

A. Charter of Liberties and Privileges of 1691

King James II's reign was to be short-lived. On December 11, 1688, he abdicated the throne under pressure that had arisen in Parliament from his commitment to both absolute monarchy and the Catholic faith. On February 13, 1688/89, William and Mary became king and queen of England. The tumult in England had profound effects in New York and throughout colonial America. The Dominion of New England collapsed, and each of the constituent parts returned to its prior form of government.[49] In New York, Jacob Leisler, a wealthy local merchant, led a rebellion. Henry Sloughter, appointed governor by the new monarchs, managed to quell it. He also called a general assembly—in effect reviving the policy initiated by James Duke of York and later vetoed by James as king. The new assembly met on April 9, 1691, and quickly enacted "An Act Declaring What are the Rights and Privileges of Their Majestyes Subjects Inhabiting within Their Province of New York." The 1691 Charter of Liberties and Privileges was virtually identical to the 1683 charter: legislative power was vested in the governor, the council, and the people's assembly; executive power resided with the governor and his council; and not a word was provided about the judiciary as a separate institution of government. The 1691 charter shared another trait with the 1683 charter: it, too, was rejected by the crown because it was perceived as a threat to the royal prerogative.[50]

The judiciary act of 1691 did not suffer a similar fate. In fact, the act remained in effect without major change until the American Revolution.[51]

---

[46] Lincoln, *Constitutional History*, 1:434–35.

[47] Galie, *Ordered Liberty*, 23.

[48] Kammen, *Colonial New York*, 120. For more on the Dominion of New England, see Viola Florence Barnes, *The Dominion of New England: A Study in British Colonial Policy* (New Haven, CT: Yale University Press, 1923).

[49] Andrews, *The Colonial Period*, 3:124.

[50] Galie, *Ordered Liberty*, 24. The two charters were technically statutes, but they functioned as grants of "constitutional powers and privileges." Lincoln, *Constitutional History*, 1:438.

[51] Martin L. Budd, "The Legal System of 1691," in Leo Hershkowitz and Milton M. Klein, eds., *Courts and Law in Early New York: Selected Essays* (Port Washington, NY: Kennikat Press, 1978), 1, 7. Budd's essay, a reprint of his 1967 *Harvard Law Review* student note, is an excellent treatment of New York's 1691 judiciary act. The general assembly renewed the

Governor Sloughter's decision to permit the legislature to draft the judiciary bill "constituted a striking departure from the historic English pattern of courts arising under the authority of the executive."[52] The governor's decision likely explains why the act endured: the legislative committee charged with writing the bill was more familiar with local needs than he was.[53] However, the governor's decision was inconsistent with the standard instructions he had received pertaining to the administration of justice. (I will discuss those instructions below after giving due consideration to the 1691 statute.)

New York embraced the prevailing practice in colonial British America of making justices of the peace the centerpiece of its judicial system, just as it had done since the time of the Duke's Laws. Justices of the peace were to be appointed by the governor. Individual justices were authorized to decide civil disputes involving forty shillings or less. All the justices of a particular county were required to meet at specified times as criminal courts of sessions to adjudicate minor infractions. Trial by jury could be requested, but rarely was. The justices performed a variety of nonjudicial functions, such as supervising road construction and issuing liquor licenses, as they did in other colonies and in England itself.

County courts of common pleas were established, and were to consist of one judge appointed by the governor sitting with three justices of the peace. The common pleas courts possessed jurisdiction, concurrent with the supreme court, over civil disputes involving more than five pounds. Both New York City and Albany had mayor's courts. These courts enjoyed jurisdiction similar to that of the county courts. The mayor's court of New York City, however, heard considerably more commercial cases than any other court in the province.[54]

The 1691 judiciary act established a supreme court with jurisdiction "of all pleas, Civill Criminall and Mixt, . . . as the Courts of Kings Bench, Comon Pleas, & Exchequer within their Majestyes Kingdome of England." As such, the supreme court possessed original jurisdiction over civil actions in which more than twenty pounds was in dispute, real property claims, and felonies. The supreme court was given appellate jurisdiction over the inferior courts. The court consisted of a chief justice and two (later three) associate justices appointed by the governor. The justices served during the governor's pleasure. A 1692 amendment required the justices to ride circuit once per year.

---

judiciary act on several occasions. Beginning in 1699, virtually the same judicial system existed via ordinances issued by New York's royal governors. Minor modifications included increasing the amount in controversy requirement from 300 pounds to 500 pounds for appeals to the crown in council.

[52] Ibid., 9.

[53] Ibid., 9, 122 n. 10.

[54] Richard B. Morris, "The New York City Mayor's Court," in Hershkowitz and Klein, eds., *Courts and Law in Early New York*, 19 (reprinting the introduction to Morris's edited book on the New York City mayor's court).

The governor and council were to serve as a court of errors for civil disputes involving at least one hundred pounds. They also were authorized to sit as a court of chancery to ensure that decisions based in law were not fundamentally unfair. The chancery court, which Governor Richard Coote, the first earl of Bellomont, eliminated in a 1699 ordinance because no one in New York knew how to conduct it, would later prove controversial—an issue that merits additional discussion in the next section.[55] Civil matters in which more than three hundred pounds was in controversy, and criminal matters in which at least two hundred pounds in fines were imposed, could be appealed to the crown in council.

Several special courts also were constituted, the most important of which were the periodic courts of oyer and terminer for the trial of felonies. Established separately from the 1691 judiciary act were a court of vice-admiralty, with a judge appointed by the governor, and a prerogative court for the probate of wills and the administration of estates, supervised by the governor.

The royal governors of New York received commissions and instructions from the crown similar to those issued to the other royal governors of British America. Their commissions authorized them to erect and constitute courts for the adjudication of matters in law and equity, while more than two dozen instructions related to the administration of justice.[56] Royal governors received an instruction to report on a regular basis to the crown on the judicial organization of the colony, an instruction to ensure regularity in court procedures, an instruction concerning the speedy and impartial administration of justice, an instruction not to erect or dissolve courts without special order from the crown, an instruction mandating the establishment of a small claims court, an instruction requiring the erection of a court of exchequer, an instruction about the appointment of special courts of oyer and terminer, and an instruction requiring appeals to the governor and council. They also received several instructions regulating appeals to the crown in council, an instruction specifying that judicial commissions issued by the governor were to be without limitations of time, an instruction that judicial appointments were to be at the crown's consent and pleasure (and a strongly worded circular letter reaffirming the instruction), an instruction that judges and justices of the

[55] Budd, "The Legal System of 1691," 15. Governor Robert Hunter reintroduced the court in 1711, and it operated almost continuously, with the governor serving as chancellor, until the American Revolution. Stanley N. Katz, "The Politics of Law in Colonial America: Controversies Over Chancery Courts and Equity Law in the Eighteenth Century," in Donald Fleming and Bernard Bailyn, eds., *Law in American History* (Boston: Little, Brown and Co., 1971), 255, 273. See also Joseph H. Smith, "Adolph Philipse and the Chancery Resolves of 1727," in Hershkowitz and Klein, eds., *Courts and Law in Early New York*, 30.

[56] Leonard Woods Labaree, *Royal Government in America: A Study of the British Colonial System before 1783* (1930; reprinted, New York: Frederick Ungar Publishing Co., 1958), 373. The royal instructions concerning the courts are collected in chapters 7 and 8 of volume 1 of Leonard Woods Labaree, ed., *Royal Instructions to British Colonial Governors, 1670–1776*, 2 vols. (1935; reprinted, New York: Octagon Books, 1967).

peace were not to be displaced by the governor without good cause, an instruction about the legal security of life and property, and an instruction to prevent exorbitant salaries and fees (and a related circular letter regarding fees).

The only significant instructions relating to the administration of justice that were issued to some British American royal governors but not to the royal governors of New York were those about the regularity of court procedures and the appointment of special courts of oyer and terminer. New York nonetheless erected special courts of oyer and terminer. However, as mentioned above, Governor Sloughter violated the instruction not to erect other courts without "especial order" from the crown when he permitted the general assembly to construct the colony's judicial system in the 1691 judiciary act, although he likely did so with the tacit assent of the crown.[57]

B. Persistent threats to judicial independence

Charles Lincoln declared in *The Constitutional History of New York* that the "departments into which a free government is deemed most wisely divided—namely, the executive, the legislature with two branches, and an independent judiciary—had already existed eighty-six years when the people of New York determined to transform the colony into a state."[58] Surely, this is incorrect. The "eighty-six years" to which Lincoln referred were those between the 1691 Charter of Liberties and Privileges and the first New York state constitution in 1777. The 1691 charter said *nothing* about the judicial power, and it also failed to "divide" the legislative power from the executive power. In fact, New York, like other British American colonies during the years building up to the American Revolution, was beset by fights about the separation of powers in general and the independence of the judiciary in particular. Three famous incidents illustrate the point: (1) Governor William Cosby's dismissal of Chief Justice Lewis Morris, Jr., in the 1730s; (2) Acting Governor Cadwallader Colden's refusal to commission judges during good behavior in the 1760s; and (3) Colden's contemporaneous attempt to interfere with the appellate process in the colony.[59]

---

[57] See Budd, "The Legal System of 1691," 10: "In deciding that the legislature should enact the required law, Sloughter probably was not seriously constrained by the explicit language of his instructions; the chief representative of a government 3,000 miles away had to have considerable leeway in interpreting his commission in light of what he knew the purposes of his superiors to be."

[58] Lincoln, *Constitutional History*, 1:470.

[59] The first incident is chronicled in Joseph H. Smith and Leo Hershkowitz, "Courts of Equity in the Province of New York: The Cosby Controversy, 1732-1736," *American Journal of Legal History* 16, no. 1 (1972): 1-50. See also Katz, "The Politics of Law in Colonial America," 273-82; and Stanley Nider Katz, *Newcastle's New York: Anglo-American Politics, 1732-1753* (Cambridge, MA: Belknap Press of Harvard University Press, 1968), chap. 4. The

The 1732/33 case of *King v. Van Dam* marked the climax of the first incident. Legalistically, the case involved a salary dispute between a governor, Cosby, and a former acting governor, Rip Van Dam: Cosby insisted that Van Dam pay him one-half of the salary, perquisites, and emoluments Van Dam had received as acting governor after the death of Cosby's predecessor, John Montgomerie, but Van Dam refused. Cosby's claim was buttressed by an instruction that Governor Montgomerie had received that an acting governor was entitled to one-half of the governor's compensation during the governor's absence from the colony, whereas Van Dam's position was bolstered by the instruction's failure to specifically address the contingency of the governor's death. To Van Dam, the instruction's silence on the matter meant that he was entitled to the entirety of the compensation, not simply half of it.

The attorney general filed an information in the king's name in the New York supreme court against Van Dam for the monies allegedly due Cosby. The equitable nature of this type of action raised a constitutional question, given the uncertain status of equity jurisdiction at this point in New York's history. More specifically, the question the supreme court was forced to confront after Van Dam filed a plea and demurrer to the attorney general's suit (what today would be characterized as a motion to dismiss for lack of jurisdiction) was whether the governor, acting pursuant to royal instruction, could establish a court—in this instance, a court of equity—or extend an existing court's jurisdiction, without an act of the general assembly. The assembly insisted that for the governor to do so would be an exercise of arbitrary power. The governor, in contrast, maintained that the executive enjoyed this power as a matter of prerogative. The supreme court split two-to-one on the question, and the governor removed the judge who disagreed with him (Chief Justice Morris) from office—an assault on the independence of the judiciary if there ever was one.[60] When this and related controversies concerning Cosby's governorship were reported in the New York press, the celebrated trial of John Peter Zenger for seditious libel was the result. Among the major grievances printed by Zenger about the Cosby administration were that "judges [were] arbitrarily displaced, [and] new courts erected without consent of the legislature."[61] Although the Zenger case is rightly proclaimed as a

---

second and third incidents are discussed in, among many other places, Milton M. Klein, *The Politics of Diversity: Essays in the History of Colonial New York* (Port Washington, NY: Kennikat Press, 1974), chap. 7. The latter two incidents were of such constitutional significance that Klein entitles his chapter about them "Prelude to Revolution in New York." All three incidents are also described, in varying degrees of specificity, in Labaree's *Royal Government in America*, chap. 9.

[60] Morris was the leader of Cosby's political opponents. Patricia U. Bonomi, *A Factious People: Politics and Society in Colonial New York* (New York: Columbia University Press, 1971), chap. 4. The financial dispute between Cosby and Van Dam was never resolved on the merits: Van Dam failed to file an answer and Cosby refused to accept process on a separate claim filed by Van Dam. Smith and Hershkowitz, "Courts of Equity," 31.

[61] As quoted in Smith and Hershkowitz, "Courts of Equity," 40.

pivotal moment for the freedom of the press—Zenger was acquitted by the jury that decided his case—the jury's decision also "brought an end to the Governor's dangerous experiment with political control of the legal system."[62]

The issue of judicial tenure obviously underlay the Cosby-Van Dam dispute. However, as mentioned above, that controversy was primarily about whether the governor could erect courts without the assent of the legislature. The question of judicial tenure took center stage during the administration of Acting Governor Colden in the 1760s. In fact, although the status of judicial tenure was being debated throughout British America at the time, nowhere was the debate more bitter than in New York.[63] The issue arose following the death of New York's longtime chief justice, James DeLancey. Colden had become convinced that DeLancey's extended tenure as chief justice from 1733 (following the removal of Morris) until DeLancey's death in 1760, had made the chief justice more powerful than the governor.[64] Colden therefore insisted on appointing the next chief justice at the crown's pleasure. The assembly protested loudly and frequently, and the province quickly reverted to the chaos that had marked the Cosby administration. A series of bills were enacted by the assembly on the matter, but Colden resisted every one.[65] Finally, the crown in council issued its famous circular letter in 1761 to the governors of all the British American colonies forbidding any governor from commissioning judges other than at the crown's pleasure "upon pain of being removed from Your Government."[66] While Colden, like Cosby before him, may appear to have won the battle, what he actually achieved was an armistice. The American Revolution would settle the rest.[67]

The final incident concerning the independence of the judiciary to be discussed in this section on New York as a royal colony culminated in *Forsey v. Cunningham* (1764). The case should have been an uneventful one: a straightforward instance of Waddel Cunningham battering Thomas Forsey, for which Cunningham paid a criminal fine and civil damages. However, Cunningham considered the jury's 1,500 pound civil award excessive—the criminal fine was thirty pounds—and he petitioned the supreme court to allow an appeal of both the law and the facts to the

[62] Eben Moglen, "Considering Zenger: Partisan Politics and the Legal Profession in Provincial New York," http://emoglen.law.columbia.edu/publications/zenger.html#s*. See also Bonomi, *A Factious People*, 105–6.

[63] Labaree, *Royal Government in America*, 391.

[64] Governor George Clinton once had liked DeLancey, and had conferred upon the chief justice in 1744 a commission during good behavior. The two later became bitter political enemies. Bonomi, *A Factious People*, 149–50.

[65] Colden consented to one bill that tied life tenure for judges to an annual appropriation for official salaries—including Colden's own—but explained the assembly's extortion (as Colden viewed it) to his superiors in England and prorogued the legislature. Klein, *The Politics of Diversity*, 164.

[66] Labaree, ed., *Royal Instructions to British Colonial Governors*, 1:368.

[67] Klein, *The Politics of Diversity*, 165.

governor and council. The court refused, invoking the well-settled practice of permitting appeals from common-law courts to the governor and
council by writ of error only (that is, for review for errors of law, not of
fact)—a practice that respected the right to trial by jury.[68]
The attorney general and the council agreed with the court. Acting
Governor Colden did not, and he requested and received backing for his
position from the crown in council. The court still refused to capitulate;
the assembly passed a series of resolutions denouncing the overreaching
by the executive; threats were made on Colden's life; and eventually he
was forced to back down by his superiors in England. Although the
matter was eventually dropped, one of the resolutions adopted by the
assembly demonstrated how seriously that body took the acting governor's threat to the independence of the judiciary. The assembly declared
that Colden's action was "illegal, an attack upon the right of the subject,
and a most dangerous innovation, tending to encourage litigiousness and
delay, promote perjury, prevent justice, subject the people to arbitrary
power, and ruin the colony."[69] In short, New York's history as a royal
colony was dominated by a familiar question: Who possessed sovereignty—
the governor, the legislature, or both?[70] The answer was provided by the
New York Constitution of 1777.

V. New York Constitution of 1777

New York's first state constitution opened by transcribing verbatim the
nation's July 4, 1776, Declaration of Independence from Great Britain.[71]
Article I then answered the question posed above: the people of New
York were sovereign in New York. With respect to the institutions of
government, John Adams's *Thoughts on Government*—his 1776 paean to
separation of powers—was "the starting point in drafting the constitution."[72] Three alternative constitutional structures were considered by
the committee charged with drafting a frame of government for the state,
but unlike in a number of other new states such as Pennsylvania, there
was unanimity in the committee for a balanced, or mixed, constitution.
Peter Galie captures the situation well: "[T]he real debate involved the

[68] The colonial practice itself made plain that the judiciary was not independent at this
point in New York's history: the governor and council exercised judicial authority. For a
discussion emphasizing the right to trial by jury in the reaction to the case, see Thomas E.
Carney and Susan Kolb, "The Legacy of *Forsey v. Cunningham:* Safeguarding the Integrity of
the Right to Trial by Jury," *The Historian* 69, no. 4 (2007): 663–87.

[69] As quoted in Labaree, *Royal Government in America,* 417.

[70] Galie, *Ordered Liberty,* 25–26.

[71] The New York Constitution of 1777 is reprinted in, among other places, Benjamin
Perley Poore, *The Federal and State Constitutions, Colonial Charters, and Other Organic Laws of
the United States,* 2 vols., 2d ed. (Washington, DC: Government Printing Office, 1878), 2:1329–39.

[72] Edward Countryman, "Legislative Government in Revolutionary New York, 1777–
1788," Ph.D. diss. (Ithaca, NY: Cornell University, 1971), 85.

nature of this mix; that is, arguments took place not between the followers of [the simple, unicameral legislative government proposed by Thomas Paine in *Common Sense* (1776)] and the followers of Adams, but between those who would follow Adams closely and those who would modify the Adams model in the direction of majoritarianism."[73]

Article II provided that the "supreme legislative power" was to be vested in an assembly and a senate that met "once at least in every year." The assembly was to consist of between seventy and three hundred members elected annually by voters in the respective counties of the state (Articles IV and XVI). The size of each county's delegation was based on population, and the assembly was to be reapportioned every seven years (Article V). Voters for assembly candidates were required to be residents of the county in which they voted, possess a freehold of at least twenty pounds free of debt, rent land whose annual value was at least forty shillings, or be a freeman in Albany or have obtained freemanship in New York City prior to October 14, 1775 (Article VII).

The senate was to consist of between twenty-four and one hundred senators elected to four-year terms (Articles X, XI, and XVI). Senators were required to own freeholds of at least one hundred pounds free of debt and were to be elected by voters who possessed the same degree of wealth (Article X). Senate seats were to be apportioned, and reapportioned, by population among the four "great districts" of the state (Articles XII and XVI).

Article XVII specified that the "supreme executive authority and power" was to be vested in a governor elected to a three-year term. There was no provision against reelection. The governor was required to be a freeholder of the state and was to be elected by the same class of voters who chose senators. He could summon the legislature into special session and prorogue it for up to sixty days. He was head of the state's militia and navy, could grant pardons and reprieves, and was to "take care that the laws are faithfully executed" (Articles XVIII and XIX). Article XX provided for a lieutenant governor, elected in the same manner as the governor, who also was to serve as president of the senate and cast tie-breaking votes. For all of these reasons, plus the governor's participation on the council of revision (discussed below), most scholars conclude that the New York Constitution of 1777 created the strongest state executive of the day.[74]

The chancellor, judges of the supreme court, and the "first judge" of every county court were to hold their offices "during good behavior or until they shall have respectively attained the age of sixty years" (Article XXIV). A proposal to permit the legislature to remove judges for "inca-

---

[73] Galie, *Ordered Liberty*, 39.

[74] For example, Peter J. Galie, *The New York State Constitution: A Reference Guide* (New York: Greenwood Press, 1991), 5.

pacity" was rejected.[75] Justices of the peace and other local judicial officials were to serve at the "pleasure" of the appointing officers, so long as
they were recommissioned at least once every three years (Article XXVIII).
Nothing was said about judicial compensation.

Judges and other nonelected government officials were to be selected
by a council of appointment (Article XXIII), a compromise between those
who favored vesting the appointment power in the executive and those
who preferred legislative selection of nonelected officials. The compromise was suggested by John Jay, one of the influential drafters of the New
York Constitution of 1777 and later the first chief justice of the United
States.[76] The council of appointment was to consist of the governor and
one senator selected annually by the assembly from each of the four
"great districts" of the state. The governor was authorized to nominate
candidates,[77] but he could only vote on their confirmation to break a tie.
Senators could not serve on the council for two consecutive years.

New York's first state constitution also created another commingled
institution of government: the council of revision. Article III is worth
quoting at length:

> And whereas laws inconsistent with the spirit of this constitution, or
> with the public good, may be hastily and unadvisedly passed: Be it
> ordained, that the governor for the time being, the chancellor, and the
> judges of the supreme court, or any two of them, together with the
> governor, shall be, and hereby are, constituted a council to revise all
> bills about to be passed into laws by the legislature; and for that
> purpose shall assemble themselves from time to time, when the leg-
> islature shall be convened; for which, nevertheless, they shall not
> receive any salary or consideration, under any pretence whatever.
> And that all bills which have passed the senate and assembly shall,
> before they become laws, be presented to the said council for their
> revisal and consideration; and if, upon such revision and consider-
> ation, it should appear improper to the said council, or a majority of

---

[75] Lincoln, *Constitutional History*, 1:535. The New York state constitutional convention also
rejected a sixty-five-year-old retirement age. Ibid.

[76] Galie, *Ordered Liberty*, 42. Scholars disagree about how large a role Jay played in writing
New York's first state constitution, but all conclude that he played an influential part.
Compare Lincoln, *Constitutional History*, 1:471, and Richard B. Morris, "John Jay and the
New York State Constitution and Courts after Two Hundred Years," in Stephen L. Schechter
and Richard B. Bernstein, eds., *New York and the Union* (Albany: New York State Commission
on the Bicentennial of the United States Constitution, 1990), 161, 163, 165 (calling Jay the
principal architect of the document), with Galie, *Ordered Liberty*, 38, and Bernard Mason, *The
Road to Independence: The Revolutionary Movement in New York, 1773-1777* (Lexington: University of Kentucky Press, 1966), 225-29 (maintaining that Jay's role has been overemphasized).

[77] Whether *only* the governor could nominate candidates under the 1777 constitution was
addressed by the New York constitutional convention of 1801. The 1801 convention decided
that the governor and the council of appointment had concurrent power to nominate candidates. Galie, *Ordered Liberty*, 64-70.

them, that the said bill should become a law of this State, that they return the same, together with their objections thereto in writing, to the senate or house of assembly (in whichsoever the same shall have originated) who shall enter the objections sent down by the council at large in their minutes, and proceed to reconsider the said bill. But if, after such reconsideration, two-thirds of the said senate or house of assembly shall, notwithstanding the said objections, agree to pass the same, it shall, together with the objections, be sent to the other branch of the legislature, where it shall also be reconsidered, and, if approved by two-thirds of the members present, shall be law.

The council of revision was unquestionably a substitute for providing the governor with the power to veto legislation. Not only does Article III read like a veto provision, but it was proposed during consideration of a draft section that would have empowered the governor with the veto.[78] The council of revision also was likely a compromise over the power of judicial review. Although many casual observers of American constitutional history credit the 1803 U.S. Supreme Court case of *Marbury v. Madison* with "inventing" judicial review, precedents for the practice existed at the time New York's first state constitution was written.[79] Article XXXIII, which created a "court" of errors and impeachments, likewise reflected an unwillingness on the part of the New York convention to confer upon the judiciary the degree of independence later afforded by the federal convention of 1787. This particular court was to consist of the president of the senate (i.e., the lieutenant governor), the senators, the chancellor, and the judges of the supreme court ("or the major part of them"). The court was to serve as the trial court for impeachments[80] and as a final appeals court on questions of law.[81] Clearly, such a court was inconsistent with the notion of an independent judiciary, joining as it did executive, legislative, and judicial officers of the state and empowering them to "correct" judicial rulings about the meaning of law. However, in an effort to limit the influence of the governor and legislators, court clerks, marshals, and registers were to be appointed by the judges of the apposite court (Article XXVII).[82] Another nod to judicial independence was found in Article XXV, which forbade the chancellor and the judges of the supreme

---

[78] Lincoln, *Constitutional History*, 1:554.

[79] See generally Scott D. Gerber, "The Myth of *Marbury v. Madison* and the Origins of Judicial Review," in Mark A. Graber and Michael Perhac, eds., *Marbury versus Madison: Documents and Commentary* (Washington, DC: CQ Press, 2002), 1–15; and William Michael Treanor, "Judicial Review Before *Marbury*," *Stanford Law Review* 58, no. 2 (2005), 455–562.

[80] If a member of the court of errors and impeachments was himself being impeached, he could not sit on the tribunal. The assembly was assigned the power of bringing articles of impeachment (Article XXXIII).

[81] Neither the chancellor nor the supreme court judges were to vote on appeals from their own courts, but they were expected to participate in the deliberations (Article XXXII).

[82] William A. Polf, "1777: The Political Revolution and New York's First Constitution," in Schechter and Bernstein, eds., *New York and the Union*, 114, 134.

court from holding any other office, except that of delegate to the conti-
nental congress "upon special occasions." The "first judges" of the county
courts were permitted to serve in the state senate. Proposals to permit the
chancellor and the supreme court judges to sit as advisory members to
the senate were replaced by the previously described council of revision.[83]

VI. CONCLUSION

New York's first state constitution was not adopted until April 20,
1777.[84] The delay occurred because New York was the scene of many
major military battles during the American Revolution and also because
of the profound disagreements between the competing forces at the convention.[85] (Leading conservative members of the drafting committee, such
as John Jay and Robert R. Livingston, were determined that New York
should not adopt an organic law in the radically democratic vein of
Pennsylvania.)[86] Certainly, New York had come a long way from its days
as a Dutch commercial settlement and as an English proprietary and royal
province in recognizing that the principal purpose of government was—as
the Third Provincial Congress phrased it on May 31, 1776, when calling
for a new congress to create a form of government for the soon-to-be-
independent state—"to secure the rights, liberties, and happiness of the
good people of the colony."[87] Intriguingly, those who wrote the 1777
constitution anticipated by a decade the Madisonian theory of separation
of powers by adding checks and balances to the mix: each department of
government was vested with some authority over the others.[88] For example, the legislature was vested with executive power through the council
of appointment, and the executive was vested with legislative power
through the lieutenant governor's status as president of the senate. How-

[83] Lincoln, *Constitutional History*, 1:537.
[84] New York's 1777 constitution was not presented to the people for ratification. In 1778,
New Hampshire became the first of the original states to submit a constitution to the people.
(The people of New Hampshire rejected the proposed 1778 constitution.)
[85] Sol Wachtler and Stephen L. Schechter, "'Liberty and Property': New York and the
Origins of American Constitutionalism," in Schechter and Bernstein, eds., *New York and the
Union*, 3, 12–13.
[86] Mason, *The Road to Independence*, 230.
[87] As quoted in Lincoln, *Constitutional History*, 1:482. Similar language was included in the
preamble of the constitution of 1777. The constitution did not contain a bill of rights,
although a number of rights were guaranteed in the body of the document (e.g., religious
freedom, trial by jury, due process). The record is silent as to why there was no bill of
rights—the convention was charged with drafting both a frame of government and a declaration of rights for the state—but it has been suggested that a bill of rights was considered
by the drafting committee to be unnecessary. Bernard Mason, "New York State's First
Constitution," in Schechter and Bernstein, eds., *New York and the Union*, 167, 180. As is well
known by students of American constitutional history, an identical argument would be
made a decade later with respect to a bill of rights for the U.S. Constitution.
[88] The distribution of powers among the branches of government was one of the central
issues of the convention. Galie, *The New York State Constitution*, 3.

ever, the New York Constitution of 1777 fell woefully short of the U.S. Constitution of 1787 in terms of creating an independent judiciary. Nothing was stated about judicial compensation; judges were required to retire at sixty; and their opinions could be reversed by a "court" of errors that included among its members the lieutenant governor and the senators. The chancellor and the supreme court judges also were required to exercise executive power in their service on the council of revision.[89]

Indeed, New York's own Alexander Hamilton criticized both the judicial tenure provision of New York's 1777 constitution and judicial service on the council of revision in two of his *Federalist Papers*. With respect to judicial tenure, Hamilton wrote:

> The constitution of New York, to avoid investigations that must forever be vague and dangerous, has taken a particular age as the criterion of inability. No man can be a judge beyond sixty. I believe there are few at present who do not disapprove of this provision. There is no station in relation to which it is less proper than to that of a judge. The deliberating and comparing faculties generally preserve their strength much beyond that period in men who survive it; and when, in addition to this circumstance, we consider how few there are who outlive the season of intellectual vigor and how improbable it is that any considerable portion of the bench, whether more or less numerous, should be in such a situation at the same time, we shall be ready to conclude that limitations of this sort have little to recommend them.[90]

Hamilton objected to a mandatory retirement age for judges primarily on practical grounds: he thought it unnecessary. He objected to commingling executive, legislative, and judicial functions on the council of revision on the principled ground of judicial independence. He wrote:

> But perhaps the force of the objection may be thought to consist in the particular organization of the proposed [United States] Supreme Court; in its being composed of a distinct body of magistrates, instead of being one of the branches of the legislature, as in the government of Great Britain and in that of this State [New York]. To insist upon this point, the authors of the objection must renounce the meaning they have labored to annex to the celebrated maxim requiring a separation of the departments of power.[91]

---

[89] The fact that the convention stripped the governor of the equity and probate jurisdiction he exercised when New York was a colony did increase the judiciary's separateness and independence. Ibid., 4.

[90] Hamilton, *Federalist No. 79*, in Rossiter, ed., *The Federalist Papers*, 474.

[91] Hamilton, *Federalist No. 81*, in ibid., 483.

To summarize, the New York Constitution of 1777 was regarded as the "best" of the original state constitutions and one that "exerted a considerable influence upon the Federal Constitution" by no less a figure than historian Allan Nevins in his celebrated study *The American States During and After the Revolution, 1775–1789.*[92] However, New York did not have an independent judiciary prior to the U.S. Constitution of 1787, a point Nevins conceded.[93] In fact, New York has *never* had an independent judiciary in the federal conception of the institution. Although the New York Constitution of 1821 abolished the council of revision,[94] and the Constitution of 1846 eliminated the court for the correction of errors and added a provision for judicial compensation (which "shall not be increased or diminished during their continuance in office"), removal of judges by "joint resolution of the two houses of the legislature"—rather than solely by impeachment—was added by the 1821 constitution,[95] and New York judges always have been subject to a mandatory retirement age (at present, seventy-six).

No discussion of judicial independence in New York would be complete without mentioning one of the most famous of the early state court precedents for judicial review, *Rutgers v. Waddington* (1784), argued by Alexander Hamilton and decided by the mayor's court of New York City.[96] At issue was whether Hamilton's client, a British citizen named Joshua Waddington, committed a trespass by occupying plaintiff Elizabeth Rutgers's property during the American Revolution. Rutgers sued Waddington pursuant to New York's Trespass Act, a 1783 statute that barred defendants from pleading that military authority justified the trespass under acts of war and the law of nations. Hamilton emphasized in his argument to the court the need for the judiciary to protect his client's rights under both the Treaty of Peace, which had canceled claims for injuries to property during the Revolution, and the law of nations. He said: "The enemy having a right to the use of the Plaintiffs property &

---

[92] Allan Nevins, *The American States During and After the Revolution, 1775–1789* (1924; reprinted, New York: Augustus M. Kelley Publishers, 1969), 161.

[93] Ibid. That does not mean New York's judiciary was not powerful. Willi Paul Adams went so far as to say that "[n]o other early [state] constitution gave so much power to the judiciary." Willi Paul Adams, *The First American Constitutions: Republican Ideology and the Making of the State Constitutions in the Revolutionary Era*, expanded edition (Lanham, MD: Madison House, 2001), 266. Adams emphasized participation by New York supreme court judges on the council of revision and the court for the trial of impeachments.

[94] The council of appointment also was abolished by the 1821 constitution. An executive veto replaced the council of revision, and the executive was empowered to nominate judges subject to the advice and consent of the senate. Both provisions mirrored the federal model.

[95] So-called removal by address was objected to as a threat to judicial independence, but proponents of the provision maintained that limiting removal to impeachable offenses made the judiciary too independent. Lincoln, *Constitutional History*, 4:556–62.

[96] The case is reported in Julius Goebel, Jr., ed., *The Law Practice of Alexander Hamilton: Documents and Commentary*, 5 vols. (New York: Columbia University Press, 1964), 1:393–419. The mayor's court was comprised of the mayor, various aldermen, a professional judge, and the city recorder.

having exercised their right through the Defendant & for valuable consideration he cannot be made answerable to another without injustice and a violation of the law of Universal society."[97]

The court was fully aware of the thrust of Hamilton's argument. The judges noted that Hamilton's defense centered on the claim that "statutes against law and reason are void." They appeared to accept his position:

> [W]e profess to revere the rights of human nature; at every hazard and expence we have vindicated, and successfully established them in our land! and we cannot but reverence a law which is their chief guardian—a law which inculcates as a first principle—that the amiable precepts of the law of nature, are as obligatory on nations in their mutual intercourse, as they are on individuals in their conduct towards each other; and that every nation is bound to contribute all in its powers to the happiness and perfection of others![98]

Despite this strong language about the importance of protecting individual rights—here, the right of Hamilton's client to use the plaintiff's property during the war—the court upheld the statute, explicitly acknowledging the supremacy of the legislature.[99] The court did, however, deny the plaintiff relief. What the court's inconsistent actions suggest is that the judges were torn between their increasing awareness of the need for judges to protect individual rights and their lingering commitment to the doctrine of legislative supremacy. And while it is impossible to know for certain, perhaps the New York judges would have been more willing to exercise judicial review if the New York Constitution of 1777 had made them as independent of the political branches as the U.S. Constitution of 1787 soon would make the federal judiciary.

Law, Ohio Northern University

---

[97] Ibid., 373.

[98] Ibid., 395, 400.

[99] Ibid., 415: "The supremacy of the Legislature need not be called into question; if they think fit *positively* to enact a law, there is no power which can controul them. When the main object of such a law is clearly expressed, and the intention manifest, the Judges are not at liberty, altho' it appears to them to be *unreasonable*, to reject it: for this were to set the *judicial* above the legislative, which would be subversive of all government" (emphasis in the original).

FOOT VOTING, POLITICAL IGNORANCE, AND CONSTITUTIONAL DESIGN*

By Ilya Somin

I. Introduction

The strengths and weaknesses of constitutional federalism have been debated for centuries. Similarly, we have had centuries of debate over the extent to which there should be constitutional constraints on the scope of government power more generally.[1] But one major possible advantage of building decentralization and limited government into a constitution has been largely ignored in the debate so far: its potential for reducing the costs of widespread political ignorance.[2]

The argument of this essay is simple, but has potentially far-reaching implications: Constitutional federalism enables citizens to "vote with their feet," and foot voters have much stronger incentives to make well-informed decisions than conventional ballot box voters. The same goes for limits on the scope of government that enable citizens to vote with their feet in the private sector.[3]

* For helpful suggestions and comments, I would like to thank Bryan Caplan, Bruce Kobayashi, Donald Wittman, and participants in conference panels sponsored by the University of California at Santa Cruz, the IVR international conference on law and philosophy, the Liberty Fund, and the Korea Institutional Economics Association. I would also like to thank Susan Courtwright-Rodriguez and Kari DiPalma for valuable research assistance.

[1] For a survey of the relevant history, see Scott Gordon, *Controlling the State: Constitutionalism from Ancient Athens to Today* (Cambridge, MA: Harvard University Press, 2002).

[2] I have myself briefly discussed these advantages in several prior publications. See, e.g., Ilya Somin, "Political Ignorance and the Countermajoritarian Difficulty: A New Perspective on the 'Central Obsession' of Constitutional Theory," *Iowa Law Review* 87 (2004): 1287–1371; Somin, "Knowledge about Ignorance: New Directions in the Study of Political Information," *Critical Review* 18 (2006): 255–78; and Somin, "When Ignorance Isn't Bliss: How Political Ignorance Threatens Democracy," *Cato Institute Policy Analysis* No. 525 (2004). However, the present essay is a much more extensive analysis. Viktor Vanberg and James Buchanan have analyzed the significance of rational political ignorance for the constitution-making process. See Viktor Vanberg and James Buchanan, "Constitutional Choice, Rational Ignorance, and the Limits of Reason," in Vanberg, *Rules and Choice in Economics* (New York: Routledge, 1994), 178–92. But this work only briefly mentions possible implications for federalism in constitutional design (ibid., 188–89).

[3] The terms "foot voting" and "ballot box voting" used in this essay are similar to Albert Hirschman's well-known distinction between "exit" and "voice." See Hirschman, *Exit, Voice, and Loyalty: Responses to Decline in Firms, Organizations, and States* (Cambridge, MA: Harvard University Press, 1970). However, Hirschman's concept of exit includes exit mechanisms other than foot voting (such as choosing to buy one firm's products rather than another's). He defines exit as any means by which people stop buying a firm's products or "leave [an] organization" in response to poor performance (ibid., 4). Similarly, his concept of "voice" includes methods of influencing an organization from within other than voting. Thus, I use

The informational advantages of foot voting over ballot box voting suggest that decentralized federalism can increase both citizen welfare and democratic accountability relative to policymaking in a centralized unitary state. Since at least the pioneering work of Charles Tiebout,[4] scholars have analyzed foot voting extensively, but its informational advantages over ballot box voting have largely been ignored.

These advantages are important both for those who believe that political ignorance is instrumentally harmful because it undermines democratic accountability in government, and for those who value democratic control of public policy for its own sake.[5] Widespread political ignorance undermines each of these potential benefits of democratic government.[6]

In Section II, I briefly elaborate on the theory of rational political ignorance, explaining why most ballot box voters have little incentive to acquire more than minimal political knowledge. In addition, the theory of rational ignorance implies that voters will often make poor use of the usually very limited knowledge that they do possess. The empirical evidence on political knowledge generally supports both of these predictions.

Section III shows that incentives for knowledge acquisition are much stronger when citizens have the option of voting with their feet rather than just at the ballot box. The same holds true for incentives to make rational use of the information that is acquired. Reductions in transportation costs and in identification with state governments in recent decades both increase the likelihood that foot voters will acquire adequate information about their alternatives, and will use that information rationally. These points hold true for the United States but may be less valid in countries where federalism tracks deep ethnic or religious divisions that make it difficult for citizens to migrate from one region to another or to admit that a regional government dominated by an ethnic group other than their own is doing a better job of governance than the one where they currently reside. With these qualifications, the benefits of foot voting strengthen the case for constitutional limits on central governments in order to facilitate decentralization.

Section IV considers some empirical evidence indicating the informational superiority of foot voting over ballot box voting. In particular, I

"foot voting" and "ballot box voting" instead of "exit" and "voice" in order to make it clear that this essay has a narrower focus than Hirschman's classic work.

[4] Charles Tiebout, "A Pure Theory of Local Expenditures," *Journal of Political Economy* 64 (1956): 516–24.

[5] See, e.g., Carole Pateman, *Participation and Democratic Theory* (Cambridge: Cambridge University Press, 1970); and Benjamin Barber, *Strong Democracy* (Princeton, NJ: Princeton University Press, 1984).

[6] See, e.g., Michael X. Delli Carpini and Scott Keeter, *What Americans Know about Politics and Why It Matters* (New Haven, CT: Yale University Press, 1996); Scott Althaus, *Collective Preferences in Democratic Politics* (New York: Cambridge University Press, 2003); and Ilya Somin, "Voter Ignorance and the Democratic Ideal," *Critical Review* 12 (1998): 413–58.

summarize evidence demonstrating that even a severely oppressed and often poorly educated group can acquire sufficient information to engage in effective foot voting. That is exactly what happened with numerous poor African Americans in the Jim Crow era South who acquired sufficient information to realize that conditions were relatively better for blacks in northern states, and also better in some parts of the South compared to others. The resulting migration significantly bettered the condition of African Americans throughout the nation.

Section V suggests that limits on the scope of government have some of the same informational advantages as political decentralization. Indeed, those advantages may be even greater in light of the fact that exit costs are usually lower in private sector markets than in the case of interjurisdictional migration. In Section VI, I discuss some implications of my analysis for constitutional design. The informational benefits of foot voting strengthen the case for constitutional limits on central governments in order to facilitate decentralization. They also strengthen the case for limits on the power of government relative to the private sector.

Finally, Section VII provides a conclusion that summarizes the implications of my analysis and notes some of its limitations.

The argument presented here is comparative. It holds that foot voting has significant informational advantages over ballot box voting, not that foot voting is without difficulty or that it overcomes all information problems completely. However, comparative analysis is important because foot voting and ballot box voting are the most important realistic alternatives facing many societies across a wide range of issues.

II. The Logic of Rational Political Ignorance

Scholars have long recognized that most citizens have little or no political knowledge.[7] An individual voter has virtually no chance of influencing the outcome of an election—somewhere between 1 in 10 million and 1 in 100 million in the case of a modern U.S. presidential election, depending on the state where one lives.[8] The chance of casting a decisive vote is

---

[7] The data is extensive. See, e.g., George W. Bishop, *The Illusion of Public Opinion: Fact and Artifact in Public Opinion Polls* (Lanham, MD: Rowman and Littlefield, 2004); Somin, "Political Ignorance and the Countermajoritarian Difficulty"; Althaus, *Collective Preferences*; and Delli Carpini and Keeter, *What Americans Know about Politics*, for recent summaries of the evidence.

[8] For the latter figure, see William H. Riker and Peter Ordeshook, "A Theory of the Calculus of Voting," *American Political Science Review* 62 (1968): 25–42; for the former, see Andrew Gelman et al., "What Is the Probability That Your Vote Will Make a Difference?" *Economic Inquiry* (forthcoming), available at http://www.stat.columbia.edu/~gelman/research/published/probdecisive2.pdf. Gelman et al. estimate that the chance of decisiveness in the 2008 presidential election varied from 1 in 10 million in a few small states, to 1 in 100 million in large states such as California (ibid., 9–10).

somewhat greater in other democracies with smaller populations, but is still extremely small.[9]

As a result, the incentive to accumulate political knowledge is vanishingly small, so long as the only reason for doing so is to cast a "better" vote. Even highly intelligent and perfectly rational citizens could choose to devote little or no effort to the acquisition of political knowledge. The theory of rational ignorance implies that most citizens will acquire little or no political knowledge and also that they will often make poor use of the knowledge that they do acquire. Both political knowledge acquisition and the rational evaluation of that information are classic collective action problems, in which individual citizens have incentives to "free ride" on the efforts of others.[10]

Some critics reject the rational ignorance theory on the ground that it allegedly also predicts that citizens will choose not to vote.[11] However, as Derek Parfit has demonstrated theoretically, and Aaron Edlin et al. have supported with empirical evidence,[12] the decision to vote is rational so long as the voter perceives a significant difference between candidates and cares even slightly about the welfare of fellow citizens, as well as his own. For example, if an American voter believes that the victory of the "right" candidate will give to each of his 300 million fellow citizens an average of $5,000 in net benefits, then it is rational to vote even if the chance that one's vote will be decisive is less than 1 in 100 million. The enormous benefit of casting a decisive vote outweighs the very low probability that it will happen. This remains true even if the potential voter values the welfare of fellow citizens who are strangers to him far less than he values his own welfare (e.g., valuing a $1,000 benefit to a fellow citizen as equivalent to $1 for himself).[13] In a 2006 publication, I extended the Parfit and Edlin analysis to show that, for most citizens, it will usually be irrational to acquire significant amounts of political information for voting purposes, even though it is rational to engage in voting itself.[14]

[9] See, e.g., André Blais et al., "The Calculus of Voting: An Empirical Test," *European Journal of Political Research* 37 (2000): 181–201, which calculates very low probabilities of decisiveness in Canadian provincial elections, despite their relatively small populations.

[10] Mancur Olson, *The Logic of Collective Action* (Cambridge, MA: Harvard University Press, 1965).

[11] There is a large literature attacking rational choice theory on the ground that it fails to explain the prevalence of voting. See, e.g., Donald Green and Ian Shapiro, *Pathologies of Rational Choice Theory* (New Haven, CT: Yale University Press, 1994); and Lars Udehn, *The Limits of Public Choice* (London: Routledge, 1996).

[12] Derek Parfit, *Reasons and Persons* (Oxford: Clarendon Press, 1984), 73–75; Aaron Edlin, Andrew Gelman, and Noah Kaplan, "Voting as a Rational Choice: Why and How People Vote to Improve the Well-Being of Others," *Rationality and Society* 19 (2007): 293–314.

[13] See Somin, "Knowledge about Ignorance," 258–60.

[14] See ibid., 259–61. For other efforts to reconcile rational choice theory and the "paradox of voting," see, e.g., John H. Aldrich, "Rational Choice and Turnout," *American Journal of Political Science* 37 (1993): 246–78; and Terry M. Moe, *The Organization of Interests* (Chicago: University of Chicago Press, 1980), 81–82.

A. Low levels of political knowledge

We cannot know for certain that the theory of rational ignorance is correct. But the available evidence strongly supports it. There is little doubt, for example, that political knowledge levels are extremely low, and have been so at least since the start of modern survey research in the United States in the 1930s.[15]

It is impossible to summarize the extensive evidence of widespread ignorance here. However, it is important to note that it covers a wide range of issues. The majority of citizens are often ignorant of the facts of specific policies, even very important ones. For example, around the time of the 2004 election, 70 percent of Americans were unaware of the recent passage of President George W. Bush's prescription drug bill, the largest new government program in decades.[16] Citizens are often also ignorant about the general "rules of the game" of politics, such as determining which officials are responsible for which issues.[17] And studies have long demonstrated that most citizens do not understand the basics of political ideologies such as liberalism and conservatism.[18]

Absent the rational ignorance hypothesis, it is difficult to explain the fact that political knowledge levels have remained roughly stable at very low levels for decades, despite massive increases in education levels and in the availability of information through the media and now the Internet.[19] The rational ignorance theory is also confirmed by data indicating that the strongest predictor of political knowledge—more important even than education—is the survey respondent's level of interest in politics.[20] This supports the prediction that those who acquire political information will do so primarily for reasons other than a desire to become better voters. Instead, they view political information as a consumption good, much as dedicated sports fans will acquire knowledge about teams and players despite the fact that they cannot affect the outcome of games.[21]

---

[15] See Delli Carpini and Keeter, *What Americans Know about Politics*; Eric R.A.N. Smith, *The Unchanging American Voter* (Berkeley: University of California Press, 1989); and Ilya Somin, "Voter Knowledge and Constitutional Change: Assessing the New Deal Experience," *William and Mary Law Review* 45 (2003): 595–674.

[16] Somin, "When Ignorance Isn't Bliss," 6.

[17] Delli Carpini and Keeter, *What Americans Know about Politics*.

[18] See Philip Converse, "The Nature of Belief Systems in Mass Publics," in *Ideology and Discontent*, ed. David Apter (New York: Free Press, 1964); Russell W. Neumann, *The Paradox of Mass Politics* (Cambridge, MA: Harvard University Press, 1986); and David RePass, "Searching for Voters along the Liberal-Conservative Continuum: The Infrequent Ideologue and the Missing Middle," *The Forum* 6 (2008): 1–49.

[19] Delli Carpini and Keeter, *What Americans Know about Politics*; Smith, *The Unchanging American Voter*; Stephen E. Bennett, "Trends in Americans' Political Information, 1967–87," *American Politics Quarterly* 17 (1989): 422–35; Althaus, *Collective Preferences*.

[20] Somin, "When Ignorance Isn't Bliss"; Somin, "Political Ignorance and the Countermajoritarian Difficulty"; Althaus, *Collective Preferences*; Robert Luskin, "Measuring Political Sophistication," *American Journal of Political Science* 31 (1987): 856–99.

[21] Somin, "Knowledge about Ignorance."

B. Illogical use of knowledge[22]

The theory of rational ignorance suggests not only that most citizens will acquire little political knowledge, but that they will often make poor use of the information they do possess. The key consideration is that the theory of rational ignorance does *not* predict that voters will choose not to acquire any information at all. Rather, it predicts that they will acquire very little or no information *for purposes of voting*.[23]

Some voters, however, will learn political information for other reasons. Obviously, scholars, politicians, political activists, journalists, and others have professional reasons for being informed about political developments. However, such professional consumers of political information are only a tiny fraction of the population. Far more common are those who acquire political knowledge because they find it interesting.[24] There are not enough such people to eliminate widespread political ignorance, but they do nonetheless form by far the largest bloc of relatively well-informed voters.

Citizens with a strong interest in politics often function like "fans" cheering on their preferred ideology or political party, rather than as rational assessors of information.[25] They evaluate information in a highly biased manner that tends to confirm rather than objectively test their preexisting views.

This prediction is supported by studies showing that people tend to use new information to reinforce their preexisting views on political issues, while discounting evidence that runs counter to those views.[26] Although some scholars view such bias as irrational behavior,[27] it is perfectly rational if the goal is not to get at the "truth" of a given issue in order to be a better voter, but to enjoy the psychic benefits of being a political "fan." Rationally ignorant voters may limit not only the amount of information they acquire but also "how rationally they process the information they do have."[28] To put it a different way, such citizens' mode of processing information may be rational for purposes of psychic gratification, but irrational for purposes of improving the quality of their votes. Pursuing

---

[22] This section recapitulates and slightly extends arguments I first presented in Somin, "Knowledge about Ignorance."

[23] Somin, "Political Ignorance and the Countermajoritarian Difficulty."

[24] Ibid.

[25] Somin, "Knowledge about Ignorance."

[26] See, e.g., Charles Lord, Lee Ross, and Mark R. Lepper, "Biased Assimilation and Attitude Polarization: The Effects of Prior Theories on Subsequently Considered Evidence," *Journal of Personality and Social Psychology* 37 (1979): 2098–2109; Charles S. Taber and Milton Lodge, "Motivated Skepticism in the Evaluation of Political Beliefs," *American Journal of Political Science* (forthcoming); and Edward Glaeser and Cass R. Sunstein, "Extremism and Social Learning," *Journal of Legal Analysis* 1 (2009): 1–62.

[27] Taber and Lodge, "Motivated Skepticism."

[28] Bryan Caplan, "Rational Irrationality," *Kylos* 54 (2001): 5; see also Bryan Caplan, *The Myth of the Rational Voter* (Princeton, NJ: Princeton University Press, 2007).

the former at the expense of the latter is itself perfectly rational, since the chance that any one vote will be decisive to an electoral outcome is infinitesimally small.

A recent study shows that the most knowledgeable voters tend to be more biased in their evaluation of new evidence than those with less preexisting political information.[29] Similarly, large numbers of relatively knowledgeable citizens believe ridiculous conspiracy theories about political events, such as claims that the 9/11 terrorist attacks were an "inside job."[30]

If those who acquire political knowledge do so in order to cast "better" votes, such findings would be difficult to explain. But if, as the rational ignorance hypothesis implies, the main goal is to enjoy psychic benefits similar to those available to sports fans, then the greater bias of the more politically knowledgeable is perfectly rational. The fact that they acquired more knowledge in the past suggests that they value the "fan" experience more than those who acquired less; thus, it is not at all surprising that they tend to be more biased in their evaluation of new data.

C. Information shortcuts[31]

Many scholars have argued that voter ignorance is not a significant problem because citizens can offset their ignorance through the effective use of information shortcuts.[32] For example, voters who know little else about a candidate can still determine a lot of useful information about him or her simply by knowing his or her party affiliation.[33] Voters who know little about the details of public policy can use "retrospective voting" to punish the party in power for poor performance if things generally seem to be going badly under its rule.[34] Elsewhere, I have criticized

---

[29] Taber and Lodge, "Motivated Skepticism"; Philip Converse, "The Nature of Belief Systems in Mass Publics," in *Ideology and Discontent*, ed. David Apter (New York: Free Press, 1964), produced similar findings many years ago.

[30] See Cass R. Sunstein and Adrian Vermeule, "Conspiracy Theories," *Harvard Public Law Working Paper* No. 08-03 (2008), available at http://papers.ssrn.com/sol3/papers.cfm?abstract_id=1084585.

[31] This section is an adapted and condensed version of my more detailed analysis of this issue in Somin, "Knowledge about Ignorance."

[32] There is a vast literature on this subject. For notable defenses of various shortcuts, see, e.g., Philip Converse, "Popular Representation and the Distribution of Information," in *Information and Democratic Processes*, ed. John Ferejohn and James Kuklinski (Urbana: University of Illinois Press, 1990); Samuel Popkin, *The Reasoning Voter* (Chicago: University of Chicago Press, 1991); Donald Wittman, *The Myth of Democratic Failure* (Chicago: University of Chicago Press, 1995); Arthur Lupia and Matthew McCubbins, *The Democratic Dilemma: Can Citizens Learn What They Need to Know?* (New York: Cambridge University Press, 1998); Morris Fiorina, *Retrospective Voting in American National Elections* (New Haven, CT: Yale University Press, 1981); and Benjamin I. Page and Robert Y. Shapiro, *The Rational Public* (Chicago: University of Chicago Press, 1992).

[33] John Aldrich, *Why Parties?* (Chicago: University of Chicago Press, 1995).

[34] Joseph A. Schumpeter, *Capitalism, Socialism, and Democracy* (New York: Holt, Rinehart and Wilson, 1950); Fiorina, *Retrospective Voting in American National Elections*.

shortcut theories on the ground that citizens must have a significant preexisting base of knowledge to use them effectively.[35] For example, retrospective voting can only be effective if citizens know which political leaders are responsible for which issues, and whether or not their policies were more effective than available alternatives. Otherwise, they might end up "punishing" incumbents for policy issues that they have no control over or for enacting policies that actually produced better results than those of their opponents would have.[36] In recent years, some scholars who were previously highly enthusiastic about the utility of shortcuts have partially conceded the validity of such criticisms.[37]

Moreover, even if information shortcuts can in theory provide an adequate substitute for more detailed knowledge, the theory underlying shortcuts implicitly assumes that voters will (1) choose the right shortcuts and (2) use those shortcuts in a logical manner to assess opposing candidates and parties. However, if rationally ignorant voters economize not only on the acquisition of information but also on the degree to which they assess it in a logical manner, these assumptions are unlikely to hold true. Empirically, voters often pick poor shortcuts or fail to use them logically. Even the most sophisticated and highly rational voters may rely on shortcuts that have little relevance to political candidates' likely performance in office. For example, a recent study of elections for the presidency of the American Economics Association (AEA) shows that the relative physical attractiveness of the rival candidates is a powerful predictor of which candidate prevails in the voting.[38] The AEA electorate consists of academic economists who are presumably knowledgeable about the functions of the AEA—and arguably more committed to rational, maximizing behavior than is the average voter in ordinary elections. If AEA voters nonetheless rely on dubious information shortcuts, it is likely that voters in other elections also do so.

Recent evidence suggests that even the most knowledgeable might systematically pick ideological shortcuts that mislead more than they inform. A study of the accuracy of predictions by experts in politics and international relations finds that their predictions of political events are

[35] See Somin, "Voter Ignorance and the Democratic Ideal"; Somin, "Resolving the Democratic Dilemma?" *Yale Journal on Regulation* 16 (1999): 401–16; Somin, "When Ignorance Isn't Bliss"; Somin, "Political Ignorance and the Countermajoritarian Difficulty"; Somin, "Richard Posner's Democratic Pragmatism," *Critical Review* 16 (2004): 1–22; and Somin, "Knowledge about Ignorance."

[36] Somin, "When Ignorance Isn't Bliss"; Somin, "Political Ignorance and the Countermajoritarian Difficulty."

[37] Samuel Popkin and Michael Dimock, "Political Knowledge and Citizen Competence," in *Citizen Competence and Democratic Institutions*, ed. Stephen Elkin and Karol Soltan (University Park: Pennsylvania State University Press, 1999); William A. Galston, "Political Knowledge, Political Engagement, and Civic Education," *Annual Review of Political Science* 4 (2001): 217–34.

[38] Daniel Hamermesh, "Changing Looks and Changing 'Discrimination': The Beauty of Economists," *National Bureau of Economic Research Working Paper No. 11712* (2005).

generally no more accurate than would be produced by random chance.[39] Of greater interest for present purposes is the finding that the most inaccurate experts are those who tend to make their predictions on the basis of broad generalizations—that is, experts who rely the most on ideological shortcuts.[40]

Such behavior is consistent with the prediction of rational ignorance theory that citizens who acquire and evaluate political information do so primarily for reasons other than becoming better voters. Biased and illogical evaluation of political information is perfectly rational behavior for people whose goal in acquiring information is something other than truth-seeking.

None of this suggests that information shortcuts are completely useless. Indeed, in my view, they often have some benefits. However, for present purposes, the only necessary inference is that information shortcuts fall far short of fully offsetting the detrimental effects of rational political ignorance. To the extent that this is true, foot voting is likely to have important informational advantages over ballot box voting.

III. Foot Voting Versus Ballot Box Voting

Foot voting provides much stronger incentives than ballot box voting for both information acquisition and rational information use. People voting with their feet are largely free of the collective action problems that lead to rational ignorance in the political process.

A. Information acquisition

As we have seen, one of the main causes of political ignorance is the fact that it is "rational." Because even an extremely well-informed voter has virtually no chance of actually influencing electoral outcomes, he or she has little incentive to become informed in the first place, at least if the only purpose of doing so is to cast a "correct" vote. By contrast, a person "voting with her feet" by choosing a state or locality in which to live is in a wholly different situation from the ballot box voter. If a "foot voter" can acquire information about superior economic conditions, public policies, or other advantages in another state, he or she can move to that state and benefit from them even if all other citizens do nothing. This creates a much stronger incentive for foot voters to acquire relevant information about conditions in different jurisdictions than for ballot box voters to acquire information about public policy. Unlike in the case of ballot box

---

[39] Philip E. Tetlock, *Expert Political Judgment: How Good Is It? How Can We Know?* (Princeton, NJ: Princeton University Press, 2005).
[40] Ibid., chaps. 3–5.

voters, information acquisition by foot voters is largely exempt from collective action problems.

In most cases, foot voters also don't need to acquire as much information as ballot box voters in order to be adequately informed. Unlike a ballot box voter, a foot voter need not connect his judgment of relative conditions in various states to specific elected officials and their policies.[41] If voters don't realize which officials are responsible for which issues or don't separate out the impact of public policy from that of other social conditions, they may end up punishing or rewarding incumbent officeholders for outcomes over which they have no control.[42] The officeholders themselves can try to take credit for positive developments that were not really caused by their policies. Presidents, for example, try to take credit for any economic prosperity that occurs during their term in office, even if they did little or nothing to cause it.

By contrast, foot voters don't need comparably detailed knowledge. It is enough for them to know that conditions are better in one state than another, and then be able to act on this knowledge by moving. So long as public officials *themselves* know that their policies can affect social conditions in ways that attract foot voters, they will have an incentive to implement better policies in order to appeal to potential migrants. Not only does foot voting create a stronger incentive to acquire knowledge than ballot box voting, it also usually requires less knowledge to implement effectively.

B. Information use

In addition to providing superior incentives for information acquisition relative to ballot box voting, foot voting also improves incentives for rational information use. Part of the reason for this is the same as that which underlies foot voters' superior incentive to acquire information: the absence of a collective action problem. But there are also other reasons to expect foot voters to make better use of the information they acquire than ballot box voters do.

As noted above, people have a strong tendency to process political information in a highly biased way that tends to confirm their preexisting ideologies and prejudices. This is true of both ordinary voters and political activists and experts. By contrast, most modern Americans lack the same kind of commitment to their states that many have to their ideologies and partisan affiliations. Over the last hundred years, citizen identification with state and local governments has largely faded away in most parts of the country, replaced by a sense of national identity as

---

[41] Somin, "When Ignorance Isn't Bliss," 12–13.
[42] Ibid.

Americans.[43] For that reason, people are likely to be more objective in analyzing information bearing on their decisions about where to live than their decisions about who to vote for. The latter decisions implicate strong partisan and ideological commitments, and sometimes also ethnic or religious ones. The former—at least in the modern United States—usually do not.

Some scholars claim that the decline of identification with state governments is an argument *against* federalism,[44] because citizens no longer have a sense of "community" that is linked to state government. However, citizens' lack of commitment to their states and localities facilitates effective foot voting, and to that extent actually strengthens the case for devolution of power away from the center.

Obviously, this point applies with much lesser force to countries where regional governments are the focus of ethnic or ideological loyalties. For example, French Canadian nationalists may be strongly attached to Quebec and reluctant to move to other provinces even if the latter have better policies. Even in federal systems of this type, however, foot voters may still be more rational in their evaluation of information than ballot box voters if their ethnic group is in the majority in more than one jurisdiction. For instance, Switzerland has multiple French-, German-, and Italian-speaking cantons. While German-speaking Swiss may be reluctant to migrate to a French-speaking canton, the same might not hold true for movement between different German-speaking jurisdictions. Moreover, even in the relatively rare cases where foot voters' biases in favor of their home jurisdiction are as powerful as those of ballot box voters in favor of their ideology or party, the former will still have stronger incentives to try to overcome their biases because of the absence of a collective action problem.

C. The role of interjurisdictional competition

Interjurisdictional competition also improves the acquisition of information by foot voters. States and localities seek to attract new residents and businesses as sources of tax revenue. Therefore, state and local governments have strong incentives to establish policies that will appeal to potential immigrants and convince current residents to stay.[45] The power

---

[43] Edward Rubin and Malcolm Feeley, "Federalism: Some Notes on a National Neurosis," *UCLA Law Review* (1994): 936–42.

[44] See, e.g., ibid., 936–51; and Malcolm Feeley and Edward Rubin, *Federalism: Political Identity and Tragic Compromise* (Ann Arbor: University of Michigan Press, 2008).

[45] Thomas Dye, *American Federalism: Competition among Governments* (New York: John Wiley, 1990), 1–33; Ilya Somin, "Closing the Pandora's Box of Federalism: The Case for Judicial Restriction of Federal Subsidies to State Governments," *Georgetown Law Journal* 90 (2002): 468–71; Barry Weingast, "The Economic Role of Political Institutions: Market-Preserving Federalism and Economic Development," *Journal of Law, Economics, and Organization* 11 (1995): 1–31.

of the competitive pressure comes from governments' constant need to attract additional revenue to finance expenditures that can pay off key interest groups and increase political leaders' reelection chances. Interstate and interlocality competition for residents facilitates the creation of public policies that advance the interests of the majority, even in the absence of informed ballot box voting.[46]

In addition, competition gives both state governments and private organizations incentives to disseminate information about the advantages of living in one jurisdiction as opposed to others. While the same is true of competitors for political office, information disseminated by competitors in the foot voting market is arguably less likely to be inaccurate or misleading than political advertising. Since foot voters have strong incentives to examine information more closely than ballot box voters, competitors in the former market are less likely to get away with deceptive or overly simplistic claims than those in the latter. Political rhetoric and advertising routinely employ misleading or deceptive rhetoric and claims,[47] some of which are quite effective. By contrast, as I discuss in Section IV, evidence suggests that competitors in the market for foot voters generally disseminate relatively accurate information to their "consumers" even in cases where the latter are extremely poor and ill-educated.

D. Implications for group migration

The informational advantages of foot voting over ballot box voting potentially extend to group migration, as well as migration by individuals and families. Historically, religious and ideological groups have sometimes chosen to migrate together in order to establish a community where they could live in accordance with their principles. Well-known examples from American history include the Pilgrims' migration from Europe to establish their colony at Plymouth, and the migration of the Mormons to Utah.[48] Such group migration differs from moving decisions by individuals or families because it requires coordination across a larger number of people, and is often undertaken for the purposes of establishing a community based on a specific religion or ideology.

[46] Somin, "Political Ignorance and the Countermajoritarian Difficulty."
[47] There is a large literature on this subject. See, e.g., Lawrence R. Jacobs and Robert Shapiro, *Politicians Don't Pander: Political Manipulation and the Loss of Democratic Responsiveness* (Chicago: University of Chicago Press, 2000); Tali Mendelberg, *The Race Card* (Chicago: University of Chicago Press, 2001); and Somin, "Voter Knowledge and Constitutional Change," 652–54.
[48] For a good discussion of the federalism issues raised by the Mormons' establishment of a new state in Utah, see Sarah Barringer Gordon, *The Mormon Question: Polygamy and Constitutional Conflict in Nineteenth-Century America* (Chapel Hill: University of North Carolina Press, 2002). For a recent account of the Pilgrims' decision to leave Europe and found a new society in Massachusetts, see Nathan Philbrick, *Mayflower: A Story of Courage, Community, and War* (New York: Viking, 2006).

Group migration within a federal system need not involve the establishment of an entirely new state or province, as happened with the Mormons. It could simply mean moving from one existing state to another whose policies are more hospitable to the group's purposes. For example, Mennonite religious groups in Canada and the United States migrated west without any intention of establishing their own state or province.[49]

Some aspects of group governance may raise informational problems similar to those that arise from ballot box voting. In a large group with a democratic governance structure, individual members might have little incentive to acquire information on which to base their votes. They could be rationally ignorant for much the same reasons as most voters in the political system are. However, group migration does generally include an individually decisive decision on the part of each member to join the group in the first place, and often an additional decision to choose to migrate along with the other members instead of staying behind. For these reasons, participants in group migrations probably have stronger incentives to acquire and rationally evaluate relevant information than do ballot box voters.

E. The problem of moving costs

The most obvious drawback of foot voting relative to ballot box voting is the problem of moving costs. People who migrate from one jurisdiction to another must pay the cost of transporting themselves and their possessions, as well as assume the burden of finding new jobs and social ties. In some cases, these costs will prevent foot voting even in situations where another jurisdiction might be more attractive to the potential migrant than her current home.

This essay is not a comprehensive evaluation of the costs and benefits of foot voting. It focuses on its advantages with respect to information-gathering. Thus, I will not fully consider the issue of moving costs. Nonetheless, a few brief remarks are in order. First, moving costs are not so great as to preclude interjurisdictional mobility for millions of people. A recent Pew survey finds that 63 percent of Americans have moved at least once in their lives, and 43 percent have made at least one interstate move.[50] Contrary to claims that foot voting is an option primarily for the affluent, census data finds that households with an income under $5,000 per year are actually twice as likely to make interstate moves as the population as a whole.[51] As I discuss in Section IV, historically poor and

---

[49] See, e.g., Adolf Ens, *Subjects or Citizens? The Mennonite Experience in Canada, 1870–1925* (Ottawa: University of Ottawa Press, 1994); and Steven Nolt, *A History of the Amish*, rev. ed. (Intercourse, PA: Good Books, 2004).

[50] Pew Research Center, *Who Moves? Who Stays Put? Where's Home?* (Washington, DC: Pew Research Center, 2008), 8, 13.

[51] Somin, "Political Ignorance and the Countermajoritarian Difficulty," 1351.

oppressed populations have often taken advantage of foot voting opportunities. Increases in societal wealth and improvements in transportation
technology have made migration cheaper than ever before. While moving
costs continue to be a shortcoming of foot voting, they fall far short of
vitiating its informational advantages. In Section V below, I discuss how
private planned communities and interjurisdictional competition that does
not require physical mobility can reduce the impact of moving costs still
further.

IV. THE POWER OF FOOT VOTING UNDER ADVERSE CONDITIONS: AFRICAN AMERICANS IN THE JIM CROW ERA SOUTH

To my knowledge, there has not yet been a study that empirically
documents the informational advantages of voting with your feet over
ballot box voting. It is difficult to construct a research design that gets at
the issue directly. However, there is telling historical evidence of impressive information acquisition by foot voters even under extremely adverse
circumstances. The case of African Americans in the Jim Crow era South
(roughly 1880–1960) is a particularly noteworthy example. During that
time, southern state governments adopted a wide variety of laws dis-
criminating against and oppressing their black populations; this extensive
system of racial oppression was collectively known as "Jim Crow."

If information acquisition for foot voting could be effective under the
severely adverse conditions endured by southern blacks in the Jim Crow
era, it is likely to be at least equally effective in other, less extreme circumstances. Moreover, the limited available evidence suggests that black
southern foot voters were better-informed than the (on average) wealthier
and more educated southern white ballot box voters of the same era.

A. Southern black migration during the Jim Crow era

African Americans in the Jim Crow era South, most of them poorly
educated and many illiterate, were able to learn enough information
about the existence of relatively better conditions in other states to set off
a massive migration to the North and also to parts of the South that were
relatively less oppressive than others.[52] Between about 1880 and 1920,
over one million southern-born African Americans migrated to the North
or the West.[53] By 1920, these migrants accounted for some 10 percent of

---

[52] See William Cohen, *At Freedom's Edge: Black Mobility and the Southern White Quest for
Racial Control, 1861–1915* (Baton Rouge: Louisiana State University Press, 1991); Florette
Henri, *Black Migration: Movement North 1900–1920* (New York: Doubleday, 1975); Daniel M.
Johnson and Rex R. Campbell, *Black Migration in America: A Social Demographic History*
(Durham, NC: Duke University Press, 1981); and David E. Bernstein, "The Law and Eco-
nomics of Post–Civil War Restrictions on Interstate Migration by African-Americans," *Texas
Law Review* 76 (1998): 782–85.
[53] Johnson and Campbell, *Black Migration in America*, 74–75.

the total black population of the United States, which then stood at 10.4 million.[54] There was an even larger black migration from South to North in the years immediately following World War II.[55] The earlier migration, however, is of special interest for present purposes, because during this period southern blacks were even more severely disadvantaged than during the later one and would have found it more difficult to acquire information about migration opportunities.

In addition to migration from the South to other parts of the country, there was also extensive African American population movement within the South itself.[56] Intraregional migration was often driven simply by the search for economic opportunity, but also by differences among southern political jurisdictions in the degree to which they oppressed the local black population.[57]

Southern blacks in the early twentieth century labored under severe disadvantages that one might expect to prevent effective foot voting. Most were extremely ill-educated, in part as a deliberate result of state government policy. As late as 1940, only 5.4 percent of southern blacks over the age of twenty-five were high school graduates, compared to 26.1 percent of contemporary American whites.[58] Even those southern blacks who did have access to education nearly always attended inferior segregated schools that were deliberately structured to provide only very limited education for black students.[59] In light of these problems, the success of so many African American migrants in acquiring the knowledge they needed is strong evidence in support of the informational advantages of foot voting.

B. Information acquisition by southern black migrants

Southern black workers relied on a variety of information sources to facilitate migration decisions. One important resource was the information provided by relatives and acquaintances already living in the North or in more tolerant southern jurisdictions.[60] Many black migrants were "armed with firsthand reports from trusted friends and relatives" about

---

[54] Ibid., 77.

[55] Ibid., 114–23.

[56] Ibid., 60–61; Cohen, At Freedom's Edge; Robert Higgs, Competition and Coercion: Blacks in the American Economy 1865–1914 (New York: Cambridge University Press, 1977).

[57] Price V. Fishback, "Can Competition among Employers Reduce Governmental Discrimination? Coal Companies and Segregated Schools in West Virginia in the Early 1900s," Journal of Law and Economics 32 (1989): 324–41; Cohen, At Freedom's Edge; Higgs, Competition and Coercion.

[58] U.S. Census Bureau 2000, Tables 3 and 11a.

[59] James D. Anderson, The Education of Blacks in the South, 1860–1935 (Chapel Hill: University of North Carolina Press, 1988).

[60] Henri, Black Migration: Movement North, 59–60.

conditions in the North.[61] Ballot box voters cannot easily rely on comparably knowledgeable and trustworthy information sources.[62]

Other information was provided by the contemporary black media, which actively encouraged migration.[63] But most scholars put special emphasis on the information-spreading activities of "emigrant agents" employed by businesses seeking to recruit African American workers.[64] The agents provided valuable information to African Americans considering moving to the North, and sometimes also helped arrange transportation for them. While agents had obvious incentives to exaggerate the benefits of moving,[65] these were to some extent kept in check by information provided by migrants who had already made it to the North,[66] and by the likelihood that workers who were deceived about the opportunities available to them might move back to the South themselves and tell others to disbelieve the agents. These mechanisms provided a check on deception by emigrant agents of a kind that is not usually available in the case of political rhetoric used to persuade ballot box voters.

In addition to successfully acquiring information about job opportunities, many black migrants also chose to move in part because they came to realize that northern state governments and social mores were less hostile to blacks than those in the South. Although economic opportunity was a key factor in motivating migration, the desire to escape racial repression was also important. Migrants themselves often cited lynching, racial discrimination, and other hostile government policies as important factors in their decision to leave the South.[67]

Some contemporary African American leaders recognized the potential of foot voting as a tool for mitigating their people's oppression, and urged southern blacks to consider migrating to the North. As early as 1886, Frederick Douglass—the most prominent African American leader of the nineteenth century—argued that *"diffusion* is the true policy for the colored people of the South," that as many blacks as possible should be encouraged to move to "parts of the country where their civil and political rights are better protected than at present they can be at the South,"

---

[61] Johnson and Campbell, *Black Migration in America*, 83.

[62] Some shortcut advocates argue that rationally ignorant voters can rely on cues from "opinion leaders" more knowledgeable than themselves. I have criticized this theory in Somin, "Voter Ignorance and the Democratic Ideal," and Somin, "Resolving the Democratic Dilemma."

[63] Henri, *Black Migration: Movement North*, 63–64.

[64] For a detailed account of these "emigrant agents" and their role in providing information to southern blacks, see Bernstein, "The Law and Economics of Post–Civil War Restrictions on Interstate Migration by African-Americans," 782–83, 792–802. See also Henri, *Black Migration: Movement North*, 60–62; Cohen, *At Freedom's Edge*, 119–27, 259–57.

[65] Henri, *Black Migration: Movement North*, 62–63.

[66] Ibid.; Bernstein, "The Law and Economics of Post–Civil War Restrictions on Interstate Migration by African-Americans."

[67] Henri, *Black Migration: Movement North*, 57–60; Johnson and Campbell, *Black Migration in America*, 84–85.

and that "[a] million of dollars devoted to this purpose [of assisting black migration out of the South] would do more for the colored people of the South than the same amount expended in any other way."[68] A 1917 NAACP publication claimed that migration north was "the most effective protest against Southern lynching, lawlessness, and general deviltry."[69]

C. Effective use of knowledge

Most scholars agree that black migration to the North during the Jim Crow era was generally effective in achieving the migrants' goals. Although the North was far from free of racism, most migrants were able to better their lot significantly, both economically and from the standpoint of protecting their civil and political rights.[70] These results suggest that the migrants made effective use of the knowledge that they acquired, and generally chose their destinations wisely.

As the theory of foot voting under competitive federalism would predict,[71] the resulting migration not only benefited the migrants themselves but also forced racist southern state governments to "grant . . . African-Americans greater educational opportunities and greater protection in their property and person" in an effort to get them to stay and continue to provide labor for white-owned farms and businesses.[72] For example, fear of losing black labor was one of the motives that led southern state governments to finally make some belated efforts to crack down on the lynching of African Americans in the 1920s.[73] Lynching was cited by many migrants as an important cause of their decision to move.[74] In a related dramatic example, interjurisdictional competition for the labor of migrating black coal miners led to successful lobbying by coal companies for a reduction in school segregation in early 1900s West Virginia.[75] As Douglass had predicted in 1886, "the condition of those [southern blacks] who must remain will be better because of those who go."[76]

---

[68] Frederick Douglass, *Selected Speeches and Writings* (1886), ed. Philip S. Foner and Yuval Taylor (Chicago: Lawrence Hill Books, 1999), 702 (emphasis in the original).

[69] Quoted in Michael J. Klarman, *From Jim Crow to Civil Rights: The Supreme Court and the Struggle for Racial Equality* (New York: Oxford University Press, 2004), 164.

[70] Henri, *Black Migration: Movement North*, 168–73.

[71] See, e.g., Dye, *American Federalism*; Weingast, "The Economic Role of Political Institutions."

[72] Bernstein, "The Law and Economics of Post–Civil War Restrictions on Interstate Migration by African-Americans," 784. See also Henri, *Black Migration: Movement North*, 75–76, 170–71; and Higgs, *Competition and Coercion*, 29–32, 59, 119–20, 152–53.

[73] Michael J. Pfeifer, *Rough Justice: Lynching and American Society, 1874–1947* (Urbana: University of Illinois Press, 2004).

[74] Henri, *Black Migration: Movement North*, 57–58; Johnson and Campbell, *Black Migration in America*, 84–85.

[75] Fishback, "Can Competition among Employers Reduce Governmental Discrimination?" For a general discussion of the ability of migration to reduce discrimination in education, see Robert A. Margo, "Segregated Schools and the Mobility Hypothesis: A Model of Local Government Discrimination," *Quarterly Journal of Economics* 106 (1991): 61–75.

[76] Douglass, *Selected Speeches and Writings*, 702.

Obviously, the ability of southern blacks to vote with their feet did not come close to fully mitigating the baneful effects of Jim Crow.[77] Foot voting was an improvement over preexisting conditions, not a panacea. It did, however, provide important informational benefits and a measure of political empowerment to a widely despised and poorly educated minority.

Although exact comparisons are difficult, it seems likely that potential southern black migrants of the Jim Crow era were able to learn considerably more about relative conditions in different jurisdictions than most modern voters have learned about the basics of our political system. At the very least, large numbers of poor and ill-educated southern blacks learned enough to understand that relatively more favorable employment opportunities and public policies awaited them in other jurisdictions, a realization that contrasts with the inability of most modern citizens to acquire sufficient knowledge to engage in effective retrospective voting.[78]

If foot voting could provide powerful informational advantages in the exceptionally adverse conditions of the Jim Crow era South, there is strong reason to expect that it is more effective under modern conditions, where education levels are much higher, information costs are lower, and no large group is as thoroughly oppressed as poor southern blacks were a century ago. People in less dire circumstances than early twentieth century southern blacks can acquire information more easily.

D. Comparison with contemporary southern white ballot box voters

In considering Jim Crow era black migration as a case of foot voting, it is difficult to make a direct comparison to ballot box voting. Most southern blacks during that period were, of course, denied the right to vote, so they did not have the opportunity to address through ballot box voting the same issues that many sought to resolve through foot voting. However, southern whites of the same period did address racial issues at the ballot box, and it is worth comparing their apparent knowledge levels with those of black foot voters.

White southerners had far higher average income and education levels than African Americans. As of 1940, 24.6 percent of southern white adults over the age of twenty-five had high school diplomas, compared to just 5.4 percent of southern blacks.[79] And this difference in quantity of education coexisted with a massive difference in quality. Income and educa-

---

[77] It should be noted, however, that its failure to do so was partly attributable to southern state governments' partially successful efforts to reduce black mobility. See Cohen, *At Freedom's Edge*, 201–72; Bernstein, "The Law and Economics of Post–Civil War Restrictions on Interstate Migration by African-Americans," 810–27.

[78] See the discussion of retrospective voting in Somin, "When Ignorance Isn't Bliss," and Somin, "Voter Ignorance and the Democratic Ideal," 427–29.

[79] U.S. Census Bureau 2000, Tables 7a and 11a.

tion are both highly correlated with political knowledge levels.[80] Despite these comparative disadvantages, southern black foot voters seem to have acquired fairly accurate information about migration opportunities, and seem to have made effective use of their knowledge of which jurisdictions had policies more favorable to blacks. By contrast, southern white ballot box voters were apparently ignorant of important basic facts relevant to Jim Crow era racial policies.

Widespread southern white support for Jim Crow policies in the early twentieth century was in part based on purely normative disagreement with racial egalitarianism. However, white support for many such policies was also in part the result of gross ignorance on factual matters and failure to make rational use of political information.

To take one of the most notorious examples, for decades large proportions of white southern voters seem to have accepted the blatantly false claim that many, if not most, black men were out to rape white women.[81] This widely accepted myth was the principal rationale justifying the southern states' policy of permitting the lynching of numerous blacks accused (often falsely) of the rape or murder of whites.[82] Although scholars and civil rights advocates demonstrated the falsity of such claims as early as the 1890s,[83] most of the white southern electorate apparently remained unaware of this fact, or unwilling to consider it.[84]

Southern white voters were also, for decades, unable to recognize that the exclusion of the region's large African American population from much of the educational and economic system was an important contributing factor to the region's underdevelopment—a point obvious to most economists. Although the relative economic backwardness of the South was a major issue in regional politics throughout the late nineteenth and early twentieth centuries, few white southerners urged desegregation as a method for promoting economic development until well after World War II, and even then such views were mostly advanced by business leaders and other elites rather than by ordinary voters.[85]

In the absence of suitable survey data from the period, it is difficult to say whether these white southern views on racial issues were driven by

[80] Somin, "Political Ignorance and the Countermajoritarian Difficulty," 1327; Delli Carpini and Keeter, What Americans Know about Politics and Why It Matters, 144–45.

[81] Sandra Gunning, Race, Rape, and Lynching: The Red Record of American Literature, 1890–1912 (New York: Oxford University Press, 1996); Pfeifer, Rough Justice.

[82] Pfeifer, Rough Justice.

[83] For a discussion of one of the best-known efforts to disprove this rationale for lynching, see Patricia Schechter, Ida B. Wells-Barnett and American Reform, 1880–1930 (Chapel Hill: University of North Carolina Press, 2000).

[84] We have no survey data documenting the precise number of southern white voters who accepted the rape myth. However, contemporary observers believed that it was widely accepted, and politicians routinely exploited it in their campaigns, and as a justification for lynching. See generally Pfeifer, Rough Justice.

[85] Numan V. Bartley, The New South, 1945–1980 (Baton Rouge: Louisiana State University Press, 1995), 245–60.

ignorance per se, or by failure to rationally evaluate the information voters did know. Most likely, a combination of both was at work. Either way, the result is consistent with the rational ignorance hypothesis, and also contrasts with the more effective acquisition and use of information on racial issues by black foot voters.

There are, of course, some important distinctions between Jim Crow era white ballot box voting on racial issues and black foot voting. Racial issues were obviously of greater importance to African Americans than to whites, and the former therefore probably had stronger incentives to be informed about them. Moreover, the knowledge necessary for effective foot voting is in some respects simpler than that necessary for ballot box voting.[86]

However, the similarities between the two cases are still strong enough to make the comparison meaningful, even if imperfect. Race and its associated economic underdevelopment were arguably the most important political issues in the Jim Crow era South, and whites had almost as great a political stake in them as blacks did. The one-party system and other political institutions of the pre–Civil Rights Movement South were organized around the objective of maintaining white supremacy.[87] Moreover, to the extent that whites did have less interest in racial issues than blacks, this factor is at least partially offset by their higher income and education levels.

V. Foot Voting in the Private Sector

The informational benefits of foot voting make the case not only for federalism as an alternative to centralization, but for the market and civil society as an alternative to government. In many situations, the private sector may be an even better mechanism for foot voting than federalism is. Voting with your feet against a product in the market usually has much lower moving costs than doing so against a regional or local government. One can switch to a different product or firm without changing one's residence. The same point holds true for most civil society organizations. In this respect, the informational argument for foot voting has implications for the balance between the government and the private sector, as well as for the relationship of one level of government to another.

Private-sector foot voting is already a reality for many services traditionally performed by local government in the United States. As of 2004, over 52 million Americans lived in private planned communities such as

---

[86] See discussion in Section III above.

[87] For the classic analysis, see V. O. Key, *Southern Politics in State and Nation* (New York: Knopf, 1949), chaps. 24–31; see also Earl Black and Merle Black, *Politics and Society in the South* (Cambridge, MA: Harvard University Press, 1987), 75–77.

condominium associations.[88] These organizations routinely provide security, trash removal, environmental protection, zoning rules, and other services that are usually the responsibility of the state.[89] Similar enterprises have proven popular in Europe, Latin America, and parts of Asia.[90]

Competing private planned communities have significant advantages over traditional interjurisdictional competition between regional and local governments.[91] A single metropolitan area can contain many more private common-interest communities than government bodies. This makes it easier for each potential resident to find the community that best fits his needs, and also cuts down on potential moving costs by reducing the distance most movers would have to travel.

Unlike state and local governments, which are often subsidized by higher-level governments,[92] most private planned communities are exclusively dependent on residents for their revenues. This increases their incentive to compete for residents and meet their demands. Should private communities fail to do so, the property values of current owners are likely to fall, and they cannot use tax revenue collected in other areas to make up the difference. By contrast, state and local government officials usually have a much weaker stake in attracting migrants and incentivizing current residents to stay.

Finally, potentially irrational attachments to a state or locality might inhibit decisions to move out of a political jurisdiction, especially in cases where that jurisdiction is closely associated with an ethnic or religious group with which the decision-maker feels a strong sense of identity.[93] By contrast, few people have strong emotional or ideological attachments to a private planned community. This factor might make foot-voting decisions involving private planned communities more rational, on average, than those where potential movers choose between competing governmental jurisdictions.

The relative advantages of the private sector over government might be even more significant for the production of goods and services not tied to particular physical locations. In such cases, people can vote with their feet without actually moving at all, thereby eliminating moving costs from the

[88] Robert Nelson, *Private Neighborhoods and the Transformation of Local Government* (Washington, DC: Urban Institute, 2005), xiii.

[89] Ibid.

[90] See generally, Georg Glasze, Chris Webster, and Klaus Frantz, eds., *Private Cities: Global and Local Perspectives* (New York: Routledge, 2006).

[91] For a related argument suggesting that private planned communities might improve the quality of decision-making and deliberation relative to government bodies, see Guido Pincione and Fernando Tesón, *Rational Choice and Democratic Deliberation: A Theory of Discourse Failure* (New York: Cambridge University Press, 2006), 228–47; see also Vanberg and Buchanan, "Constitutional Choice, Rational Ignorance, and the Limits of Reason," 186–90, which argues that individuals might make better-informed choices between alternative constitutional arrangements in the market than through voting.

[92] Somin, "Closing the Pandora's Box of Federalism."

[93] See the discussion of this issue in Section III above.

equation. Here, too, the informational advantages of foot voting suggest that private provision has an important advantage over government.

In recent years, the Swiss economist Bruno Frey has argued that regional and local governments can take on some of the characteristics of private-sector firms, breaking the link between territory and jurisdiction.[94] Frey claims that various government bodies specializing in different issue areas could have overlapping jurisdictions, and that individual citizens could change government service providers without a physical move. It is too early to give a definitive verdict on these proposals. If Frey's theories turn out to be viable, they could provide a blueprint for ensuring that foot voting will often be as effective in the public sector as in the private. Something resembling Frey's proposal already exists in the field of commercial transactions in the United States, where businesses and others are often able to choose for themselves which state's law will govern their dealings with each other, often without making a physical move.[95]

A complete comparison of private planned communities and political bodies is outside the scope of this essay. My aim here is to note a potentially important and underanalyzed advantage of private communities over ones controlled by political bodies. I do not assert that this advantage necessarily outweighs all competing considerations. To the extent that the informational benefits of foot voting are even greater in the case of private-sector institutions than political jurisdictions, they argue for increasing the authority of the former relative to the latter.

VI. Implications for Constitutional Design

Widespread political ignorance and irrationality strengthen the case for constitutional limits on the powers of central governments, and also for constitutional constraints on the size and scope of government power.

As I discussed above, foot voting has major informational advantages over ballot box voting. It reduces incentives for both ignorance and irrationality. Even if this conclusion is accepted, however, it is possible that the benefits of foot voting can be left to legislatures to balance as they see fit. Since determining the size and degree of centralization of government involves many complex trade-offs, it is possible that legislatures will be in a better position to balance the relevant considerations than constitutional drafters or courts exercising the power of judicial review.

---

[94] See Bruno Frey, "A Utopia? Government without Territorial Monopoly," *Independent Review* 6 (2001): 99–112; Bruno Frey, *Happiness: A Revolution in Economics* (Cambridge: MIT Press, 2008), 189–97; and Bruno S. Frey and Reiner Eichenberger, *The New Democratic Federalism for Europe: Functional, Overlapping, and Competing Jurisdictions* (London: Edward Elgar, 2004).

[95] See Erin O'Hara and Larry Ribstein, *The Law Market* (New York: Oxford University Press, 2009).

Despite this concern, there is reason to believe that ordinary legislative activity will undervalue the informational benefits of both decentralization and limited government. Perhaps the famous "political safeguards of federalism" would make constitutional limits on central government power unnecessary. Some scholars argue that the political power of regional governments is sufficient to prevent excessive centralization, because the regions can use their clout to prevent it, and voters will punish overcentralization at the polls.[96]

Unfortunately, the very political ignorance that makes decentralization and limited government desirable also reduces the chance of achieving them through the ordinary legislative process. Few voters have a solid understanding of federalism, and fewer still are likely to be aware of the interconnection between limits on federal government power and "foot voting."[97] For these reasons, they are unlikely to punish elected officials who promote overcentralization.

This might not be a problem if central and regional governments had other incentives that would lead them to avoid excessive centralization. In fact, however, both regional and federal governments often have strong political incentives to concentrate power at the center. Central governments have incentives to expand their power in order to capture more revenue and use it to buy political support; subnational governments have incentives to lobby for central-government grants and to use the central government as a cartel enforcer that suppresses competition among them.[98] Strikingly, subnational governments in most federal systems get the vast majority of their funds from central-government grants.[99] This occurs despite the fact that dependence on central-government grants severely reduces regions' incentives to compete for foot voters in order to attract tax revenue, and increases the central government's ability to use grants to suppress regional policy diversity.[100]

The political reality that overexpansion of central-government power often advances the interests of regional governments undermines claims

---

[96] For well-known arguments that the political safeguards of federalism make judicial intervention unnecessary in the United States, see Larry D. Kramer, "Putting the Politics Back into the Political Safeguards of Federalism," *Columbia Law Review* 100 (2000), 215–311; Jesse H. Choper, *Judicial Review and the National Political Process* (Chicago: University of Chicago Press, 1980); Jesse H. Choper, "The Scope of National Power vis-à-vis the States: The Dispensability of Judicial Review," *Yale Law Journal* 86 (1977): 1552–84; and Herbert J. Wechsler, "The Political Safeguards of Federalism: The Role of the States in the Composition and Selection of the Federal Government," *Columbia Law Review* 54 (1954): 543–64.

[97] These points are elaborated in greater detail in John McGinnis and Ilya Somin, "Federalism vs. States' Rights: A Defense of Judicial Review in a Federal System," *Northwestern University Law Review* 99 (2004): 89–130.

[98] See ibid.; and Weingast, "The Economic Role of Political Institutions." See also James Buchanan and Geoffrey Brennan, *The Power to Tax: Analytical Foundations of a Fiscal Constitution* (Cambridge: Cambridge University Press, 1980), 214–15.

[99] See Barry Weingast, "Second Generation Fiscal Federalism: Implications for Decentralized Democratic Governance and Economic Development," draft paper (2007), 13–16, 42–43.

[100] See ibid.; and Somin, "Closing the Pandora's Box of Federalism."

that "political safeguards" are enough to ensure an optimal level of decentralization. Virtually all such arguments rely on the political power of regional governments to serve as a check on the center. But if regional governments actually help promote centralization, their influence in the national legislature becomes a liability for federalism rather than an asset.

Moreover, ordinary political processes often cannot be relied on to prevent government from growing unduly at the expense of the private sector. Political ignorance may prevent voters from being able to effectively monitor government interventions that benefit narrow interest groups at the expense of the general public. Most of the items in government budgets are ones that the majority of voters are probably not even aware of.[101] Even when voters are aware of the existence of a given program, "rational irrationality" will often prevent them from making effective use of the information they possess. Economist Bryan Caplan's recent research indicates that public opinion is distorted by "antimarket bias" and "antiforeign bias," which lead the majority of voters to systematically overestimate the effectiveness of government interventions in the economy, and of protectionism and restrictions on immigration.

For these reasons, widespread voter ignorance and irrationality are likely to prevent the political process from producing the appropriate level of decentralization and limits on government needed to restrict the harm. This suggests that constitutional restraints on centralization and the growth of government are needed. How strict should those constraints be? Unfortunately, analysis of the dangers of political ignorance does not, in and of itself, provide an answer to this question. Obviously, political ignorance is not the only factor that must be considered in determining the optimum level of constitutional constraints on government power. A wide range of other considerations—some of which vary from one society to another—must be weighed. However, our analysis does suggest that the need to combat the effects of political ignorance justifies stronger constitutional constraints on centralization and the growth of government than we might otherwise wish to impose.

VII. Conclusion

The informational advantages of foot voting over ballot box voting have important implications for normative theories of federalism. Perhaps the most significant is the way in which they reinforce the case for political decentralization. The more policy issues are under the control of regional or local governments as opposed to the national government, the greater the range of policy choices over which citizens can exercise lever-

---

[101] As I noted above, 70 percent of Americans were unaware of the creation of the new Medicare prescription drug benefit, the largest new government program in forty years.

age through foot voting and the more they can make use of its informational benefits.

In addition to strengthening the case for decentralization more generally, the informational benefits of foot voting also bolster the argument for competitive as opposed to cooperative federalism.[102] The greater the incentive for regional governments to compete with each other for citizens, taxpayers, and businesses, the greater the likely effectiveness of foot voting as a tool for imposing democratic accountability on government. This consideration strengthens the argument for policies associated with competitive federalism, such as limiting central-government subsidies to regional governments, so that the latter have stronger incentives to compete.[103]

Further, the ability of even a severely oppressed minority such as Jim Crow era blacks to acquire the knowledge necessary for effective foot voting suggests the need for a partial rethinking of the traditional view that such groups necessarily benefit from political centralization.[104] While central-government intervention to protect minority groups is often desirable, this potential advantage of centralization should be weighed against the disadvantages of eliminating foot voting. To the extent that oppressed minority groups often have lower income and education levels and therefore lower political knowledge levels than others, the relative informational advantages of foot voting for them may be even greater than for other citizens. Such benefits of decentralization are even more important in periods when the central government has little or no interest in alleviating the plight of oppressed regional minorities—as was certainly true of the United States during much of the Jim Crow era.[105] The gains for oppressed groups from foot voting within a federal system imply that there may be even greater foot-voting benefits from international migration, a possibility I discussed in another recent essay.[106] The differences in quality between regional governments within one society are generally much smaller than those between nations. Foot voting through international migration is the best hope for many of the most oppressed people in the world.

At the same time, it is essential to recognize that the argument of this essay is limited in scope. The informational benefits of foot voting are likely to vary from issue to issue, from nation to nation, and perhaps also from group to group. Obviously, foot voting cannot be used by people

[102] For a particularly influential argument for competitive federalism, see Weingast, "The Economic Role of Political Institutions."

[103] Ibid.; Somin, "Closing the Pandora's Box of Federalism."

[104] For a recent restatement of that view, see Douglas Laycock, "Protecting Liberty in a Federal System: The U.S. Experience," in *Patterns of Regionalism and Federalism: Lessons for the UK*, ed. Jörg Fedtke and B. S. Markesinis (London: Hart, 2006), 121–45.

[105] Klarman, *From Jim Crow to Civil Rights*.

[106] Ilya Somin, "Tiebout Goes Global: International Migration as a Tool for Voting with Your Feet," *Missouri Law Review* 73 (2008): 1247–64.

who are unable to leave a particular area, or by those who seek to protect immobile assets such as land. Examples include people with very high moving costs because they cannot find employment for their special skills outside a given locality, and those precluded from moving by serious health problems. Similarly, foot voting may not be effective for "network industries" that must operate in every part of a nation simultaneously in order to operate anywhere.[107]

Finally, democracy and political ignorance are far from the only issues that must be taken into account in determining the degree of decentralization that a society should have.[108] Various other considerations may in some situations outweigh the advantages of foot voting. The argument advanced here is not intended to be a comprehensive theory of federalism or of the appropriate role of government in society. It does, however, raise an important consideration that is too often ignored.

Law, George Mason University

---

[107] These two limitations of foot voting are effectively discussed in Richard A. Epstein, "Exit Rights under Federalism," *Law and Contemporary Problems* 55 (1992): 147–65. Telecommunication is one example of a network industry.

[108] For a recent survey of the literature on the various considerations involved, see Larry Ribstein and Bruce Kobayashi, "The Economics of Federalism," in *The Economics of Federalism*, ed. Larry Ribstein and Bruce Kobayashi (New York: Edward Elgar, 2007).

PLURALIST CONSTITUTIONALISM

By William A. Galston

I. Introduction

The purpose of this essay is to explore the ways in which a broadly pluralist outlook can help illuminate long-standing issues of constitutional theory and practice. I begin by adopting a common-sense understanding of pluralism as the diversity of observed practices within a general category—in this case, constitutions (Section II). In the light of this understanding, many assumptions that Americans and others often make about constitutional essentials turn out to be valid locally rather than generically. I turn then to pluralism in a more technical and philosophical sense—specifically, the account of value pluralism adumbrated by Isaiah Berlin and developed by his followers. After offering a rough and ready account of this version of pluralism (Section III), I bring it to bear on a range of constitutional issues (Section IV). In doing so, I distinguish between, on the one hand, areas of variation among constitutions and, on the other, some basic truths about political life that define core constitutional functions. I conclude (Section V) with some brief reflections on the normative thrust of pluralist constitutionalism—in particular, its presumption in favor of the maximum accommodation of individual and group differences consistent with the maintenance of constitutional unity and civic order.

II. Constitutional Diversity

It is easy for scholars working within particular national traditions to assume that the features of their own constitutions are definitive of constitutionalism as such. A brief glance across time and space suffices to dispel such parochial illusions.

While constitutions are usually written, they need not be; there is nothing paradoxical about tomes devoted to the British constitution.[1] Nor need they be democratic; as the late Carl Friedrich pointed out, autocracies and even dictatorships have managed to provide themselves with serviceable constitutions.[2] Similarly, constitutions need not be "liberal" in

---

[1] Larry Alexander, "Constitutions, Judicial Review, Moral Rights, and Democracy: Disentangling the Issues," in Grant Huscroft, ed., *Expounding the Constitution: Essays in Constitutional Theory* (New York: Cambridge University Press, 2008).

[2] Paul Sigmund, "Carl Friedrich's Contribution to the Theory of Constitutional-Comparative Government," in J. Roland Pennock and John W. Chapman, eds., *Constitutionalism* (New York: New York University Press, 1979), 38.

the sense of protecting individual rights, immunizing a private sphere from public interference, or limiting the powers of government as a whole (as distinct from particular institutions within government). Nor, finally, need they rest on a foundation of popular sovereignty. For example, Article 1 of the Iranian constitution refers to the "sovereignty of truth and Qur'anic justice," while Article 2 cites "the One God . . . , His exclusive sovereignty and the right to legislate, [and] Divine revelation and its fundamental role in setting forth the laws."[3]

By contrast, there are some things that all constitutions must do, either explicitly or by implication. First, constitutions rest on, and often declare, a principle of authorizing legitimacy. When the preamble to the U.S. Constitution says, in part, that "We the People of the United States . . . do ordain and establish this Constitution for the United States of America," it does more than describe a collective action. It suggests that the people (and only the people) have the authority to perform such an act: the identical document, if imposed on the people without their consent, would lack legitimacy.

Second, constitutions establish governing institutions and set forth their respective responsibilities and powers. Put simply, constitutions constitute—create and define—a political community's governing powers. This apparently straightforward proposition conceals an ambiguity, however. Political scientist and comparative constitutionalist Stephen Holmes suggests that "Constitutions may be usefully compared to the rules of the game or even to the rules of grammar. While regulative rules (e.g., 'no smoking') govern preexistent activities, constitutive rules (e.g., 'bishops move diagonally') make a practice possible for the first time."[4] But whether we see a constitution as regulative or constitutive depends on how we understand the activity or practice that it governs or, alternatively, brings into being. It is reasonable to believe that while the rules of chess create the game of chess, they do not create the human capacity, or desire, for structured play.

Recall Aristotle's famous thesis: "Man is by nature a political animal. . . . And yet the one who first constituted [a city] is responsible for the greatest of goods."[5] Like many other species, we might say today, humans are genetically configured to live in collectivities. But unlike all (or nearly all) other species, *how* we live together is not genetically or

---

[3] Constitution of Iran, available at http://www.iranonline.com/iran/iran-info/government/constitution.html. Article 1 does note, however, that the form of government of the Islamic Republic had been endorsed by 98.2 percent of eligible voters, suggesting that popular belief and endorsement has a role to play. But there is no suggestion that the truth of the Koran and the bindingness of sharia law rest on popular sentiment.

[4] Stephen Holmes, "Precommitment and the Paradox of Democracy," in Jon Elster and Rune Slagstad, eds., *Constitutionalism and Democracy* (New York: Cambridge University Press, 1988), 227.

[5] Aristotle, *Politics* 1251a3, 1251a30, trans. Carnes Lord (Chicago: The University of Chicago Press, 1984).

instinctually determined. Our sociality is unscripted. In one sense, then, constitutions are regulative: they shape but do not create human communities, the collective acts such communities perform, and the relations of dominance and subordination that make such acts possible. In another sense, however, constitutions are constitutive, because they create and give shape to legitimate authority as opposed to simple force. If X is to be a directive or "law" that requires rightful compliance, it must pass through institution Y in accordance with procedure Z. If it does not, it reflects only the will of the speaker, backed by whatever personal or collective power the speaker may command.

A third defining feature of constitutions is their orientation toward distinctive ensembles of public purposes. Consider again the preamble to the U.S. Constitution. Prior to ordaining and establishing national political institutions, it specifies, albeit in general terms, the ends that these institutions are designed to serve. They are created "in Order to" promote the goods of unity, justice, order, security, well-being, and liberty—*not* virtue or piety or perfection. (Other institutions may be thought responsible for cultivating the second list, or perhaps individuals are left alone to work out their own destiny.) Compare this again to the Iranian constitution. In Section 1, Article 3, we find an enumeration of sixteen purposes that the Islamic Republic of Iran is created to promote, the first of which is "the creation of a favorable environment for the growth of moral virtues based on faith and piety and the struggle against all forms of vice and corruption."

A key implication is that constitutional purposes help define each regime's distinctive orientation. No political community is, or can be, wholly neutral regarding all ends that individuals and associations may seek to pursue; each community encourages some while discouraging others (or prohibiting them outright). While some regimes are more capacious than others, none can accommodate on equal terms the full range of human possibilities. It is often said that to govern is to choose; so too is to create a government.

Fourth, constitutions are held to be "higher" than ordinary law. As the legal scholar Larry Alexander puts it, "constitutions are what validate ordinary law—the law produced by legislative and administrative bodies and by common-law courts."[6] We may trace this conception back to the Hebrew Bible, where each newly anointed king is commanded to write for himself a copy of "this law" (the Torah), to keep it with him at all times, and to read it "all the days of his life," so that he may act in accordance with "all the words of this law and these statutes" (Deuteronomy 17:18-19). This same passage suggests that only submission to higher law can check the natural tendency of the ruler toward arrogance, so that "his heart be not lifted above his brethren" (17:20).

[6] Alexander, "Constitutions, Judicial Review, Moral Rights, and Democracy," 119-20.

The understanding of a constitution as higher law is at its least problematic when the constitution is regarded as the word of God, *nec plus ultra*, and it is nearly as unproblematic when the constitution is regarded as the expression of natural law or "right reason" refracted through human experience. Complications arise when the people are the ultimate sovereign, because it is not obvious how some of their acts can enjoy a higher status than others. One possibility is that unlike ordinary law, a constitution represents a conscious decision by the people acting in their collective capacity. In this vein, the American Declaration of Independence speaks of the right of the people "to institute new Government, laying its Foundations on such Principle, and organizing its Powers in such Form, as to them shall seem most likely to effect their Safety and Happiness." A related possibility, captured in legal scholar Bruce Ackerman's "constitutional moments" thesis, is that the people are more thoroughly involved, and more likely to engage in meaningful deliberation, when they know they must decide questions that will reshape their community.[7] A third possibility, not exclusive of the others, is that constitutional decisions are both broader and deeper than others, requiring the people to act in accordance with their overall conceptions of human nature and human purposes.

Constitutions are almost always harder to change than ordinary laws. The amendment process set out in Article V of the U.S. Constitution is unusually rigorous, which may explain why the Constitution has been amended (officially) only seventeen times (roughly once every twelve years) since the Bill of Rights was ratified in 1791. The need for a framework of reliable expectations if citizens are to make long-term plans is often cited as the key argument in favor of constitutional stability. In fact, its justification goes deeper, as U.S. constitutional discussions illustrate.

Debate about the Constitution's engineered resistance to change broke out even before it was ratified. In *Federalist No. 49*, James Madison replied to Thomas Jefferson's view that it was wrong in principle to give the past a controlling interest in the present, and that, in practice, it should not be onerous to amend a constitution whenever the people so desired.[8] Madison's response merits extended quotation:

---

[7] Bruce A. Ackerman, *We the People, Volume 1: Foundations* (Cambridge, MA: Harvard University Press, 1991).

[8] Madison was explicitly replying to the argument Jefferson had made in a draft constitution appended to his *Notes on the State of Virginia*. He probably had in mind, as well, Jefferson's oft-repeated view that because human affairs were unpredictable and mutable, their institutional arrangements should be open to regular change. In a letter he wrote to Madison in 1789, for example, Jefferson declared: "I set out on this ground which I suppose to be self-evident: 'That the earth belongs in usufruct to the living;' that the dead have neither powers nor rights over it. . . . We seem not to have perceived that by the law of nature, one generation is to another as one independent nation to another." Alpheus T. Mason, ed., *Free Government in the Making: Readings in American Political Thought* (New York: Oxford University Press, 1965), 374.

[A]s every appeal to the people would carry an implication of some defect in the government, frequent appeals would, in great measure, deprive the government of that veneration which time bestows on everything, and without which perhaps the wisest and freest governments would not possess the requisite stability. If it be true that all government rests on opinion, it is no less true that the strength of opinion in each individual, and its practical influence on his conduct, depend much on the number which he supposes to have entertained the same opinion. The reason of man, like man himself, is timid and cautious when left alone, and acquires firmness and confidence in proportion to the number with which it is associated. . . . In a nation of philosophers, this consideration ought to be disregarded. A reverence for the laws would be sufficiently inculcated by the voice of an enlightened reason. But a nation of philosophers is as little to be expected as the philosophical race of kings wished for by Plato. And in every other nation, the most rational government will not find it a superfluous advantage to have the prejudices of the community on its side.[9]

Reason may justify law, in short, but it does not suffice to secure its acceptance. Time, habit, and what Madison calls "prejudices" (community-based beliefs decoupled from background justification) are needed to close the gap.

This is not a new thought. In the *Politics*, Aristotle criticizes the analogy between progress in the arts and sciences and political progress: "Change in an art is not like change in law; for law has no strength with respect to obedience apart from habit, and this is not created except over a period of time. Hence the easy alteration of existing laws in favor of new and different ones weakens the power of law itself."[10]

As Aristotle stresses, this is not an argument in favor of stubborn conservatism. Circumstances change, and our understanding improves. He did not deny the possibility of what Alexander Hamilton asserts in *Federalist No. 9*: "The science of politics, . . . like most other sciences, has received great improvement. The efficacy of various principles is now well understood, which were either not known at all, or imperfectly known to the ancients."[11] It is sometimes necessary and proper to alter laws, and even the arrangements of ruling institutions that the Greeks called "regimes." But as Aristotle and Madison both argue, the superior rationality of a proposed new law or constitution is not a dispositive argument in favor of adopting it: projected gains must be balanced against

---

[9] James Madison, *Federalist No. 49*, in *The Federalist Papers*, ed. Clinton Rossiter (New York: New American Library, 1961), 314–15.

[10] Aristotle, *Politics* 1269a20–24.

[11] Alexander Hamilton, *Federalist No. 9*, in Rossiter, ed., *The Federalist Papers*, 72.

the disruption of habitual acceptance, the confusion of settled opinion, and the diminution of the veneration that rests, however unreasonably, on long-established custom.

These reflections on the psychology of obedience are one thread in a larger tapestry. To a much greater extent than does ordinary legislation, constitution-making rests on broad assumptions about (inter alia) human nature, moral principles, and the way the world works. The Framers of the U.S. Constitution famously did not share the hopes of the French revolutionaries about creating a republic of virtue; the Framers' view was not that virtue in public life was impossible or even rare, but that we would be unwise to rely too heavily upon it.

Of the inferences Madison drew from his political psychology, the best known is his invocation of "auxiliary precautions"—institutional barriers against the weaknesses of human nature—in *Federalist No. 51*. But other inferences are equally noteworthy. Consider, for example, his declaration in *Federalist No. 47:* "The accumulation of all powers, legislative, executive, and judiciary, in the same hands, whether of one, a few, or many, and whether hereditary, self-appointed, or elective, may justly be pronounced the very definition of tyranny." [12] Wise and virtuous philosopher-kings have an exemplary existence, but only in our imagination. In the real world, no one is wise and virtuous enough to be trusted with unchecked and unaccountable power.

Despite these cautionary notes, however, Madison warns against going to an extreme of pessimism about human nature that could undermine confidence in the possibility of republican government. He insists in *Federalist No. 55* that "[a]s there is a degree of depravity in mankind which requires a certain degree of circumspection and distrust, so there are other qualities in human nature which justify a certain portion of esteem and confidence. Republican government presupposes the existence of these qualities in a higher degree than any other form." [13] For better or worse, the American constitutional tradition is Janus-faced, resting on a delicate, easily disrupted balance between optimism and pessimism. Optimism expresses itself in periodic outbursts of utopian political expectations, the most recent of which occurred in the 1960s, while pessimism manifests itself in mistrustful efforts to abolish discretionary authority in favor of precise rules, such as those that have proliferated throughout the U.S. regulatory system in recent decades.

III. PLURALISM AS A BASIS FOR CONSTITUTIONALISM

The previous section emphasized the diversity and pluralism of constitutional traditions, with U.S. constitutionalism as one among many

---

[12] James Madison, *Federalist No. 47*, in ibid., 301.
[13] James Madison, *Federalist No. 55*, in ibid., 346.

possibilities. In next two sections, I explore the constitutional relevance of pluralism understood more precisely and philosophically, taking as my point of departure the account of the moral world offered by Isaiah Berlin and known as value pluralism.[14] During the past decade, moral philosophers have clarified and debated many of the complex technical issues raised by value pluralism, as well as broader objections to the overall approach. For the purposes of this essay, a few basics will suffice.

1. Value pluralism is not relativism. To be a human being is to operate within a shared horizon of moral meaning and justification. In this respect, the distinction between good and bad, and between good and evil, is objective and rationally defensible. Pluralism enters at a different level— for example, the clash between pagan pride and Christian humility that we encounter as an aspect of a systematic difference between two enduring moral outlooks.

2. Objective goods cannot be fully rank-ordered. This means that there is no common measure for all goods, which are qualitatively heterogeneous. It means that there is no *summum bonum* that is the chief good for all individuals. It means that there are no comprehensive lexical orderings among types of goods. It also means that there is no "first virtue of social institutions,"[15] but rather a range of public goods and virtues whose relative importance will depend on circumstances.

3. Some goods are basic in the sense that they form part of any choice-worthy conception of a human life. Few would willingly place themselves in situations in which goods such as sustenance, civic order, and familial and social relations were insecure or absent. To be deprived of such goods is to be forced to endure the great evils of existence. All decent regimes endeavor to minimize the frequency and scope of such deprivations, which provide a ground of unity on which diverse individual and collective lives may be built.

4. Beyond a parsimonious list of basic goods, there is a wide range of legitimate diversity—diversity of individual conceptions of good lives, and also of public cultures and public purposes. This range of legitimate diversity defines the zone of individual liberty, and also of deliberation and democratic decision-making. Where necessity (natural or moral) ends, choice begins.

5. The denial of value pluralism is some form of what Berlin and others call "monism."[16] A theory of value is monistic if it either (a) reduces

---

[14] The *locus classicus* of this discussion is in the final section (entitled "The One and the Many") of Berlin's most famous essay, "Two Concepts of Liberty," in Isaiah Berlin, *Four Essays on Liberty* (Oxford: Oxford University Press, 1969), 167-72.

[15] John Rawls asserts that justice is the first virtue of social institutions in *A Theory of Justice* (Cambridge, MA: Harvard University Press, 1971). If Berlin is right, Rawls's claim is unsustainable as a general proposition, which does not mean that particular communities cannot choose to elevate justice to this position as a regulative principle of their own social life.

[16] See Berlin, "Two Concepts of Liberty," 170.

goods to a common measure or (b) creates a comprehensive hierarchy or ordering among goods.

One may well ask why value pluralism is to be preferred to the various forms of monism that thinkers have advanced since the beginning of philosophy as we know it. A few nontechnical remarks may be helpful.

To begin, monistic accounts of value lead to Procrustean distortions of moral argument. Utilitarians notoriously have a hard time defending some of the concrete consequences of their ruling principle; the standard example is that given certain plausible factual assumptions, slavery might turn out to be defensible on utilitarian grounds. But the difficulty is not confined to utilitarianism. Even Kant could not maintain the position that the good will is the only good with moral weight; hence his account of the "highest good," understood as a heterogeneous composite of inner worthiness and external good fortune.

Second, our moral experience suggests that the tension among broad structures or theories of value—consequentialism, deontology, and virtue theory; general and particular obligations; regard for others and justified self-regard—is rooted in a genuine heterogeneity of value. If so, no amount of philosophical argument or cultural progress can lead to the definitive victory of one account of value over the rest. Moral reflection is the effort to bring different dimensions of value to bear on specific occasions of judgment and to determine how they are best balanced or ordered, given the facts of the case.[17]

Many practitioners (and not a few philosophers) shy away from value pluralism out of fear that it leads to deliberative anarchy. Experience suggests that this is not necessarily so. There can be right answers, widely recognized as such, even in the absence of general rules for ordering or aggregating diverse goods.

It is true, as John Rawls pointed out more than thirty years ago, that pluralism on the level of values does not, in principle, rule out the existence of general rules for attaching weights to particular values or for establishing at least a partial ordering among them.[18] But in practice these rules prove vulnerable to counterexamples or extreme situations. As Brian Barry observes, Rawls's own effort to establish lexical priorities among heterogeneous goods does not succeed: "[S]uch a degree of simplicity is not to be obtained. We shall ... have to accept the unavoidability of balancing, and we shall also have to accept a greater variety of principles than Rawls made room for."[19] But, to repeat, the moral particularism I am urging is compatible with the existence of right answers in specific cases;

---

[17] For a fuller exploration of objections to value pluralism, see William A. Galston, *The Practice of Liberal Pluralism* (New York: Cambridge University Press, 2004), chap. 2.

[18] Rawls, *A Theory of Justice*, 42.

[19] Brian Barry, *Political Argument: A Reissue with a New Introduction* (Berkeley: University of California Press, 1990), lxxi.

there may be compelling reasons to conclude that certain trade-offs among competing goods are preferable to others.

IV. PLURALIST CONSTITUTIONALISM

Even though value pluralism is not relativism, pluralism certainly embodies what Thomas Nagel has called the fragmentation of value.[20] But political order cannot be maintained without some agreement. It is not unreasonable to fear that once value pluralism is publicly acknowledged as legitimate, it may unleash centrifugal forces that make a decently ordered public life impossible. Within the pluralist framework, how is the basis for a viable political community to be defined?

A. The minimum conditions of public order

While pluralists cannot regard social peace and stability as dominant goods in all circumstances, they recognize that these goods typically help create the framework within which the attainment of other goods becomes possible. They recognize, then, that anarchy is the enemy of pluralism and that political community is (within limits) its friend. Pluralists must therefore endorse what I shall call the minimum conditions of public order.

For modern societies, these conditions form a familiar list. Among them are clear and stable property relations, the rule of law, a public authority with the capacity to enforce the law, an economy that does not divide the population permanently between a thin stratum of the rich and the numerous poor, and a sense of membership in the political community strong enough (in most circumstances, at least) to override ethnic and religious differences.

It follows that pluralists are also committed to what may be called the conditions of the conditions—that is, those economic and social processes that experience suggests are needed (at least in modern and modernizing societies) to secure the minimum conditions of public order. Among these are a suitably regulated market economy, a basic level of social provision, and a system of education sufficient to promote not only economic competence but also law-abidingness and civic attachment.

I do not mean to suggest that this public framework constitutes an ensemble of goods and values that always outweighs other goods and values. Under unusual circumstances, the moral costs of public life may become too high to be endured, and individuals may feel impelled toward conscientious objection or outright resistance. Nonetheless, pluralists will understand that in the vast majority of circumstances, reliable public

---

[20] Thomas Nagel, "The Fragmentation of Value," in Nagel, *Mortal Questions* (Cambridge: Cambridge University Press, 1979).

order increases rather than undermines the ability of individuals to live in accordance with their own conceptions of what gives life meaning and value. This does not mean that each can live out his or her conception to the hilt. The ensemble of conditions of public order will typically require some modification of each individual's primary desires. In the absence of public order, however, the threat to those desires will almost always be much greater. It is rational and reasonable, therefore, for pluralists to incorporate a shared sense of the minimum conditions of public order into the ensemble of goods they value and pursue.

One of the strengths of the U.S. Constitution is that its preambular purposes closely track, and do not move much beyond, these conditions of public order. The Constitution mirrors, on the secular plane, a deservedly famous theological proposition, "In necessary things, unity; in uncertain things, liberty; in all things, charity,"[21] which might well serve as the motto of pluralist constitutionalism.

We may argue about what is necessary for purposes such as protecting liberty, order, or security, of course; all the more so when exigent circumstances reveal tensions among basic goods. Early in the Civil War, for example, President Lincoln was confronted with a clash between domestic tranquility and the rule of law. He famously responded by suspending the writ of habeas corpus, an act that the leading jurist of his day, Joseph Story, deemed to be under the authority of Congress only. Some months later, presenting a formal defense of his action to a special session of Congress, Lincoln asked (rhetorically), "[A]re all the laws, *but one*, to go unexecuted, and the government itself go to pieces, lest that one be violated?"[22] The crux of his argument was that in the specific circumstances in which he found himself, his duty to preserve public order overrode another basic public good with which order could not be reconciled: *Salus populi suprema lex.*[23]

One might argue, of course, that the requirements of public order sometimes depend on how leaders define the boundaries of the "people," a matter of controversy in Lincoln's day. "No Union with Slaveholders," preached William Lloyd Garrison five years before the Civil War; "Our first duty is to pronounce the American Union accursed of God—to arraign every man who supports it, and tell him, as Jesus told the rich young man in the Gospel, that whatever else he may have done, one thing he yet lacketh: *he must give up support of the Union.*"[24] In the two months of fragile peace after the

---

[21] Often attributed to St. Augustine, this maxim seems to have been used first in the seventeenth century by a German Lutheran theologian, Peter Meiderlin. It now serves as the motto of numerous religious denominations and associations. Pope John XXIII quoted it in his encyclical *Ad Petri Cathedram.*

[22] Quoted in Mark E. Neely, Jr., *The Fate of Liberty: Abraham Lincoln and Civil Liberties* (New York: Oxford University Press, 1991), 12 (emphasis in the original).

[23] That is: "The welfare of the people is the supreme law."

[24] William Lloyd Garrison, "Dissolution of the Union Essential to the Abolition of Slavery," September 28, 1855, in *American Datelines: Major News Stories from Colonial Times to the*

secession of the southern states, prominent northerners counseled acquiescence. "If the cotton States shall decide that they can do better out of the
Union than in it, we insist on letting them go in peace," said Horace Greeley,
writing in the leading Republican newspaper, *The New York Tribune*. General Winfield Scott, the commander of the American Army, put it more pith-
ily: "Wayward sisters, go in peace." (If Jefferson Davis, the president of the
southern confederacy, had not chosen to fire on Fort Sumter, a decision
fiercely opposed within his own Cabinet, a peaceful dissolution of the Union
might well have taken place.)[25] Without Lincoln's stubborn, often lonely
determination to preserve the Union at all costs—to defend the perimeter
of "We the People" defined in 1787—the outcome we now regard as inevitable could have been very different. But the route to the *salus* of that people, so defined, ran through rivers of blood. In public matters, necessity
and contingency are intertwined.

B. *Constitutionalism*

Constitutionalism offers a response to the challenge posed by the centrifugal tendencies of moral pluralism. Beyond the common foundation
and requisites of public decency and order, every political community
assumes a distinctive form and identity through its constitution. A constitution, we may say, represents an authoritative partial ordering of public values. It selects a subset of worthy values, brings them to the
foreground, and subordinates others to them. These preferred values then
become the benchmarks for assessing legislation, public policy, and even
the condition of public culture.

Various aspects of this thesis require further elaboration.

Within the pluralist understanding, to begin, there is no single constitutional ordering that is rationally preferable to all others—certainly not
across differences of space, time, and culture, and arguably not even
within a given situation. Nonetheless, the worth of a constitution can be
assessed along three dimensions: call them *realism, coherence,* and *congruence*. A constitution is realistic if the demands it places on citizens are not
too heavy for them to bear. A constitution is coherent if the values it
embodies and promotes are not too diverse to coexist within the same
community. A constitution is congruent if its broad outlines correspond to
the moral sentiments of the community and to the situation the community confronts.

For the pluralist, there is no single account of how a given constitution
comes to be authoritative. One model is covenantal acceptance: the peo-

---

Present, ed. Ed Cray, Jonathan Kotler, and Miles Beller (Champaign: University of Illinois
Press, 2003), 42.

[25] For all this and more, see the extraordinary article, "How the Great Struggle Began,"
The New York Times, April 4, 1915.

ple of Israel at Sinai.[26] Another is public ratification of the work of a constitutional convention, as in the United States. A third is bargaining among representatives of large forces in a divided society—the process that led to the post-apartheid South African constitution, for example. A fourth flows from the ability of a great leader to express the spirit and needs of a people in a practicable manner—the Napoleonic Code, or the French Fifth Republic. It is even possible for a conqueror to establish an authoritative constitution for a conquered people, as the Allies did for Germany (and the United States for Japan) after World War II.

Authoritativeness, we may say, has two dimensions. No proposed constitution can become authoritative if it falls below the minimum requirements of realism, coherence, and congruence. Nor can it be authoritative if it fails to gain broad acceptance within the community—perhaps not immediately, but within a reasonable period of time. While the post-World War II German constitution met this condition, it seems clear in retrospect that the post–World War I Weimar Republic never did.

A constitution represents only a "partial ordering" of value in three senses. In the first place, there is no guarantee that a community's distinctive constitutional values will always be consistent with the minimum requirements of public order, or that in cases of conflict public order must yield to constitutional values. Second, it is not the case that constitutional values will always dominate an individual's ensemble of personal values. There are circumstances in which it is not unreasonable for individuals to place the values at the core of their identity above the requirements of citizenship.

Third, a constitution is only a partial ordering because the plurality of values that it establishes as preferred will unavoidably come into conflict with one another. Such conflicts are a familiar feature of U.S. constitutionalism. Public purposes understood in the consequentialist manner (e.g., "domestic tranquility") may clash with individual rights understood deontologically (e.g., a "fair trial"). And individual rights may themselves come into conflict; consider the tension between the right to a fair trial and freedom of the press.

From a pluralist standpoint, it is inevitable that many of these conflicts will have no single rationally compelling solution. Reasonable men and women may well disagree about the relative weight to be attached to competing values, and many will be able to make legitimate appeal to different features of the constitutional framework. There are no strict lexical orderings, even in theory, among basic values.

In *Federalist No. 51*, James Madison poses a famous rhetorical question: "[W]hat is government itself but the greatest of all reflections on human nature?" And he continues: "If men were angels, no government would

---

[26] The Talmudic rabbis debated, inconclusively, the extent to which the acceptance of the Torah could be understood as voluntary rather than coerced.

be necessary."[27] A philosophical pluralist must disagree. Even if every individual were, in Madison's sense, angelic—perfectly capable of subordinating ambition and self-interest to reason and public spirit—the incapacity of reason to resolve fully clashes among worthy values means that authoritative mechanisms for resolving disputes would remain indispensable.[28] The more reasonable individuals are, the more clearly they will understand the need for such mechanisms. And this is true even if there is broad public consensus on constitutional matters—that is, on the ensemble of values that are to be brought into the foreground.

From a pluralist standpoint, individuals vested with the power to make authoritative decisions—whether judicial, legislative, or executive—must understand that many of the controversies they are called on to resolve represent the clash, not of good and bad, but rather of good and good. This means that these individuals must carry out their duties in a particular spirit: to the maximum extent feasible, their decisions should reflect what is valuable, not only to the winners, but also to the losers. Sometimes this will not be possible. But when not required by the logic of the matter to be resolved, winner-take-all decisions needlessly (and therefore wrongfully) diverge from the balance of underlying values at stake.

V. Conclusion

In the previous paragraph, I moved from a structural question—What must constitutions do?—to a normative question—What should they do? The reader may wonder whether I have offered adequate grounds for that transition. After all, I argued earlier that no constitutional ordering can be equally hospitable to all ways of life. Even when they do not explicitly prohibit choices, by placing a particular ensemble of values in the foreground, constitutions create social contexts that encourage some ways of life and discourage others.

This does not mean that all constitutions are created equal, however. Some are more restrictive, others less so. The pluralist approach implies a preference for capaciousness. To the greatest extent possible, constitutional orders should strive to accommodate the range of worthy ways of life—the ones that comport with the minimum conditions of public decency and order. This need not mean equal treatment, or even equal protection. It does mean that whenever the enforcement of public norms significantly interferes with individual or group practices that pluralists cannot deem unworthy, those in positions of authority within a constitutional order should look for ways of diminishing the human costs without eviscerating the norms.

---

[27] James Madison, *Federalist No. 51*, in Rossiter, ed., *The Federalist Papers*, 322.
[28] In the Talmud, angels are sometimes depicted as arguing, civilly, about important questions—much as the rabbis themselves did.

Consider the much-discussed case of *Employment Division v. Smith* (1990),[29] where the issue was whether the free exercise clause of the First Amendment would permit the state of Oregon to ban the use of peyote, even for Native Americans who had long used it in their religious rituals, and to deny unemployment benefits to individuals who had been fired for such religiously inspired use. Writing for the majority, Justice Antonin Scalia argued that if a law is neutral on its face, is of general application, and is reasonably related to a legitimate state purpose, the mere fact that its enforcement selectively burdens certain individuals or groups (even in exercising their religion) is neither here nor there. Quite the reverse, he argued: Any society adopting a presumption in favor of accommodation would be "courting anarchy." The greater the diversity within the society, the greater the risk. So even fundamental interests of individuals must be subject to collective decisions. If that means that certain views, otherwise legitimate, are systematically repressed, so be it: "That unavoidable consequence of . . . government must be preferred to a system in which each conscience is a law unto itself."[30]

In my judgment, this approach combines the worst of Hobbes with the worst of Kant. It not only privileges authority over all other values but also assumes that asking "What if everyone did this?" is always the right test. Reasonable determinations based on the facts of particular cases need not (and should not) be transformed into universal decision-rules. There is no evidence that a more accommodating holding in *Smith* would have gutted Oregon's drug laws, any more than permitting certain draftees to be "conscientious objectors" undermined the military draft.

Whether in morals, legislation, or adjudication, pluralism points to a measure of particularism in all decision-making. Constitutional goods and principles create a framework within which decisions are made, and they often contain rules and presumptions that give some kinds of considerations more weight than others. Even so, there is no escaping the need for judgment that we cannot reduce to a collection of algorithms. For that reason, among others, constitutional contestation will never cease, no matter how firmly rooted and venerable a constitution may be.

Governance Studies, The Brookings Institution

---

[29] *Employment Division v. Smith*, 110 S. Ct 1595 (1990).
[30] Id. at 1605.

DELIBERATIVE DEMOCRACY AND CONSTITUTIONS

By James S. Fishkin

I. Introduction

What we expect of constitutions depends on what we expect of democracies. Depending on our theory of democracy, we can plausibly have very different notions of how constitutions ought to be founded and how they ought to change. All over the world, constitutional processes have alternated between applications of two particular democratic theories. As a shorthand, I will call them Elite Deliberation and Participatory Democracy. Elite Deliberation for constitutional politics is probably best exemplified in the idea of a constitutional convention: a manageably small body of representatives who can deliberate about the appropriate design of institutions and the constraints they operate under. The American Founding offered the most prominent and successful case, inspiring many later ones, including the ill-fated convention that was supposed to provide a constitution for the European Union. Participatory Democracy can also play a role in constitutional politics. Many American states and many countries provide for constitutional changes via referendum. The rationale is that a referendum allows all voters subject to a constitution to approve it or approve changes to it. Sometimes the referendum proposals come from the people via initiatives; sometimes they come from legislatures (and hence from Elite Deliberation). But once a proposal has been made, and is to be approved via a mass referendum, completely different campaign dynamics determine the result, as any resident of California or some of the other western states will attest. All over the world, constitutional processes tend to involve one approach or the other, or some mixture of the two.

Neither of these two theories, nor the institutions that best express them, offer a credible role for deliberation *by the people* in constitutional processes. Constitutional conventions offer deliberation by elites or representatives. A similar point could be made about legislatures. Referenda offer a nondeliberative process for approval by the people in what are typically plebiscitary campaign processes. I believe an ideal theory of constitutional change would give the mass public a deliberative role. But the institutional requirements for doing so remain a matter of wide contention.

A Madisonian aspiration for "successive filtrations" of public opinion in manageably small select gatherings such as the 1787 Constitutional

Convention, the ratifying conventions, the Senate, and even the Electoral College in its original form drove the original American constitutional design. Publius's theory, like that of John Stuart Mill a century later, was one of Elite Deliberation. But the "reflective" views of deliberating representatives can conflict with the "reflected" views of actual mass opinion. In the ratification of the U.S. Constitution, the battle was soon joined in one of the American states, between Elite Deliberation and direct mass consultation characteristic of Participatory Democracy: Rhode Island considered the issue of ratification by referendum rather than by the convention prescribed in the proposed constitution. Federalists objected on grounds of insufficient deliberation—there would not be a forum in which arguments offered could be answered and in which the same body could consider all the competing arguments on their merits at the same time and in the same place. A convention appeared to be the only known means of accomplishing that purpose. Even if all the population of Rhode Island were gathered on "some spacious plain," no such deliberation would be practicable.[1] Federalists boycotted the referendum, and the Constitution was voted down. Only under threat of blockade and invasion by the neighboring states of Massachusetts and Connecticut did Rhode Island eventually relent and approve the proposed constitution through the required convention.

Many U.S. states now make constitutional changes by initiative and referendum—by an application of Participatory Democracy rather than Elite Deliberation. And a drama with parallels to the Rhode Island one has been playing out with respect to proposed constitutional changes in the European Union. The proposed "constitution" was voted down in referenda by the French and Dutch in 2005, and a revised version, called the Lisbon Treaty, was voted down by the Irish in a referendum in June 2008. For the Lisbon round, all the states but one used elite processes to approve, but the Irish were required by their constitution to take it to a vote of the people. Of course, no one has threatened to invade Ireland of late, but, like Rhode Island, the Irish were under enormous pressure from the other states to approve. Eventually, the Lisbon Treaty was approved by the Irish in a referendum in October 2009.

While a referendum embodies actual mass consent, it is not a deliberative instrument but rather one of plebiscitary mass democracy. The Irish referendum defeat of the Lisbon Treaty probably turned more on high gas prices than on the content of the proposal. California ballot propositions, such as Proposition 8 in 2008 changing the state constitution to ban gay marriage, involve typical referendum campaigns with television ads, mobilized constituencies, and a minimum of substantive public debate. We

---

[1] See "Rhode Island's Assembly Refuses to Call a Convention and Submits the Constitution Directly to the People," and "The Freemen of Providence Submit Eight Reasons for Calling a Convention," in Bernard Bailyn, ed., *The Debate on the Constitution*, Part II (New York: The Library of America, 1993), esp. 277.

seem to face a forced choice between politically equal but relatively nondeliberative masses and politically unequal but relatively more deliberative elites. The famous "democratic deficit" in the European Union constitutional processes—the perceived distance between public preferences and elite decisions behind closed doors—is a measure of the gap between the two.

However, these two poles of elite deliberation and mass participation represent a truncated view of democratic possibilities. To place the normative options within a broader framework, let us distinguish four theories of democracy. Elsewhere I have argued that the complexity of possible democratic theories can usefully be boiled down to these four.[2] As I will discuss below, two of the four place great emphasis on deliberation. These two raise the issue of how, if at all, deliberation is to be incorporated into constitutional processes.

More broadly, my argument will be that there are both impediments and possible solutions to the core problem: how to incorporate public deliberation into the higher lawmaking of constitutional processes. First I will try to outline the issue and then discuss the impediments. At the end, I will suggest the outlines of a possible solution.

II. Four Democratic Theories

There is not one democratic theory, but many. In order to get a handle on the range of possible positions, it is useful to think of some core component principles—political equality, (mass) participation, deliberation, and avoiding the tyranny of the majority (which I will call non-tyranny). Three of these principles are internal to the design of democratic institutions, and one (non-tyranny) is about the effects of democratic decision, effects that have long worried critics of democracy. If we consider these four principles to be essential components of a democratic theory, then the variations in commitment to them provide a kind of rudimentary grammar that allows us to specify the range of alternative theories. In other words, we can get a handle on different democratic theories according to whether they accept or reject these component principles.

By *political equality*, I mean, roughly, the equal consideration of one's views as these would be counted in an index of voting power. These views can be tabulated in response to poll questions or in secret ballots in an actual voting process. Does the design of a decision process give each person a theoretically equal chance of being the decisive voter (or having the decisive opinion in achieving a majority)? Or, to take an obvious

---

[2] I develop this discussion of competing democratic theories in James S. Fishkin, *When the People Speak: Deliberative Democracy and Public Consultation* (Oxford: Oxford University Press, 2009).

TABLE 1. *Four theories of democracy*

	Competitive Democracy	Elite Deliberation	Participatory Democracy	Deliberative Democracy
Political equality	+	?	+	+
Participation	?	?	+	?
Deliberation	?	+	?	+
Non-tyranny	+	+	?	?

example, do voters in (less populous) Rhode Island have far more voting power than voters in (more populous) New York when it comes to selecting members of the U.S. Senate? By *participation*, I mean actions by voters or ordinary citizens intended to influence politics or policy or to influence the dialogue about them. By *deliberation*, I mean the weighing of reasons under good conditions in shared discussion about what should be done. The good conditions specify access to reasonably good information and to balanced discussion with others who are willing to participate conscientiously. This summary is a simplification, but it should do for now. By *non-tyranny*, I mean the avoidance of a policy that would impose severe deprivations when an alternative policy could have been chosen that would not have imposed severe deprivations on anyone.[3] Obviously, there are many interesting complexities with regard to the definition of severe deprivations, but the basic idea is that a democratic decision should not impose very severe losses on some when an alternative policy would not have imposed such losses on anyone. The idea is to rule out only some of the most egregious policy choices and leave the rest for democratic decision.

Each of the four theories in the table above embraces an explicit commitment to two of the principles just mentioned. The commitment is signaled by a "+." The theory is agnostic about the other two (the agnosticism is represented by a "?"). While there are obviously sixteen possible theories defined by acceptance or rejection of the four principles, I have argued elsewhere that the useful theories reduce to these four.[4] On the one hand, variations that aspire to more than two of these principles turn out to be utopian or vacuous, since they just paper-over hard choices that need to be faced in the typical patterns by which these principles conflict. We will look in detail at some of those conflicts when we discuss a

---

[3] For more on non-tyranny as a principle of democratic theory, see James S. Fishkin, *Tyranny and Legitimacy: A Critique of Political Theories* (Baltimore, MD: Johns Hopkins University Press, 1979).

[4] See Fishkin, *When the People Speak*, "Appendix: Why We Only Need Four Democratic Theories."

trilemma of democratic reform in Section III below. On the other hand, those theories that aspire to less than two of these principles include elements of one of our four theories, but are less ambitious than necessary.

The four theories have all been influential. In some cases, I modify a familiar theory to make it more defensible, in order to get the strongest version of each theory.

By *Competitive Democracy*, I mean the notion of democracy championed by Joseph Schumpeter and more recently by Richard Posner.[5] On this view, democracy is not about collective will formation but is just a "competitive struggle for the people's vote," to use Schumpeter's famous phrase. Legal guarantees, particularly constitutional ones, are designed to protect against the tyranny of the majority. Within that constraint, all we need are competitive elections. While Schumpeter did not even specify political equality in competitive elections, I have included it here, on the grounds that it makes the position more defensible than it would be if it allowed political inequality. The theory is agnostic about the other two principles (participation and deliberation). Some variants of this position avoid prizing participation, viewing it as a threat to stability or to elite decision-making. Better not to arouse the masses, as their passions might be dangerous and might motivate factions adverse to the rights of others, threatening the position's commitment to protect against the tyranny of the majority. Because of collective action problems and incentives for "rational ignorance" (to use Anthony Downs's famous phrase), little can be expected of ordinary citizens. This position makes that minimalism a virtue.[6]

By *Elite Deliberation*, I mean the notion of indirect filtration championed by James Madison in his design for the U.S. Constitution. The Constitutional Convention, the state ratifying conventions, and the U.S. Senate were supposed to be small elite bodies that would consider the competing arguments. They would "refine and enlarge the public views by passing them through the medium of a chosen body of citizens," as Madison said in *Federalist No. 10* in discussing the role of representatives. Madison held that the public views of such a deliberative body "might better serve justice and the public good than would the views of the people themselves if convened for the purpose."[7] A similar position was given further development in John Stuart Mill's *Considerations on Representative Government*, particularly in Mill's account of the "Congress of Opinions," which was supposed to embody a microcosm of the nation's views "where those whose opinion is over-ruled feel satisfied that it is heard, and set aside not

[5] Joseph A. Schumpeter, *Capitalism, Socialism, and Democracy* (New York: Harper and Row, 1942); Richard A. Posner, *Law, Pragmatism, and Democracy* (Cambridge, MA: Harvard University Press, 2003).

[6] See, for example, Posner, *Law, Pragmatism, and Democracy*, 172–73.

[7] James Madison, *Federalist No. 10*, in *The Federalist Papers*, ed. Clinton Rossiter (New York: New American Library, 1961).

by a mere act of will, but for what are thought superior reasons" (pre-figuring Jürgen Habermas's famous notion about being convinced only by the "forceless force of the better argument").[8] This position, like the last one, avoids embracing mass participation as a value. The passions or interests that might motivate factions are best left unaroused. The American Founders, after all, had lived through Shays's Rebellion (an armed uprising of indebted farmers in Massachusetts in 1786–87) and had an image of unfiltered mass opinion as dangerous. If only the Athenians had had a Senate, they might not have killed Socrates.[9]

By *Participatory Democracy*, I mean an emphasis on mass participation combined with political equality. While, of course, many proponents of Participatory Democracy would also like deliberation, the essential components of the position require participation (perhaps prized for its "educative function")[10] and equality in considering the views offered or expressed in that participation (even if that expression is by secret ballot). Advocates of Participatory Democracy might also advocate voter handbooks, as did the Progressives, but the foremost priority is that people should participate, whether or not they become informed or discuss the issues.[11] Part of the problem with this position is that it is sometimes advocated based on a picture of small-scale decision-making such as that which occurs in a New England town meeting, in which discussion is facilitated, but then implemented in the social context of mass democracy. Another example is the California process of ballot initiatives, where essentially plebiscitary processes are employed for constitutional change.

By *Deliberative Democracy*, I mean a theory that attempts to combine deliberation by the people themselves with an equal consideration of the views that result (whether those views are counted in votes or in a tabulation of opinions, as in a poll). One method for implementing this twofold aspiration is the deliberative microcosm chosen by lot, a model whose essential idea goes back to ancient Athens. It was realized in institutions such as the Council of 500 (whose members were chosen by lot and met for a year, setting the agenda for the Assembly), the *nomothetai* (legislative commissions that were convened for a day to make the final decisions on some legislative proposals), the *graphē paranomon* (a procedure whereby a person could be prosecuted before a jury of five hundred

---

[8] John Stuart Mill, *Considerations on Representative Government* (New York: Prometheus Books, 1991; originally published 1862), 116; Jürgen Habermas, *Between Facts and Norms: Contributions to a Discourse Theory of Law and Democracy* (Cambridge, MA: MIT Press, 1996), chap. 7.

[9] See James Madison, *Federalist No. 63:* If the Athenians had only had a Senate, "[p]opular liberty might then have escaped the indelible reproach of decreeing to the same citizens the hemlock on one day and statues on the next."

[10] An argument made notably by Carole Pateman, *Participation and Democratic Theory* (Cambridge: Cambridge University Press, 1976).

[11] For an overview, see David Magleby, *Direct Legislation: Voting on Ballot Propositions* (Baltimore, MD: Johns Hopkins University Press, 1984). For the relative ineffectiveness of voter handbooks and other efforts to get voters more informed, see ibid., 137–39.

chosen by lot for making an illegal proposal in the Assembly), and the citizen juries (which also typically had five hundred members chosen by lot and which had a purview far greater than modern juries).[12] Modern instances of something like this idea include the Citizens' Assemblies in British Columbia and Ontario and the Deliberative Polling (DP) research program I am involved in. Deliberative Polling administers a survey to a scientifically chosen random sample of the population and then engages that sample in extensive deliberation, either face to face or online, after which the same survey is administered again. Many Deliberative Polls have control groups and are full-fledged scientific experiments.[13] Some cases of DP have been involved in constitutional processes or have provided input to them in countries such as Australia and Denmark. I will return to uses of deliberative microcosms before referenda in Section VI.

It is worth noting that the deliberative microcosm is not the only method of realizing deliberative democracy that engages the people themselves. Another way to satisfy the combination of political equality and deliberation would be to engage the entire population with the deliberative discussions, followed by a voting or tabulation process. Bruce Ackerman and I have worked out an institutional design for achieving that aspiration, in a scheme called "Deliberation Day."[14] I will return to that idea in Section VII.

III. The Trilemma of Democratic Reform

Under normal conditions, the three principles internal to the design of democratic institutions—political equality, mass participation, and deliberation—pose a trilemma. Serious efforts to realize any two will reliably run into clear roadblocks with respect to the third.

The major strategy of democratic reform since the American Founding has been to bring decisions more and more directly to the people. Election to the Senate was made the subject of popular vote rather than of decisions by the state legislatures; candidate selection was put increasingly in the hands of electorates in mass primaries rather than remaining in the hands of party elites; some substantive decisions were given over to ballot propositions rather than decisions by state legislatures and elected officials; the Electoral College has changed from an institution originally thought to require deliberative choice to a crude vote-counting mechanism in which those who decide independently can be prosecuted as "faithless electors."

---

[12] For a good overview of these ancient institutions, see Mogens Herman Hansen, *The Athenian Democracy in the Age of Demosthenes* (Oxford: Blackwell, 1991).
[13] See Fishkin, *When the People Speak*, for an overview of this research program.
[14] Bruce Ackerman and James S. Fishkin, *Deliberation Day* (New Haven, CT, and London: Yale University Press, 2004).

In all these cases, the strategy of reform has focused on combining political equality and mass participation. But by placing decisions that were once the province of elites into the hands of mass electorates, the social context that might make deliberation possible has been lost. Not that elites were always deliberative. In fact, problems of corruption and electoral calculations among elites often meant that substantive policy deliberation was lacking among representatives—leading to the very Progressive reforms that make the system more plebiscitary now. However, once decisions are placed directly into the hands of the mass public, ordinary citizens have little incentive to become seriously informed, and they have an increasingly vanishing context for citizen deliberation—that is, for weighing competing reasons for one policy solution or another in circumstances where citizens can be effectively motivated to become well informed. Hence, one option is political equality and mass participation without much deliberation. A second option is to get deliberation and some mass participation; but such deliberation, among self-selected groups who are especially motivated, will predictably violate our third principle, political equality. Self-selected microcosms of deliberators will, at their best, be like the League of Women Voters. They will be thoughtful and conscientious but far from representative of the broader population. Voluntary efforts to foster discussion are, of course, immensely useful from the standpoint of civic education. But they will inevitably be unrepresentative and, in that sense, violative of political equality. A third option, embracing political equality and deliberation, leaves out mass participation. Via a deliberative microcosm chosen by lot or random sampling, one can achieve both political equality and deliberation to a high degree. But the deliberations of such a representative microcosm hardly touch the value of mass participation. Once again, we can get only two of the three basic principles, and we face serious impediments against any real progress on the third.

IV. Ideal Theory and Second Best

Ideally, if one thought that the formation of public will was meaningful, then there would be a case for implementing all three principles in any process of higher lawmaking. Each principle contributes to a constitutional process adding up to the public's collective informed consent. Political equality means that the people's views are counted equally. Deliberation means that the public has arrived at considered judgments after it has weighed competing arguments. Participation is a kind of token for actual consent.

The problem, as we have seen with the trilemma, is that it is difficult to get all three principles satisfied simultaneously. If we get mass participation, we are unlikely to get deliberation because of the incentives for rational ignorance and disconnection characteristic of "audience democracy" in the large-scale nation-state.[15] We can achieve political equality and deliberation, but only for a microcosm—under the good conditions of balanced, face-to-face discussion required for deliberation. So if we get deliberation and political equality, we leave out mass participation. And if we pursue participation and deliberation, we get the distortions that result when only the interested and maybe the more advantaged citizens participate, thus sacrificing political equality. With the tool-kits of democratic reform that have been used since the Founding, running right through the Progressive era and the modern reforms of the presidential primary process since the 1970s (as well as parallel democratic reforms in most countries around the world), we cannot satisfy all three principles simultaneously.

Ideal theory plausibly specifies the full-scale realization of all three principles at the same time, in order to represent the considered judgments of the public will, counting all views equally, with actual mass consent. But if full-scale realization of all three at the same time is not feasible, what is the most plausible approach to second best? The common picture of the role of second best, popularized by Rawlsian theory, is that one should simply attempt, so far as possible, to approximate the ideal (even if one cannot fully realize it).

But there are two complexities here, one causal and one having to do with the definition of the ideal itself. The causal issues have been worked out in the economic "theory of the second best," which states that if one factor is constrained (i.e., cannot be fully realized), then it may be less than optimal to try to achieve the maximum value of the other factors. At first it may seem counterintuitive that if we cannot maximize A, we shouldn't still try to maximize B and C. But it may be that when A is less than its full value, getting the full dose of B and C leads to an inferior result. Sometimes for example, if one is trying to make the economy more competitive, increasing competition in some industries may not be optimal if other industries are constrained not to be competitive.[16] But note that this is a causal issue. It has to do with what will achieve the best result on an underlying dimension, which is ultimately that of utility. All other issues are instrumental ones. And there is no dispute that maximizing utility is the goal even within the ordinal intrapersonal framework of modern welfare economics.[17]

To the extent that we are confronted with a trilemma, we have a different situation, which I have characterized as "ideals without an ideal." We have a plurality of competing principles, but they do not

---

[15] I take the term from Bernard Manin, *Principles of Representative Government* (Cambridge: Cambridge University Press, 1997), chap. 6.

[16] R. G. Lipsey and Kelvin Lancaster, "The General Theory of Second Best," *The Review of Economic Studies* 24, no. 1 (1956–57): 11–32.

[17] If a Paretian, ordinalistic framework is applied, then at least there is no clearly better (or Pareto-superior) alternative.

add up to a unified ideal that we can try to approach step by step. If we try to approximate it as best we can, we find, for example, that we have increased mass participation and political equality but to the detriment of deliberation (as with the rise of direct consultation and mass democracy). If we prize self-selected deliberation, increasing both participation and deliberation, then we sacrifice political equality, etc. We are faced with conflicts among valuable principles, and if we forthrightly pursue any two, we find we are stumped, or even set back significantly, on the third.

However, if instead of trying to *approximate* the ideal, we attempt to *proxy* it, we can do so with Deliberative Democracy as realized with the revived Athenian notion of the deliberative microcosm, whose members are chosen by lot or random sampling. Such efforts offer a representation of what the realization of all three principles would be like under good conditions. The deliberative microcosm offers a *representation* of what the entire public would think, if it were thinking and engaged under good conditions—if, in a word, it were deliberating. Or at least that is the potential of the research program in applied philosophy to which these efforts, including Deliberative Polling, contribute. In the language of social research, the project is meant to combine (1) *internal validity,* so that we know it is the good conditions of deliberation that are producing the opinions at the end of the process, and (2) *external validity,* so that we know the results are generalizable to the whole population. Such a project, if it maintains both internal and external validity of the relevant sorts, can speak credibly for "we the people."

But what are good conditions for deliberation, or what is the sort of deliberation and/or discussion that we should be aspiring to achieve? To encapsulate issues I have pursued elsewhere, I would like to specify some criteria for quality in deliberation.[18]

By *deliberation,* I mean the process by which individuals sincerely weigh the merits of competing arguments in discussions together. We can talk about the *quality* of a deliberative process in terms of five conditions:

(a) *Information:* the extent to which participants are given access to reasonably accurate information that they believe to be relevant to the issue.

(b) *Substantive balance:* the extent to which arguments offered by one side or from one perspective are answered by considerations offered by those who hold other perspectives.

(c) *Diversity:* the extent to which the major positions held by members of the public are represented by participants in the discussion.

(d) *Conscientiousness:* the extent to which participants sincerely weigh the merits of the arguments.

---

[18] These criteria are discussed in greater detail in Fishkin, *When the People Speak,* 33–42.

(e) *Equal consideration:* the extent to which arguments offered by all participants are considered on the merits, regardless of which participants offer them.

When the process of discussion realizes these five conditions to a high degree with a representative sample, then it provides a basis for inferring that the judgments of the sample are the considered judgments that members of the public would reach under good conditions for considering the issue. The research program I am involved in—Deliberative Polling—has been focused on how to accomplish this. It has looked empirically at the information gains from deliberation, at the substantive balance of the discussions, at the diversity of the small groups, at the degree to which people are participating sincerely (rather than strategically), and at the degree to which they consider the merits regardless of the social locations of the other participants. We have found that, when properly structured, a deliberative discussion among ordinary citizens can avoid distortions from small-group psychology such as polarization and domination by more privileged groups. We have also found that, in balanced discussions, ordinary citizens achieve high gains in information, and that it is these gains that drive changes of opinion.[19]

V. Realizing Core Principles

The difficulty is that each of the three core principles—political equality, deliberation, and mass participation—serves a different normative function. Without political equality, there is a distorted picture of public opinion. Without deliberation, there is not a considered weighing of the arguments for one alternative or another. Without participation, there is no act of actual choice that can be taken as a token of mass consent. The situation is analogous to that of the voters of Rhode Island, who objected to the use of a convention to ratify the U.S. Constitution because such a convention would leave them out of the process; they thought that each person's liberty was at stake, and that this justified having an opportunity to vote. Likewise, citizens who were not chosen in a random microcosm would think they were left out if a final decision were left to the microcosm, without an opportunity for voting by the mass public. For these reasons, a fully developed ideal theory would include the realization of all three core principles. But second-best issues show that a proxy strategy at least gives us the punchline of what the public's considered judgments would be, under appropriately good conditions for thinking about the

---

[19] The polarization argument has been made most notably by Cass R. Sunstein. See, for example, Sunstein, "The Law of Group Polarization," in James S. Fishkin and Peter Laslett, eds., *Debating Deliberative Democracy* (Oxford: Blackwell, 2003), 80–101. For an overview of results, see Fishkin, *When the People Speak*, chap. 4.

issue. But because the resulting views may not be the actual views of the public, there is the potential for a gap—a democratic deficit.

Two basic strategies suggest themselves for overcoming this deficit. First, there is the possibility of a connected sequence of decisions that together overcome the trilemma by first maximizing some principles and then maximizing others. An alternative to the sequential strategy is a new design, such as the one that Bruce Ackerman and I have proposed for Deliberation Day. As we will see, these two strategies offer some design synergies.

VI. Sequential Strategies

In his wide-ranging critique of the U.S. Constitution, Sanford Levinson charts many deficiencies in the U.S. system by the criteria stated here. Some are deficiencies in terms of political equality, some in terms of participation, and some in terms of deliberation. At the end of his book *Our Undemocratic Constitution*, Levinson proposes variants on a new constitutional convention to get us out of the "iron cage" of the current constitution, which is exceedingly difficult to amend. In thinking about democratic reform, he mentions three institutional strategies and endorses all three in combination: a Deliberative Poll, a referendum, and a convention. He does not, however, make a recommendation about the sequence in which these strategies might be employed or how they might relate to each other.[20]

Looking at the issue as a matter of constitutional/political theory, without getting into issues of how any of these strategies might connect to an existing constitution, at whatever level, in the United States or elsewhere, there are, in theory, six possible sequences of the three institutions. Each has distinctive characteristics.

A. Convention—Deliberative Microcosm—Referendum

A version of this pattern occurred in Australia in preparation for the 1999 referendum on the Republic (whether Australia was going to continue as a constitutional monarchy or have a president as head of state). First, a "constitutional convention" was convened to write a referendum proposition for possibly changing Australia from a monarchy to a republic. This convention was composed primarily of political elites but also had some representation from "ordinary Australians." Second, there was a national Deliberative Poll, a scientific sample of the entire country con-

---

[20] Sanford Levinson, *Our Undemocratic Constitution: Where the Constitution Goes Wrong (and How We the People Can Correct It)* (New York: Oxford University Press, 2006). For the "iron cage" posed by the amendment process, see pp. 20–24. For the constructive proposals, see pp. 178–80.

vened to deliberate about the question for three days in the Old Parliament House in Canberra. The process and the results of this DP were nationally televised. Third, there was a national referendum vote on the proposition to change the Australian Constitution from a monarchy to a republic with a president appointed by Parliament replacing the governor general.

Strikingly, the convention and the Deliberative Poll both came to the same conclusion, that the proposed constitutional change, to a republic with a president appointed indirectly by two thirds of the Parliament, was a good change. However, the referendum campaign was fiercely contested, with political advertising and some misleading sound bites about the supposed effects of making the change. As a result, despite large-scale publicity for the recommendations of both the convention and the DP, the referendum was defeated. Setting aside a substantive discussion of the merits, the weak link in this design appears to be the connection between the two deliberative phases (elite deliberation in the form of a convention; microcosmic deliberation in the form of the DP) and the mass participatory phase of the referendum voting. If the aspiration is for the deliberations to have an effect on the decision, it looks as if mere media coverage of deliberative results is not enough for those results to really impact a concluding referendum process. We will return to this linkage below.

B. Deliberative Microcosm—Convention—Referendum

To my knowledge, this pattern has not been actually realized. But one could imagine a Deliberative Poll testing out the issues and providing input to a representative body who would participate in a convention to formulate a proposed constitutional change to be ratified by the people. The legislature of the Virgin Islands proposed convening a DP to advise the constitutional convention that met to formulate its new constitution. However, funds were not found to conduct the DP, so the convention went ahead without systematic public input. But the proposal would have realized this pattern. In China, my research colleagues and I have used DPs to successfully provide input to a local People's Congress for budgetary decisions. If the people's representatives are to "refine and enlarge the public's views," there is always the question of where they get those views from. If they get only "top of the head" opinion, or only intensely voiced views from organized interests, then they do not have input that is both thoughtful and representative. On something as momentous as a constitutional change, it might be useful to have a Deliberative Poll provide the public's considered judgments as an input to elite deliberation. Then the elites could formulate the actual proposal for constitutional change and submit the proposal for ratification by the people themselves. Once again, however, the likely weak link in the chain of causation is the connection between the deliberations of a representative group (whether a statistical microcosm or elected representatives) and the conclusions of the whole public in a referendum process. If this link could be strengthened beyond mere media coverage, then a powerful ideal process could be fashioned.

One difficulty with having the referendum at the beginning is that once the people have spoken in a referendum, it is difficult to imagine contravening their conclusion with some other democratic decision process. Of course, courts have set aside referenda on the grounds that other constitutional provisions have been violated, but that is not the same as having a microcosmic decision overrule a decision by the whole population (or at least all of those who turn out to vote). Such a scenario would involve one version of democracy, with limited participation, overruling another with maximal participation. Even if the subgroup in a convention or a deliberative microcosm is more deliberative, even if it is more representative, and even if the people in the broader population are misled by campaign tactics, it is the people themselves who speak in a referendum, however misguided they may be. A second limitation of this pattern is having a small group make the conclusive decision. Of course, that was the original pattern in the state ratifying conventions for the U.S. Constitution. It was approved not by referenda and not by state legislatures, but by state conventions. Still, that was the very challenge faced in Rhode Island, where critics said that every man's freedom was at stake so every man should be able to vote on the issue.

It is not completely implausible to have a decision actually made by a deliberative microcosm. In modern Greece, one of the country's two major parties used Deliberative Polling to actually select candidates instead of using a mass primary. This effort was greeted as a return of Athenian democracy to a part of Athens after a gap of 2,400 years.[21] But the candidate selected in this alternative to a mass primary, while he was nominated, still had to run in the general election. In ancient Athens, the *nomothetai* (legislative commissions chosen by lot) made the final decisions on some legislation. So there are precedents, lost in the dust of history, for a microcosm making the final decision.[22] Nevertheless, modern democratic norms of mass consent would suggest that once all the people vote, it is difficult to overrule their decision with a decision from a microcosm, no matter how representative or deliberative the latter might be.

---

[21] See James S. Fishkin, Robert C. Luskin, John Panaretos, Alice Siu, and Evdokia Xekalaki, "Returning Deliberative Democracy to Athens: Deliberative Polling for Candidate Selection," paper presented at the American Political Science Association, Boston, September 2008, available at http://cdd.stanford.edu/research/papers/2008/candidate-selection.pdf.
[22] See Hansen, *The Athenian Democracy*, 167–69.

C. Other possibilities

If the referendum is to be held last, then the only viable possibilities are the two we have already considered: "Convention—Deliberative Microcosm—Referendum" and "Deliberative Microcosm—Convention—Referendum."

Consider the other four possibilities:

(1) Referendum—Deliberative Microcosm—Convention
(2) Referendum—Convention—Deliberative Microcosm
(3) Convention—Referendum—Deliberative Microcosm
(4) Deliberative Microcosm—Referendum—Convention

These patterns all have the referendum in some place other than the end. As I have noted, there is a strong presumption of finality if the great mass of the public are actually asked to consent to a constitutional change. It is hard to then lay that consent aside on the basis of deliberations in either a convention or a deliberative microcosm. Hence, it would seem that these four patterns, which share the characteristic that serious decisions come after the referendum vote, are not viable.

Thus, the referendum should be last in the process, and it should be preceded in order either by the convention and then the deliberative microcosm or by the deliberative microcosm and then the convention.

In the British Columbia Citizens' Assembly of 2004, the deliberative microcosm had the power to put a ballot proposition for constitutional change directly on the ballot, without further filtering by any elite deliberative body. This mandate was empowering to the group. While there are some serious questions about the research design for recruiting the microcosm, it was an instance of the basic idea of a random sample deliberating.[23] And its members showed an extraordinary, indeed an inspiring, willingness to devote a year to the process. While the process had some considerable success, it suffered from the same weak link found in

---

[23] In this case, a stratified random sample of 23,034 was invited via letter to participate. Of these, 1,715 responded saying they were interested. After some demographic criteria were applied, 1,441 of these were invited to come to "selection meetings," and 964 did so. Of the 964, a total of 158 were selected randomly. The issue is that we do not have any way of evaluating how the 1,715 who selected themselves compared to the initial pool of 23,034. How much more interested or knowledgeable about politics and public affairs were they? How much more skewed to one political viewpoint or another? Similarly, we do not know anything about how the representativeness of the microcosm was affected by the other stages of selection. It is a demanding task to volunteer to give up nearly a year of one's life. How did those who put themselves forward for this opportunity compare to those who did not, or, in other words, how did they compare to the rest of the population for whom they were supposed to be a random microcosm? See Technical Report, pp. 35ff., available at http://www.citizensassembly.bc.ca/resources/TechReport(full).pdf. The response rate as a proportion of the original 23,034 is miniscule, and the data for comparing participants and nonparticipants is not collected in this design. The DP design avoids both problems. See Fishkin, *When the People Speak*.

the Australian project in 1999: despite considerable media coverage, delib-erations by the representative microcosm did not carry the day in the referendum. Of course, in both British Columbia and Australia, the bar for success was set high—by supermajority requirements in Canada, and by the double majority requirement for constitutional change in Australia (a national majority of voters and a majority in a majority of the states). But both experiences dramatize the potential gap between the delibera-tive conclusions of a microcosm and the results of mass participation.

VII. DELIBERATION DAY

In these various scenarios, the weak link is the causal connection between the deliberations of a representative group (whether Elite Deliberation in a convention or deliberation in a statistical microcosm) and the actual decision by the mass public in a referendum. In *Deliberation Day* (2004),[24] Bruce Ackerman and I offer a scenario for combining, if only briefly, serious deliberation, mass participation, and political equality. Our initial focus is a presidential election in the United States. However, the basic idea could be applied to any country where the people can be consulted in a constitutional process. It would be particularly applicable before a national referendum, which many countries employ, or even require, for constitutional changes. The discussion below is generic and not focused on any given country. Rather, it is focused on bringing the people—all of them—into a higher lawmaking process that is also deliberative.

This strategy is different from the sequential strategies outlined above. In Deliberation Day, there is a single proposed institution that attempts to realize all three principles at once—deliberation, political equality, and mass participation. The effort is costly and ambitious, in that it would require a national holiday and payment to millions of deliberators who would actually experience a day's discussions modeled closely on the Deliberative Poll, with alternating small-group sessions and plenary ses-sions with experts or representatives answering questions from the small groups, just as in the DP. One way to get a good representation of informed public opinion is to get a scientific sample to deliberate. Another way is to get the actual population—to get most people to actually participate. The basic idea is that such an experience would close the gap between "top of the head" opinion (the pre-deliberation views of most of the mass public) and deliberative mass opinion (as represented by the concluding views of the scientific sample in a Deliberative Poll). By inviting all voters to sites near them where they could experience daylong deliberations before an election or referendum, deliberations structured much like a DP, and by incentivizing participation through a reasonable stipend to ensure widespread participation, the project would produce something compa-

24 See Ackerman and Fishkin, *Deliberation Day*.

rable to deliberative views on the question at issue for the whole society rather than for a microcosm.

On this view, Deliberation Day would strengthen the weak link between deliberative opinion in a microcosm and normally nondeliberative mass opinion in a referendum. To give the maximum deliberative input to a design culminating in a mass referendum, the latter could be preceded by both a DP and a convention, in either order (that is, "DP, convention, referendum" or "convention, DP, referendum").

A clearly practical scenario would be to have a Deliberative Poll which would expose the way the mass public would deliberate about an issue, and which would clarify the trade-offs that were of greatest concern. Those concerns might then be the subject of a constitutional convention which would debate the referendum proposal in detail and formulate it for national decision. In preparation for a referendum vote, official committees would prepare briefing materials for national discussion (representing, respectively, the "yes" and "no" positions on the proposal). Those materials would then be the substance of a one-day national deliberation (or statewide deliberation, if it is a state constitution that is being changed), and then the entire population would go through a process akin to that experienced by the microcosm in a Deliberative Poll. Instead of the connection between deliberation and voting being provided by media coverage, it would be provided by the actual engagement of the mass public in a balanced process of discussing the issues—a process that would be decentralized in many small-group and plenary sessions on the model of the DP. The reason the effort is expensive is that to be effective it would require large-scale participation. Ackerman and I believe that a significant incentive (we have suggested $300) would motivate participation, when combined with the holiday.

VIII. Conclusion

The entire debate leading up to Deliberation Day would be altered, we believe, by the anticipation that on a given day the public would be much better informed about the issues. One cannot offer misleading or trivial arguments and expect to succeed if one knows that the public will soon see through them.

The aspiration is to combine three principles—political equality, deliberation, and mass participation—to a high degree in order to achieve, not just mass consent, but mass consent via something approaching the public's actual considered judgments. Constitutional processes are characterized as a form of "higher lawmaking."[25] What makes the higher lawmaking higher? It can only be that it satisfies appropriate normative criteria to a

[25] See Bruce A. Ackerman, *We the People*, vols. I and II (Cambridge, MA: Harvard University Press, 1991 and 1998).

higher degree than required in normal politics. In the view outlined here, the fundamental democratic criteria are the three principles already mentioned. While normally we cannot have all three, a transformation of the frontier of possibilities by a dramatically higher investment of resources in a new kind of institution (Deliberation Day) offers the prospect of evading the trilemma with a different kind of tool for public consultation.

While there are plausible arguments about the order of elite deliberations and deliberations by a microcosm, both have a contribution to make. Most importantly, the insertion of Deliberation Day would strengthen the connection between the deliberations of a representative body and the eventual result in a referendum by allowing a mass participatory version of deliberation to affect the votes of all the people. Now, one might ask, why should we even have the other phases of deliberation if Deliberation Day would be so effective? First, there is the question of how the agenda for a referendum is to be set. Here the current initiative process in many states is obviously defective. The initiative is a lobbying tool for organized interests to avoid legislative decision and to use constitutional changes to decisively alter decisions.[26] Much care must be taken in the deliberations that set up a public consultation. Some scenario of elite deliberation drawing on a representative microcosm (or having its views evaluated by a representative microcosm) in preparation for mass decision should be very helpful, both in framing the choice to be voted on and in framing the arguments around it.

Of course, the scenarios just described have ignored federalism and have treated a unitary electorate as the target population for deliberative democracy. The United States has no national referenda, and constitutional choices require ratification on a state-by-state basis. Still, there is the unused and perhaps dangerous clause about the convention route to constitutional change,[27] and it was Sanford Levinson's intention to build on that route which stimulated his proposal to attempt to combine the three institutions just described—a Deliberative Poll, a convention, and a referendum. It is worth noting, as Bruce Ackerman has pointed out in *We the People*,[28] that the original Constitutional Convention of 1787 was, strictly speaking, illegal in that it was supposed to simply revise the Articles of Confederation and not create a new constitution. So there may be circumstances where radical new experiments are required, though I am not claiming that we have reached that point yet, even if some of our eighteenth-century institutions are stifling (the Electoral College and the constitutional amendment process come to mind).

[26] See, for example, David Broder, *Democracy Derailed: Initiative Campaigns and the Power of Money* (New York: Harcourt, 2000).

[27] Article V of the U.S. Constitution provides that "Congress . . . on the Application of the Legislatures of two thirds of the several States, shall call a Convention for proposing Amendments. . . ."

[28] See note 25 above.

In any case, my account here is not offered with any particular constitution in mind; rather, my aim has been to sketch what might be called an ideal theory of higher lawmaking. If we were starting from scratch to determine, under favorable conditions, the most compelling scenario for constitutional change, how would such a system be designed for application in the large-scale nation-state? My proposal is meant as a contribution to democratic theory. The institutional design issues discussed here are meant to sketch how core democratic principles could be satisfied, if one wished to build an ideal theory for higher lawmaking into one's constitutional design. If "governments derive their just powers from the consent of the governed," then the institutional design for soliciting collective informed consent is central to higher lawmaking.

Communication and Political Science, Stanford University

THE CONSTITUTION OF NONDOMINATION*

By Guido Pincione

I. Introduction

I argue in this essay that procedural constitutional guarantees of market freedoms best protect individuals from domination. One corollary of my argument is that political theorists who attach paramount importance to freedom as nondomination should embrace market freedoms no matter what other divergent commitments they may have. In particular, Philip Pettit's claim that various forms of state interference with private markets are needed to forestall domination will prove to be unwarranted.[1] Another corollary of my argument is that market freedoms are best protected by procedural rules for political decision-making, as opposed to constitutional guarantees of private property and other substantive rules.

A moral presumption against interference has been more or less explicitly advocated by the political tradition known as "classical liberalism" or (sometimes to denote the versions least sympathetic to the state) "libertarianism." On this tradition, a legal system ought to protect spheres of mutual noninterference. To be sure, classical liberals allowed for conditions under which I am morally authorized, or even required, to interfere with someone's actions—say, to prevent her from violating my, or someone else's, rights. But classical liberals typically saw such cases of legitimate interference as the price to be paid for a legal system that minimized the total amount of interference.[2] In contrast, the political tradition known as "republicanism" is not hostile to interference as such but rather to *arbitrary* interference. Republican theorists embrace an ideal of *freedom as nondomination,* according to which persons ought not to be subject to the arbitrary will of others.[3] Notice, however, that libertarians, modern liberals, and egalitarians are also arguably committed to a principle of

* I am grateful to Bas van der Vossen, Carlos F. Véliz, and audiences at Torcuato Di Tella University Law School and Bowling Green State University for helpful comments on an earlier draft of this essay. I owe special thanks to Ellen Frankel Paul and Harry Dolan for their acute and detailed editorial comments. I completed work on this essay while visiting the philosophy department at Bowling Green State University (2009–2010).
[1] See Philip Pettit, "Freedom in the Market," *Politics, Philosophy, and Economics* 5, no. 2 (2006): 131–49, esp. 144–46.
[2] For a contemporary defense of this view, see Loren Lomasky, *Persons, Rights, and the Moral Community* (New York: Oxford University Press, 1987).
[3] For a historical and analytical discussion of the differences between the classical liberal and republican conceptions of freedom, see Philip Pettit, *Republicanism: A Theory of Freedom and Government* (Oxford: Clarendon Press, 1997), 17–126.

nondomination, whether or not they explicitly endorse it. Libertarians uphold a strong moral right of self-ownership, a right that those who dominate others violate, or at least threaten to violate. Liberals cherish personal autonomy, a value that domination destroys. And since domination is surely offensive to any attractive understanding of equality, egalitarians should condemn it.

Given this convergence of four major strands of political thought, the thesis that I announced at the outset—that constitutional guarantees of market freedoms best protect individuals from domination—may sound implausible to many readers. How can the free market be less prone to domination than *any* statist alternative, including those typically favored by egalitarians and modern (as opposed to classical) liberals? Indeed, some might want to argue that the extreme form of domination in which slavery consists may emerge from an exercise of market freedoms: it is not obvious why the contractual freedom that is so central to a free market should not extend to selling oneself voluntarily into permanent servitude. Perhaps libertarians have theoretical resources to resist this conclusion consistently with their commitment to self-ownership and the contractual freedom they derive from it,[4] but in that case the modern liberal and egalitarian complaint might persist that free markets in *external* resources give rise to forms of domination that can only be averted by a regulatory state (or one that is, in some appropriate sense, socialist). Since I am interested in evaluating this latter complaint, I shall assume that slavery contracts are invalid both in a free market and in any plausible statist alternative, and I shall confine my discussion to the spheres of freedom and domination created by more or less statist legal regimes for external resources.

By a "free market" I mean a legal regime that confers full ownership rights to persons over their own bodies and labor and over those external things that they have acquired through consensual methods. Such rights include the power to voluntarily transfer their rights over external things. I will also say that legal regimes that restrict such rights are (more or less) *statist*. Of course, this characterization of the free market is in need of clarification at various points. Thus, in some contexts we must say more about just what counts as labor and what counts as a voluntary method of transferring rights. Still, I believe that the characterization of the free market that I offered is clear enough for present purposes. In particular, it helps us to distinguish the free market from its most familiar alternatives, such as the welfare state and all versions of socialism (apart from, as we will see, those forms of collective ownership that result from permissible moves in the free market and that some may want to designate

---

[4] John Stuart Mill famously argued in *On Liberty* (1859), chap. V, that slavery contracts are void because the person who sells himself as a slave "defeats . . . the very purpose which is the justification of allowing him to dispose of himself," namely, "consideration for his liberty."

as "socialist"). I should stress that, on the present understanding, a free-market society is composed of persons entitled with property *rights,* as opposed to *revocable* authorizations to control and transfer things: this essay purports to offer a nondomination-based argument for the free market, as distinct from free-market *economic policies* that the government is constitutionally authorized to change for more or less statist alternatives.

Two additional notes on terminology are in order. First, we should distinguish freedom as nondomination both from other conceptions of freedom and from personal autonomy. Roughly put, under the so-called *negative* conception of freedom, my freedom to do *x* is the absence of other people's interference with my doing *x*. My *positive* freedom to do *x* is my ability to do *x*. My *personal autonomy* is usually characterized as my ability to design and carry out plans that are responsive to my reflective self. Thus, my personal autonomy vanishes when I am taken over by drives that I would reflectively like to get rid of (as when my addiction to certain drugs prevents me from pursuing endeavors that I value more than retaining my addiction), or when my desires or beliefs do not flow from my original self (as when they were instilled in me through nonconsensual brain surgery).[5] If Robinson Crusoe had been both accidentally crippled and, after inadvertently eating a poisonous mushroom, temporarily confused, he would have been both less positively free and less autonomous than most of us, even though he would have enjoyed full negative freedom—and necessarily so, before Friday arrived on the scene.

Second, while freedom (whether negative or positive) and personal autonomy are facts that we can describe without reference to rules, nondomination presupposes rules, typically legal immunities against interference. This normative dimension of nondomination distinguishes republicans from typical classical liberals, despite their shared hostility to interference with people's actions. Negative freedom in a society—"social freedom," in Pettit's terminology—is, as he correctly observes, just one component of nondomination, the other one being "protection against arbitrary interference."[6] Indeed, on Pettit's favored interpretation of the republican conception of freedom, nondomination demands "protection against arbitrary interference, not just probabilifying the absence of such

[5] I am simplifying a lot here. For detailed analyses, see Isaiah Berlin, *Four Essays on Liberty* (Oxford: Oxford University Press, 1969), 118–72; Lawrence Crocker, *Positive Liberty* (The Hague: Martinus Nijhoff, 1980); Gerald MacCallum, "Negative and Positive Freedom," *Philosophical Review* 76, no. 2 (1967): 312–34; and Horacio Spector, *Autonomy and Rights: The Moral Foundations of Liberalism* (Oxford: Clarendon Press, 1992), 9–63. For an interesting attempt to show that the republican and negative conceptions of freedom are vulnerable to objections that do not confront "freedom as the nonobstruction of planning" (i.e., something close to personal autonomy), see Steven Wall, "Freedom as a Political Ideal," *Social Philosophy and Policy* 20, no. 2 (2003): 307–34.

[6] Pettit, "Freedom in the Market," 132–38. See also Christian List, "Republican Freedom and the Rule of Law," *Politics, Philosophy, and Economics* 5, no. 2 (2006): 201–20, at 202 (noninterference is neither sufficient nor necessary for republican freedom). Nevertheless, republican freedom does entail the absence of *arbitrary* interference.

interference."[7] Such protection consists in *legal* means to resist interference. More precisely, it consists in legal immunities against interference (for instance, a legal immunity against arbitrary arrest). As the case of benevolent despots illustrates, the absence of such protections may well coexist with a low probability of being interfered with by the despot. In such cases, persons are nevertheless *subject* to the despot's arbitrary will. Legal issues, and in particular effective constitutional barriers against the concentration of power, are crucial to determining the extent to which domination obtains.[8]

The remainder of this essay is organized as follows. Section II shows how the dispersion of economic power is a barrier against domination, and why free entry into markets furthers such dispersion. As against the idea that the state is in a better position to disperse economic power, I argue that the constitutional provisions needed to implement that idea are contestable, and to that extent require interpretive powers that themselves involve domination. Section III reinforces the argument of Section II by showing that only a procedural constitution that generates full private property rights can shield citizens from domination. Section IV shows that a plurality of suppliers of goods and services is a structural feature of the free market, in a sense of "structural" that matters for measurements of domination based on fairly uncontroversial claims about persons and resources. Finally, Section V offers a brief conclusion.

II. Nondomination, Dispersion of Economic Power, and Free Entry

The institution of slavery illustrates how legal systems can uphold extreme forms of domination. Now legal systems may also engender domination in less direct ways. If, for example, someone (whether a ruler or a citizen) has a legal monopoly on the supply of some good essential to most life-plans (say, drinkable water), then domination is likely to obtain, for that monopolist is legally entitled to make access to her supply of water conditional on a variety of consumers' behaviors. This example suggests that the extent to which domination occurs varies inversely with the number of suppliers of goods essential to people's life-plans. In this section, I will defend a less obvious claim, namely, that a free market generates more suppliers of goods that matter for a theory of freedom as nondomination than alternative arrangements, *including* regulatory powers officially aimed at eradicating monopolies or counteracting their power.

---

[7] Pettit, "Freedom in the Market," 132–38.
[8] Legal realists equate legal rules with certain facts, e.g., judicial decisions. Were they right, I would say that, while negative freedom and personal autonomy consist in *nonlegal* facts, nondomination consists in those facts which, according to legal realism, are identical to legal rules against arbitrary interference.

As we have already seen, domination involves *subjection* to another's will. X dominates Y if X controls Y's behavior and Y lacks any legal means to escape such control. The sort of control relevant here should be distinguished from X's inducing Y to perform a *particular* act (whether through coercion, persuasion, information, or any other means). If republican freedom is to differ from negative freedom, domination has to affect more pervasively those subject to it than particular instances of coercion and other ways of influencing another's behavior. I am not dominated by *anyone* if *everyone*, one at a time and independently, coerces me into doing something they (arbitrarily) want me to do. In contrast, you dominate me if, over a relatively extended period, you decide, typically through coercive means, how I am to behave, and I lack any legal means of resisting your commands. We might introduce a comparative notion of domination, one that would allow us to say that a person is dominated to a degree determined by a weighted sum of (i) the scope of activities over which she is subject to external control, (ii) the centrality to her life-plans of the goals for which actions within such a scope are constitutive or instrumental, and (iii) the duration of such external control. Context will make it clear, I hope, whether the notion of domination in play in my argument admits of degrees or refers instead to an all-or-nothing condition.

Clearly, domination cannot possibly arise in Crusoe-like scenarios. Societies, too, can aspire to a complete absence of domination, provided they adopt certain rules. Nondomination is achieved under the rule of law, whereas domination is another name for the rule of persons. Those who embrace the ideal of freedom as nondomination (or the ideals that, as we saw in the previous section, should lead libertarians, modern liberals, and egalitarians to abhor domination) should therefore feel pressure toward supporting *legal* remedies against domination. In the remainder of this essay, I offer a rather general and abstract version of the argument they should employ.

A first step in that argument is to contend that competition averts domination. You cannot dominate me if, at no significant personal cost, I can refuse to behave as you ask me to. Competition reduces such costs. Imagine that the only seller of a good essential to my life-plans starts facing competition. This will increase my bargaining power with that seller, forcing her to reduce the price of that good. My bargaining power will increase with the number of competitors. The very existence of a single supplier of a certain good—a monopoly, in one of the senses of the term[9]—gives potential suppliers of goods perceived as homogeneous by consumers an incentive to undercut the price set by the monopolist. It

---

[9] For a discussion of the variety of meanings of "monopoly," both in economics and in public political discourse, see Murray N. Rothbard, *Man, Economy, and State*, rev. ed. (Auburn, AL: Ludwig von Mises Institute, 1993), 587–95.

follows that free entry into markets reduces suppliers' ability to control consumers' lives. Conversely, barriers to entry increase such control. The idea that firms *compete* for larger shares of *dominated* people is internally inconsistent. Domination shrinks with the dispersion of economic power.[10]

It might be countered that a suitable trade-off between the state and the market as potential sources of domination would favor a legal system that empowers the state to *subsidize* the destitute and other potential victims of domination without increasing state domination. On this view, the institutions of a liberal democracy, with their bill of rights and separation of powers, go a long way toward bringing such subsidies within the boundaries of the rule of law. One problem with this proposal is that public policies based on essentially contestable concepts—such as fairness, equality, justice, and perhaps even domination itself—are doomed to be arbitrary and hence unable to guide constitutional design inspired by the ideal of the rule of law. (A moral or political *concept* is said to be "essentially" contestable when disputes among people holding rival *conceptions* of that concept cannot be rationally settled.[11] Consider, for example, the dispute over whether equality of resources is a better conception of the concept of equality than equality of welfare is.)

But even if, as Ronald Dworkin famously argues, there is a "right answer" to every question of legal interpretation, "hard cases" included,[12] citizens, legislators, and judges *will* in all likelihood hold widely divergent views on which specific subsidies best forestall domination. In other words, even if essential contestability is illusory or overstated, *actual* contestability might well be an ineradicable feature of our political prac-

---

[10] An increase in the number of suppliers of an essential good, as well as the new options thus created for consumers, are facts, as opposed to rules or norms, but some such facts have legal consequences. Thus, an increase in the number of suppliers of a certain type of good entails that consumers acquire the *legal power* to buy elsewhere that type of good. So the thesis that competition averts domination does not involve a shift toward a (purely) factual (including probabilistic) notion of domination, which I, following Pettit, rejected in the previous section.

[11] See Christine Swanton, "On the 'Essential Contestedness' of Political Concepts," *Ethics* 95, no. 4 (1995): 811–27. I explore the tension between essential contestability and the rule of law in Guido Pincione, "Market Rights and the Rule of Law: A Case for Procedural Constitutionalism," *Harvard Journal of Law and Public Policy* 26, no. 2 (2003): 397–454. In addition to essential contestability, there is what I call "causal" contestability, i.e., persistent disagreement among reasonable persons regarding the most effective ways of bringing about outcomes mandated by the constitution, such as decent housing for all under a constitutional right to decent housing (ibid., 413–15). The present essay counts as evidence, I think, for the claim that freedom as nondomination, in addition to being an essentially contestable conception of freedom (which in turn is, as I pointed out in Section I, an essentially contestable concept), is causally contestable—unless we believe that Pettit and the other writers who claim that some forms of statism fare better than the free market on a scale of domination are uncontroversially correct or mistaken. We will see in Section IV.B why it is important for constitutional design that freedom as nondomination be itself (i.e., as distinct from freedom *simpliciter*) an essentially contestable notion.

[12] Dworkin defends the right-answer thesis in, for example, Ronald Dworkin, *Law's Empire* (London: Fontana Press, 1986). For another defense of interpretive determinacy, see Gerald F. Gaus, *Contemporary Theories of Liberalism* (London: SAGE, 2003), 106–8.

tices. Wide interpretive powers will then be required to arbitrate among clashing interpretations of the demands of freedom as nondomination. In a world of scarce resources, the state will have to choose whom to *deny* goods that they perceive as central to their most cherished life-plans. Thus, policymakers may have to discontinue subsidies to students of art in order to increase the provision of food stamps for the destitute, or vice versa, even if both groups need the subsidies to accomplish their most cherished goals in life.[13] To the extent that the state is effectively able to deny people those subsidies *at will* (as entailed by the discretionary powers it needs in order to arbitrate among widely divergent interpretations of the demands of freedom as nondomination), citizens will remain at the mercy of the state. It is no reply to say that, by hypothesis, no one will supply in the free market the goods made available to the beneficiaries of such subsidies. This consideration may be relevant for a *welfarist* case for subsidization, but not in the present context, where we are comparing (1) the amount of domination inflicted by a government entitled to take redistributive measures over a vast range of resources and groups with (2) the amount obtaining in a regime where *nobody* is entitled to do so.

Regulatory powers have an even darker side when looked at from the perspective of a theory of freedom as nondomination. Contestable political concepts spawn rhetorical pathologies that render public political justification both epistemically unreliable and inimical to any attractive conception of distributive justice. Fernando R. Tesón and I argue elsewhere that there is a mutually reinforcing interaction between citizens' rational ignorance (due to the individual voter's prohibitive costs of casting a well-informed yet nondecisive vote) and political posturing (due to politicians' and rent-seekers' incentives to reinforce the patterns of political error fostered by rational ignorance). This interaction leads public opinion in a liberal democracy (let alone in illiberal regimes) to a rhetorical equilibrium in which certain patterns of factual and moral mistakes will prevail.[14] Reasonable, sincere, and well-informed citizens will not consent to public policies that stem from such discursive pathologies (much less to the *consequences* of such policies), on any morally relevant notion of consent.[15] This lack of consent should surely count in an assessment of the extent to which the coercion involved in implementing such

---

[13] I do not think that confining the authority of legislators and judges to arbitration among *reasonable* interpretations of constitutional rules would impose a significant restriction on the scope of my argument. For the notion of reasonableness is itself de facto contestable. Hence, it is utopian to hope that public policies will enjoy consensual support, and for that reason will not evince domination, if policymakers publicly defend them with arguments that they sincerely believe no one will reject on reasonable grounds. See Gaus, *Contemporary Theories of Liberalism*, 136–40.

[14] See Guido Pincione and Fernando R. Tesón, *Rational Choice and Democratic Deliberation: A Theory of Discourse Failure* (New York: Cambridge University Press, 2006).

[15] Tesón and I discuss democratic consent in *Rational Choice and Democratic Deliberation*, 204–11.

policies is symptomatic of governmental domination, especially if such coercion is arbitrary. Let me explain.

We have seen that domination involves arbitrariness (Section I). Now we should distinguish between a narrow and a wide understanding of arbitrariness. On the narrow understanding, an interference is arbitrary just in case the rules that authorize it are not consented to by the person who undergoes it, or would not be consented to by that person under suitably idealized epistemic and motivational circumstances. This is the sense of "arbitrariness" I assumed when I said, in the previous paragraph, that the discursive pathologies involved in the public justification of public policies deprive such policies of consensual bases.[16] More specifically, the statist (even if democratic)[17] strategy to reduce domination by subsidizing the entry of new suppliers, or the poor, thereby increasing consumers' bargaining power, itself involves domination, because the subsidization criteria rest on contestable views regarding who is to contribute how much to finance the subsidies, who their beneficiaries will be, and what sorts of behavior the subsidies will reward or their denial will penalize. Moreover, such subsidies cannot be continuously implemented without rationing based on criteria that many reasonable people will, in turn, reject (e.g., rationing based on queues, waiting lists, types of consumers' needs, degree of industry concentration, etc.).[18]

On the wide interpretation of arbitrariness, interference is arbitrary if it is morally groundless, and especially if it is morally impermissible; in the typical case, the interferer acts on sheer selfish motives. Policies stemming from the above discursive pathologies are, again, arbitrary in the wide sense, because they fail any plausible moral test. Tesón and I substantiate this claim elsewhere; suffice it to say here that part of the problem is that such discursive pathologies are disproportionately sensitive to special interests that no attractive political morality would uphold.[19] Thus, on

---

[16] According to Pettit, "I control the interference of the state [and so make it nonarbitrary] so far as that interference is forced to track the interests that I am disposed to avow in common with my fellow citizens" ("Freedom in the Market," 136). If Tesón and I are right, this condition is not met by Pettit's advocacy of various sorts of regulations of markets, as stated, for instance, in the following passage: "Let freedom as non-domination be a central ideal in political life and not only will it be likely to make a case for a variety of forms of regulation, it will also explain how regulation by a coercive state need not be viewed with quite the reluctance that other ideals would generate" (ibid., 147).

[17] Tesón and I argue that the discursive pathologies of nondemocratic or nonliberal polities will be more severe than those we diagnose in liberal democracies. See Pincione and Tesón, *Rational Choice and Democratic Deliberation*, 244–46.

[18] Wouldn't subsidization by lotteries evade the objection that subsidies cannot help being arbitrary? No, because any characterization of the class of suppliers that the state ought to subsidize will be sincerely contested by some reasonable citizens: they would contest, for instance, whether candidates for the subsidies are to be characterized in terms of the structure of their corporate governance, the nature and price of their products, or the location of their plants.

[19] See Pincione and Tesón, *Rational Choice and Democratic Deliberation*, 194–98, 211–13, and 224–27. The critique of theories of "deliberative democracy" that we mount in that book

either interpretation of arbitrariness, regulatory powers aimed at preventing the emergence of domination in private markets themselves involve domination by the state—or by those who occupy key positions in political decision-making.

III. Manipulability, Compossibility, and Domination

How can we subject everyone, including the government, to rules? Clearly, we need an adequate answer to this question to devise constitutional rules that shield citizens from arbitrary interference by others—that is, to devise a constitution of nondomination. I argued in the previous section that a constitution that disperses economic power best protects citizens from domination. In this section, I want to show that purely procedural constitutional guarantees of market freedoms hold out a better hope of dispersing economic power than constitutional guarantees of private property and other substantive protections of market freedoms advocated by classical liberal constitutionalism.

Constitutional checks on governmental power will be effective only if they are nonmanipulable. I cannot be constrained by a (putative) rule if I am allowed to interpret that rule at will. Such a "rule" provides me with no guidance or constraint on my behavior, because I am allowed to determine the normative status of my behavior in the light of the "rule," which is tantamount to being subject to no normative requirement at all—to being free to do as I wish. Interpretive manipulation should be of obvious concern to theorists of nondomination. No one can dominate me unless they can manipulate the interpretation of the rules that set limits on how they may affect me. The more interpretive leeway those rules allow, the more power those persons will have over me.

Unfortunately, we cannot aspire to fully univocal constitutions, if only because vagueness is an ineradicable feature of the natural languages in which constitutions are written. The essential (let alone actual) contestability of substantive constitutional rights compounds this problem of constitutional indeterminacy. Even a cursory look at the scholarly literature on substantive constitutional rights, such as the right to free speech and the right to private property, reveals that these rights are highly contestable and vague. It is no surprise, then, that such rights are taken to countenance quite divergent policies and rulings.[20] In contrast, electoral

---

applies to those versions of republicanism that deny that state interference is arbitrary when it occurs after an open deliberative process that somehow weighs fairly everyone's interests. For a different critique of those versions of republicanism, see Geoffrey Brennan and Loren Lomasky, "Against Reviving Republicanism," *Politics, Philosophy, and Economics* 5, no. 2 (2006): 221–52.

[20] Thus, while Owen Fiss thinks that a constitutional protection of free speech warrants a variety of restrictions on private property, Milton Friedman argues that only a strong protection of private property, and the market freedoms it entails, can afford the amplest opportunities for free speech. See Owen Fiss, *The Irony of Free Speech* (Cambridge, MA:

systems (e.g., a system of proportional representation in Congress) and voting rules for the enactment of laws and for the appointment of high-ranking officials and justices (e.g., approval by majorities in the two chambers of Congress) are much less contestable.[21] I will call these two latter types of constitutional rules "procedural rules." Disagreements over the normative implications of a substantive constitutional right—that is, over which actions violate that right—tend to persist because they are anchored in deep controversies over what the best conception of such a right is (this is the essential-contestability problem I have alluded to in the previous section), as well as over how to protect the interests or choices that the right so conceived protects.[22] Because procedural rules lack essentially contestable concepts, they are likelier targets of convergent interpretations than substantive rules are. Accordingly, procedural rules can aspire to unambiguous consensual support: those who consent to being governed by them know what they are consenting *to*. Given that, as I argued in Section II, consent excludes arbitrariness (at least under the narrow interpretation of arbitrariness), the fact that procedural rules are better candidates for consensual support is of crucial significance for a theory of freedom as nondomination.

Saying that procedural rules are less manipulable than substantive rules does not mean, of course, that rights or other substantive notions should play no *justificatory* role in constitutional design. Indeed, constitutional drafters keen on protecting certain rights might well conclude that a

---

Harvard University Press, 1996); and Milton Friedman, *Capitalism and Freedom* (Chicago: Chicago University Press, 1962), chap. 1. The very notion of private property is in turn contested, as shown by such divergences as that between Richard Epstein, *Takings: Private Property and the Power of Eminent Domain* (Cambridge, MA: Harvard University Press, 1985); and Cass Sunstein, *The Partial Constitution* (Cambridge, MA: Harvard University Press, 1993), chaps. 1-6, on the constitutional underpinnings of the regulatory state in the United States. Leif Wenar offers a nice discussion of the changing interpretations of the takings clause by the U.S. Supreme Court in Wenar, "The Concept of Property and the Takings Clause," *Columbia Law Review* 97, no. 6 (1997), 1923–46.

[21] Authoritarian regimes characteristically repeal constitutional bans on presidential reelection—procedural rules, in my terminology. Interestingly, such regimes take care to follow quite cumbersome *procedural* rules for the requisite constitutional amendment, even though they feel no social pressure to refrain from jailing dissidents, confiscating hostile newspapers, and taking other tyrannical measures that violate *substantive* constitutional protections of free speech and other civil liberties. It would seem that tyrannies manage to retain, at least in the eyes of many, an aura of constitutional/democratic legitimacy by abiding by procedural rules only. The 1949 constitutional amendment under Juan Perón in Argentina illustrates this point: ample majorities in the Senate and the House allowed General Perón to repeal the constitutional ban on reelection, thereby enabling his second presidential term and its attendant suppression of civil liberties. Interestingly, the military revolution (with considerable popular support) that deposed Perón in 1955 and banned the Peronist Party on the grounds that it supported "tyranny" (meaning the suppression of substantive civil liberties) was followed by several decades of frequent military takeovers, with Peronists urging the "end of dictatorship" (meaning the return of majority rule). See Félix Luna, *Perón y su Tiempo*, 2nd unified edition (Buenos Aires: Editorial Sudamericana, 1993), esp. 217–42.

[22] See note 11.

purely procedural constitution best serves their goals. If asked for a justification of their constitutional proposal, they would sincerely refer to their commitment to rights, along with their beliefs about how society works. They may add that explicit substantive declarations are counterproductive. Constitutional drafters may foresee, for example, that legislators and judges will be affected by epistemic or motivational flaws that lead them to adopt a conception of a constitutional right that differs from the one favored by the drafters, or to implement that right through counterproductive laws or judicial decisions. The structure of this problem parallels the familiar structure that leads indirect utilitarians to advocate decision procedures that make no reference to the maximization of utility. Agents might better conform to the utilitarian standard of rightness, which judges actions as right just in case they maximize aggregate utility, only if they try to follow the Golden Rule, God's commands, Kantian ethics, or any other decision procedure that maximizes aggregate utility as a side-effect.[23] By the same token, my previous remarks on manipulability, along with theoretical and empirical work on public choice theory,[24] suggest that substantive constitutional rules are vulnerable to the sorts of epistemic and motivational shortcomings that make it advisable for constitutional drafters committed to freedom as nondomination to adopt a procedural approach to constitutional design.

The advantages of the procedural strategy against domination are best perceived by considering the shortcomings of the substantive alternative. A substantive approach to constitutional design sets either *goals* for public officials—such as general prosperity, (some version of) equality, or universal health care—or *constraints*, such as the U.S. bill of rights, on the pursuit of legitimate goals. I argued in this section that substantive constitutional rights are contestable, and to that extent are vulnerable to manipulation. But even if constitutional rights were noncontestable, the substantive strategy would engender the following sort of indeterminacy. Given its highest position in the legal hierarchy, a constitution tends to be both abstract and general. In these respects, constitutions are at the opposite extreme of particular legal orders or instructions, such as a criminal court's instruction to the correctional authorities to keep in jail a certain person for a certain time, or a traffic officer's instruction to a driver to turn left. Now we can easily conceive of an indefinite number of mutually consistent particular commands: we just need to imagine legal authorities commanding distinct persons to perform particular actions at different

---

[23] An example of the extensive literature in favor of this indirect form of utilitarianism is the early John Rawls. See his "Two Concepts of Rules," *The Philosophical Review* 64, no. 1 (1955): 3–32.

[24] See James D. Gwartney and Richard E. Wagner, "Public Choice and the Conduct of Representative Government," in James D. Gwartney and Richard E. Wagner, eds., *Public Choice and Constitutional Economics* (Greenwich, CT: JAI Press, 1988), 29–56; and Pincione and Tesón, *Rational Choice and Democratic Deliberation*, 8–64.

places or times. However, it is also easy to conceive of an indefinite number of mutually *inconsistent* particular commands derivable from (let us assume, noncontestable interpretations of) distinct substantive constitutional rules. This is so because it is of the nature of a substantive constitutional rule that it provides that citizens may, or may not, perform certain *types* of action. As Hillel Steiner argues, a plurality of rights to perform types of actions is not *compossible;* that is, those rights entail mutually inconsistent *particular* norms.[25]

Consider the following example. On a natural, unqualified interpretation of the First Amendment of the U.S. Constitution, which provides that "Congress shall make no law . . . abridging the freedom of speech," fraud committed through speech acts is a protected act; yet fraud arguably violates the protection of private property inferable from various constitutional provisions. Conspicuous among these are the Fifth Amendment, which provides that "no person . . . shall be . . . deprived [by the federal government] of . . . property . . . without due process of law" and that "private property [may not] be taken [by the federal government] for public use, without just compensation" (the "takings clause"); the Fourteenth Amendment, which applies the due process clause to the states; and Article I, Section 10, which prohibits states from passing any "law impairing the obligation of contracts" (the "contract clause").[26] Some particular exercises of an unqualified right to free speech, such as those involving fraud, violate an unqualified right to private property, and some particular exercises of an unqualified right to private property, such as boycotts on the sale of paper to a newspaper, violate an unqualified right to free speech. The upshot is legal indeterminacy: *as far as the constitution is concerned* (at least prior to judicial balancing of conflicting rights),[27] certain actions are both permitted and forbidden.

Constitutional drafters responsive to the value of freedom as nondomination will avoid the legal indeterminacies created by noncompossible rights, because such indeterminacies furnish advocates of expanded political power with the rhetorical advantages of appealing to constitutional rights. Since, as we just saw, substantive constitutional rights are noncompos-

---

[25] See Hillel Steiner, *An Essay on Rights* (Oxford: Blackwell, 1994). For a discussion of degrees of contestability of legal rules, see Gaus, *Contemporary Theories of Liberalism*, 75–77.

[26] The concept of private property I am using here, and arguably the one assumed by the framers of the U.S. Constitution, takes the right to private property to encompass the rights to possess, use, exclude others from the use of, and voluntarily transfer a certain thing (e.g., by selling, donating, or bequeathing it). By definition, fraud renders transfers of property involuntary. See Wenar, "The Concept of Property and the Takings Clause."

[27] Whether judicial balancing of conflicting rights makes an otherwise noncompossible system of rights compossible depends in part on how we conceive of a legal system. If we take judicial decisions and/or the doctrines they adopt, along with certain rules of precedent and legal hierarchy, as components of the legal system, then it may be possible to reconstruct a legal system whose general rules establish mutually conflicting rights as a compossible legal system. The argument that follows in the text does not turn on any specific view on such conceptual issues.

sible, the state is called upon to adjudicate their conflicts. Thus, the flip side of legal indeterminacy is the interpretive leeway conferred to legislators and courts to adjudicate such conflicts one way or the other. The essential contestability of such rights compounds, as we also saw, such indeterminacies. The upshot is that contestable or noncompossible constitutional rights deprive courts of constitutional grounds to limit the scope of legislative activity, since such activity can be arguably portrayed as responsive to *some* constitutional right. The rhetorical pressure toward increased legislative powers is all the more intense when legislators can appeal to constitutional *rights*, as opposed to general welfare or other aggregative goals, in defense of their preferred ways of filling out constitutional indeterminacies. The classical liberal desideratum that rights trump utility and other aggregative goals of public policy is thus bypassed by turning rights against themselves: any constitutional right can be overridden by another constitutional right, with the legislature deciding which right prevails over which as political expediency dictates. A proliferation of substantive constitutional rights tends to increase political power, and correspondingly exposes citizens to the arbitrariness that the classical liberal rhetoric of rights was supposed to shield them from.

Notice, however, that noncompossible or contestable constitutional rights do not *entail* governmental domination. Noncompossible or contestable constitutional rights will not engender domination if parties to conflicts of rights agree to have their disputes settled by an arbiter. The availability of such arbiters transforms a system of noncompossible or contestable rights into a system of compossible and noncontestable ones. Even if reasonable people held divergent interpretations of a constitutional provision, they would still be governed by that provision (as opposed to being ruled by persons) if they agreed on a procedure for settling their interpretive dispute. The availability of arbiters widely regarded as legitimate is an operational test for the existence of effective legal barriers to domination, especially if such arbiters occupy the highest position in the legal hierarchy. Another way to put this is to say that noncompossible or contestable rules engender domination only if their interpretation does not emerge from consensual arbiters.

We should not hasten to conclude, however, that a constitution that rules out domination should just contain a single provision to the effect that "conflicts of rights shall be settled by consensual courts," or something of that sort. Indeed, the foregoing arguments from contestability and compossibility point to a procedural route to the very creation of consensual courts. Accordingly, a constitution animated by the ideal of freedom as nondomination would contain those procedural rules from which the jurisdiction, composition, and modus operandi of consensual courts would emerge. Such a strategy for constitutional design is dictated by the fact that the very notion of consent lends itself to all kinds of interpretive conflicts. Just consider this question: Are citizens of the United

States consenting to the rulings of the Supreme Court? Among the issues that are arguably relevant to answering the question are the availability of emigration at reasonable cost and the existence of constitutional requirements of congressional supermajorities to confirm nominees for the Supreme Court. Of course, reflection on such issues involves, in turn, highly contestable questions about (1) the relevance of residence as an implicit manifestation of consent, (2) how reasonable emigration costs are (and what "reasonable" means in this context), (3) how close to unanimity a social decision rule must be in order for it to qualify as an expression of consent, (4) how representative members of Congress are, etc. Constitutional designers committed to freedom as nondomination will foreclose these interpretive issues by choosing the right procedural rules. The upshot is that consensual arbitration as a remedy for contestability and noncompossibility holds out hope of success only if it emerges from appropriately procedural, and hence noncontestable and compossible, rules.

I am now in a position to deploy a powerful argument from freedom as nondomination for a procedural constitution that upholds free markets. Its first premise has already been substantiated. It asserts that the proliferation of noncompossible constitutional rights increases political domination, especially if such rights are contestable in the sense indicated in Section II. A second premise asserts that an exhaustive and nonoverlapping allocation of private property rights is both compossible and noncontestable. Here property rights are to be understood as exchangeable rights to control particular things, including rights to participate in mutually agreed collective decision procedures to control particular things (as in condominiums and joint stock companies). For any thing, there is an uncontroversial legitimate owner of it (albeit there might be some *factual* controversy about who that owner is).[28] From these two premises it follows that constitutional procedural rules that generate effective legislative and judicial protection of particular private property rights forestall political domination. What protects citizens from domination is not so much a *generic* constitutional right to private property but rather a procedure for political decision-making that yields particular titles to property as a side-effect of the passions and interests of political actors, who need not have the creation of such titles as their goal.[29] How exactly a

---

[28] I assume that rational agreement on factual claims is easier to obtain than rational agreement on normative matters, yet I am not assuming moral skepticism. My argument purports to show that a regime of private property rights is less prone to domination than statist alternatives. For a detailed classical analysis of the notion of private property, or "full ownership," involved here, see Tony Honoré, "Ownership," in G. A. Guest, ed., *Oxford Essays in Jurisprudence* (Oxford: Clarendon Press, 1961), 107–47.

[29] For illustrations of the idea that even abstract rights to property and contract have indeterminate particular applications, see Arthur Ripstein, "Authority and Coercion," *Philosophy and Public Affairs* 32, no. 1 (2004): 2–35, at 26–32. For an overview of procedural constitutional rules that generate private property rights on particular things, with due allowances for the production of public goods (see Section IV), see James D. Gwartney and

constitution that effectively guarantees such rights should be worded is a question I cannot address here except to offer a couple of examples. A strongly federalist system, with states autonomously deciding on tax and spending policies over a wide range of issues, induces states to compete with each other for investment and inhabitants (and thus for taxpayers) by offering an optimal bundle of taxes and genuine public goods (as opposed to redistributive policies). Similarly, a supermajority voting rule in the federal legislature would increase the cost of rent-seeking (that is, of "buying" legislative votes through campaign contributions and other means) and ensuing special-interest legislation, thereby fostering legislation aimed at the production of public goods, including that overarching public good in which (the maintenance of) a free-market economic system consists. In general, although the literature on constitutional economics is officially guided by welfarist or contractarian ideals, a good number of the procedural rules that literature advances are defensible instead as responsive to the ideal of freedom as nondomination.[30]

IV. PLURALITY OF SUPPLIERS AS A STRUCTURAL FEATURE OF A FREE MARKET

In Sections II and III, I argued that the political power needed to subsidize suppliers of goods and services, or the poor, itself involves domination. This thesis is compatible with the claim that the concentration of economic power enabled by a fully free market, and its attendant decrease in consumers' bargaining power, is a more serious threat to freedom as nondomination. In this section, I argue that this latter claim is unwarranted: empowering the state to fight private domination just makes things worse. This completes my case for relying on market mechanisms, instead of the state, as a weapon against domination.

The argument I am going to offer for the claim that the free market best protects persons from domination should be distinguished from other well-known, yet ultimately weaker, arguments. I begin by indicating the shortcomings of those other arguments (subsection A), and then proceed to my own argument (subsection B).

Richard Wagner, "Public Choice and Constitutional Order," in Gwartney and Wagner, eds., *Public Choice and Constitutional Economics*, 44–49.

[30] For a seminal contractarian defense of procedural constitutional rules that protect market freedoms and help overcome market failures (see Section IV.B), see James Buchanan and Gordon Tullock, *The Calculus of Consent: Logical Foundations of Constitutional Democracy* (Ann Arbor: University of Michigan Press, 1962). Notice that economic approaches to constitutional design need not be procedural. Examples of largely substantive (and welfarist) discussions of the constitutional protection of market freedoms are Dennis Mueller, *Constitutional Democracy* (New York: Oxford University Press, 1996), 209–36; and Robert Cooter, *The Strategic Constitution* (Princeton, NJ: Princeton University Press, 2000), 241–308.

A. Misguided strategies

Some libertarians might wish to claim that there is a conceptual connection between the free market and the absence of domination. They might say that the free market bans arbitrary (aggressive, violent, unjust, etc.) interference, and thus makes domination impossible. Such arguments invoke conceptual, as opposed to empirical, links between the free market and the absence of domination. A usual strategy of this sort has it that the free market presupposes, by definition, private property rights over one's body and labor, as well as private property rights over external resources acquired through consensual means (e.g., labor on unowned land, contracts, and bequests, provided third parties are not thereby made worse off). If we then define "arbitrary interference" as any violation of such property rights, we can deductively infer that the free market bans arbitrary interference. On this view, then, the moral justification of the free market lies in its unique compatibility with a prohibition against arbitrary interference.[31] Conversely, any regulation of the market to the detriment of property rights so defined—any form of statism, in my terminology—will sanction arbitrary interference and the potential for domination that comes with it.

This argument suffers from circularity, because "arbitrary interference" and like notions are defined in terms of the very property rights the argument purports to justify.[32] The sort of interference inflicted by a thief on his victim may be physically indistinguishable from the sort of interference inflicted by a police officer to force the thief to return a stolen item to its legitimate owner, yet the grounds on which the argument distinguishes "arbitrary" interference from "legitimate" or "defensive" interference are not purely physical. The police officer's interference is assumed to be legitimate in that it is interference authorized by a legal system that protects property rights. More specifically, such an authorization is granted to enforce a legal prohibition of theft, where "theft" is defined, in turn, as an *unlawful* taking of somebody else's property. Moreover, who owns what—what property rights there are over what—is determined by the law of property. But, of course, it is the very law of property, and the particular property rights it generates, that the argument was supposed to justify. The kind of free marketeer I am considering must say that a legal system that upholds free markets bans *arbitrary* (aggressive, violent, unjust, etc.) interference with sets of options *defined by property rights*. She cannot rest content

---

[31] Murray N. Rothbard offers an argument of this sort in "Society without a State," in Tibor R. Machan, ed., *The Libertarian Reader* (Totowa, NJ: Rowman and Littlefield, 1982), 53–63, at 54.

[32] For versions of this critique, see G. A. Cohen, "Capitalism, Freedom, and the Proletariat," in Alan Ryan, ed., *The Idea of Freedom: Essays in Honor of Isaiah Berlin* (Oxford: Oxford University Press, 1979), 9–26, esp. 12; and Spector, *Autonomy and Rights*, 14–22, esp. 20.

with a purely physicalist notion of noninterference: she does not want to condemn, for instance, the police officer's interference with the thief's use of the stolen goods. Indeed, all forms of statism may be conceptualized as bans on arbitrary interference with the property rights *they* recognize (e.g., interference with the ways in which a single mother with children wants to use her welfare entitlements).[33]

Free marketeers aware of the difficulties of the conceptual route to establishing a nondomination case for the free market might want to invoke an empirical correlation between free markets and the absence of domination. Yet it is hard to come up with uncontroversial arguments of this sort. Take, for example, the claim that free markets spread economic power by increasing the number of suppliers of goods and their close substitutes. As we saw in Section II, the extent to which people exert monopoly power over the sale or purchase of things, including labor, obviously bears on the question of how much domination obtains. A competitive market for labor, for example, might be deemed to reduce or eliminate workers' dependency on any particular employer.[34]

Such arguments are open to dispute, though. On the empirical front, the literature on antitrust legislation abounds in controversies about the extent to which the free market will give rise to monopolies.[35] To be sure, a monopoly (short of a monopoly over much of a whole economy) may not dominate its workers: many of them may find a job elsewhere. But many others may depend on their jobs in ways that render them vulnerable to domination by their employer. Thus, technological change may result in layoffs of those workers whose specific skills will not be demanded elsewhere; they will accordingly be vulnerable to domination by their

[33] Gaus embraces a presumption against nonmoralized interference, and takes it to be the kernel of the limited-government ideal advocated by classical liberals. Following Stanley Benn, he contends that "there is a basic asymmetry between you acting and another interfering with your actions" (Gaus, *Contemporary Theories of Liberalism*, 223). As it stands, this claim is not vulnerable to the circularity objection, because it refers to purely physical interference. However, some of Gaus's illustrations of the presumption against interference rely on a moralized conception of interference. Thus, he argues that "a specific national health care scheme could only pass the test of liberal legitimacy if there is a conclusive justification—a justification that no citizen has sound reasons for rejecting—that there be some sort of national health care. . . . If there is no conclusive justification for a principle or a type of policy, then the 'wait and see' stance seems dictated by the Liberal Principle: if thus far no conclusive justification has been given, then thus far no government action is justified" (ibid., 221). But is government not "taking action" when it protects people's private property rights to the resources that would otherwise be redistributed (typically, through taxation) to the national health care scheme? It would seem that at some point Gaus's argument shifts from a physicalist to a moralized notion of interference; to that extent, his argument for the sort of limited government praised by classical liberals is circular.

[34] See Pettit, "Freedom in the Market," 142; and John Gray, "Against Cohen on Proletarian Unfreedom," in John Gray, *Post-Liberalism: Studies in Political Thought* (London: Routledge, 1996), 123–55, at 149–54; reprinted from *Social Philosophy and Policy* 6, no. 1 (1988): 77–112.

[35] For an overview of the economics of antitrust law, see Richard A. Posner, *Economic Analysis of Law*, 5th ed. (New York: Aspen, 1998), 309–46. For the view that antitrust law is counterproductive, see Thomas Sowell, *Knowledge and Decisions* (New York: Basic Books, 1996), 202–13. See also notes 52 and 53 below.

current employer (or prospective ones). How likely such plights are is itself an issue open to dispute. Also open to dispute is the extent to which unregulated markets will give rise to monopolistic supply of highly wanted or urgently needed goods, and the forms of domination that go with it. Moreover, the project of establishing an empirical correlation between free markets and the absence of domination faces hardly tractable measurement problems, of both a practical and a theoretical nature. We would have to determine the impact of various kinds of monopolies, including the monopoly of regulatory powers to fight monopolies, on the total amount of domination—a task that involves counterfactual comparisons among an indefinite variety of more or less statist alternatives.

The free marketeer might look for shortcuts. She might say that there are well-established positive correlations between the extent of market freedoms and the amount of general prosperity, hoping that the general prosperity effected by free markets enhances the bargaining power of workers and consumers and consequently reduces domination by employers and sellers.[36] But even if we granted (as I think we should) that free markets bring about general prosperity, some theorists might wish to resist the claim that general prosperity reduces domination. Thus, some writers argue that capitalist labor relationships revolve around "coercive wage offers"—a fact that would be inherent to capitalist "relations of production" regardless of prosperity.[37] To be sure, I have distinguished domination from particular instances of coercion (see the second paragraph of Section II), but many wage relationships are long and demanding enough to shape a worker's life-plans: if such relationships were coercive, they would in all likelihood evince domination of workers by employers.[38]

Thus, to offer an effective reply to the coercive-wage-offer argument, the free marketeer committed to freedom as nondomination cannot rest content with showing that free-market societies are generally more prosperous than alternative regimes; she must show in addition that, whatever their social costs, safety-nets like those provided by the welfare state will fail to grant workers a higher bargaining power with employers than that possessed by the worst-off in the free market. Admittedly, it is hard to maintain such safety-nets permanently, because those eager to qualify

[36] Publications such as the *Index of Economic Freedom* (http://www.heritage.org/Index/), by the Heritage Foundation and the *Wall Street Journal*, offer the kind of evidence that might be invoked by the argument I am considering.

[37] See David Zimmerman, "Coercive Wage Offers," *Philosophy and Public Affairs* 10, no. 2 (1981): 121–45; and Allen Buchanan, *Ethics, Efficiency, and the Market* (Oxford: Clarendon Press, 1985), 87–95.

[38] Notice that free marketeers cannot say that wage offers constitute exercises of the right to private property, which entails the alienability of labor, and that *for this reason* wage offers are not coercive: that move would presuppose the very property rights that are in need of justification. Such an argument would therefore be guilty of the kind of circularity I diagnosed earlier in this section.

for welfare benefits will adjust their behaviors to the very existence of the safety-nets (we should expect increased numbers of single mothers with children if they qualify for welfare benefits).[39] But it is hard to show that a commitment to freedom as nondomination rules out *any* trade-off between current and future domination, so that any reduction in current poverty through statist measures would involve an overall decrease in domination, no matter how uncertain and less serious the long-term adverse effects on poverty rates (and attendant domination) might be. Unless we could make interpersonal (and intergenerational) comparisons of domination, we could not know whether harming the current beneficiaries of welfare programs (by dismantling such programs) is more apt to engender less overall domination (including that obtaining in the more or less distant future) than currently harming the foreign poor or increasing domestic poverty for future generations—the two groups that are arguably impoverished by welfare programs.[40]

Here is still another type of empirical argument that a free marketeer committed to freedom as nondomination might offer. Some writers argue that free markets rein in politics because they disperse economic power. Such dispersion should surely count in measurements of freedom as nondomination for reasons that should be distinguished from those that supported my claim in Section II that free markets disperse economic decision-making. There the idea was that the free market increases the bargaining power of workers and consumers in their negotiations with employers and firms. The present claim assumes instead that *politics* is an especially powerful source of domination in that it legally monopolizes one key component of domination, namely, physical coercion. Accordingly, other things being equal, reining in politics should be a paramount goal of those who embrace the ideal of freedom as nondomination. On this view, then, the dispersion of economic power fostered by the free market is a good thing not just because it enhances the independence of workers and consumers from employers and firms, but also, and primarily, because it enhances everyone's independence from the most threatening source of domination—the state.

For all the strengths that I find in this argument, reasonable people may demur. To be sure, societies largely based on free markets have fared vastly better than centrally planned economies as providers of freedom as nondomination, as shown by the infamous record of communist regimes

---

[39] Indeed, such behavioral adjustments pose a serious threat to proposals such as an unconditional basic income, which might be thought to circumvent the worries about arbitrariness that affect traditional welfare schemes. For a related point, see the text accompanying note 18.

[40] See David Schmidtz, "Taking Responsibility," in David Schmidtz and Robert E. Goodin, *Social Welfare and Individual Responsibility: For and Against* (Cambridge: Cambridge University Press, 1998), 1–96; and Tyler Cowen, "Does the Welfare State Help the Poor?" *Social Philosophy and Policy* 19, no. 1 (2002): 36–54. As Cowen argues, granting equal rights to immigrants would render welfare states financially unsustainable.

in matters of civil liberties, deprivation, and arbitrariness, a record that is certainly indicative of relationships of domination. Yet there is strong evidence that private firms operating in formally free markets have been able to sway politics in favor of the rich, typically by sponsoring regulations that restrict the entry of competitors.[41] Perhaps we should conclude that unhampered markets engender their own destruction through anti-competitive regulations sponsored by rent-seekers and politicians who stand to gain from the disproportionate influence of small, well-organized, and well-informed groups vis-à-vis dispersed and ill-informed taxpayers and consumers.[42] On this view, unhampered markets are unlikely to disperse power to the benefit of freedom as nondomination. Others would conclude instead that further layers of regulation, such as antitrust legislation, could foster competition. Such meta-regulations have been attacked, in turn, as unduly sensitive to the political influence that they were expected to neutralize.[43] Be that as it may, it seems fair to conclude that the issues involved here are, once again, far more controversial than the type of argument that I offer next.

B. The structural argument

As a first approximation to that argument, let me say that I have in mind the sort of argument advanced by Thomas Hobbes in his account of the emergence of the state from a "state of nature," by David Hume in his explanation of the origins of property rights, and by H. L. A. Hart in his account of the various types of legal rules found in a modern, developed legal system.[44] Such arguments rely on empirical generalizations connecting, on the one hand, broadly characterized facts about legal systems, persons, and resources, and, on the other hand, broadly characterized social outcomes. More specifically, such arguments infer fairly abstract and general patterns of social outcomes from (i) fairly uncontroversial claims about people's perceived needs and basic types of desires, as well as their relative physical and mental abilities and vulnerabilities, (ii) assumptions about technological conditions, (iii) fairly uncontroversial claims about the scarcity of resources relative to people's needs and desires, and (iv) assumptions about legal rules, broadly characterized (e.g., whether such rules protect private property or some form of communal ownership, whether

---

[41] See Roderick Long, "Toward a Libertarian Theory of Class," *Social Philosophy and Policy* 15, no. 2 (1998): 303–49.

[42] For a seminal rational-choice analysis of such asymmetries, see Mancur Olson, *The Logic of Collective Action* (Cambridge, MA: Harvard University Press, 1965).

[43] See note 35, especially the reference to Sowell. See also William C. Mitchell and Randy T. Simmons, *Beyond Politics: Markets, Welfare, and the Failure of Bureaucracy* (Boulder, CO: Westview Press, 1994), esp. chaps. 4–11.

[44] See Thomas Hobbes, *Leviathan* (1651), Part II; David Hume, *Enquiry Concerning the Principles of Morals* (1751), chap. IV and appendix 2; and H. L. A. Hart, *The Concept of Law* (Oxford: Clarendon Press, 1961), chap. 5.

damages are awarded on the basis of fault or strict liability, and how judges are selected and removed). Let us call arguments of this sort *structural*. Structural arguments yield empirical predictions and explanations of broad patterns of social outcomes. Such predictions and explanations follow deductively from the propositions about agents, technology, scarcity, and the legal system. Notice that the premises of a structural argument— especially (ii) and (iv)—do not have to be true in order for it to perform *justificatory* functions. For example, Hobbes famously argued that rational, self-interested inhabitants of a "state of nature," that is, an imaginary and hardly ever existent situation in which there is no state or legal system, will devote most of their efforts to plundering others and resisting other people's attempts at plundering them, thus living lives that are "solitary, poor, nasty, brutish, and short."[45] They will accordingly realize that it is in their interest to appoint a political sovereign that monopolizes overwhelming physical force and thus is in a position to deter plundering and other barriers to mutually beneficial interaction, thereby making productive activities beneficial to all. Hobbes implies that such a potential explanation[46] of the emergence of the state is a justification of the state.

Structural explanations point to rational (though not necessarily reflective) choices—stories about agents pursuing their perceived goals through choices that are personally cost-effective, given their beliefs. The totality of such choices shape broadly characterized aggregate outcomes (e.g., more or less general prosperity, more or less poverty, more or less equality). Structural explanations feature an *a priori* component in that, given the relevant assumptions about persons, resources, and legal systems, no empirical research is needed to figure out what those aggregate outcomes will be: the outcomes can be deduced from the assumptions. Many of those deductions may be unexpected and interesting, even to those who find the assumptions obvious. Thus, in Hobbes's argument, it is not immediately obvious that inhabitants of a state of nature for whom it is rational to engage in a "war of all against all" will ever find it rational to make a covenant with an eye to surrendering all of their weapons to a sovereign. Hobbes's argument depends on propositions about strategic behavior that we can nowadays formulate more precisely with the tools of game theory. Some of the game-theoretical insights involved in his argument are fairly counterintuitive (e.g., the claim that, sometimes, rational agents will *not* adopt strategies leading to their most preferred collective outcome), yet this fact does not detract from the deductive validity of (appropriate reconstructions of) his argument.[47]

---

[45] Hobbes, *Leviathan*, chap. XIII.

[46] For an explication of the notion of potential explanation involved here, see Robert Nozick, *Anarchy, State, and Utopia* (New York: Basic Books, 1974), 6–9.

[47] Hobbes defends the rationality of obeying the law in his imaginary discussion with "the Fool," in *Leviathan*, chap. XV. Some of Hobbes's insights here anticipate modern analyses of iterated prisoner's dilemmas, as theorized by Robert Axelrod, *The Evolution of Coop-*

A particularly interesting type of structural argument postulates an *invisible-hand* process, that is, a sequence of interactions whose aggregate outcome is an unintended effect of different people's actions aimed at local objectives.[48] *Visible-hand* processes, in contrast, bring about aggregate outcomes aimed at in concert by the relevant agents. Conspiracy theories conspicuously postulate visible-hand processes. Invisible-hand theories are usually more interesting than their visible-hand counterparts because invisible-hand theories ground unexpected predictions. Moreover, they have greater predictive power because their premises can be independently tested, as opposed to being ad hoc. The concerted actions postulated by many visible-hand explanations of overarching societal features, such as a country's relative economic backwardness, are inferred from the occurrence of the facts one is trying to explain. The fact that such inferences are ad hoc explains, in turn, the lack of predictive power of such visible-hand explanations.

We normally know the types of goals pursued by ordinary people in their everyday activities—goals such as making money, being amused, or fulfilling the duties of friendship—yet we may have a hard time trying to figure out even the broadest patterns of aggregate outcomes inferable from such knowledge. Good invisible-hand explanations bridge this gap. Thus, the branch of economics known as public choice theory enables us to explain, and predict, otherwise puzzling societal patterns, such as the systematic patterns of exploitation of taxpayers and consumers by small and well-organized groups, even under well-functioning liberal democratic institutions. Such explanations and predictions rest on independently testable hypotheses about the types of local goals pursued by voters, bureaucrats, and rent-seekers.[49]

Crucially for present purposes, invisible-hand processes rule out domination because domination involves *intentional* interference.[50] Invisible-hand theories are a subset of rational-choice theories (visible-hand theories, too, may well assume that agents are rational, as typical conspiracy theories do). As such, invisible-hand theories postulate that agents pursue certain goals, but these are *local* goals (e.g., buying a pound of apples, eating sweet fruits, plundering a plot of land, or resisting plunder), and

---

eration (New York: Basic Books, 1984). See also Russell Hardin, *Liberalism, Constitutionalism, and Democracy* (New York: Oxford University Press, 1999), 82–119; and Gregory Kavka, *Hobbesian Moral and Political Theory* (Princeton, NJ: Princeton University Press, 1986), chaps. 3–6.

[48] The metaphor of the invisible hand was famously introduced by Adam Smith in *The Wealth of Nations* (1776), Book IV, ii.

[49] See Olson, *The Logic of Collective Action*; and Robert Tollison, "Rent Seeking," in Dennis C. Mueller, ed., *Perspectives on Public Choice: A Handbook* (Cambridge: Cambridge University Press, 1997), 506–25.

[50] That dominating power is exerted through intentional interference was implicit in my analysis in Section II. See also Pettit, "Freedom in the Market," 135; and Guido Pincione, "Welfare, Autonomy, and Contractual Freedom," in Mark White, ed., *The Theoretical Foundations of Law and Economics* (New York: Cambridge University Press, 2009), 214–33.

the agents who pursue them do so without intending to do their share in bringing about the aggregate outcomes that those theories are expected to explain (e.g., the equilibrium price of apples, changes in the price of substitute goods, low average investment in farming, or high average investment in self-protection). Whether a process whereby members of a group of people G worsen their situations is constituted by the concerted actions of members of group H seeking to benefit themselves at the expense of members of G, or is rather an invisible-hand process that worsens the members of G and benefits the members of H, is surely relevant to determining whether the members of H dominate the members of G.

I can now deploy two nondomination-based structural arguments for the thesis that freer markets involve less domination. The first argument is premised on the idea that tearing down legal barriers to entry into markets sets in motion forces against domination. What I have in mind here differs from a thesis I defended in Section II, namely, that competition reduces domination. This latter thesis is compatible with the claim that freer entry will not, as a matter of fact, increase competition, a claim that the first structural argument disputes. Imagine that a monopoly on goods essential to consumers' leading minimally meaningful lives has emerged in a free market. As we saw in Section II, the holder of such a monopoly arguably dominates consumers; she can, for example, refuse to sell a life-preserving drug to a patient unless he complies with whatever requests the monopolist happens to make.[51] Economists have shown that a monopoly emerges in a free market just in case certain market structures obtain. More specifically, technology, along with supply and demand for substitute goods, must be such that the monopolist maximizes her profit by charging a price that exceeds her marginal cost. Call these the *market conditions*. Nobody has an incentive to compete with a monopoly under current market conditions. However, the very existence of a monopoly gives entrepreneurs an incentive to change the current market conditions. This is especially true of the market conditions that matter for a theory of freedom as nondomination. The existence of a single supplier of a good that consumers perceive as necessary to carrying out their most cherished life-plans sets in motion forces that check domination: a monopolist's very ability to increase revenue by raising her price above the equilibrium price for a competitive market[52] generates incentives for others to invest in new technologies or otherwise change the market conditions under which it is unprofitable to compete.

---

[51] The argument I am offering holds, mutatis mutandis, for a monopsony (i.e., a single buyer) as well. Thus, a single employer (i.e., a buyer of labor) can threaten disobedient employees with dismissal.

[52] Such ability rests on the fact that the demand curve for the monopolist's output becomes more inelastic just above the competitive price, a fact that enables the monopolist to obtain, beyond that point, per-unit gains that are higher than required to compensate for a reduction in sales. For a fuller, though still nontechnical, explanation, see David Friedman, *Law's Order: What Economics Has to Do with Law and Why It Matters* (Princeton, NJ: Princeton University Press, 2000), 244–46.

Moreover, the very existence of monopoly prices increases consumption of substitute goods, including goods invented in response to the "excessive" monopoly price.[53] But then, showing that a firm is a monopoly fails to prove domination, even if the firm monopolizes goods necessary to leading a minimally decent life—unless, of course, it is a *legal* monopoly, and as such prevents the emergence of the countervailing forces described above. It seems far-fetched to assume that no amount of investment in new technologies, exploration, and substitutes (including new substitutes) will upset monopolistic positions, or even that inordinately high levels of investment will be necessary. I want to suggest, then, that the free market has built-in incentive structures that correct for monopolistic tendencies, *especially* if a monopoly engenders domination. Moreover, even if a monopoly retained its position for long enough to dominate its consumers, the self-defeating structure of incentives under which it operates would have no parallel in the structure of incentives created by the regulatory powers needed to fight private domination. The fact that some kind of regulation of a monopolistic market (e.g., a price control) would be needed to simulate the outcome that such a market would have attained under competitive conditions does not entail that the regulatory powers that are needed to implement such regulation will not be subject to the sort of perverse incentives theorized by public choice economists. Nor does it entail, in particular, that such powers will not involve the forms of domination that I described in Section II. In short, any sound argument for the claim that statist alternatives to private monopoly best realize freedom as nondomination must meet the burden of proving that the forms of domination spawned by statism are less serious or come with better self-correcting mechanisms.

Notice, also, that freer markets facilitate mutually beneficial interaction—a fact that surely prevents the emergence of domination. Saying that freer markets facilitate mutually beneficial interaction may sound platitudinous, because the free market by definition involves contractual freedom, a freedom that allows persons to interact in ways that they perceive as worth their personal cost. It is well known, however, that barriers to mutually beneficial interaction may arise in a free market. Economists have studied such nonlegal barriers under the heading of *market failures*. A common example of market failure takes place when transaction costs prevent a firm from making contracts with neighbors over levels of pollution they are willing to tolerate, thereby inducing the firm to increase output, and the attendant pollution, beyond the point at which marginal social benefits and marginal social costs are equal. More generally, market failures prevent rational agents from attaining aggregate outcomes that they rank higher in their

---

[53] See Rothbard, *Man, Economy, and State*, 586–620 and 632–60. The relatively short history of the personal computer contains many examples of what David Friedman calls "serial competition," i.e., dominant (in a sense, monopolistic) products quickly replaced by other dominant products. See Friedman, *Law's Order*, 259.

respective preference orderings than the outcomes they in fact attain.[54] Such divergences between individual rationality and what we might call "collective rationality" are usually taken to prove the inefficiency of real-world markets (as compared with "perfectly competitive markets").

It would be pointless to challenge the theory of market failure without challenging the assumptions under which it is derived, given the deductive validity of the arguments premised on such assumptions.[55] Indeed, some writers propose to revise the rationality assumptions, such as the transitivity of preferences, contained in such arguments.[56] I want to challenge instead the use of the theory of market failure to model real-world economies, as described by fairly uncontroversial claims about human psychology, relative physical and mental abilities, scarcity, and technology—hence the structural nature of my argument. Conceptual truths about market failure need not undermine the proposition that actual markets will tend to fail less often in ways that matter for a theory of freedom as nondomination than *feasible* statist alternatives. My previous remarks in this subsection on changes in market conditions—as well as those made in Sections II and III on dispersion of economic power, manipulability, and compossibility—suggest that this latter proposition holds true with regard to private monopolies. But the point can be generalized in the following way.

For any amount of market failure, there will be correspondingly strong incentives to invest in changing the market conditions that give rise to that failure. For example, there will be correspondingly strong incentives to find new sources of a scarce resource, or to use (and if necessary invent) technologies to reduce transaction costs and exclude free-riders in the production of collective goods worth their social cost. While, as we saw, it is by hypothesis unprofitable to compete with monopolies *under current market conditions,* the very existence of a monopoly provides people with incentives to alter such conditions in order to make competition profitable. To be sure, this is an empirical hypothesis, yet we do not need regressions and other usual techniques of empirical research to validate it.[57] It rests on fairly uncontroversial propositions about persons and their circumstances, propositions that should surely figure in any empirical interpretation of formal economic models aspiring to possess predictive/explanatory power. Of course, empirical testing of that hypothesis may ultimately undermine it, but its *structural* nature—the fact that it rests on

[54] See Alan M. Feldman and Roberto Serrano, *Welfare Economics and Social Choice Theory,* 2d ed. (New York: Springer, 2006), 119–93.

[55] For a simplified formal proof of the inefficiency of externalities—a major source of market failure—see ibid., 143–50.

[56] Fernando Tesón and I defend standard rational-choice assumptions in *Rational Choice and Democratic Deliberation,* 65–86.

[57] The realism and verifiability of the assumptions under which standard economics proves the inefficiency of monopolies have been questioned by the Austrian school of economics, as illustrated by Rothbard, *Man, Economy, and State,* 560–660. See also note 35.

fairly uncontroversial propositions about human psychology, relative physical and mental abilities, scarcity, and technology—places the burden of
proof on those who advocate state intervention as a remedy for the forms
of domination that free markets may produce. Given my arguments in
Sections II and III to the effect that such interventions themselves involve
various forms of domination, I am skeptical that statists could meet such
a burden of proof under moderately realistic assumptions.

My second structural argument rests on the fact that the processes
whereby free markets disperse economic power need not involve especially virtuous agents. On the contrary, the invisible-hand nature of such
processes ensures that the free market economizes on those virtues that
would otherwise be necessary to prevent domination. Virtue, understood
as a disposition to act on duties that sometimes demand self-sacrifice, is
a scarce resource, and, for this reason, well-informed, rational, and morally motivated constitutional drafters will economize on it.[58] They will
design constitutions that provide the right people with the right incentives to bring about good social outcomes. Whether those drafters seek to
improve the lot of the poor, to promote general prosperity, to secure
equality, or to achieve any other social outcome sanctioned by their preferred political morality, they will avail themselves of invisible-hand processes to achieve those goals as long as they take seriously the fact that
virtue is scarce. They will not design constitutions that *empower* public
officials to attain certain goals.

Constitutional design guided by the goal of nondomination is no exception. Constitutional drafters committed to freedom as nondomination
and persuaded by my first structural argument will not seek to protect
freedom through solemn constitutional declarations, or even through more
or less detailed lists of rights that can naturally be thought to shield
persons from domination. They will not, for instance, provide that "labor
in its several forms shall be protected by law, which shall ensure to
workers: dignified and equitable working conditions; limited working
hours; paid rest and vacations; fair remuneration; minimum vital and
adjustable wage; equal pay for equal work; participation in the profits of
enterprises, with control of production and collaboration in the management; protection against arbitrary dismissal; stability of the civil servant;
[and] free and democratic labor union organizations."[59] Even though
there arguably is *some* plausible interpretation of such rights that makes
them effective tools against "coercive wage offers" and other sources of
domination discussed in the previous subsection, the constitutional drafters that I have in mind will not draft the constitution along those lines.

---

[58] For a formal analysis of institutions that economize on virtue, see Geoffrey Brennan
and Alan Hamlin, "Economizing on Virtue," *Constitutional Political Economy* 6, no. 1 (1995):
35–56.

[59] These are provisions of the Argentine Constitution, section 14bis. (Section 14bis is a
section introduced by amendment between sections 14 and 15.)

We saw in Section III how such substantive provisions make room for interpretive manipulations that furnish legal cover for the very relationships of domination that they are expected to eliminate.[60] My present point is that, in addition, such provisions do not economize on virtue: at least one alternative route toward freedom as nondomination requires less virtue, namely, the invisible-hand process depicted in my first structural argument. Constitutional drafters committed to freedom as nondomination will seek to generate, through the sort of procedural rules advocated in Section III, an invisible-hand process of governance whose side-effect is another invisible-hand process—a free-market process—whereby freedom as nondomination is, in turn, an aggregate side-effect of agents pursuing their separate goals.[61]

V. Conclusion

Cuba is currently (2009) a member of the United Nations Human Rights Council. Due to its harsh suppression of political dissent, its lack of free elections, and the absence of effective legal safeguards against arbitrary executions and imprisonments, organizations such as Amnesty International, Freedom House, and Human Rights Watch have long denounced Cuba for serious violations of human rights.[62] Supporters of the regime typically note that Cuba makes health care and education available to all citizens, and for this reason it respects basic human rights to a larger extent than liberal democracies do. Many opponents of the regime object either that those achievements exist only as pieces of the regime's propaganda or that they do not make up for Cuba's violations of civil rights and liberties. Such opponents tend to regard advocates of the Cuban regime as either misinformed or insensitive to the paramount importance of liberal rights; and when, as is too often the case, Cuba's defenders condemn a liberal democracy for its occasional curtailments of civil rights and liberties, many charge them with hypocrisy.

The argument I have developed in the course of this essay suggests another way of looking at things. It suggests that, whatever the accuracy of the factual premises on which supporters of the Cuban regime rely, whatever the weight of the human rights they invoke as a reason to

---

[60] For a study of the capture of Argentine society by vast amounts of special-interest legislation dressed up in a rhetoric of constitutional rights, see Jorge E. Bustamante, *La Argentina Corporativa* (Buenos Aires: EMECE, 1988).

[61] Notice that a free market, on the understanding of it that I adopted in Section I, excludes appeals to the types of rights illustrated by the passage from the Argentine Constitution quoted above.

[62] See Amnesty International USA, http://www.amnestyusa.org/all-countries/cuba/page.do?id=1011139; Freedom House, http://www.freedomhouse.org/template.cfm?page=22&country=7592&year=2009; and Human Rights Watch, http://www.hrw.org/en/search/apachesolr_search/Cuba.

suppress civil rights and liberties, and whatever their sincerity, their very advocacy of a manipulable set of rights amounts to supporting tyranny (and the corresponding violations of nonmanipulable human rights against torture, arbitrary arrest, and other forms of domination). Indeed, the more seriously they take the alleged achievements of the Cuban regime as a matter of rights, and not merely as a matter of public policies that are, as such, systematically outweighed by rights-based considerations, the more plausible it is to interpret their ostensible reasons for supporting the Cuban regime as reasons for supporting tyranny. Those of us who abhor domination should regard the lists of "human rights" contained in the United Nations Charter and so many constitutions and international treaties as rhetorical tools for tyranny. We should accordingly not take the membership of Cuba in the United Nations Human Rights Council (merely) as an aberration of the language of human rights. On the contrary, it is precisely people's willingness to treat all of the rights contained in those documents as genuine that *commits* them, for the reasons I have offered throughout this essay, to embracing a huge concentration of arbitrary power.

I end with two caveats. First, the kind of procedural constitution that I have advocated should not be taken as an infallible recipe against domination, or even as a recipe that will often work well. Nondomination may well be unattainable in societies where social conventions induce people to breach formal legal rules, for example, through bribes and informal sanctions for whistle-blowing. In the jargon of game theorists, in such societies noncompliance with formal legal rules and compliance with the rules of organized crime or other groups capable of subjecting others to their arbitrary power is the strategic equilibrium.[63] Under those circumstances, not even a procedural constitution will shield citizens from the forms of domination that such groups may impose. But this is not to say that we cannot do anything to prevent the emergence of domination in societies where noncompliance with procedural constitutional rules does not pay. To the extent that societies of this latter sort exist, my argument for a procedural constitution against domination will be applicable.

Second, I have offered a presumptive case for the advantages of the free market when nondomination is our primary concern, yet I do not mean to downplay the significance of other principles or values for an overall assessment of the free market. Indeed, I indicated at the outset why those who embrace self-ownership, personal autonomy, or equality should be attracted to a principle of nondomination—and, if I am right, to the

---

[63] See Robert Cooter, "The Rule of State Law versus the Rule-of-Law State: Economic Analysis of the Legal Foundations of Development," in Edgardo Buscaglia, William Ratliff, and Robert Cooter, eds., *The Law and Economics of Development* (Greenwich, CT: JAI Press, 1997), 101–48.

market freedoms it sanctions.[64] Theorists of freedom as nondomination who support statist solutions have the burden of disproving the presumption in favor of the free market that I have endeavored to establish. They will have to show, in particular, why the concentration of political power needed to implement their preferred policies, including those officially aimed at curbing private domination, should not itself loom large in our measurements of domination.

Philosophy and Law, Torcuato Di Tella University, Buenos Aires

---

[64] Perhaps less transparently, welfarist political moralities also seem responsive to the value of freedom as nondomination. Thus, I have argued elsewhere that welfarist and autonomy-based arguments converge on justifying a strong presumption of contractual freedom and are ultimately based on a hypothetical contract that embodies the value of freedom as nondomination. See Pincione, "Welfare, Autonomy, and Contractual Freedom."

CAN WE DESIGN AN OPTIMAL CONSTITUTION?
OF STRUCTURAL AMBIGUITY AND RIGHTS CLARITY*

By Richard A. Epstein

I. Introduction

Constitutionalism is all the rage around the world today. Every serious student of the topic recognizes, indeed insists, that each nation, especially each emerging nation, should adopt a written constitution to shape the organization of its government. As a matter of common agreement, these constitutions are set apart from the ordinary business of lawmaking that every nation has to undertake on a routine basis. The usual conceit is that a national constitution entrenches the basic and more permanent elements of political governance, sufficient to justify their insulation from the political stresses of the day. It is also commonly agreed that the individuals entrusted with forming new constitutions in modern times do not have the luxury of making incremental improvements on preexisting institutions. The strategy of slow evolution did work within the English context, but it has not been imitated since. Unwritten constitutions necessarily require a period of time for evolution that is no longer feasible when constitutions are self-conscious documents written with a clear instrumental purpose. Conscious design, not Hayekian gradualism, is a necessity, not an option.

What judgments should inform the design of an optimal constitution? To flesh out this discussion, three interrelated questions have to be addressed. The first goes to an assessment of human nature: it seeks to identify the forces that drive individual and collective action. The last two go to the key issues of constitutional design. Of these last two questions, one deals with the structure of government. Does a constitution adopt a presidential or parliamentary system? How does it organize its legislature? Does it preserve judicial independence and allow for judicial review of legislation? The other question deals with the protection of individual rights such as due process of law, freedom of speech and religion, and the protection of economic liberties and private property.

In dealing with these questions, the fundamental inquiry is how best to deal with the size and scope of government institutions. To this, two approaches are possible. The first is the Lockean vision of limited gov-

* I should like to thank Jack O. Snyder, University of Chicago, Class of 2010, Sharon Yecies, University of Chicago, Class of 2011, and Michael Nadler, New York University Law School, Class of 2011, for their valuable research assistance.

ernment; the second is the progressive vision of a larger but more expert and benevolent government. I stand strongly in favor of the Lockean tradition, and seek in this essay to offer additional justifications for that set of insights. In order to take steps toward this end, I proceed as follows. In Section II, I briefly set out the three major questions that any regime of constitutionalism must face. In Section III, I outline the differences between the Lockean and progressive visions of constitutionalism. In Section IV, I defend the Humean account of "confin'd generosity" as the best brief summation of the nature of man. In Section V, I address the key structural issues that constitutional framers must confront. Section VI addresses the question of individual rights, and Section VII provides a short conclusion.

II. The Three Fundamental Constitutional Inquiries

A. Human nature

The first inquiry is as follows: What assumptions should designers of constitutions make about human nature, given that they themselves are flawed individuals? Will these assumptions change when constitutional designers think about the population at large, as opposed to the leaders of the nation? Are people to be regarded as virtuous or self-interested, and in what proportions?

Admittedly, it would be easy to design a workable constitution if the virtuous were in control. But it is far more difficult to do so when political actors are emboldened by their willingness to advance their own excessive self-interest at the expense of others. As James Madison memorably wrote in *Federalist No. 51*: "If men were angels, no government would be necessary. If angels were to govern men, neither external nor internal controls on government would be necessary."[1] And certainly, no constitutional government will be sustainable in the long run if all individuals are devils. The hard question is how to proceed with the task of constitutional design when the bulk of the population consists of individuals who fall somewhere between the two extremes, possessing both selfish and altruistic traits. This challenge is not made any easier given that political leaders often turn out to be more devilish and less angelic than the population at large. Stated otherwise, the wisdom of the Madison quotation lies in its awareness that character problems of the governed are often less critical than character problems of the governors, with their extreme and outsized personalities.

B. The institutions of government

Our second inquiry asks what institutional features a constitution can put into place—legislatures, executives, judges, administrative agencies—to

[1] James Madison, *Federalist No. 51*, in Alexander Hamilton, James Madison, and John Jay, *The Federalist Papers*, ed. Clinton Rossiter (New York: New American Library, 1961).

help constrain the manifest and pervasive human imperfections in both the governed and the governors. On this point, there is a common understanding that any system of sound governance must decide which bodies can pass what laws. The simplest form of government is a single legislative body that operates by majority vote. But the advantage of speed may well be offset by the danger of oppression. The operation of legislative bodies is often slowed to avoid this risk. But which system should be adopted? Federalism? Bicameralism? Supermajority votes? Presidential vetoes? The range of possibilities is quite large, and the relative advantages are difficult to determine. As we shall see, no strong theory emerges to define these optimal structural features, so that it is difficult to draw any inference regarding what will work, or fail, in one country from what works, or fails, in another. The translation of social institutions across nations is often more difficult than the translation of legal doctrine, which often follows similar lines in quite dissimilar places.

C. The protection of individual rights

The third inquiry has to do with the entrenchment of individual rights against government interference. The two major questions here are the following: What are the particular rights that should be entrenched? And what state justifications should be allowed to override them? On this score, two kinds of individual rights can be identified. The first kind is comprised of personal rights such as freedom of religion, freedom of speech, and freedom from invidious discrimination. The second kind is comprised of economic liberties, including the rights to contract and own private property. With respect to the first, it is possible to believe in the protection of freedom of speech and still think that fraud, defamation, bribery, and assault should be subject to civil and/or criminal penalties. One can be in favor of freedom of religion and be opposed to human sacrifice, even when done in the name of religious liberty. One can be in favor of equal treatment regardless of race and sex, and still be in favor of state-run affirmative action programs or sex-segregated sports. With respect to the second kind of individual rights, one can believe in the protection of freedom of contract and also in the limitation of cartels. One can believe in the protection of private property but also allow for its taking for public use with the payment of just compensation. One can also believe that the justifications for the limitation of individual rights should be far broader, so as to encompass the imposition of antidiscrimination laws on religious hiring, campaign finance limitations, minimum wage laws, and zoning and antigrowth ordinances.

III. LOCKEAN VERSUS PROGRESSIVE VISIONS

Armed with these distinctions, the thesis of this essay is simple enough. The imperfections of human nature drive us toward the creation of complex constitutional structures that limit the speed and efficiency of government action in order to control the risk that government action poses to individual rights. As is evident from the previous discussion, the nature and extent of these dual constitutional protections—dealing with institutions and entrenched rights, respectively—depends in large part on the answer to the initial question on human nature.

On this score, there are two different visions. One originates in the Lockean tradition that finds—in answer to the danger of unbridled individual self-interest—a legal regime that couples strong property rights (broadly conceived) with limited government. Under this vision, the broad conception of property rights covers more than external objects; it also covers an individual's political and religious views, and the full use of his natural faculties.[2] This vision powerfully, albeit imperfectly, motivated the design of the American Constitution. At every stage, the original design of the American Constitution evidences a tradition of limited government and strong property rights that relies on the contribution of such figures as Montesquieu, David Hume, Adam Smith, William Blackstone, James Madison, and Alexander Hamilton.

Yet this approach to constitutionalism hardly commands universal assent today. In opposition there is a strong modernist tradition, starting in the late nineteenth century, which believes that intelligent legislation and administrative expertise are strongly needed to control the abuses that take place in unregulated markets. Government is regarded not as some necessary evil, but as a positive source for good that can ease the difficult transitions from a simple agrarian society to a post-industrial one.

This conflict in views between classical liberals and progressives is readily apparent in the American tradition, particularly in the post–Civil

[2] See James Madison, *Property* (1792), in *The Papers of James Madison* (Charlottesville: University of Virginia Press, 1983), vol. 14, pp. 266–68. The relevant passage reads as follows:

This term [i.e., "property"] in its particular application means "that dominion which one man claims and exercises over the external things of the world, in exclusion of every other individual."

In its larger and juster meaning, it embraces every thing to which a man may attach a value and have a right; and which leaves to every one else the like advantage.

In the former sense, a man's land, or merchandize, or money is called his property.

In the latter sense, a man has a property in his opinions and the free communication of them.

He has a property of peculiar value in his religious opinions, and in the profession and practice dictated by them.

He has a property very dear to him in the safety and liberty of his person.

He has an equal property in the free use of his faculties and free choice of the objects on which to employ them.

In a word, as a man is said to have a right to his property, he may be equally said to have a property in his rights.

Note that the first line quoted is a softened redaction of the famous definition of property from William Blackstone, *Commentaries on the Laws of England: Book the Second of The Rights of Things* (1766): "That sole and despotic dominion which one man claims and exercises over the external things of the world, in total exclusion of the right of any other individual in the universe." Missing are the words "despotic" and "total."

War period. The choice of outcomes was sealed in favor of the progressive vision with the judicially crafted constitutional revolution that culminated in the October 1936 term of the United States Supreme Court. In rapid succession, the Supreme Court issued its explicit repudiation of key elements of the Lockean tradition on matters of both institutional structure and individual rights. In addition, the role of separation of powers at the federal level as a check on the size and power of government was cut back by decisions that explicitly endorsed the rise of independent administrative agencies,[3] which could act pursuant to broad grants of delegated authority from Congress.[4]

A similar transformation took place within the basic federalist structure of the United States Constitution. The original grant of legislative power to Congress under Article I of the Constitution was organized by an implicit reference to the doctrine of enumerated powers, under which the federal government could act only in certain well-specified fields, leaving the rest of the governance to the states. One advantage of this system of enumeration was that it minimized the likelihood that both the national and the state governments could control a single economic activity. That approach to limited government power was upheld when the commerce clause of the Constitution—"Congress shall have the power to . . . regulate commerce with foreign nations, among the several states, and with the Indian tribes"[5]—was read by Chief Justice John Marshall (in 1824) to cover all forms of cross-border trade, transportation, and communication,[6] but to leave all internal commerce and other economic activities within a state to that state's sole regulation. But that definition of commerce was not broad enough to allow the federal government to impose comprehensive labor regulation and agricultural regulation on local businesses. To facilitate the expansion of federal power in the 1930s, in a stunning about-face, the commerce clause was interpreted far more expansively to allow the federal government to regulate all aspects of manufacturing, agriculture, and mining, so long as they had some "indirect effect" on interstate commerce, which they inherently always do.[7]

Last, the nineteenth-century understanding of rights, which allowed for government control over monopolistic practices but not competitive

---

[3] See *Humphrey's Executor v. United States*, 295 U.S. 602 (1935) (holding that the president cannot dismiss an FTC commissioner except for cause).

[4] For the modern formulation of delegated authority, see *Whitman v. American Trucking Association, Inc.*, 531 U.S. 457 (2001) (allowing any delegation informed by an "intelligible principle").

[5] U.S. Constitution, art. I, sec. 8, cl. 3.

[6] See *Gibbons v. Ogden*, 22 U.S. 1 (1824) (voiding a state law that blocked out-of-state ships from using steam power in New York waters); *E. C. Knight and Co. v. United States*, 156 U.S. 1 (1895) (dismissing antitrust suit against sugar refiners as outside the scope of the commerce power).

[7] See, e.g., *National Labor Relations Board v. Jones and Laughlin Steel*, 301 U.S. 1 (1937) (sustaining national labor statute against commerce clause challenge); *Wickard v. Filburn*, 317 U.S. 111 (1942) (sustaining national labor statute for regulation of agricultural production).

ones,[8] gave way to a far more elastic vision of government power that allowed government to prop up monopolies or rip them down in accordance with its own policy preferences.[9] The clear import of the new constitutional structure was that all classical liberal devices, intended to slow down the expansion of government, were consciously replaced by a new set of doctrines that facilitated government growth. The justification was that only government administrative agencies—imbued with public spirit, enabled with technical expertise, and insulated from the pressures of market forces—could best run a complex economic system.[10] Within this framework, judicial review was regarded as a profound irritation that relied on a primitive defense of property rights in order to block the orderly introduction of the administrative state. The function of courts was to bless, not block, the new constitutional arrangements.

This post-1937 progressive constitutional vision does not entirely embrace this potent combination of majoritarian politics and the administrative state. Quite strikingly, on certain other questions, the triumph of the modern administrative state was tempered by the recognition of the massive dangers that majoritarian politics posed on explosive subjects, such as race relations in the United States. Before the ink was dry on the modern constitutional order as it pertained to economic liberties, a judicial reaction set in to make sure that no combination of majoritarian politics and administrative expertise could consign large portions of the American population to second-class citizenship. The only method to achieve this end was to reverse the move away from judicial review in those fields. Thus, in 1938, only one year after the consolidation of the New Deal hegemony over economic affairs, the Supreme Court held that it had an active role to play to ensure that "discrete and insular minorities" were not systematically disenfranchised by more powerful groups.[11] The momentum for judicial oversight led nearly inexorably to the 1954

---

[8] See, e.g., *Adair v. United States*, 208 U.S. 161 (1908) (striking down federal law that required collective bargaining in interstate commerce); *Coppage v. Kansas*, 236 U.S. 1 (1915) (voiding a statute prohibiting employers from blocking attempts by their employees to associate with labor unions).

[9] See, e.g., Daniel A. Crane, "The Story of *United States v. Socony-Vacuum:* Hot Oil and Antitrust in the Two New Deals," in Eleanor M. Fox and Daniel A. Crane, eds., *Antitrust Stories* (New York: Foundation Press, 2007), 91–119 (recounting the switch in government policy, within a very short period of time, from supporting industry-wide cartels to subjecting them to criminal prosecution). For the criminal prosecution, see *United States v. Socony-Vacuum Oil Co.*, 310 U.S. 150 (1940) (upholding a conviction for antitrust violations).

[10] For landmarks in that tradition, see Woodrow Wilson, *Congressional Government: A Study in American Politics* (1885; Cleveland, OH: Meridian Books, 1956), 187 ("It is, therefore, manifestly a radical defect in our federal system that it parcels out power and confuses responsibility as it does. The main purpose of the Convention of 1787 seems to have been to accomplish this grievous mistake."); and James M. Landis, *The Administrative Process: Integrating Theory and Practice* (New Haven, CT: Yale University Press, 1938), 11–12 (attacking the principle of separation of powers, which Landis adjudged to be inadequate when government agencies had concerns with "the stability of an industry").

[11] See *United States v. Carolene Products*, 304 U.S. 144, 152–53 n. 4 (1938) (imposing heightened scrutiny on laws harmful to "discrete and insular" minorities).

decision of *Brown v. Board of Education*,[12] in which the Supreme Court undertook a massive federal intervention into local public policy when it ordered the end of segregated public schools throughout the nation.

This highly truncated version of American history shows how difficult it is to come to grips with the simplest of questions that face any system of constitutionalism—when to accept the outcome of majority votes and when to override them in order to take into account either institutional limitations on the organs of government, or the protection of individual rights. I now turn to a closer examination of three basic issues: How do we understand human nature? What does it tell us about the choice of government structures? And what does it tell us about entrenched individual rights?

IV. THE NATURE OF MAN

As to the working account of human nature, I believe that constitutional designers should be guided neither by the relentless Hobbesian account of individual self-interest, nor by the naïve republican accounts of an animated citizenry that deliberates anxiously in search of the public good. We have neither devils nor angels. Rather, two points stand out. First, as a general matter, the most accurate account of the median individual is that of a self-interested person who has, in Hume's memorable phrase, a "confin'd generosity" to other individuals.[13] Second, the Humean account of the *median* position needs to be supplemented, as noted earlier, by an account of the *variance* around that mean. Thus, the Humean insight is consistent with some small fraction of any population having deeply antisocial traits, just as some fraction will have highly laudatory ones. The function of constitutionalism can be best understood as an effort to structure governmental arrangements so that individuals in the bad tail of the distribution do not run roughshod over those who lie everywhere else on the distribution.

Hume's point has received a powerful reformulation in modern public choice theory—which I date from James Buchanan and Gordon Tullock's *The Calculus of Consent* (1962).[14] Their book starts with a simple question: How do self-interested individuals interact in both markets and political settings? Unfortunately, the analysis starts on what I think to be an oversimplified and incorrect assumption: that a form of relentless self-interest—good old-fashioned selfishness—animates all the activities of private individuals. In this case, at least, the stark assumption is an instructive one, for if it is possible to design institutions that have

---

[12] *Brown v. Board of Education*, 347 U.S. 483 (1954).

[13] David Hume, *A Treatise of Human Nature* (1740), ed. P. H. Nidditch (Oxford: Oxford University Press, 1978), 519.

[14] James M. Buchanan and Gordon Tullock, *The Calculus of Consent: Logical Foundations of Constitutional Democracy* (Ann Arbor: University of Michigan Press, 1962).

some chance of success in that hostile environment, those same institutions will surely do better in nations where at least some fraction of the citizenry displays some modest public spirit in support of its internal institutional arrangements.

Starting from Buchanan and Tullock's initial assumption, we get very different results for market and political institutions. In the former, we employ a naïve conception of laissez-faire that says individuals everywhere and always are free to do whatever they want, whenever they want,[15] so long as, at the very least, they keep their promises and avoid the use of force and fraud. On these very modest assumptions, the worst that can emerge is a set of private economic monopolies that crop up through voluntary mergers and cartelization. Yet these economic monopolies receive no special franchise or grant from the state, and thus are constantly at risk of erosion from new entry by outside parties, which they are powerless to resist. Put otherwise, if neither buyers nor sellers can organize themselves, the result of interactions of self-interested individuals is a move toward the formation of a competitive market.

That market will never assume the idealized form in which all parties have perfect information and in which transaction costs are zero. But such a utopian standard of competition makes the best the enemy of the good. The key variable is free entry of both capital and labor in all markets, which offers choices to consumers, workers, and businesses to undermine the power of extant monopolies.[16] So long as the state does not impose legal barriers to competition, through licensing or certification requirements, the other short-term obstacles to competition tend to wither, so that, in an imperfect way, open markets will move closer to a competitive ideal that maximizes social output for any given configuration of scarce resources, be they human, physical, or intellectual. Any residual problem with cartelization and mergers can be constrained by an intelligent antitrust law, whereby courts refuse to enforce contracts in restraint of trade. Cheating on cartels is likely to be pervasive, as each cartel member tries to chisel on prices to increase its market share. When everyone engages in this conduct, the cartel crumbles, which further minimizes the social losses from anticompetitive practices.

This model does not allow for any state support of the poor through mandated programs of redistribution. And in a world in which everyone is selfish, we can expect high levels of output but no voluntary support of the needy outside the contexts of families and friendships. But if we relax the assumption that all individuals are selfish, then nothing in this system prevents persons who have more than average levels of generosity from helping less fortunate individuals or groups. Efforts of this sort were

---

[15] See, e.g., Grant Gilmore, *The Death of Contract* (Columbus: Ohio State Press, 1974), 95.

[16] This, of course, is the great theme of F. A. Hayek, *The Road to Serfdom* (Chicago: University of Chicago Press, 1944).

common in laissez-faire regimes, with high levels of giving to hospitals, churches, and universities, and extensive assistance to the needy.[17] In the United States, for example, the late nineteenth century witnessed the founding of the University of Chicago by John D. Rockefeller, Stanford University by Leland Stanford, and Johns Hopkins University by Johns Hopkins.

It is worth noting that the levels of charitable giving in the United States, even today, are far higher than they are in Europe.[18] The older tradition of American individualism always called for extensive charitable giving on the ground that all individuals had some "imperfect obligation" to assist others in need, even if they retained full power to decide which persons received what benefits.[19] Ironically, levels of charitable giving have always been far lower in Europe (Great Britain is an important exception) than in the United States precisely because the care of the poor has traditionally been regarded largely as a government function.[20] The strong private response to the risks of deprivation and poverty should not be dismissed as idle talk. Indeed, the secret of voluntary charity is often the use of intermediate social groups—churches, schools, hospitals, youth groups—which organize giving so that individual donors no longer have to run background checks on potential recipients.

This vision of markets is, however, incomplete. No market can generate sufficient resources to combat the use of force and fraud. Nor will uncoordinated voluntary efforts lead to the organized provision of public goods—streets, defense, courts, and infrastructure—a deficiency which has long been the bane of some extreme forms of libertarian theory that rule both taxation and the power of government to take private property completely out of bounds.[21]

So we need a state after all. Nonetheless, before we lurch to the other extreme, we must pay some attention to institutional arrangements. As a matter of ideal political theory, unanimous consent should be obtainable

---

[17] One representative early quotation:

> There is a time when a Christian must sell all and give to the poor, as they did in the Apostles times. There is a time allsoe when Christians (though they give not all yet) must give beyond their abillity, as they of Macedonia, Cor. 2, 6. Likewise community of perills calls for extraordinary liberality, and soe doth community in some speciall service for the Churche. Lastly, when there is no other means whereby our Christian brother may be relieved in his distress, we must help him beyond our ability rather than tempt God in putting him upon help by miraculous or extraordinary meanes.

John Winthrop, "A Modell of Christian Charity" (1630), quoted in Arthur Brooks, "Religious Faith and Charitable Giving," *Policy Review* (October and November, 2003), http://www.hoover.org/publications/policyreview/3447051.html. Brooks also notes the higher rate of giving among conservative religious people.

[18] Brooks, "Religious Faith and Charitable Giving."

[19] See Joseph Story, *Encyclopedia Americana* (Clark, NJ: The Lawbook Exchange, 2006).

[20] See Brooks, "Religious Faith and Charitable Giving."

[21] See Mancur Olson, *The Logic of Collective Action: Public Goods and the Theory of Groups* (Cambridge, MA: Harvard University Press, 1965).

by all rational persons acting from behind the veil of ignorance: each, after all, receives *in principle* the benefits of greater security that outweigh his loss of liberty and property. In practice, however, no one is tucked entirely behind the veil of ignorance in the design of political institutions; serious risks (such as oppression) necessarily arise in the exercise of power by any collective body. In light of these risks, the ideal political system need not, and probably should not, operate by simple majority vote. It is for this reason that many constitutions divide power between two houses of a legislature, intended to offset each other. In other instances, super-majority votes are required to pass key kinds of legislation, or, in presidential systems, legislation can be blocked by an executive veto, subject to some legislative override.[22] Political institutions have a territorial and not a membership base. Accordingly, they cannot rely on the initial authority obtained by unanimous consent at formation of the institution to justify their monopoly of force within a given territory.

The precarious justifications for political institutions should shape our attitudes toward them. The key point here is that within the context of political institutions, any model that posits political actors who act out of individual (or group) self-interest generates implications that are far more chilling than those raised by the power of businesses that are constrained by the prospect of new entry into the market. Every system of political organization must, at some time, bind individuals who have not consented to the particular program at hand. The dangers of political paralysis are too great otherwise. But any system that does not have complete unanimous consent faces the risk of faction and capture. Depending on the particular political configuration at any moment, certain majority or minority groups may be able to take advantage of the inevitable gaps and glitches within the constitutional order to wield a disproportionate influence over political processes for their own narrow purposes. And gaps there will be, for constitutions inevitably make wrong institutional choices or use phrasing whose ambiguity only becomes clear when it is too late to change the text.

In light of these imperfect institutional structures, the basic point can be put in a simple way. Any society has individuals that array themselves along a distribution from very good to very evil. There is little that can or need be done to deal with the former. There is much that needs to be done to combat the corrosive influence of the latter. Unfortunately, political institutions can operate by a one-way ratchet, so that once evil persons take over power, it can only be pried from them by massive protests or overt coups, many of which fail.

The lesson we learn about politics is that it hardly matters that Thomas Hobbes was wrong in his insistence that *all* human beings are animated by a relentless self-interest. It is daunting enough that some small fraction

---

[22] See U.S. Constitution, art. I, sec. 7, cls. 2 and 3.

of the population fits that description. The need to maintain order is the first order of political business, and this can be subverted by authoritarian figures. But even if that risk is controlled, the less serious but more pervasive risks of corruption and favoritism still remain. The question is what set of institutions and entrenched rights are best able to deal with these multiple prospects. As a general matter, there is little reason to be optimistic in light of the staggering number of failed efforts at decent government. Any discussion about how constitutions create institutional arrangements and entrench individual rights should not proceed on the assumption that the counterweights to these destructive political forces are always at hand. Sound constitutions do not provide safe havens. They only improve the odds of good government.

V. Constitutional Safeguards

There are, roughly speaking, four different kinds of institutional protections that could be included in a constitution: democratic elections; federalism; separation of powers; and an independent judiciary. Under the broad category of elections, constitutional framers must decide such issues as who is eligible to vote and which systems are used to aggregate individual votes in order to represent the collective choice. Is majority vote sufficient, for example, or is some supermajority required? Under federalism, framers must decide how political power should be distributed between two layers of government, where one has a larger geographical reach than the other.

The third kind of protection, separation of powers, could arise at any level of government. Under this general framework, the framers must decide whether political power should be funneled through a parliamentary system, in which the ministers who wield executive power are members (indeed leaders) of the legislative branch, or whether we should adopt a presidential system in which the executive branch is outside the legislative branch and holds some form of veto power over it. Both systems leave open the following further question: Which kinds of tasks should be taken out of the realm of legislative control and delegated to legislatively created agencies? Finally, the framers must organize the judicial power within this system. How should judges be appointed, and should they at all times be independent from the political branches of government by being unaccountable to them? If so, should judges have the power to override political decisions in order to protect either the structural or individual-rights elements of the constitution? And if they have such power, should the political branches, in turn, be able to override their judgment, and if so, by what mechanism?

I shall review each of these permutations in turn in order to establish this depressing thesis: There is no sure way to deduce the optimal structure of a constitution, even for those who are sensitive to the risk of excessive concentration of government power. Some combination of these four kinds of institutional protections is strictly necessary, but the relative advantage of one set of institutional arrangements relative to another is hard to sort out in the abstract, as so much of institutional design depends on factors such as territorial expansion, ethnic composition, and social infrastructure, which vary widely across nations. Quite simply, there is no strong theory of constitutionalism that clearly demonstrates the dominance of one structure over another.

A. Democratic elections

The first and most powerful constraint on political actors is the use of general election procedures that are intended to take ultimate political authority out of the hands of dangerous political factions. But these safeguards are far from fail-safe, and in too many contexts they degenerate into a democratic kleptocracy in which a single individual who gains power through a phony election can reduce a nation to ruin by acts of terror and confiscation. Think of such notable heads of state as President Saddam Hussein, President Robert Mugabe, President Kim Jong Il of North Korea, President Vladimir Putin, President Mahmoud Ahmadinejad, and (lagging not too far behind) President Hugo Chavez. None of these despotic leaders have repudiated the form of elections. None have used the title King. But they have all rigged elections and disregarded constitutional provisions in their successful efforts to consolidate unacceptable levels of political power.

No sound constitutional order can tolerate the unconstrained concentration of power in the hands of a single man, meaning that creating institutions capable of preventing the domination and manipulation of public elections has far greater urgency than is commonly recognized. This also demonstrates the attractiveness of binding term limits for powerful individuals in public office, in order to create a check against the possible abuses of power in democratic politics. Even here, however, there are no impregnable fortifications if President Putin can switch from president to prime minister in a regime with term limits.

Fortunately, in many Western democracies at least, national political cultures are marked by a willingness of elected leaders to allow themselves to be voted out of power.[23] That simple practice of orderly political succession rules out a descent into disguised presidential dictatorships. But even if orderly succession can be maintained, the prospects for democratic political institutions operating well without any additional checks are still quite grim. Sometimes the risk can be countered by an indepen-

---

[23] For a discussion of some of the mechanisms that help keep constitutional institutions in place, see Daryl J. Levinson, "Parchment and Politics: The Positive Puzzle of Constitutional Commitment," Social Science Research Network, http://papers.ssrn.com/sol3/papers.cfm?abstract_id=1577749.

dent judiciary or by civilian control of the military, but these innovations in the end are subject to the same corrupting influences that plague all key constitutional design choices.

Ultimately, it is exceedingly difficult to develop effective institutions to guard against even evident perils, given the multiple ways in which bad actors can abuse their power. For example, a simple majority, without shame, may decide to expropriate the property of a minority (often individuals in a different region or members of a different ethnic group). Or a small group may hold out for a larger share of a future gain by taking advantage of different voting rules to block an important social improvement. The supermajority requirements that protect against the first form of abuse could easily intensify the second. Because of this, the exact choice of basic voting rules is difficult to state in advance, and it is difficult to maintain these rules even when they are embodied in a constitutional order.

The bottom line from this quick discussion is that the framers of national constitutions should seek to minimize these problems of political faction by increasing, through every available means, the scope of market institutions relative to political institutions. The justification for slimming down government does not rest on some optimistic ground that markets are always efficient and always immune to various forms of corruption. Nothing reaches that level of perfection. The reason is more modest: warts and all, the corrective forces of competition are likely to prove more resilient and effective than any set of political checks against the use of government power. The fewer matters that are left to regulate, the more robust any set of elective political institutions will turn out to be. It is easier to constrain a government that has fewer powers than it is to constrain one with many.

B. Federalism

The question of whether to adopt federalist institutions does not have a firm answer as a matter of general political theory. Much depends on the configuration of two key variables: population size and geographic distribution of ethnic groups. The latter point deserves some special attention here, because there is often good reason to believe that ethnic tensions, accumulating over decades or centuries, cannot be mediated by government structure at all. For example, the political separation into Protestant Northern Ireland and Catholic Ireland may have reduced the level of conflict, but it surely has not eliminated it. Distrust on both sides has precluded any effective unification of the country, no matter what safeguards could be built into the constitution. Even the separation itself has not put an end to all the violence. The same can be said of the painful separation in 1947 of Pakistan from India, which involved major migrations of populations across large distances in an effort to reduce the ethnic tensions in what quickly became two separate nations. Whatever the border tensions that arise after separation, these are less threatening to peace and good order than massive internal violence verging on civil war. More recently, the breakup of the former nation of Yugoslavia into the new nations of Slovenia, Croatia, Bosnia and Herzegovina, Macedonia, Montenegro, and Serbia (which contains two autonomous provinces, Kosovo and Vojvodina) shows how fragile and bloody the business of nation building can be.[24] In a sense, it is best to look at the territorial separation as a failed merger between two or more firms that could not overcome the cultural differences between them. But even the territorial divisions are not perfect; they often expose the ethnic minorities that are left behind to various forms of retaliation and political discrimination. It is difficult to mend deep divisions.

The problem of integration is also acute within corporate cultures, where mergers are often greeted with dread by employees who (if they are retained) suspect that two cultures will not mesh. In the case of Daimler/Chrysler, the sardonic joke before its breakup was: "How do you pronounce Daimler/Chrysler? Answer: Daimler, the Chrysler is silent." All joking aside, it is also best to think of territorial division as a most imperfect solution. After all, the trapped minorities on either side of the border may be left more vulnerable by virtue of a territorial realignment than they would have been in a unified state. But in the grim business of international statecraft, it is all too predictable that imperfect accommodations will lead to horrific outcomes.

In some situations, strong national pressures lead to the decision to retain a single nation, notwithstanding evident tensions. That seems to have been the right call with respect to Iraq after Saddam Hussein was deposed. The Kurds, Sunnis, and Shiites have multiple grievances against each other that no outsider can quite begin to fathom. Separation by territories within a confederation is a sensible idea because it allows for local governments to take up some essential functions (e.g., education and social welfare programs) in a way that has little impact on other groups.

Separation by territories within a confederation may also explain why the principle of "subsidiarity" has emerged to take such a central role in modern discussions of federalism.[25] Under that principle, each particular decision is assigned to the smallest political unit in which the bulk of its economic and political consequences are likely to be felt:

The principle of subsidiarity is defined in Article 5 of the Treaty establishing the European Community. It is intended to ensure that

---

[24] See "The Break Up of Yugoslavia: 1990–1997," http://www.thenagain.info/WebChron/EastEurope/YugoBreakup.html.

[25] See, e.g., Denis J. Edwards, "Fearing Federalism's Failure: Subsidiarity in the European Union," *American Journal of Comparative Law* 44, no. 537 (1996).

decisions are taken as closely as possible to the citizen and that constant checks are made as to whether action at [European] Community level is justified in the light of the possibilities available at national, regional or local level. Specifically, it is the principle whereby the [European] Union does not take action (except in the areas which fall within its exclusive competence) unless it is more effective than action taken at national, regional or local level. It is closely bound up with the principles of proportionality and necessity, which require that any action by the Union should not go beyond what is necessary to achieve the objectives of the Treaty.[26]

The principle of subsidiarity represents a careful compromise. Land use disputes are assigned to cities; commuter rail systems are assigned to state or regional authorities; airline grids and defense are assigned to national bodies. That system helps ensure that government officials and private citizens with the greatest knowledge and interest address a particular problem. But that system also runs the risk of exposing local minorities to political retaliation unless the national body has some power to veto local decisions. And there is no rule for deciding whether an action is "more effective" at one level or another. Subsidiarity is a broad standard that is intended to guide discussion, not resolve it. Everyone agrees that there is a core of good sense in the principle. No one is sure how far it goes.

General standards work relatively well when levels of trust are high, but when trust is lacking, indeterminate standards often yield to rules. Consistent with this principle, the procedures that set out government powers tend to become more explicit as the depth of ethnic divisions increases. At this point, the fear of exploitation tends to shift the control mechanisms from broad principles to specific veto rights.

Just that type of institutional design is found in the elaborate constitutional structure in Bosnia-Herzegovina, which sports *three* separate presidents (representing the Bosnian Muslims, Croats, and Serbs), each of whom is given the ability to veto any government decision that he or she deems to be "destructive of the vital interests" of the representative population.[27] This proposition is meant to remove the veto power from decisions that do not pose a threat to the stability of each independent ethnic group, but to leave a second-order mechanism to control decisions that pose a threat to the discretion of the presidents. Thus, the presidents' discretion is subject to both a political check and an independent legal check—a presidential veto must be ratified by a two-thirds majority of what is termed a "home" parliament, whose ethnic composition tracks the ethnic constituency of each of the three

---

[26] Europa Glossary, "Treaty of Lisbon," http://europa.eu/lisbon_treaty/index_en.htm.

[27] For discussion, see Samuel Issacharoff, "Constitutionalizing Democracy in Fractured Societies," *Journal of International Affairs* 58, no. 1 (2004).

presidents. All these solutions were introduced only after a period of extended ethnic strife. The object lesson is that the only regimes that have a chance to cope with the residual distrust are those that take explicit cognizance of the previous high levels of ethnic hostility in order to guard against its corrosive effects.

In other places, like Canada, where the French-English split is a constant tension, total separation into two independent nations always remains an option. Yet the federal arrangement in Canada seems to limp along tolerably well, because it too is filled with local options that, in turn, blunt the power of national authorities. Thus, under the Canadian Charter of Rights and Freedoms adopted in 1982, no judicial decision striking down a legal provision has the final say, for the national parliament or state legislature, as the case may be, is free to reenact the same provision for a period of five years by simple majority vote, which in turn can be extended for additional five-year terms.[28] The Quebec legislature has done just that on multiple occasions, in refusing to respect the bilingual provisions of the Canadian Charter.[29]

In the United States, it took a civil war to eliminate slavery, but not its deep racial tensions. Thus, in the aftermath of the Civil War, the United States adopted the Fourteenth Amendment, which allowed states to initiate legislation but also assigned to either the Congress or the courts the task of ensuring that these state laws did not violate certain extensive guarantees of fundamental rights.[30] It was a determined effort to respect the principles of federalism, on the one hand, and to limit their scope, on the other. It was impossible, however, to predict how the issue would play out. The initial effectiveness of the strategy was blunted by the acceptance of "separate but equal" in the 1896 decision of *Plessy v. Ferguson*,[31] which at once legitimated school segregation, segregation in public transportation, and antimiscegenation laws. The campaign for racial equality then took a long and painful backtracking until the 1954 decision in *Brown v. Board of Education*,[32] which held simply that there was "no place" for racial segregation under the equal protection clause of the Fourteenth Amendment. There were no constitutional amendments that could account for a shift in judicial holdings. Instead, national reflection and nonstop litigation led to a total change in worldviews.

[28] Canadian Charter of Rights and Freedoms, para. 33 (1982).

[29] *Attorney General of Quebec v. Blaikie*, 2 S.C.R. 1016 (1979).

[30] See U.S. Constitution, amend. XIV, sec. 1: "All persons born or naturalized in the United States and subject to the jurisdiction thereof, are citizens of the United States and of the State wherein they reside. No state shall make or enforce any law which shall abridge the privileges or immunities of citizens of the United States; nor shall any State deprive any person of life, liberty, or property, without due process of law; nor deny to any person within its jurisdiction the equal protection of the laws."

[31] *Plessy v. Ferguson*, 163 U.S. 537 (1896).

[32] *Brown v. Board of Education*, 347 U.S. 483 (1954).

The situation in the European Union today is driven in part by the importance of national divisions and distrust, which have both worked to limit the central power in Brussels. The EU functions best as a free-trade zone, and less effectively as a federal regulator that uneasily divides its power with its nation-state members. This is due, in part, to the fact that the internal divisions in the EU are far more profound than those in the United States. Each of the member states of the EU has long been an independent national sovereign and continues to act independently in military and international affairs.

The EU thus presents the converse of the United States, whose constitutional order puts control over foreign affairs squarely at the national level, where it is divided between Congress and the president, with occasional intervention from the courts.[33] The simple point here is that high levels of internal trust make the difficult task of organizing power across a federal system far easier in the United States than it would be elsewhere. Americans today think nation first and state second[34] — a change in personal identity that did not create any convulsions.

This arrogation of power to the center of government may have profound economic consequences in the creation or control of monopoly power, but that has to be put in perspective. The key point is that no configuration of American federalism increases the chances that national power will be used to kill, imprison, or rob dissenting individuals. The worst that the United States did as a nation was the creation, during World War II, of the Japanese internment camps whose validity was upheld in *Korematsu v. United States* (1944).[35] This was, in my view, both a constitutional blunder and a colossal mistake of public policy,[36] for which the United States rightly apologized in 1976[37] and voted reparations in 1988.[38] At no time, however, did that internment ever pose a threat to the lives of the detainees. Similarly, the entire episode surrounding the prisoners in Guantanamo Bay has brought forward a level of judicial resistance that was not evident during World War II; indeed, with respect to Guantanamo, the antigovernment forces (of which I was one)

[33] See U.S. Constitution, art. 1, sec. 8, cls. 10–16; art. 2, sec. 2, cl. 1.

[34] See, e.g., Bruce Ackerman, "2006 Oliver Wendell Holmes Lectures: The Living Constitution," *Harvard Law Review* 120, no. 1737 (2006): "After two centuries of development, America's political identity is at war with the system of constitutional revision left by the Framers. We understand ourselves today as Americans first and Californians second."

[35] *Korematsu v. United States*, 323 U.S. 214 (1944).

[36] For a full account of the fiasco, see Geoffrey R. Stone, *Perilous Times: Free Speech in Wartime* (New York: Norton and Company, 2004).

[37] Gerald Ford, "Proclamation 4417—An American Promise" (February 19, 1976), http://www.presidency.ucsb.edu/ws/index.php?pid=787: "We now know what we should have known then—not only was the evacuation wrong, but Japanese-Americans were and are loyal Americans."

[38] The Civil Liberties Act of 1988, Pub. L. No 100-383, 102 Stat. 903 (2000), codified at 50 U.S.C. App. sec. 1989(b).

managed to win in the courts what they could not win with the president or Congress.[39]

For all its weaknesses, the American federal system does not regularly spin out of control on a mass scale, and this relative stability allows the U.S. to prevent the kinds of massive abuses that are found elsewhere. There is no American exceptionalism here, as other democracies exhibit similar forms of political stability. But there is at least some sense in which the federal structure, in the U.S. and elsewhere, creates a diffusion of power that avoids the risk of wholesale breakdown.

Constitutional framers are always in a position to ask whether a federalist system is an effective diffuser of power. But it is hard to determine in the abstract which federal system is best. What is clear is that the more ambitious the total level of government activities, the harder it is for constitutional drafters to design an ideal set of institutions. Shrinking the scope of government activities should ease the burden of system design, but will by no means eliminate it. Even the smallest of modern governments has an impressive portfolio of activities. A good deal more work remains to be done.

C. Separation of powers

The third key structural choice concerns the separation of powers, which is normally coupled with the extensive use of checks and balances among different branches of government. A system of separation of powers reserves certain distinct government functions for different branches of government. The most common division dates back to Montesquieu's 1748 masterpiece, *The Spirit of the Laws*.[40] That book was written at a time when the English king was rapidly losing his control over executive matters within the realm, and about forty years before the American Constitutional Convention of 1787 and the French Revolution of 1789.

Montesquieu's articulation of the ideal division between the executive, legislative, and judicial functions was not new, for many of the same ideas can be found in John Locke's *Second Treatise of Government*. Both books have left their imprint on the American Constitution. The first three articles of the U.S. Constitution start with a sharp tripartite delineation between the making of the law, the enforcing of the law, and the adjudication of disputes under the law. This arrangement still retains a common-sense aspect that is not completely obliterated by the endless efforts to draw

---

[39] For the judicial reaction, see *Hamdan v. Rumsfeld*, 548 U.S. 557 (2006) (holding that Congress had not authorized the use of military commissions to try detainees at Guantanamo Bay); *Boumediene v. Bush*, 128 S. Ct. 2229 (2008) (giving detainees at Guantanamo Bay the protection of habeas corpus, or an equivalent proceeding to challenge the legality of their detentions, even after Congress authorized the use of military commissions to resolve these proceedings).

[40] Charles de Secondat, baron de Montesquieu, *The Spirit of the Laws* (1748).

sharp lines between legislative and executive functions. A legislative decision to build post offices in major towns generally allows the executive to decide which towns to include and where to build the post offices.[41] The legislative decision to impose tariffs on foreign goods normally leaves it to the executive to figure out which tariff should be put on which class of goods. The legislature may authorize the hiring of executive branch employees, but may it create a civil service to combat the spoils system, whereby the new administration is able to replace all routine employees with members of its own party? Ultimately, Chief Justice William Howard Taft held, in an exhaustive opinion, that civil service regulations did not impinge on the executive function for routine employees, but did so for a first-class postmaster in Portland, Oregon.[42]

The situation becomes still more complex when the demands of the administrative state lead to efforts to change the checks and balances between the separate branches of government. Within the American system, there are constant efforts on the part of the various constitutional players to alter their respective powers by mutual agreement, and these efforts provoke extended controversy because of the challenge they pose to both separation of powers and checks and balances.

One instructive American example concerns whether a duly passed statute can authorize a single house of Congress to overturn a decision of the Immigration and Naturalization Service granting asylum to an alien. That procedure does not comply with the usual requirements for enacting a law, which requires passage by both houses of a bill that is then presented to the president for signature.[43] The Supreme Court answered the question in the negative in *Immigration and Naturalization Service v. Chadha* (1983), properly in my view.[44] The doctrine of separation of powers is put in place precisely to limit the freedom of contract among the political branches. The beneficiaries of these structural restrictions are members of the public at large, so that only a constitutional amendment, not a political agreement, may deprive them of such protection. Elected officials have fiduciary duties to the public at large, and cannot act solely out of personal or political expediency. Other theorists disagree, and insist that so long as the overall framework by which these agreements take place is adopted through legislation that meets the constitutional requirements of

[41] For a discussion of early congressional debates over whether and how to designate postal routes, see David P. Currie, *The Constitution in Congress: The Federalist Period, 1789–1801* (Chicago: University of Chicago Press, 1997), 146–49.

[42] *Myers v. United States*, 272 U.S. 52 (1926).

[43] For the various requirements, see U.S. Constitution, art 1, sec. 1; art. 1, sec. 7, cls. 2 and 3.

[44] *Immigration and Naturalization Service v. Chadha*, 462 U.S. 919 (1983) (striking down statute permitting one house to veto an executive branch decision not to deport an alien). See esp. id. at 945: "[P]olicy arguments supporting even useful 'political inventions' are subject to the demands of the Constitution which defines powers and, with respect to this subject, sets out just how those powers are to be exercised. Explicit and unambiguous provisions of the Constitution prescribe and define the respective functions of the Congress and of the Executive in the legislative process."

bicameralism and presentment, it is simple folly to insist that the administrative treatment of individual cases, such as an application for asylum in the United States, be handled in the same fashion as a basic statute.[45] To that response there is the further reply that single cases should never be regarded as matters for the Congress to resolve, so that any ability to challenge these decisions must be taken through the courts.[46] However, notwithstanding the holding in *Chadha*, legislative vetoes are more common in the United States than ever before. Administrative imperatives can trump constitutional text.

Clearly, any system of separation of powers faces a constant tension between the need for prudence and the need for speed. The key point for these purposes is not whether these various decisions are right under the specific provisions of the U.S. Constitution. The key, rather, is to remind people that a few hard choices at the margins do not undermine the basic conceptual distinction between legislation and its executive enforcement. Under the American system, it would be wrong for the president to build any roads or post offices without receiving any authorization from Congress, which could, if desired, specify the exact location for such post offices. It should also be evident at some level that the expansion of government roles from the eighteenth century to the twentieth would have posed immense challenges to the operation of government without the creation of independent agencies, whose status under the original American Constitution is dubious at best (except for those who think that it makes perfectly good linguistic sense to locate in the executive branch agencies that act, as Justice George Sutherland put it, "quasi-legislatively and in part quasi-judicially").[47]

There is little doubt that the demands of rate regulation (for example) would lead a new constitution to be more tolerant of independent administrative agencies than the framers of the U.S. Constitution were, since they had no reason to foresee the magnitude of this particular problem.[48] Indeed, the law on this point is so difficult that most people within the United States do not know which administrative functions are securely in the executive branch (like the Environmental Protection Agency) and which are inde-

---

[45] Id. at 967 (White, J., dissenting): "Without the legislative veto, Congress is faced with a Hobson's choice: either to refrain from delegating the necessary authority, leaving itself with a hopeless task of writing laws with the requisite specificity to cover endless special circumstances across the entire policy landscape, or in the alternative, to abdicate its lawmaking function to the executive branch and independent agencies."

[46] Id. at 959 (Powell, J., concurring): "When Congress finds that a particular person does not satisfy the statutory criteria for permanent residence in this country it has assumed a judicial function in violation of the principle of separation of powers."

[47] See *Humphrey's Executor v. United States*, 295 U.S. 602, 628 (1935).

[48] For an early discussion of the issue, see *State ex rel. Railroad and Warehouse Commission v. Chicago, Milwaukee, and St. Paul Railroad*, 37 N.W. 782, 787 (1888). Mitchell, J., laid out powerful reasons why a legislature could not undertake to set thousands of different rates by itself. But he did miss one piece of the ultimate solution. If rates are to be set by a special commission, they should be subject to judicial review, given the fear of confiscation.

pendent agencies (like the Securities and Exchange Commission and the National Labor Relations Board). And in general, the melding of executive and legislative functions is less problematic than the melding of either the legislative or the executive branch with judicial functions, where concerns with institutional bias play an important part. For these purposes, the key point is that the principle of separation of powers tells constitutional framers that, while some lines between functions must be drawn, a constitution cannot itself specify with precision where those lines should be drawn.

Once these lines have been drawn, however, the complementary principle of checks and balances allows each branch of government to block actions by the others. The American Constitution allows the president to block legislation by veto, which in turn can be overridden by a two-thirds vote of each house of Congress. Once again, the details of the system of checks and balances matter, but the system is not clearly constrained by any general theory. For example, there is no deep division as a matter of principle between a two-thirds vote and a three-fourths vote to override a presidential veto. But a veto override is far less likely with the three-fourths provision, which would give a major boost to the power of the president.

The question then arises: How should these two principles (separation of powers and checks and balances) be put together? On this score, Americans should be careful about exporting their constitutional arrangements to the rest of the world.[49] One obvious concern here is that a stable political environment reduces the pressures to get the perfect system of separation of powers, just as it reduces the pressures to have the perfect brand of federalism. Americans do well on constitutional issues because the relatively high level of political cohesion and internal stability in the U.S. enables cooperation between the different branches of government.

Classical liberal principles demand at least some division of powers to prevent the excessive concentration of political power. Nonetheless, a commitment to the principle of separation of powers does not require a presidential system or rule out-of-bounds a system of parliamentary control, whereby the electorate may vote for its representative but has no direct say on the selection of the ruling party or its key officials. The split ticket—voting for one party for president, and the other for the House or Senate—is a hallmark of the American political system. Necessarily, it has no place in any parliamentary system, where all voters are restricted to a

---

[49] See, e.g., Bruce Ackerman, "The New Separation of Powers," *Harvard Law Review* 113 (2000): 633–729, which opens by taking to task Steven Calabresi's paean to American constitutional solutions in Steven G. Calabresi, "An Agenda for Constitutional Reform," in William N. Eskridge, Jr., and Sanford Levinson, eds., *Constitutional Stupidities, Constitutional Tragedies* (New York: NYU Press, 1998), 22. Ackerman's preferred alternative is a "constrained parliamentarism," which rejects the presidential systems based in France and the United States ("The New Separation of Powers," 640), and which adds in doses of federalism and national referenda.

single choice of their local representative. Due to party loyalty, a party with a bare majority is better able to dominate the British Parliament than the United States presidential system, where party discipline is weaker. Under the latter, for example, a bill must have 60 percent support in order to close off debate in the Senate, and a byzantine committee structure can hamper the passage of many popular bills before they reach the floor of either house. We learn, then, that swiftness and caution can be forces for either good or evil, depending on who is in charge.

The performance of a parliamentary system can also depend critically on whether its elections are carried out under a Westminster system, which gives all power to the party first past the post, or a proportionate representation system, which lets small parties gain a far larger say in the political process. Such a slight shift in voting rules profoundly alters the political landscape. The differences between the two forms of parliamentary governments may well dwarf those between presidential and parliamentary systems that share the common feature of operating with two dominant parties. Since minority parties have no say in a parliamentary first-past-the-post system, they tend to shrivel and die. Conversely, since minority parties can often hold the whip hand in proportionate representation systems, they tend to proliferate and flourish under such systems. The incentives in these systems are so powerful, and the effects so predictable, that the basic pattern has long been called Duverger's law.[50]

It would, however, be unwise to insist on the superiority of proportionate representation solely because it weights minority interests more heavily. One risk is that the small parties will systematically exert excessive influence in the formation of new government coalitions, which will no longer map well onto the preferences of the voting public. Let there be three parties with 40 percent, 40 percent, and 20 percent of the legislative seats, respectively, and the smallest party can form a winning coalition with either of the two dominant parties. The politics become only more complex as the number of splinter parties increases. This endless bargaining rises to an art form in such places as Italy, Israel, and New Zealand (after it retreated from the Westminster system).[51]

There are other differences between the presidential and parliamentary systems that are hard to assess. The definite four-year term for the American president, for example, differs sharply from the outer limit of five-year terms before national elections must be called in parliamentary systems. The ability of the ruling party, or its prime minister, to dissolve

---

[50] Maurice Duverger, *Political Parties: Their Organization and Activity in the Modern State* (Hoboken, NJ: Wiley, 1954).

[51] For my evaluation of the New Zealand system, see Richard A. Epstein, *MMP—The Right Decision?* (Wellington: New Zealand Business Round Table, 1999). MMP refers to a "mixed member proportional" system, which does not allow for a single party to obtain exclusive control over government. Any system (such as MMP) that lets minor parties gain leverage at the polls tends to give those minor parties disproportionate influence in setting up a government.

parliament on short notice and call for a new election gives the incumbent
an advantage that is denied to presidents in presidential systems. Yet
under a parliamentary system, the ability to force a vote of confidence
against the ruling coalition puts it at a disadvantage, holding it hostage to
the small groups within the coalition.

There is no easy translation from a belief in limited government to
either of these two systems. Parliamentary systems are more likely
to change dramatically, as England's did with Margaret Thatcher's rise
to power in 1979, since she did not have to face the more chaotic institutional framework of the U.S. Congress. Conversely, the parallel rise to
power of Ronald Reagan in 1981 in the United States was less transfor-
mative because the House of Representatives remained in Democratic
hands throughout Reagan's two terms, and the Senate remained in Republican hands only through 1986. That high variability is again both a blessing and curse, for the system that gave Great Britain Margaret Thatcher
had previously produced leaders with far lower wattage—which can also
be said of the run of American presidents from the founding of the nation
onward. It is hard to identify which system produces abler leaders or
why.

Ultimately, therefore, the choice of government form reduces to a battle
of relative imperfections that trades off risks of hasty action and debili-
tating paralysis, both accentuated by factional discord. It may well be that
inertia will prove the deciding factor in stable systems. Change is costly,
and usually unwise unless some manifest defect cries out for correction.
Yet at the same time, when difficulties become crises, the empirical evidence shows a rapid shift from presidential to parliamentary systems or
the reverse. Thus, one exhaustive review concludes that between 1950
and 2003, there were, worldwide, 123 constitutional changes, of which
sixty-seven went from presidential to parliamentary forms of government
and fifty-six in the opposite direction.[52] It is very difficult to detect a
global consensus in the wake of this evidence.

Figuring out the desirability of these changes is an even more difficult
challenge, given the ebb and flow in both directions. One set of studies
purported to find that presidential systems that had lower levels of government spending also had about 6 percent lower GDP than parliamentary systems, and that welfare spending was about 2 to 3 percent less,
with somewhat lower levels of corruption and, more dubiously, somewhat lower levels of production.[53] But these findings have been challenged on a variety of technical grounds, including the model's inability
to explain why the choice of governmental form should be treated as

[52] See Bernd Hayo and Stefan Voigt, "The Determinants of Constitutional Change: When
and Why Do Countries Change Their Form of Government?" http://www.mps2009.org/
files/Voigt.pdf.
[53] T. Perrson and G. Tabellini, *The Economic Effects of Constitutions* (Cambridge, MA: The
MIT Press, 2003).

independent of other historical and political forces.[54] Skepticism seems warranted for the simple reason that there is no unique presidential or parliamentary system, and it is likely that the variations within each type could prove as important as the variations across types. The powers of presidents and legislatures can be tweaked in so many ways that differences within each group could easily matter as much as differences between the two groups.

Some lawmaking power could be taken out of the legislative process, either by initiative or referendum,[55] and given directly to the electorate. That approach would avoid the factions in government, and it would produce a clean up-or-down vote on a given question. But it could also lead to results that are politically divisive, as was proven in California in 2008, where the passage of Proposition 8 has prohibited gay marriage, at least for the moment,[56] but only at the cost of much bitterness and mutual recrimination in the aftermath. One important dynamic relates to the complex interactions when referenda on controversial issues appear on Election Day, for by altering the overall electoral turnout, they can easily alter the outcome of general elections. It is commonly thought, for example, that the strong support for Proposition 8 among African Americans boosted the turnout in the presidential election to the advantage of Barack Obama, who carried the state handily.

Yet here, as with federalism, it is appropriate to end on a note of caution. There are many nations where ethnic conflicts are so embedded that no system of separation of powers and checks and balances can work. Deep ethnic conflicts in the mottled distribution of a population within a small nation make it impossible to orchestrate any physical separation or federal system. At this point, ornate checks and balances are the last feeble hope. A textbook example is the highly unstable situation in Lebanon, where the fragile 1943 accommodation called for a Christian Maronite President, a Sunni prime minister, and a Shiite parliamentary speaker.[57] That arrangement started from the correct political presump-

---

[54] Daron Acemoglu, "Constitutions, Politics, and Economics: A Review Essay on Persson and Tabellini's *The Economic Effects of Constitutions*," NBER Working Paper No. W11235, http://papers.ssrn.com/sol3/papers.cfm?abstract_id=693096. See also, Lorenz Blume, Jens Muller, Stefan Voigt, and Carsten Wolf, "The Economic Effects of Constitutions: Replicating— and Extending—Persson and Tabellini," *Public Choice* (forthcoming).

[55] For a general, if qualified, endorsement of referenda, see Robert Cooter, *The Strategic Constitution* (Princeton, NJ: Princeton University Press, 2000), 143–48. See also Ackerman, "The New Separation of Powers," where Ackerman suggests ways to avoid the California excesses by limiting the number of issues that can be raised in this fashion, and by requiring two or more separate votes to pass a referendum.

[56] Prior to the Proposition 8 referendum, the California Supreme Court recognized the right of same-sex couples to marry. See *In re Marriage Cases*, 183 P.3d 384 (Cal. 2008).

[57] Gary C. Gambill, "Lebanon's Constitution and the Current Political Crisis," http://www.mideastmonitor.org/issues/0801/0801_3.htm: "It was the informal 1943 National Pact that reserved the presidency for Maronite Christians, the office of prime minister for Sunni Muslims, and (a few years later) the office of parliament speaker for Shiite Muslims, while apportioning parliament seats according to a fixed sectarian quota."

tion that each interest group should hold veto power over major structural changes, a feature that is indispensable in any political setting driven
by ethnic distrust. But this compromise proved short-lived given the
relative growth in Shiite population, which resulted in the first of many
ethnic civil conflicts in the late 1950s. The country's subsequent history
has hardly proved easier, for the internal instability in Lebanon has led to
partial occupations by Israel and Syria, as well as huge internal conflicts
with the rise of Hezbollah. There are some situations that are beyond
cure, absent political miracles.

D. Judicial power

But what of the judicial power? That discussion divides itself conveniently into three questions. The first asks the purpose and organization
of the judicial system. The second addresses the selection of judges. The
third concerns the power of judicial review, that is, the ability of a court
to strike down a properly formulated action of the legislative or executive
branch in either a presidential or parliamentary structure, on the ground
that it is inconsistent with the constitution.

In a classical liberal regime, courts exist to resolve individual disputes
that arise under the general law. The key obligation in this system is to
make sure that neither the executive nor the legislature denies any person
or organization the opportunity to have his, her, or its grievances resolved
before a neutral tribunal. That conception of judicial power is clearly
found in Locke's *Second Treatise*[58] and in Montesquieu's *Spirit of the Laws*.[59]
On this point, the American Constitution follows the English practice,
guaranteeing access to the courts both as a matter of due process and by
the writ of habeas corpus, which cannot be suspended except under
extraordinary circumstances.[60]

This model of judicial power works well for traditional legal disputes,
but it has been called into question by the rise of the modern administrative state, which often places greater stress on the identification and
use of judicial power. For example, specialized rate courts are often used
in states to deal with the heavy burden of rate-making proceedings. And
it is common to assign high-volume issues, such as workers' compensa-

---

[58] As Locke insisted, in the state of nature, "[t]here wants an established, settled, known
law, received and allowed by common consent to be the standard of right and wrong, and
the common measure to decide all controversies between them." John Locke, *Second Treatise
of Government* (1690), sec. 124. The needed rules should be (as they are often not today)
"plain and intelligible" (ibid.). State power also remedies the want of a "*known and indifferent
Judge*, with authority to determine all differences according to the established law" (ibid.,
sec. 125).

[59] Montesquieu, *The Spirit of the Laws*, Book VI, sec. 3 (discussing the decrease in judicial
discretion).

[60] U.S. Constitution, art. I, sec. 9, cl. 2: "The Privilege of the Writ of Habeas Corpus shall
not be suspended, unless when in Cases of Rebellion or Invasion the public Safety may
require it."

tion cases, to specialized tribunals that deal with these issues on a regular basis, with matters of law often resolved by appeal to the ordinary court.

In general, there is little that an optimal constitution should do to eliminate the rise of these specialized tribunals. Nonetheless, some limits should be set on the use of such tribunals. For example, specialized courts outside the judicial system are used in the United States in labor relations cases, where the National Labor Relations Board (NLRB) operates under a five-person board whose chairman is appointed by the president and whose other four members are by custom divided evenly between the two political parties.[61] The NLRB oversees an extensive statutory regime that organizes union elections, resolves unfair labor practices, and formulates general policy. This field is fraught with sharp divisions along party lines. Even though some level of judicial review by independent courts is available, the NLRB mixes judicial functions with legislative and administrative ones. There is no reason why the judicial function in these cases should be lodged in a single body whose members are chosen exclusively because of their partisan positions. Polarization along political lines is thus the order of the day. Keeping the deciding vote in the hands of the president thus tends to increase the dominance of the party in power, which is inconsistent with strong separationist principles. Keeping specialized tribunals within the political branches of government is, on balance, a risk that no sound system of constitutional law needs to run.

In choosing judges, once again, there is no uniform approach. Within the American system, federal judges are nominated by the president but only appointed after they have been confirmed by a majority of senators, with no participation of the House of Representatives.[62] At the time of the founding, senators were chosen by state legislatures, and a deliberative body, the Electoral College, chose the president. The most popular element of government, the House of Representatives, was shut out of the process altogether.

To further insulate members of the judiciary, their terms are for life, or technically during "good behavior." This goes far beyond term limits to insulate judges from political pressures.[63] The reason for the adoption of this practice under the American Constitution was doubtless the conception that the purpose of judges was to protect propertied interests from political expropriation. The criticism is that such protection entrenches people of privilege who already exert too much power over the political branches of government. The move for direct election of judges, often for limited terms, has taken hold in some states, which in turn generates a pressure on judges to play to the gallery on critical decisions. The anti-

---

[61] National Labor Relations Act, 29 U.S.C. sec. 153(a).
[62] U.S. Constitution, art. 2 sec. 2, cl. 2.
[63] U.S. Constitution, art. 3, sec. 1.

elitist impulse is quite evident here. But the choice between methods of selection remains highly controversial everywhere.

Even more controversial than the role of specialized administrative tribunals or the rules for selecting judges is the hot-button issue of judicial review. Judicial review, of course, gives courts the power to strike down legislation that falls outside the permissible boundaries of the constitution. Judicial review in the United States was established in the 1803 case of *Marbury v. Madison*,[64] in which there was an explicit contradiction (on a narrow question of the Supreme Court's jurisdiction) between what the Constitution required and what the legislature decreed.

Unfortunately, most constitutional issues do not have such matchless clarity. Many key judgments on federalism, separation of powers, and individual rights depend on controversial readings of basic texts. The difficult question is whether unelected judges should be allowed to override proposals (e.g., minimum wage or maximum hours laws) that command strong levels of political support in a highly polarized political situation. On this, there is nothing inevitable about the American solution, which has produced decisions as appallingly misguided as *Dred Scott v. Sandford* in 1857 (upholding the second-class status of slaves by denying that they could become citizens of the United States even when freed)[65] and as inspired, if controversial, as *Brown v. Board of Education* in 1954 (ordering desegregation of public schools throughout the United States, chiefly in the South).[66]

The usual way of phrasing the problem of judicial review is to ask whether unelected judges should be able to negate the power of democratic majorities who act after prudent political deliberations. On that question, much depends on which public decisions one believes should be made by government authorities in the first place. Thus, from the classical liberal perspective, any collective deliberation concerning financial appropriations for war and peace is not a suitable area for judicial intervention, and on these matters courts everywhere have long taken a hands-off position. But the case for judicial intervention can easily shift in the opposite direction when the conflict concerns the protected right of an individual to a fair trial when charged with an offense that could result in the loss of life, liberty, and property. In this case, a strong role for the judiciary is far more appropriate in light of the dangers of individual oppression.[67]

Finding an appropriate test to decide when courts should intervene is more difficult when dealing with economic and social matters. Classical liberals tend to prefer definitions that tie the public interest to classic

---

[64] *Marbury v. Madison*, 5 U.S. 137 (1803).

[65] *Dred Scott v. Sandford*, 60 U.S. 393 (1857).

[66] *Brown v. Board of Education*, 347 U.S. 483 (1954).

[67] For a discussion of these issues, see *Hamdi v. Rumsfeld*, 542 U.S. 507 (2004); *Hamdan v. Rumsfeld*, 548 U.S. 557 (2006); and *Boumediene v. Bush*, 128 S. Ct. 2229 (2008).

economic definitions of a public good that stress nonexcludability, that is, actions in which the supply of a particular good or service to one individual necessarily provides it to a second.[68] At this point, judicial intervention is appropriate to ensure that some individuals do not free-ride off the contributions and labor of others. But other theorists tend to think that any burning issue of public dispute is a proper subject for legislative action, which calls for a far narrower scope for judicial review than classical liberals endorse.

There is little question that, globally, the call for some system of judicial review has gained ground recently, often through adjudication of major constitutional questions in specialized constitutional tribunals set up exclusively for that purpose. But it is far from obvious that any judicial decision of constitutional import should necessarily be immunized from political review. In some instances, that review is exceedingly hard to obtain, as under the highly restrictive amendment process set out in Article V of the United States Constitution. It is therefore always possible to avoid that process by using a weaker system of judicial review, such as some variation of the legislative override that is found in the Canadian Charter, which provides that if a court strikes down a legislative act or provision, "Parliament or the legislature of a province may expressly declare in an Act of Parliament or of the legislature, as the case may be, that the Act or a provision thereof shall operate notwithstanding" the court's decision.[69]

The Charter outlines the fundamental social and legal rights of Canadians. Note that the Canadian provision does not call for any supermajority vote to override the determinations of any court, which has allowed Quebec to use this provision to resist the imposition of English-language requirements—long a source of tension between Quebec and Canada as a whole.

Regardless of the particulars of this dispute, the Charter's legislative override sets too low a bar on normative grounds. A more sensible approach would probably be to follow the model of the veto provisions in the United States Constitution, such that a two-thirds vote in each house of a bicameral system would be sufficient to undo the decision. That approach gives a dual form of protection. First, the legislation in question has to pass muster at two separate times. Second, it takes a substantial majority to override judicial claims that protect individual rights.

What, then, does the optimal structural constitution look like when all the moving parts are considered together? The issue is clearly difficult to resolve. At best, we can identify a set of constraints through separation of powers, checks and balances, and judicial review. But these animating principles are consistent with both presidential and parliamentary sys-

---

[68] See, e.g., Olson, *The Logic of Collective Action*.
[69] Canadian Charter of Rights and Freedoms, para. 33 (1982).

tems, leaving it quite undecided which of these is in better harmony with sound governance. On this point, the classical liberal will differ from the champion of the modern social democratic state, given that the latter has far greater confidence in the impartiality and expertise of administrative tribunals to which a social democratic state routinely extends extensive powers. But the fact here is that it is hard sledding to think of any universal truth that guarantees the supremacy of one form over the next. The plusses and minuses of any proposed change are often so evenly matched that there is much to be said for the view that the status quo should endure in democratic societies. The truth is that nations become more adept in dealing with familiar structures, so that the costs of transition are likely to swamp the gains from some alternative state of the world that may well be less attractive than the one that has been abandoned. This recognition of the simple point that established institutions may work better than they appear to on paper is not a call for stagnation, but a call for care in making changes that could prove to be more disruptive than valuable. This is a Burkean gloss on a classical liberal constitution.[70]

VI. INDIVIDUAL RIGHTS AND LIBERTIES

Let me now turn to the last topic, where the question is what stance the optimal constitution ought to take on matters of individual rights to liberty, property, or equal treatment before the law. On this question, I believe it is possible in principle to reach conclusions more categorical than those that are possible under the structural questions. More precisely, the preference for competition over monopoly is a *sine qua non* for sound social and economic relationships.

Start with the economic side of the coin. Constitutional framers should rely on general demonstrations that monopolies are inferior to competition on the ground that monopolies create welfare losses by allowing parties to restrict entry into markets, raise prices, and reduce output. This set of consequences does not depend on the peculiar historical evolution of any country. One reason why a sensible version of antitrust laws in the United States, or competition laws in the European Union and elsewhere, makes sense is that such laws translate well from one society to the next. Indeed, there may not be any peculiar set of local circumstances that displace the proposition that monopolies are inferior to competition. This is an ideal topic for constitutional protection that can easily be couched in the language of freedom of contract, private property, or ordinary economic liberties by constitutional framers who are so inclined to act.

---

[70] For the recent infatuation with Edmund Burke, whose evolutionary approach meshes at best imperfectly with a written constitution, see Thomas W. Merrill, "Bork v. Burke," *Harvard Journal of Law and Public Policy* 19 (1996): 509. See also Cass Sunstein, "Burkean Minimalism," *Michigan Law Review* 105 (2006): 353.

This constitutional preference for competitive markets does not offer any refuge for those forms of behavior that are suspect within the classical liberal framework. Protections against force and fraud, against tortious interference with contract, against defamation, and against monopolization are all consistent with this point of view. The pre-1937 Supreme Court in the United States has often been attacked for its unprincipled protection of the rich and the powerful. That charge certainly has traction on matters of race relations, with the rise of the separate but equal doctrine of *Plessy v. Ferguson* (1896). But on economic matters, there is no evidence that the Supreme Court was consciously unprincipled in its decision-making. With the occasional lapse, it sought to protect competitive forces against anticompetitive regulations (at the time called "labor regulations") that all too often masqueraded as rules intended to protect health or safety.[71] The ten-hour maximum workday struck down in *Lochner v. New York* (1905),[72] for example, surely was intended to blunt the competition of nonunion laborers.[73] And the major decisions that repudiated *Lochner* were all efforts to introduce cartel-type arrangements in either labor or agricultural markets.[74] Regardless of constitutional structure, it should always be possible to construct a coherent system of individual rights to property and liberty by giving due weight to the power of the state to maintain ordered liberty, without tolerating state sponsorship of various barriers to entry or state-supported monopolies.

The same insights, on the importance of competition and the dangers of monopoly, apply with equal force to various noneconomic liberties. The importance of freedom of speech means that no person should be allowed to prevent the free entry of others into political or artistic markets. Efforts, therefore, to impose limitations like the now-discredited Fairness Doctrine in telecommunications, whereby individual stations are required to give both sides of a divisive issue equal airtime, should be stoutly resisted.[75] Efforts to burden the speech of one party with obligations to present the views of another reduce the total amount of speech on matters of public concern. The task of getting well-rounded views in a marketplace is best accomplished by allowing others to enter, not by forcing current speakers to subsidize their rivals. Print or

---

[71] See Richard A. Epstein, *How Progressives Rewrote the Constitution* (Washington, DC: The Cato Institute, 2006).

[72] *Lochner v. New York*, 198 U.S. 45 (1905).

[73] For an exhaustive demonstration from the historical sources, see David Bernstein, "Lochner Era Revisionism, Revised: Lochner and the Origins of Fundamental Rights Constitutionalism," *Georgetown Law Journal* 92, no. 1 (2003).

[74] See *National Labor Relations Board v. Jones and Laughlin Steel*, 301 U.S. 1 (1937) (sustaining national labor statute against commerce clause challenge); *Wickard v. Filburn*, 317 U.S. 111 (1942) (sustaining national labor statute for regulation of agricultural production).

[75] For the doctrine's repudiation in the United States, see *Miami Herald Publishing Co. v. Tornillo*, 418 U.S. 241 (1974).

broadcast media should not be treated as isolated miniature markets when consumers can move within and across media instantaneously. It is quite sufficient if the overall market has balance, even if none of its components do. The same applies to the misguided history of campaign finance law, whose major effect is to entrench incumbents and to invert the protections of freedom of speech so that it no longer allows ordinary people and citizens to express their views close to election times when they matter most.[76] The culprit here is the progressive mind-set that misunderstands the overall structure of information markets by thinking falsely that all corporate speech is lined up on the same side of all issues.

Similar arguments apply to religious freedom, where the elaborate body of law that developed in the United States on free exercise and establishment is best understood as an effort to prevent the state from favoring, through either taxes or subsidies, one religion over another, or all religions over none.[77] The ban on cross-subsidies that animates any coherent account of the state regulation of religion is vintage classical liberalism. In contrast, the classical liberal should not insist on strict separationist principles when cooperation between religious and nonreligious organizations works for the mutual advantage of both.

Indeed, one can go further and say that any coherent constitutional account of individual liberties and property rights creates a sphere of protection that guards against the two major problems that plague any political order. The first of these deals with negative externalities such as aggression and pollution, whereby one person has an incentive to undertake actions that lead to private advantage and social losses at the same time. The second is the inability of private markets to overcome a range of coordination problems such as those that exist in network industries like telephones and railroads, where the need for the cooperation of all on key matters of interconnection precludes the realization of competitive markets. The first of these problems dates from the start of government, and the second arose with the increased pace of industrialization that required, and still requires, a complex social infrastructure.[78]

This vision of constitutionalism is not compatible with the modern social democratic state, which lurches between competition and monopoly in the ways indicated at the outset of this essay. And to what end—to make the world safe for restrictive practices that reduce over-

---

[76] For the validation of the Bipartisan Campaign Reform Act, Pub. L. 107-155, 116 Stat. 81 (2002), see *McConnell v. Federal Election Commission*, 540 U.S. 93 (2003).

[77] Michael W. McConnell, "The Origins and Historical Understanding of Free Exercise of Religion," *Harvard Law Review* 103 (1990): 1409.

[78] I sought to deal with many of these problems from a constitutional point of view in Richard A. Epstein, *Takings: Private Property and the Power of Eminent Domain* (Cambridge, MA: Harvard University Press, 1985).

all welfare, compromise individuals' liberty, increase administrative costs, create undue uncertainty, and generally subject politics to a set of factional pressures from which it finds it difficult to recover? The American experience reveals this simple picture. Where courts care about the classical liberal conception of matters of free speech and federalism, they do a fine job in preventing these various ills from taking place. The ability to keep commerce open across state lines is but one example. Where courts do not care, they claim that it is impossible to distinguish right from wrong and smart from dumb, so that all questions are resolved through legislation that produces a dizzying array of protectionist actions, whereby local businesses, in league with local governments, systematically exclude out-of-state competitors.

In some instances, the situation gets worse. Not only is it possible for modern constitutions to give short shrift to classical liberal rights of property and liberty, but they may also move strongly in the direction of positive rights—rights to housing, jobs, welfare, health care, or anything else that could be provided by ordinary markets if they were allowed to operate. Indeed, this massive program of government subsidies for all lay at the heart of Franklin D. Roosevelt's Second Bill of Rights,[79] which was comprised of rights whose correlative duties he nowhere specified. In these cases, of course, it is not possible to specify the quantities of the rights so allowed. All such details depend on the level of resources in society, the state of technology, the distribution of income, and myriad other variables that lack the permanence necessary for any kind of a constitutional order to grasp. And even if we accept that states may legitimately be committed to some constitutional articulation of positive rights, they should be careful about how far they go. Constitutions should

---

[79] See Franklin D. Roosevelt, State of the Union Address, January 11, 1944:

> We have come to a clear realization of the fact that true individual freedom cannot exist without economic security and independence. "Necessitous men are not free men." People who are hungry and out of a job are the stuff of which dictatorships are made.
>
> In our day these economic truths have become accepted as self-evident. We have accepted, so to speak, a second Bill of Rights under which a new basis of security and prosperity can be established for all—regardless of station, race, or creed.
>
> Among these are:
>
> The right to a useful and remunerative job in the industries or shops or farms or mines of the nation;
>
> The right to earn enough to provide adequate food and clothing and recreation;
>
> The right of every farmer to raise and sell his products at a return which will give him and his family a decent living;
>
> The right of every businessman, large and small, to trade in an atmosphere of freedom from unfair competition and domination by monopolies at home or abroad;
>
> The right of every family to a decent home;
>
> The right to adequate medical care and the opportunity to achieve and enjoy good health;
>
> The right to adequate protection from the economic fears of old age, sickness, accident, and unemployment;
>
> The right to a good education.

not provide for these rights, but at most should make it clear that the legislature does nothing wrong when it provides for them in abundance.[80]

There is massive danger in this effort to make government the provider of key support for all its citizens. The state creation of entitlements by fiat is a game without an end. Scarcity is a powerful constraint, no matter what choices are made on constitutional design. The positive rights in question can only be funded from taxes or other forms of exaction. The provision of positive rights therefore limits the scope of negative rights on the opposite side of the equation. The pattern that follows is yet another illustration of the downward spiral that comes when political actions are not constrained in areas where there is no strict necessity for collective action. The current malaise within the American system, which has been replicated worldwide, is not a function of faithful adherence to a constitution that tries in its substantive phase to limit the power of government. It stems from the opposite attitude, which holds that, on matters of entitlement, there should be no limits on the state to craft positive rights at will, funded by whatever device seems opportune at the moment. The cumulative deficit as program piles on program should be evident to anyone who examines the costs of health and welfare in the "out" years, that is, those years for which the present administration was not duty-bound under law to include future losses outside the budget window in its budget appropriations. Politics without constitutional constraint will always break down. And the current remedy of more government intervention will only compound the problem.

VII. Conclusion

The task of making constitutions is, on any account, harder than the task of making ordinary laws. The cardinal feature of constitutional structures is that they must have a certain degree of permanence; they must be resistant to nullification through ordinary legislation. At this point, the choices in design are hard for two reasons. First, the required level of ambition is greater. Second, the information available to make these choices is harder to come by. Any constitution that is drafted with respect to a particular controversy is not likely to outlive that controversy. Different rules will be required when the issues and the players change. It is therefore necessary to step back from particulars and look at the enduring features of human nature, in order to choose that structure that is likely to prove most resilient in the wide range of future disputes, whose content can only be dimly perceived.

---

[80] For a thoughtful defense of this position, see Kim Lane Scheppele, "Social Rights in Constitutional Courts: Strategies of Articulation and Strategies of Enforcement," http:// polisci.berkeley.edu/faculty/gsilver/ScheppeleFull.pdf.

Within this framework, the two enduring elements remain the scarcity of resources and the strong self-interest of individuals and groups. Any constitution born of short-term optimism will tend to ignore these restraints, which will lead to the formation of governments with excessive powers over the personal and economic affairs of their citizens. To avoid this problem, two key sets of choices must be made. The first set of choices is structural. It regards the processes by which laws are made by legislatures, enforced by executives, and interpreted by courts. On these complex questions, the general maxim remains that it is best to divide power so that the ambitions of one group or individual are checked by those of another. But that insight does not yield any clear articulation of which powers should be delegated to what bodies under what circumstances. In any particular case, the success of a constitution could depend on the size of the state, the ethnic mixture of its population, its ability to transition from colonial rule, and a thousand other contingent facts. Lawyers and political theorists can say little about the concrete choices. But on the question of what system of private rights should be preserved, I have little doubt that the fewer the positive rights created under a constitution, the more durable it will be.

It is better, therefore, to start with the second set of choices, which concerns the protection of property, contract, speech, and religion from government control. These rights, of course, cannot be absolute just because they are constitutional. But here, too, there is a theory that indicates how they should be structured. Competition is preferable to monopoly whenever it can be achieved. Constitutions should thus preserve competitive markets when possible, and should cautiously allow for the regulation of private monopolies when competition is not possible.

The implications of this overall analysis should be clear. The classical liberal objectives of limited government are, if anything, more important in societies that are divided by deep ethnic clashes. The strategy here is to reduce the pressures on the structural elements of government by reducing the number of decisions that government has to make. By stressing the control of force, fraud, and monopoly, and shying away from questions of positive rights and redistribution, the classical liberal conception relies on government force in those cases where it is likely to be backed by the strongest national consensus, across ethnic lines, for the exercise of government power. By reducing their span-of-control problems, governments would not have to dip deep into the pool of potential hires for public office. That selectivity, in turn, should allow government officials to recruit abler individuals into public service, and to devote more public resources to reaching sensible solutions on those questions that remain within the sphere of government action.

The same instinct applies with equal force to economic and noneconomic affairs. Setting up a constitution is no easy matter. It is altogether clear why so many constitutions that start with a flourish end in disaster. False optimism is the bane of this enterprise. No national framers can avoid risks, but they will do best if they recognize that their task is to design institutions and rules that cope with scarcity and self-interest in ways that are intended to preserve the life, liberty, and property of their citizens.

Law, New York University

INDEX

Aaron (scriptural figure), 60, 65
Abram/Abraham, 58
Ackerman, Bruce, 108–9, 231, 248, 253, 257
Acts (book of), 66
Adam, 52
Adams, John, 84, 194–95
Adams, Willi Paul, 150
Aegean Sea, 31, 33
Affirmative action, 154
Afghanistan, 105
Alcibiades, 31, 37
Alexander, Larry, 1, 230
Alexy, Robert, 12–14
Alien and Sedition Acts (1798), 84, 94
Alien Tort Statute, 143
Alito, Justice Samuel, 110
American Civil Liberties Union (ACLU), 101
American Economics Association (AEA), 209
American Founders, 25, 44, 46, 80, 106
American Revolution, 73, 80, 151, 198
Amnesia (forgetting-ness): as a law to end vengeance, 38
Amnesty International, 287
Amsterdam chamber, 181
Anarchy, 53–54, 58, 235–36
Andocides, 43
Andros, Edmund, 186, 188
Antifascist Council of National Liberation of Croatia (1943), 175
Antifederalists, 79, 94
Antiphon, 34
Arbitration, 273
Archelaus, 36
Aristophanes, 35, 38, 47
Aristotle, 26, 72, 150; on "composite tyranny" of the Assembly in Athens, 28; on legal change, 232–33; on Protagoras, 35; on the distinction between a *nomos* and a *psephisma*, 40 n. 60; on the nature of law, 48; on the political nature of human beings, 229; on the problem of the authority of the Athenian Assembly, 42
Article 116 of 1990 Nepalese Constitution, 164
Article I of United States Constitution, 95, 98, 130, 144, 155, 159, 161

Article II of United States Constitution, 90, 95, 98, 99, 100, 105, 161
Articles of Capitulation (1664), 183
Articles of Confederation, 23, 46, 68, 150, 151
Assembly, ancient Athenian, 28, 29, 31; contrasted with *nomothetai*, 38–39; irrationality in war with Sparta of, 30–31; violation of Athenian custom, 33, 36
Assembly of XIX, 181–82
Atheism, 37
Athens, 27–28, 33
Authority, 6–7; and problems with social contract theory, 51; constitutional, 90–91; of states, 50; of Oral Law in New Testament, 66; of United States Constitution, 67, 69; to execute war, 130; to use political power, 154; via assent, 59
Autonomy: 263

Bailey, Jeremy, 85
Ballot box voting, 202 n. 3
Barry, Brian, 235
Battle at Arginusae, 30
Berger, Raoul, 98–99, 100, 101
Berkeley, Lord John, 185
Berlin, Isaiah, 228
Berman, Mitchell, 17 n. 43, 21
Bessette, Joseph, 104, 105
Bible: interpretation of, 66
Bicameralism, 154
Bill of Rights, 118, 266; of the United States Constitution, 67, 73, 84, 94, 110, 157
Bills of attainder, 46
Black Sea, 33
Blackstone, William, 95
Bosnia-Herzegovina: constitutional structure of, 304
Boumediene v. Bush (2008), 109, 113
Brandeis, Justice Louis, 153
Brandon, Mark, 103
Breslin, Beau, 162, 177
Briscoe, Robert, 170
British Columbia Citizens' Assembly (2004), 256
British Parliament, 20
Brown v. Board of Education (1954), 296, 305, 316

Lightning Source UK Ltd.
Milton Keynes UK
UKOW032320120412

190625UK00002B/17/P